Searching for Aboriginal Languages

Chloe Grant (Jirrbal and Girramay dialects of Dyirbal) (on right) with her daughter-in-law Mamie Grant whose mother was Mbabaram and father Warungu, but who didn't know any Aboriginal language herself. (1964)

Searching for Aboriginal Languages

Memoirs of a Field Worker

R. M. W. DIXON

The University of Chicago Press

Chicago and London

The University of Chicago Press, Chicago 60637
The University of Chicago Press, Ltd., London

University of Chicago Press edition 1989
Printed in the United States of America

98 97 96 95 94 93 92 91 90 89   5 4 3 2 1

Library of Congress Cataloging in Publication Data

Dixon, Robert M. W.
   Searching for aboriginal languages : memoirs of a field worker /
R. M. W. Dixon.
      p.   cm.
   Reprint. Originally published: St. Lucia ; New York : University of
Queensland Press, 1983.
      1. Australian languages—Australia—Queensland. 2. Linguistics—
Australia—Queensland—Field work.   3. Dixon, Robert M. W.
4. Linguists—Australia—Biography.   I. Title.
PL7091.Q4D59   1989   89-34383
499′.15′09943—dc20   CIP
ISBN 0-226-15430-0 (alk. paper)

⊗ The paper used in this publication meets the minimum requirements of
the American National Standard for Information Sciences—Permanence of
Paper for Printed Library Materials, ANSI Z39.48-1984.

Contents

Illustrations

Acknowledgments

Acknowledgment is made to Slim Dusty and Castle Music Pty Limited for their generous permission to reproduce extracts from the song "Namatjira". Acknowledgments are also extended to Southern Music Publishing Co (Australasia) Pty Ltd for extracts from "My Old Pal" by Rodgers and McWilliams and "Gambling Polka Dot Blues" by Rodgers.

Since Imperial measures were in use in Australia in 1963, when the author began field work, they have been retained in the narrative. By the time the author returned in 1967, Australia had converted to decimal currency.

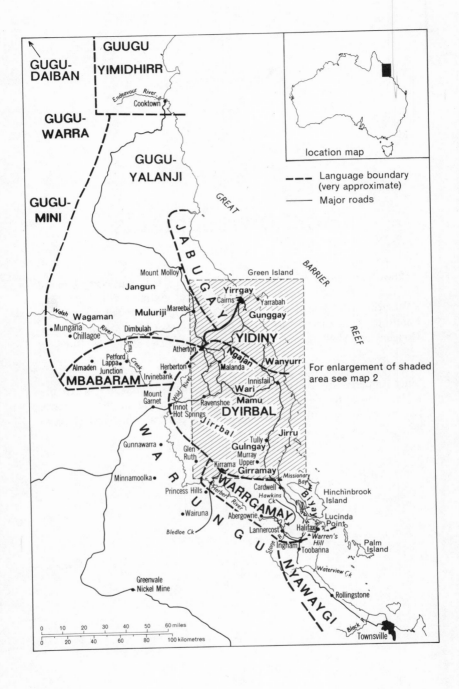

location map

- - - Language boundary (very approximate)
——— Major roads

GUGU-DAIBAN

GUUGU YIMIDHIRR

Endeavour River
Cooktown

GUGU-WARRA

GUGU-YALANJI

GUGU-MINI

GREAT

BARRIER

REEF

JABUGAY

Mount Molloy
Green Island
Jangun
Yirrgay
Cairns
Yarrabah
Muluriji
Mareeba
Gunggay

Walsh Wagaman
Mungana
Chillagoe
River
Dimbulah
YIDINY
Atherton
Ngajan
Wanyurr

Emu Creek
Petford
Lappa
Junction
Almaden
Herberton
Malanda
Irvinebank
Innisfail

MBABARAM
Wari

Mount
Garnet
Wild River
Ravenshoe
Mamu
Innot
Hot Springs
DYIRBAL

Jirrbal

W
A
R
U
N
G
U

Gunnawarra
Tully
Jirru
Glen
Ruth
Gulngay
Murray
Kirrama
Upper
Girramay

Minnamoolka

For enlargement of shaded area see map 2

Missionary
Bay

WARRGAMAY
Cardwell
Hinchinbrook
Island
Princess Hills
Herbert River
Hawkins
Ck
Wairuna
Abergowrie
Lucinda
Point
Bledloe Ck
Lannercost
Halifax
Warren's
Hill
Palm
Island
Stone R.
Ingham
Toobanna

Biyay

Greenvale
Nickel Mine
Waterview Ck

NYAWAYGI
Rollingstone

Black R.

0 10 20 30 40 50 60 miles
0 20 40 60 80 100 kilometres

Townsville

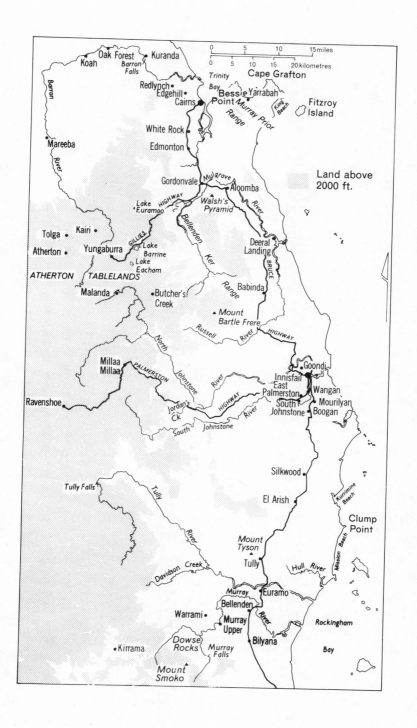

1

Setting off

The rain was only heavy when Chloe Grant began her story:

"Captain Cook, first one", as a title, and then she commenced the narration, in Jirrbal: *"Garulgu bayi baninyu warrjanda."*

Rosie Runaway assented *"nga"* as Chloe continued, *"yanggumanggandu buran warrjanda bayingalu, janangu ganangga, banangga . . ."*

We were sitting in a small, dirty hut at an abandoned mission in the dense tropical forest of north-east Queensland. The first big storm of the wet season had just started. Chloe continued her story, telling of the first contact with Europeans. Captain Cook came into Cardwell in his boat — she used the word *warrjan* which means a vessel, usually a raft, made of planks of wood — and was seen by all the Girramaygan tribe. At first sight, Cook appeared to them to be standing up in the middle of the water.

The storm worsened and we had to strain to catch her words. *"Anyja baybu buyan.* He talk in the English now. 'Man,' he say, 'you want a smoke?' *Banggumanggandu buran. Minya minya ginyan yanggul ngangungga ngiyijan gandanyu. Bunu gandagandaygu wanya . . ?"* Cook and his group smoked a pipe. All the Aborigines watched, and wondered: "What is that burning thing this man has stuck in his mouth? What is making all the smoke?"

The rain by now had become so hard that, although I could see Chloe's lips moving, I couldn't catch any of the words. The microphone, on the table between us, did pick up the story although the noise of the storm recorded as loud as Chloe's voice.

Captain Cook boiled up a billy of tea, to the incredulity of Chloe's ancestors, and offered them a drink.

Fig. 1. Rosie Runaway (Girramay), the author, and Chloe Grant at the "mission", Murray Upper, just after telling the stories of Captain Cook and Kennedy. (1963)

"Gamu nguju", they replied "that's just dirty water." Then "White man say again. 'This good, look, I drink him, I drink him.' " The scalding liquid drew no takers.

"White man say again: 'I put a-cold water there, you drink him!' "

The corrugated iron on the roof rattled, the rain sounding like bullets. Drops were beginning to fall on us and I closed the lid of the recorder to safeguard the tape. Captain Cook was now baking a Johnny-cake on the coals, turning it over — front to back, back to front, top to bottom. Lifting it up to see if it was yet light and cooked. He put it down to cool, then cut pieces off and handed them around. They looked to the Girramaygan like roast *wila,* cakes of brown walnut, one of their staple foods. They customarily prepared these before the summer rains began, wrapping them in leaves and burying them in the sand, to eat later when food was scarce.

But the Johnny-cake didn't measure up to its looks. It smelt stale — quite unlike walnut — and they threw it away, untasted. The beef, which Cook offered next, was better received. They had never before seen boiled meat, but it smelled all right, the salty skin could be wiped off, and the taste was new but acceptable.

As the tale continued, Cook was portrayed by Chloe as a considerate and respectful explorer, much the character one would infer from his journal. The storm outside the hut eased a little, but was then rekindled with a sudden whipcrack of thunder. The explorers in Chloe's tale were preparing for departure, much to the consternation of the Girramaygan who had inferred from their white skins that they were spirits, deceased ancestors returning to visit and advise them. Cook stepped into his boat.

"Nguma, nguma, gawu bani, banaga. Father, father, come here, come back to us," they wailed, beating their fists on the ground in desolate sorrow. But Cook and his party sailed away to the north. And as the story ended, so did the rain.

Rosie Runaway, who had prompted Chloe and argued with her throughout the story, was only four foot six in height. The few score survivors of the Girramaygan and Jirrbalngan tribes were still — after a century of white contact — living in their traditional territory. Much of the forest had been cleared to make way for bananas, and for the sugar cane that was carried along the narrow tramway to the crushing mill at Tully. But the jungle was untouched on the coastal fringe — in the swamps and along the crocodile-infested streams. There is a legend that, in the long distant past, the larger trees decided they would like to come down from the hills to live on the coast. But the mangrove trees down by the sea thought little of the idea, so they made boomerangs from their elbow-shaped roots and used them to bombard the bull oak, the water gum, the black walnut and the other invading inland trees. That is why today only mangroves, and just a few other quite small trees, grow on the lowlands.

The European invaders had not so far thought it worthwhile putting agriculture or livestock on the foothills of the range, which rose to more than three thousand feet only twenty miles from the ocean. So the original forest still grew around the pool at the base of Murray Falls where the rainbow serpent is said to live, and around the large stones near Davidson Creek that are said to be transmogrified forms of a chicken-hawk nest and eggs, one of the many conception sites from which people's spirits came before their birth, and to which they returned at death.

These people, and their jungle setting, echo traditions that are many thousands of years old. They have legends that clearly relate to the end of the Ice Age, and to such geological events as volcanic eruptions that took place at least ten millennia ago. Their stories, places and ceremonies are of an antiquity that is of a different order from that which we consider "old" in Europe or America. Sitting in that dank, dark hut at Murray Upper — with the water now dripping off the trees on to the roof in an uneven clatter — it was difficult to remember the world I had left behind. The world of academic sophistry, confrontation and intrigue.

It had been in a dormitory room at the Massachusetts Institute of Technology, the previous year, that I had listened to a private debate between Noam Chomsky, of MIT, and Michael Halliday, of Edinburgh, that was supposed to determine the future direction of linguistic theory. That room had been bigger than the hut at Murray Upper and, although it was drizzling outside in the New England night, the room itself had been warm and carpeted and comfortable.

Bob Stockwell, the aggressive chairman of linguistics at Los Angeles, believed that there were just two major innovators in linguistic theory at that time, in 1962 — Chomsky's transformational grammar was beginning to receive international renown, while Halliday had that year published on a quite different way of looking at grammar, "scale-and-category theory". During the Ninth International Congress of Linguists, Stockwell decided to set them at one another, like two fighting cocks, to find out which was the mightier. I don't believe that either Chomsky or Halliday was too taken with the idea but it would have been impossible to refuse. There was, as might be expected, no worthwhile linguistic debate. Instead, antagonistic attitudes between the different "schools" of linguistics hardened, and were to set more firmly over the years. Halliday had taught me linguistics. Chomsky is a charismatic figure with a stunning intellect; he is probably the cleverest man I have ever met. For me, the confrontation in that MIT dormitory room was a sobering experience. It released a number of worries that did not begin to be resolved until, in November of the following year, I began to unravel the structure of Jirrbal. By gaslight, in a caravan deep in the rain forest.

The path which had led me to North Australia was a fairly straight-forward one. I had come to Edinburgh, in July 1961, to learn linguistics. Halliday taught how this rather new branch of social science looks for "universals", properties that are held in common by all human languages. It asks questions like these: do all languages have nouns, verbs and adjectives? Do they all have tenses on their verbs, and a masculine/feminine distinction in third person pronouns?

Michael Halliday's grammatical theory was new and exciting. He maintained that the grammar of any language was best formulated in terms of a number of "units" (sentence, clause, group, word, morpheme) showing complex interrelations through a network of "structures", "systems" and "classes". Halliday emphasised that linguists should work simultaneously on two fronts. Detailed description of the grammars of a wide range of languages is necessary as input to high level generalisations about "the general nature of any grammar". From the first, I felt the need to relate the general linguistic ideas I was being taught to some actual language data.

After four or five months of learning about phonemes and morphemes, I went to Halliday and said that I wanted a language of my own — some interesting and complicated tongue that was in need of study. I had been reading Boas and Sapir, so when Halliday asked what language I had in mind, I replied — remembering the daunting polysynthetic complexity of Nootka, in British Columbia — that I'd been thinking of an American Indian language.

"No," said Halliday, "leave those to the Americans. What you want is an Australian language."

We had been taught at school in Nottingham that Australian Aborigines were the lowest type of man, scarcely better than animals, with no idea of property or work; they were explicitly contrasted with Maoris who were said to be at the top of the blackman league, only a jump away from Europeans in their capacity to be civilised. I'd long since worked out my own views on such matters, but it was still a surprise to be told that Australian languages had complex grammars that could provide as strong an intellectual challenge as any linguistic system known.

"I want an Australian language? Do I?"

"Yes," said Halliday, "go and look at Capell's paper in Volume Ten of the Australian anthropological journal *Oceania*, about the Kimberley languages. They have lots of gender classes and extensive grammatical concord, perhaps even more than the Bantu languages of East Africa."

I found that the language of the Worora people had just the kind of grammatical detail that fascinated me. They had lived for thousands of years in the mountainous ranges of north Western Australia, where they developed an elaborate kinship system and code of social behaviour. In 1838, the explorer George Grey had described their Wondjina figures, rock paintings showing the brightly coloured outline of a head with no mouth or ears but with two staring blue eyes connected by a long nose. They reminded me of drawings of "Chad" above a motto "What no eggs?" (or whatever other vital commodity we were short of in post-war Britain). The Reverend J.R.B. Love had established a Presbyterian mission at Kunmunya in the 1920s and had gradually weaned the Worora from their nomadic hunting and gathering ways to a sedentary "Christian" life.

Capell's paper led me to a sketch grammar of Worora by Love in the *Journal of the Royal Society of Western Australia* for 1930–32. He reported, amongst much else, that there were no less than four hundred and forty-four forms of the verb "to be", each carrying information about the subject and object of the sentence. I returned to Halliday and said: "Yes, you're quite right. I do want to work on an Australian language."

By a lucky coincidence, an Institute for Aboriginal Studies was just being established in Canberra, and applications were being sought from people interested in describing Aboriginal anthropology, music, languages, and the like. Halliday put me in touch with Dr Capell, Reader in Oceanic Linguistics at the University of Sydney, and for twenty years the only person in any Australian university who taught linguistics.

I wrote an enthusiastic letter to Capell, saying how intrigued I was by Worora and other North Kimberley languages, and asking whether I should write direct to the Reverend Mr Love for information about going to Kunmunya.

"I shouldn't advise writing to Rev Love," replied Capell, in what I came to recognise as his characteristic laconic style. "He died several years ago. There are only a handful of Worora remaining and they have now been moved down to Mowanjum, just out of Derby."

He went on to say that Anindilyagwa, spoken on Groote Eylandt, off the east coast of Arnhem Land, had probably the most complicated grammar of any Australian language, but that the AIAS (the Australian Institute for Aboriginal Studies) was setting priorities as to which areas were in most urgent need of linguistic study.

I applied for a position with AIAS, but there were still twelve months before I could leave Edinburgh and start my field work. Ideas about where I should go had time to gel and then shift again.

For a while, the islands of the Torres Strait, between Queensland and New Guinea, were my first choice. The idea of spending some months on Miriam, a coral atoll at the northern extremity of the Barrier Reef that was described as a "tropical paradise", was appealing, especially when contemplated in the middle of a dark, windy Edinburgh winter. The languages of the Torres Strait had not been studied since the Cambridge Anthropological Expedition of 1898–99.

Then Capell suggested the languages of the Cairns rainforest region, at the lower end of the Cape York Peninsula (to the south of the Torres Strait). In 1942, two anthropologists – Norman Tindale from Adelaide and Jo Birdsell from Harvard – had suggested that the rainforest people were of a different physical type from other Aborigines, and were perhaps related to the extinct Tasmanians. They were reported to be of short stature, with crisp curly hair, yellow-brown skins and a distinctive blood type. Tindale had quoted eleven words from one language, Barbaram, that looked very unlike words in other Australian languages. There were monosyllables, such as *ka*; words ending in stop consonants, such as *mok* "man"; and words beginning with consonant sequences, as in *mbe:ra* "grass basket". Yet Father Worms, a friend of Capell's, had gathered a few score words of Djirubal, another rainforest language, and these were unexceptional, many of them being obviously cognate with forms from languages in other parts of the continent. When I showed interest in working on these languages, Capell passed on the information that many speakers were now to be found on, as he half-typed it, "Pa m island".

I searched the map of Queensland. The only island to be found with a four-letter name that began with *pa* and ended with *m* was Palm Island, out from Townsville towards the Great Barrier Reef. It certainly sounded all right, and seemed a fair swap for Torres Strait (I'd been planning to go there for so long that the idea was getting a little stale). But when I wrote expressing willingness to go to Palm Island and study the rainforest languages, Capell replied that he had now made further inquiries and was sorry to report that Palm Island would be the worst possible place to begin my investigation!

Meanwhile, the AIAS, who had just completed a tribal listing, said they would like me to work on the languages of the Cape York Peninsula, from Torres Strait right down to the rainforest region. All of them! And they listed 136 language names. In the year at my disposal, this would be about two days per language, allowing some time for travelling, making contacts, having the odd weekend off, and so on.

I carefully made the point that I was inexperienced in this work, that it took a good while to get under the skin of a language, as it were, to work out its linguistic system, and that I really was interested in testing out various linguistic theories on Australian languages. They reluctantly accepted my suggested compromise — to work intensively on one language for about six months, and then spend the second half of the year in a more extensive survey (one day per language?). It was decided that I should begin in the rainforest area. Although there were many speakers in the Aboriginal settlement on Palm Island, they tended to speak a sort of pidgin, mixing in bits from many different languages, and I should start by trying to locate groups of speakers on the mainland, in their original tribal territory.

Arthur Capell's solid, grey exterior hides a whimsical sense of humour and a weakness for dreadful puns — as when he referred to the "semantics" of a language as "some antics". He had been a school-master, and then was ordained and became a locum tenens in the parish of Morpeth, near Newcastle, for the Reverend A. P. Elkin, who had just been appointed professor of social anthropology at the University of Sydney. Elkin returned to the parish during vacations and was so impressed by Capell's linguistic knowledge and skills that soon he appointed him to a lectureship in linguistics in his department.

When Capell was promoted to Reader it was in the field of Oceanic linguistics, and his major interest was always the languages of the Pacific and of New Guinea. It could almost be said that he worked on Australian languages "at the weekends". Yet he did work of the greatest importance on the languages of Australia, spending lengthy periods in the Kimberleys and in Arnhem Land. Capell's surveys — he spent a day or two on this language, a week on that — opened the way for the intensive studies that are now being undertaken of these languages. He says, ruefully, that he feels as if he was a wine-taster, with the pleasure of quaffing the bottle being left to his successors.

He had a solitary life, with few close friends. When his old house-keeper became ill, he hired another housekeeper to look after the first. When she also became ill, Capell was left caring for the two of them. They always called him "Dr Capell". Indeed, he addressed me formally for ten years, beginning letters "Mr Dixon", then "Dr Dixon" and then "Professor Dixon", although I had signed mine more casually from the beginning. Only in 1972 did he begin "Dear Bob (I think informality is called for)". I asked Stephen Wurm — the only person I knew who called him Arthur — whether I should do likewise. In fact, Capell seemed perfectly happy when after that I always referred to him as Arthur, even in meetings and committees.

He arrived at his austere, sunless, book-lined office in the university at about 10 a.m. His research assistant, who shared his room, would always greet him with, "Good morning, Doctor." Capell then attended to his considerable correspondence, prepared and delivered his lectures, ate his sandwiches, and made coffee with an electric jug in the corner of the room. He was never known to offer coffee to the research assistant.

Capell singlehandedly taught first and second year linguistics to a wide range of students, and even prepared his own textbook for the course. Sadly, he had no research students working under him — there was just one, funded by AIAS, in the last couple of years before his retirement in the late sixties.

Despite his shy manner, Capell could be warm and welcoming. When I got married, soon after gaining a grant from AIAS, the Institute went into a flurry over whether or not they could pay Alison's fare out. Capell simply wrote, "Now there will be two of you to welcome."

We stopped off in New York, in San Francisco, and then in Papeete. From the boat ride round Manhattan Island, to trying to negotiate the roads of Tahiti on a motor scooter with a dud spark-plug, it seemed a good beginning. After this, Fiji was distinctly dull. We'd been booked in at a colonial hotel in Nandi, where we were served tinned peaches and custard, despite the mangoes growing outside. So we cut short this segment of the trip.

Capell was quite taken aback when I rang him in Sydney and said that we'd arrived a few days early: "I'll say you have!" But he left his sandwiches that day and took us for lunch in the students' union.

The next day, Capell introduced us to La Mont West, Jnr., a casually dressed, bearded American anthropologist who had spent some years travelling around the continent, mostly studying sign language. He explained that he hadn't yet worked out what were the basic units, in order to crack the system — in the way that spoken language was revealed once the letters of the alphabet were invented. Monty West was something of a legend for his trying to live the freest possible life. It was said that, as a little boy, he had been given a sailor suit with a whistle attached; but he was not allowed to blow the whistle, in case it had germs. Most of his life now seemed to be a reaction to this — but somehow it didn't quite ring true. When he went to an Aboriginal settlement, he would only record material from the oldest, most senile and scabrous individuals, rejecting younger, neater and more intelligent people — although they were sometimes in a better position to give him the information he sought. And when Monty decided to travel rough and live off the country, he almost starved, since he had little real idea of how to go about things.

Monty West lived cheaply, making a twelve-month grant last for two years. He had been almost everywhere in Australia, and had given Capell the information about Palm Island. West immediately invited us to dinner and provided all sorts of useful advice. Most importantly, he had heard of a group of rainforest Aborigines still living a fairly traditional life somewhere near Tully, although he hadn't been there himself.

Capell was fascinated by Monty West and — quite uncharacteristically — asked what exactly he had given us to eat. He seemed rather disappointed that it was just a good beef stew. Capell himself was equally helpful, letting me see all the data he had — although it wasn't much — on the languages of Cape York Peninsula. He lent me a tape he had made of the Western Torres Strait language (the only recording he knew of for that language) and also a key to his office so that I could listen to it on his tape recorder on Sunday. He was as disappointed as I when the tape turned out to be completely blank.

The Australian Institute of Aboriginal Studies is a funny sort of body; and it had rather peculiar beginnings. In about 1960, the Australian government joined with others in criticising South Africa's racist policies. The story goes that South Africa turned round and told Australia to put its own house in order. This was fair comment, since Australia's treatment of its coloured people had been just as bad as anything in South Africa. But Aborigines make up such a small part of the Australian population that they pose no threat; their plight is scarcely noticed.

R. G. Menzies is said to have agreed to establish AIAS partly in response to this criticism and partly to try to placate W. C. Wentworth, an obstreperous backbencher from Menzies' own party who had been championing the need for more documentation of things Aboriginal. In fact Wentworth continued, exactly as before, to be thorn in Menzies' side, openly criticising his fiscal and other policies. Wentworth's undoubted intelligence was offset by a radical impetuosity and inconsistency. And his attitude towards Aborigines was equivocal. I have heard it characterised as "document, then bulldoze", and that may be only somewhat unfair.

A conference of interested scholars, which was sponsored by the government, recommended in 1961 that an Institute be established. During my year in Australia, it was on an interim basis, attached to the prime minister's department, but was later made a permanent statutory body. The major professional impetus behind its foundation came from W. E. H. (Bill) Stanner, an outstanding anthropologist who worked at the Australian National University. Stanner had the misfortune to be an Australian, and was passed over for critical chairs in favour of people from overseas (a common failing in Australia – the worth of home-grown scholars is seldom recognised until they have been appointed to a good job overseas, by which time it is often too late to persuade them to return and work in an Australian university). But the Institute did not work out in the way Stanner had hoped and – much to its misfortune – he never played any significant role in running it.

There is a story that an Aborigine – and they were few and far between in Canberra in the early sixties – once passed a door in the suburb of Dickson on which was the legend "Australian Institute of Aboriginal Studies". He'd always wanted to study and ventured inside, only to be ejected with the explanation that it was *we* who did the studying of *them.* In the seventies, AIAS did start to employ some Aborigines – firstly as janitors, but later in more responsible positions – and put some Aborigines on their committees. But decisions were still made white-style, and almost all the money went to white people. AIAS has never quite known what it was doing — then, as now. But every now and again it has tried to find out. In the six months before leaving Edinburgh, I'd written letters to superintendents of missions in the Cape York Peninsula, and to the Bishop of Carpentaria, asking permission to undertake linguistic work. Suddenly the Institute requested copies of all the letters I had written. I couldn't oblige, because I hadn't made carbons; AIAS accepted this, and never did say why they'd wanted them.

Then there was an urgent letter asking if I could drive; if not, it was imperative I learn at once. Apparently a German musicologist called Wolfgang Laade, who had arrived six months before me, was found to have never been behind a driving wheel. So he had to have lessons in Canberra, which took about three months — and all the time he and his wife were living in a private hotel, and no one invited them home for dinner, we were told. Laade learnt to drive on a Volkswagen and then flew up to Brisbane to pick up an International truck. It was decided that he shouldn't also attempt to pull the caravan he had been assigned — which was lucky for us, since we took it instead.

Laade drove north as far as Coen, where the road gave out, spending all his travellers' cheques on fuel for the juggernaut. He then found he could only get in by plane to Lockhart River Mission and the Torres Strait islands, where AIAS had told him to work. So the truck stayed in Coen. It wasn't exactly idle — the policeman drove it a bit, and then some farmers, until it eventually got a bash in the side and the Department of Supply had to fly a man up to drive it back to Brisbane. Laade disappeared into Torres Strait and eventually became so tired of AIAS asking — perfectly justifiably — for details of his expenses, that he stopped writing to them. He and I were in contact, since I was planning to move on to Torres Strait, and I eventually had to act as an intermediary, passing news of Laade's welfare and movements on to the Institute.

AIAS had been reassured that I could drive. We were planning to spend a week or ten days in Canberra before going up north, but Monty West felt we'd be lucky to get away in under three months. In fact, there turned out to be little to detain us there.

The Institute was situated in a set of pokey little rooms, separated by thin partitions, above the offices of the state automobile association, the NRMA. It had a staff of about a dozen middle-aged ladies, most of whom knew nothing about Aborigines or anthropology or linguistics. One afternoon there was a torrential rainstorm at about half-past three; within minutes the building was deserted — they'd all gone to give their children lifts home from school. There was a full-time bibliographer, and also the beginnings of a useful library; the only difficulty was that the librarian and bibliographer weren't on speaking terms.

John Greenway published a comprehensive *Bibliography of the Australian Aborigines and the Native Peoples of Torres Strait to 1959* late in 1963; it contains a great deal of useful information, but also many errors. In his reminiscences, *Down Among the Wild Men* (1973), Greenway commented that his compilation "remains the standard general reference, though the Australian Institute of Aboriginal Studies is still working out of the book for improved local lists. I caught them at it once — four people grubbing away with the book and thousands of cross-reference cards — and was greatly amused, since I had had in the meantime a fight with the Institute's then director, who was apparently unable to see me."

I am sorry to report that this is too flattering. The AIAS bibliographers did *not* go through Greenway's listing. I once asked them about this and they said that they had started, but gave up when they were unable to trace many of his references. They also failed to go through the superlative linguistic bibliography in Wilhelm Schmidt's *Die Gliederung der Australischen Sprachen* (1919), which is inexcusable since the AIAS had paid to have this work translated into English — and then didn't use it!

I'd written from Edinburgh to the Institute asking about living costs in North Queensland. It was somewhat unnerving to be told that they had no idea — that I probably knew more about it than they, since I'd been in correspondence with people in the north. Anyway, they promised to reimburse what it cost to live in the field, over and above what it would have cost in Canberra.

And there was the rub. We were booked in to University House, a graduate residence at the Australian National University, which charged £A30 per week for full board. But the salary I had asked for and been granted — based on what I had been paid as Research Fellow in Edinburgh — was £A1,500 per annum. That is, I was being paid less than £A29 per week gross (and taxes would reduce it further), but accomodation was £A30. And expenses would only be paid if they exceeded £A30 per week!

We settled it in the end, as I remember, by agreeing that expenses should be allowed over what it would cost the two of us to live in Edinburgh, which I estimated at £A12 per week (allowing for a liberal diet of kippers). We still had to estimate expenses so that the Institute could grant an advance. A major item was obviously going to be petrol for the Land Rover we were to pick up in Brisbane. The AIAS administrative officer remarked that standard grade was three shillings and fourpence in Sydney, but three and nine in Canberra, some miles inland. She suggested it might be six or seven shillings a gallon in Cairns, and we estimated on that basis. When we reached Cairns, we found the price was in fact just three shillings and fourpence a gallon. Cairns is a port, like Sydney.

In 1963, the languages of Australia were very much a terra incognita. Pitifully little work had been done in the 175 years since the first white invasion, and half-way decent grammars were only available for three or four of the two hundred distinct Aboriginal languages. During my period in the field, there was just one other linguist at work — the Sanskrit scholar Luise Hercus, who was recording the languages of Victoria from their last speakers. (She was also financed by AIAS.) And the Summer Institute of Linguistics had its first four missionary linguists in far North Queensland.

Perhaps no other place in the world — outside the swamps of New Guinea or the dense forests of Brazil — had so many languages in desperate need of professional description. And Australia was an easy country to work in, with its sealed roads, good health system, and an English-speaking population.

Except that they didn't talk precisely my kind of English. British people are aware of differences between their speech and American English — "trailer" for "caravan" and the like — but it had never occurred to me, at least, that Australian would present any difficulties. Some things were quite easy — we soon picked up "bitumen roads" where an Englishman would talk about "tarmacadam" and an American "asphalt". But these were exceptions. Once when Chloe Grant was giving me the names of fishes, and said that *yabi* was *yigarra*, I wrote both words down, but had no idea which was supposed to be English and which Jirrbal. A kindly farmer later explained the "yabby" is the Australian name for a type of crayfish, quite probably borrowed in the last century from some now-extinct Aboriginal language in the south-

east. And then I was told that *gubarrngubarr* was the Jirrbal word for
— something I wrote down as "scrubbage" (it rhymed with roughage).
This turned out to be scrub-itch, a parasitic red mite a bit like ring-
worm. We learnt that "bogey" — a loan into bush English from the
original Sydney language — meant "bathe", and to beware of young
larrikins getting into mischief. "Larrikin", originally an English word,
had all but dropped out of use in Britain while increasing in popularity
in Australia; there are signs that it may now be being borrowed back
from Australian into British English.

We made our escape from Canberra within about a week — to
Brisbane, a friendly city of frame houses with long gardens, strung
along a winding river. The Department of Supply directed us to the
Bureau of Mineral Resources' warehouse to draw supplies for the
caravan Dr Laade had left behind. Government-issue blankets, a
tow-rope, pots and pans, a tea-pot that turned out to be caked with
rust . . . and, finally, a tin-opener. Language difficulties intruded again.
Our kitter-out — a friendly English immigrant who had lived twenty
miles from the sea in County Durham and visited it once a year, but
now lived twenty-five miles away and went there every weekend —
asked what sort of opener we wanted. Getting no response, he said:
"Well, the question is, are you going to be having any plonk?" We
had absolutely no idea what plonk was, but from his tone of voice it
was obviously a good thing, so I said: "Yes, of course we are going to
be having plonk." We drove off with a tin-opener that had a corkscrew
attached, for use on the corks of bottles of cheap wine.

In Canberra I'd had to get a permit to drive a government Land
Rover. After my tentative stabs at the mystery of four-wheel driving,
the instructor paused and said: "Oh well, you'll be driving out of
Brisbane into the bush. You'll pick it up there."

When we enquired whether Alison would be allowed to take a turn
at driving, we were told that she wasn't even permitted to be in the
vehicle in the first place, since she wasn't a Commonwealth government
employee! This was something of a setback. But the AIAS, who were
always friendly and often helpful through their web of disorganisation,
said we were not to worry, as they would stand by us. We never did get
permission, but of course Alison did go — and shared the driving.

So we set off from Brisbane. The last section of the road to Cairns
had just been bitumenised, but for a lot of the way there was only a
narrow strip of hard-top. When two cars met, they both moved over

onto the gravel in order to pass. A bus driver in Brisbane had told us of "horror stretch", between Rockhampton and Mackay, which had no town or filling station for two hundred miles. But the Land Rover had a twenty-four-gallon reserve petrol tank and a thirty-gallon water tank. We felt ready for most things.

Halliday had provided a thorough training in most branches of theoretical linguistics, but during my time at Edinburgh I'd had virtually no exposure to actual analysis of languages. We hadn't been asked to "solve" sets of data in an unknown tongue, working out the significant units of sound and meaning. Still less had there been anything like a field methods course — which is a normal requirement in most linguistics programmes nowadays — with an instructor demonstrating how to ask questions of an informant and how to build up a grammar from scratch.

While in Canberra, I'd had a most useful chat with Stephen Wurm, the only linguist in the Department of Anthropology of the Australian National University. Wurm had done a tremendous amount of field work in Australia and New Guinea (although he still hasn't written up and published more than a fraction of it) and was full of hints on how to get by officialdom, remain on good terms with the local whites, and — most important of all — how to establish good relations with the Aborigines.

"Always offer round cigarettes when you meet a new man. Before you start asking questions."

"But I don't smoke," I protested.

"Neither do I. Doesn't matter. If you offer a smoke you must be a friend. Leave them out for them to help themselves as they talk. Helps them to relax. And leave the pack when you go. Say you've got some more back home, huh."

Stephen Wurm's advice was given in quick, clipped sentences with a stress pattern that revealed his Central European origins, and with a grin — almost a grimace — as each new hint was unfolded, and a questioning "huh" to mark the conclusion of a point. As time went by, I realised how useful his advice had been. Whenever I went up to a door at a strange settlement, someone would call "Look out, *bulijiman* here." But the cigarettes had a magical effect — policemen don't go around offering smokes. Ever.

There is a special brand of cranky old Aboriginal lady who will give any stray visitor a steady, piercing stare and say "What do you want?" in a croaky voice that drips with suspicion and uncooperativeness. But then I'd offer the pack of Rothmans (the most popular brand in Aboriginal Australia).

"I'll take two," she would say, extending her claw-like hands with their broken, dirty nails.

When I said, "Take three," she'd grin. And we'd like as not be friends for life.

But all this was some way off when we headed north from Brisbane along Route 1. The first thing was to find our Aborigines. I hadn't set eyes on even an urbanised Aborigine in Sydney, Canberra or Brisbane. We had Tindale's map of tribal territories, published in 1940, but people had warned us that some tribes were extinct and the remnants of others might now reside on government settlements many miles from their traditional homes. Our mission was to drive a thousand miles up to the Cairns rainforest and see if there were any people left who still spoke any of the languages of that region.

I felt quite jaunty as we set off, stopping in Maryborough to buy a wide-brimmed ex-Army hat, and in Townsville to get some tropical shorts and sandals. But as we got nearer to the field location, I realised that I had absolutely no idea what to do. We drove a shorter distance each day — only a little more than half of what we'd managed the previous day. Finally — and really against my better judgment — we unavoidably reached Ingham, at the southern end of the rainforest.

The 1897 Queensland Act for the Protection (!) of Aborigines was still in force. Under this Act, each local policeman was "protector" for his area. Stephen Wurm had warned me to contact the policeman as soon as I arrived in a new town, before doing anything else.

"If he sees a strange white man talking to his niggers, he'll have you in the lock-up in a flash, and you'll have a hard time talking yourself out."

The Ingham Sergeant was most helpful and recommended we talk to Willie Seaton, who lived at Toobanna, five miles back along the road we had just travelled.

Ingham is a pleasant town, situated on coastal flats just to the south of the Herbert River. Many of the cane farmers are Italians, and next to the bakeries selling crusty European bread, are newsagents with more papers and magazines in Italian than in English. We walked around the town until I could think of no excuse for delaying further.

Willie Seaton's house was easily located from the policeman's directions — it was between the Toobanna store and Trebonne Creek. "House" was perhaps too flattering a label. The two rooms were put together from corrugated iron, with board shutters covering the glassless window holes. The front room seemed full of people, but I was made welcome and invited to sit down. Willie Seaton was a tallish, white-haired man, about seventy and blind. He sat very upright on a metal stretcher bed behind the door, accepted a cigarette, and answered my questions.

He said he came from Waterview Creek, a few miles further south, and remembered a bit of the Nyawaygi language. Only he and one other old man, Long Heron, knew anything of it now that the "old people" were dead. But if I went north, I'd find lots of people speaking the language up there — Jirrbal, he thought it was called. They used it all the time, in the way Nyawaygi had been spoken when he was a boy.

It was dark in Seaton's front room, but I could just make out the breakfast things still on the table — a tin of powdered milk, a packet of tea, and some left-over crusts. I offered him another cigarette and plucked up courage to ask the Nyawaygi names for some simple body parts. "Foot", *jina*. "Eye", *buyin*. "Tongue", *dhalany*. I could only just see to write them down and wasn't too sure what symbols to use for some of the sounds — there was no time to mull over and discuss the possibilities, as we had in the phonetics classes at Edinburgh. Willie Seaton had to remind me gently that he was blind, when I pointed at things I wanted the Nyawaygi terms for, such as "this part of the leg".

I was convinced, from what I had read and been taught at Edinburgh, that the best results would come from analysis of running text (monologue or conversation) rather than from direct questions of the type, "How do you say this?" So I asked Seaton to tell a story into the tape recorder, perhaps something about his early life. He responded with a few halting sentences and then told me in English what they meant. I thanked him, said I hoped to come back sometime to ask a few more questions, and left the remainder of the cigarettes before beating a nervous retreat.

Later, I found the recording level had been turned up so high that it was completely inaudible, and that the few words I had taken down were scarcely legible. I'd spent no more than half an hour with Willie Seaton. But at least it was a start.

2

"Haven't you got a machine?"

The next morning we continued northwards, over the low wooden bridge that spanned the Herbert River. Seaview Range comes down close to the coast here, and it was slow work pulling the caravan up the steep, winding road. We were driving through the fringes of tropical rainforest — ferns and creepers covered and joined the trees. Then, at the top of the range, we came to a lookout over to Hinchinbrook Island, which was separated by a jagged blue channel from the mangrove swamps of the mainland coast. The island was completely uninhabited at that time, a swathe of brown vegetation rising uninterrupted to meet the clouds that shrouded its mountain peaks.

The road descended and then ran straight for thirty miles through the marshes, crossing and recrossing the single-track railway to Cardwell. The town had been founded in 1864 as a major port. But, as so often in Queensland, the site selected by the government proved impracticable, for the high mountains behind Cardwell had made it impossible to establish a path to the interior. Now only about five hundred people lived there, not many more than in 1870.

Cardwell has just one long street, running parallel to a shady, sandy beach. A few hundred yards across the sea to the east is Missionary Bay, at the end of Hinchinbrook Island. A Reverend Mr. Fuller had gone over there in 1870 to establish a mission for the Biyaygiri tribe. He stayed for five months, during which time not a single Aborigine came near him, and so was forced to return south where the natives were at least approachable!

In retrospect, the Biyaygiri might have done well to seek his protection. In 1872, Sub-Inspector Robert Johnstone — who was convinced that there was only one real way to "teach the Aborigines a lesson" — led a party of police and troopers who beat a cordon across the island and cornered almost the whole tribe on a headland. Those who were not massacred on land were shot as they attempted to swim away. There are no Biyaygiri left today, and scarcely any records of the language.

It took a while to find the police station, tucked away off the main street. The policeman came straight to the point, showing that little had changed in Cardwell during the last ninety years: "There are no niggers in this town." When I pressed him, he said that there were some at Murray Upper, twenty miles to the north, but they were under the jurisdiction of the Tully police. So we drove straight on up to Tully, a metropolis with a population of almost three thousand, and the seat of government for Cardwell Shire.

It would be hard to find a greater contrast to Cardwell, with its clean white houses and scattered palm trees, fanned by languid sea breezes. Tully looked as if someone had stopped half-way through building it. Or perhaps more as if it were half-way to demolition. The setting is imposing enough — its main street runs uphill, at right-angles to the coast highway, right under the huge, forested bulk of Mount Tyson. But there were odd gaps along the street where something had burnt down and had never been rebuilt. Too many panes of glass were cracked, too many windows boarded-over, and there was not enough paint.

The only place to put our caravan was in the council park, next to the lower of the two cinemas. The first night we went in, sat in deck-chairs and watched Robert Mitchum and Deborah Kerr in *The Sundowners,* a rousing story about an itinerant sheep-shearer who just couldn't bring himself to settle down. And we heard it loud and clear every night for the rest of the week, through the wooden walls of the cinema.

There was a tap nearby, which was the only facility provided. Well, the town toilets *were* situated there, but they didn't get cleaned between Friday morning and Monday morning and the people of Tully didn't seem too clean in their habits — perhaps especially at weekends.

Tully had a single redeeming feature — one that was rather unexpected. To mark one hundred years of white settlement, the council had just published *Cardwell Shire Story* by Dorothy Jones, wife of the shire engineer. It was nicely printed in Brisbane and had an attractive cover with an Aboriginal firestick design. This model work traces the shire's history from the first explorers who sailed up the coast, the early settlers and their encounters with Aborigines, the establishment of the sugar mill at Tully in 1925, up to the present day. It is well researched and judiciously written. There was only one snag: the tiny Tully library didn't have a copy because the council thought everyone should buy one.

I went up the hill to ask Mrs Jones if she could suggest the best place to go to study a language. We stood at the door and spoke for a few minutes. Yes, there were some Aborigines at Murray Upper, but they often wouldn't talk and it was a rough place. The best people to try were Joe Kinjun and Joe Chalam, two old men who lived by the Tully River. Mrs Jones warned that I should not believe everything they told me — they tended to say whatever they thought someone wanted to hear. And she warned me especially not to sit down in their camp, because of the likelihood of catching a disease.

(I didn't see Dorothy Jones again for fourteen years, when I was still doing some work on Jirrbal and she was by then registered as a higher-degree student at the James Cook University in Townsville. Mrs Jones had become very interested in the Aborigines, and was planning a thesis on cognition. In the intervening years, she had gathered a good deal of linguistic information from Joe Kinjun, but hearing and transcribing strange words was not her forte. Although I was able in 1977 to resolve most of her queries, Dorothy quoted a few things that I just couldn't recognise. So I suggested that we drive out to see Joe Kinjun and get him to repeat them. We were able to clear things up, and in fact had a good long chat with him. Sitting down.)

Having established contact with the Tully policeman, Alison and I drove back south a few miles to the Tully River. It was getting towards the end of the cane season when some of the fields were eight or ten feet tall. A cassowary poked its head out of one stand of cane, waddled across the road accompanied by a chick, and made for the forest. It was almost as big as an emu, with glossy black feathers on its flightless wings and a bright blue neck. On its head was a bony helmet which protects it from the impact of low branches as it speeds through the jungle. Although it walks a bit like a duck, gyrating its behind, the cassowary can outrun a horse, and disembowel a man.

We came to Euramo, named after the Jirrbal word for "river", *yuramu.* There were about a dozen houses, a store, and a tumbledown hotel. In Queensland, liquor licenses are only granted to hotels, which must undertake to provide food and accomodation for travellers. But no one had ever been known actually to stay at the old Euramo hotel. It was said that a traveller had once thought about it, but when he was shown a room, decided that he just might push on a bit further.

A road ran off to the right at Euramo, parallel to the Tully River. Cane farmers' houses were located every few hundred yards, and by asking the way a couple of times, we found a track through to the river. A white-haired old man with his shirt buttoned erratically was sitting on a log. He said he was Joe Chalam, waiting for Joe Kinjun and his family to return from a fishing trip. When I got out a notebook and pencil and shyly enquired whether I could ask a few words, he expressed surprise.

"Haven't you got a machine?"

I admitted that we did have a tape recorder.

"Well, get it out then. You got to do it properly."

I later learnt that a couple of years before, Ken Hale, an American and doyen of field linguists, had worked there for a couple of hours. Chalam remembered Hale's recorder and was anxious to repeat the experience. He spoke a sentence or two of his language into the machine, then translated and embellished in English and demanded to hear it replayed. Chalam was in total charge of the session, and I really couldn't follow all that was being said — it was too much and too fast. But Chalam's relaxed enjoyment of the situation put me at my ease, and a lot of good language was being recorded onto the tape. I felt I was really getting somewhere.

Joe Chalam told us about Mrs Henry, a white woman living up the road who was writing a book about the local legends and place names. She wasn't in, but we talked to Les Grant, an Aborigine who was working around the yard. He said he knew a bit of the language, but not really enough to help us. We should go and see his mother, Chloe Grant, who lived at Murray Upper. She knew all of the languages from around here and could tell us everything we wanted to know.

So that afternoon we drove south from the Tully River, over Bellenden Plains with its swamps and pools, a flock of brolgas dancing over the long green kangaroo grass, and a crocodile skulking by the river. This was the Murray River — not to be confused with its longer and better-known namesake in the south. It rises at several places in the mountains, no more than thirty miles from the coast, and then cascades down *Guyurru,* the majestic Murray Falls. The pool at the base of the falls is said to have been made by the dragonfly, *yirrinyjila,* shaking his wings as he tried to get free from a group of tormenting children. The river then flows into the sea two dozen miles north of Cardwell.

Cane farms had been left behind at the Tully River, and when we turned off the bitumen and crossed the railway line we were in original rainforest. Only a thin strip had been cleared, for the dirt road to Murray Upper.

In 1963, perhaps sixty white people, and about an equal number of Aborigines, were living in the Murray Upper valley. A few acres had been fully cleared, here and there, for bananas or beans or cabbages. Some land had been partly cleared of bushes and low scrub and its grass improved, so that cattle now grazed among the black bean trees, the Moreton Bay Figs, and the imported oranges and mangoes. But most of the bush remained uncleared. Among the rich jungle vegetation — trees with edible fruit like the black pine, the finger cherry and the wild nutmeg — bustled wallabies, long-nose bandicoots, spiny echidnas and, of course, cassowaries.

I've often had arguments about Murray Upper with George Watson, a member of the Mamu tribe from the tablelands fifty miles to the north. I find it so majestic as to be overwhelming — a long flat valley, with the two branches of the Murray coming together in the middle, sheltered on three sides by tall mountain peaks that seem both to dwarf the valley and to give it an air of stillness and peace. George simply says that he finds it shadowy and depressing and that he doesn't like to be hemmed in like that. (Just possibly his aversion is connected with the traditional antipathy between the Mamu and the Murray Upper tribes.)

We drove to the centre of Murray Upper: the school, the post office, and Cowan's store. Two elderly Aboriginal ladies in the store were buying flour, corned beef and epsom salts. A white farmer in a ten-gallon hat was drinking a bottle of sarsaparilla. Mrs Cowan — trim, bustling, fiftyish — found time to talk to us in between serving and answering the telephone.

"You ought to go and see old Jimmy over at our place, Warrami. He'd know all the old stories. He's always telling me that I should write the words down, then I'd learn them, and I'd like to, but I've got so much to do in the shop that I just don't seem to find the time. Old

Tommy Sullivan, up at the mission — he'd know a lot, too, but he's a cranky old fellow. If you found him in a good mood he'd tell you everything he knew. He helped Gladys Henry with her book. Went over the names of every bend in the river, from Bellenden right up to the Falls."

We asked about Chloe Grant.

"Oh yes, Chloe'd know a good bit too. Been with the whites a fair amount, but she was brought up by the tribe. You could try her. Follow the road down here past the school, straight on past the turn-off on the right to Warrami, go over the bridge, past the mission on the right and it's about the third house on the right. I think it's called Yabbon. But do go across and see our Jimmy Murray. He's the best fellow for all the old songs."

Thanking Mrs Cowan and promising to follow her advice, we drove on, over the hundred yards of bitumen that went from the store to the school, and then westward down the valley. The track got rougher, and we had to weave slowly around the worst of the potholes. A brown sand-wallaby jumped out of the jungle in front of our Land Rover and, braking to miss it, we almost hit our heads on the windscreen. Over a rickety wooden bridge that rattled as we crossed, with the forest on our right, and on our left, a cleared patch knee-high in bladey grass. And there was Yabbon: a white-painted wooden house set on blocks about two feet off the ground, with a water-tank and windmill off to the right. The yard was fenced and bare, except for a few clumps of grass and weed among which the dogs — and a goat — ran.

Chloe invited us up to sit on a wooden bench and chairs on the front verandah. We said what a nice house it was.

"Yes," she agreed, "used to be white people live here until two months ago. But I'm a poor widow since my husband pass away, and I've got these three girl to bring up. One of my own still at school and then there's my daughter's kid — she don't come, she just leave them with me and she go off with her husband and work on a station out Garnet way. So old Ormy Butler he let me live here. But now he say he want me to move. I'm not *going*." Chloe's voice moved up an octave as she almost sang the last word. "I've got nowhere to go." Then without any pause and in a matter-of-fact tone: "Yes, what can I do for you?"

I explained, stammered, that I'd come from England to learn something about the original language of Murray Upper and that Les had said Chloe might help us. What I really wanted was stories, just telling a traditional tale, or something about her early life, talking into the microphone for five or ten minutes.

"I don't think I can help you there." There was a pause, while Chloe fiddled with her cigarette. "There were two languages on the Murray, not just one."

"No, I didn't know that."

"Oh yes. The other side of the river that was Jirrbal and this side was Girramay."

"Were they very different?" I asked.

"Oh, long way. Jirrbal call 'water' *bana* but Girramay say *gamu*. And 'fire', that's *buni* over there but this side they call *yugu*."

"Yes, I see. What about other words? Parts of the body. Were they different?"

"*Jina*, that's 'foot' in both languages. And *mala* is 'hand' and *gayga* 'eye'. Most words the same, only a bit different. You could understand one another. But those Girramay, they fierce people. I'm Girramay, I was born Girramay but I brought up Jirrbal. My father he was Irish but I never see him much. My auntie she bring me up and everyone talk Jirrbal then."

Chloe told us she had eight children living. Her eldest son, Edgar, lived with his family in a sad-looking shack, made of old bits of wood and iron, just behind her house. Ernie still lived at home. Ernie and Edgar were working with Mrs Cowan's son Max, cutting timber on a property that King Ranch was clearing to create more grazing land. The second daughter, Irene, and her three children were staying with Chloe for a few weeks while her white husband looked for a job up north.

Black-haired, bespectacled, of medium-height, Chloe exuded a vivacity and intelligence that made it hard for me to keep up. Her eyes danced as she told us about the people in Murray Upper — mostly stories of how they couldn't quite do what they should do. "Poor old thing" seemed to sum up most situations — Mrs Cowan trying to look after that shop all on her own, opening it seven days a week; Joe Chalam who was too old to work anymore; Tommy Sullivan, an old Aborigine at the mission who was neither fully man nor fully woman.

Then her chatter suddenly halted.

"Well, what can I do for you?" Chloe turned to us. I asked a few more names of animals and body parts.

"That wallaby around here, you seen any?"

"Yes, we saw a brown one just down the road."

"Oh. Well, he's *barrgan*. And the big kangaroo, up on the range, he's *yuri*. Little kangaroo rat is *barngan*. And that one climb up in the tree — you ever seen him?"

"No, not yet."

"Well, he *is* a kangaroo but he climb up in the tree and if he see you he jump down and jump away on the ground so he easy to catch that way. Silly-looking thing. Call him *mabi*."

A few more words were different between Jirrbal and Girramay, which seemed really to be two dialects of one language, as linguists define the term (in terms of mutual intelligibility). "Woman" is *gumbul* in Girramay but *jugumbil* in Jirrbal, while both have *yara* "man". And "ear" is *garba* in Girramay, as against Jirrbal *manga*.

Chloe laughed, "You know what those kids call what-is-it in the store? Come on Irene! They call them *manga*."

Irene explained that dried apricots, which Mrs Cowan had just begun to stock, had been dubbed *manga,* because they looked a bit like dried ears!

We were disappointed that Chloe steadfastly maintained she knew no stories and couldn't give us a running monologue in Jirrbal. But she was a real find — tremendously friendly, obviously bright, and able to explain things in a clear and instructive way. We thanked her for an informative afternoon and promised to come back in a day or two.

The next day we decided to follow Mrs Cowan's advice. Leaving Tully quite early, we drove back down to Murray Upper and took the turning to Warrami, a mile past the school, over a low flat wooden bridge crossing the northern branch of the Murray, up a steep bank — and there was the flat, cleared expanse of the Cowans' farm. It was divided up into areas for bananas, grass-seed and cattle, with a field of water-melons, and extended to the strip of dense scrub that had been left by the edge of the meandering river.

Jimmy Murray lived a few hundred yards down towards the river from the Cowans' homestead, in a clean wooden house with a fenced garden in front, in which he grew pineapples and other introduced foodstuffs. He was a plump, round-faced, bow-legged man who was always short of breath. The epsom salts we had seen being bought in the store had been for Jimmy. He told us he got fifteen packets every two weeks (but never said what the extra one was for). A full-blood Girramay, he had spent years away as native tracker for the police at Bowen.

"Then they decide in Brisbane 'no more black tracker', so they send me back here."

Jimmy Murray was in his sixties; his spouse, Mary Ann, looked a dozen years older. She knew much more about traditional life, but was kept in the background during our conversation. Jimmy had to turn to her every couple of minutes, though, to check something of which he wasn't quite sure himself.

Mary Ann had been married to Wild Jimmy, an incredible character whose exploits are recounted with gusto by both white and black.

Fig. 2. Jimmy and Mary Ann Murray (Girramay) outside their house on the bank of the Murray River. (1963)

Legend has it that he killed a man and then lived around the upper Herbert River for several years, all by himself, to avoid the police. And even when he emerged, Wild Jimmy was able to avoid capture for a considerable time. One of the nicest stories concerns a policeman from Herberton who decided to catch Wild Jimmy. He hired an Aborigine from Herberton as a tracker and went off towards the Herbert. His guide was most helpful and they found some of Wild Jimmy's recent tracks but not Jimmy himself. On returning to Herberton, the policeman told the tracker to rub down his horse while he refreshed himself in the hotel. A settler in the bar congratulated him on bringing in Wild Jimmy.

"What do you mean?"

He pointed out of the window. The policeman had hired Wild Jimmy to track himself down!

Mary Ann had taken up with Jimmy Murray when Wild Jimmy had finally been sent to prison. There had been a worry that he might try to claim her when he was released, but that hadn't happened and Wild Jimmy was now dead. Mary Ann had long, straggly hair and a loose dress hanging off her bent shoulders, contrasting with Jimmy's upright stance, his clean white vest and belted shorts. I never heard her speak more than a word or two of English, although she could undoubtedly understand it a bit.

We were shown a boomerang that Jimmy Murray had just made — and painted, although that was never done in the old days. He gave us a few names of animals and trees, making us repeat them after him, and complimenting Alison on how well she got her tongue around the words. But it was hard to keep him on track — every other word would prompt some long, egocentric reminiscence. When we got out the tape recorder, Jimmy said he could sing a song, but not tell a story. Accompanying himself by tapping two boomerangs — with Mary Ann beating out a rhythm on her thigh — Jimmy Murray sang about a pelican, circling over the sea looking for fish and then diving down and grabbing a meal into its beak. His voice was high and intense, the words running together and broken by a swallow of breath after every dozen syllables.

Jimmy told us that he'd see about arranging a corroboree while we were there — perhaps on Saturday night. All the men from Murray Upper would paint themselves and act out the songs — and they'd invite across the people from the Tully. Jimmy would speak to Mrs Cowan about organising transport for it.

We were still keen to record some running text. Mrs Cowan had mentioned Tommy Sullivan and Jimmy said he would be all right, if he would talk to us. But he liked to be called Tommy Warren now. "Sullivan" was out of favour because it had been a white man's name.

It seemed that everyone had one or more Girramay or Jirrbal names — Jimmy Murray was Girrinyjany and Mary Ann, Minyajanggay — and also an official European name. A regular forename, such as Joe or Jack or Rosie, would be followed by a surname that could be the designation of one's tribal country (Jimmy Murray, from the Murray River), the name of a white man one's father or grandfather had worked for (Spider Henry had been brought up on the property of Hughie Henry), or an adaptation of one's Aboriginal name. Joe Chalam's Jirrbal name was Jalam and Tommy Sullivan's was Warruny (the *n* and the *y* are pronounced together, as a single sound, at the end of the word); he now wanted to be known as Tommy Warren.

Just as we were leaving, Jimmy Murray added another piece of information about Tommy Warren.

"That fellow, he's hermaphrodite."

It was perhaps the most surprising vocabulary item I've ever heard from someone whose English was really fairly rudimentary, very much a second language to the Girramay he used in everyday discourse. When we mentioned this to Mrs Cowan, she said that although she had heard the word, she wouldn't have been able to recall it at will, and Jimmy certainly hadn't got it from her. It seemed that as Tommy had got older, his feminine characteristics had become more pronounced, with mammary development backing up his high, shrill girlish voice.

Even if it hadn't been the most obvious move from a linguistic point of view, we couldn't have controlled our curiosity any longer. Our next stop must be the mission, and Tommy Sullivan/Warren.

Actually it wasn't a mission any longer. A couple of years before, a self-appointed missionary from an ersatz sect had leased a few acres just beyond the Warrami turn-off and erected some wooden huts and a small wooden church. Then, after only a few months, he had left. In 1963, someone used to drive out there once a week to hold services, but soon afterwards that stopped and the people gradually moved away.

The mission was filthy. There was obviously no proper sanitation and nothing was ever cleaned. Everything there seemed to stink. Someone said that Tommy Warren lived in the second hut on the left and we were able to talk to him — but not really to see him — through a raised shutter.

The conversation was quite simple, and very short. Tommy wanted twelve pounds before he'd tell us anything. I was of course offering payment — but it was ten shillings or a pound, and it was payment for results. I suggested that he first tell a story and then I could give him one or perhaps two pounds. That was no good. He wanted twelve pounds, on the nail, in advance, or he wasn't saying anything. Mrs Marnie Digman, who was passing by, told us that her husband Mosley would help us for free when he got home from work. She advised us not to mess with Tommy Warren: "You give him twelve pounds and he tell you three words, then he say he want more money."

So, cutting our losses, we left the mission. Following another suggestion of Mrs Cowan's, we travelled further up the track, past Chloe Grant's house, crossed the Murray by a ford and drove up a steep bank to Birdy Curtis's place. Three old Aboriginal ladies lived there, and Mrs Cowan was certain they'd talk for us.

Birdy Curtis was a weather-beaten, wiry, old farmer. With his young white wife and the three old Jirrbal ladies to help around the place, he could afford to be laconic. Birdy was obliging enough to us. He let out a holler that seemed to make the banana plants bend back.

"Lena, you get those two other old ladies, Biddie and Lassie. Come and talk language for this man here. He come long way to record you fellows talk."

It was scarcely the ideal situation. Birdy and his wife stood in the background, directing the Jirrbal ladies to talk straight at the microphone and offering a steady stream of encouragement:

"That's right. . . . You tell it now! . . . Talk to — go into that there. . . . Keep going — oh, heck, I don't want to be in it."

The conversation was hardly fast-moving — perhaps the whole farm was laconic. But at least something was being said.

"*Wunyjangum — baninyu — wunyjarri — wunyjangum — bangum dawulu* or *balbulu* or *gunggarri* or *guyngguru* — you now . . .*"

Birdy thought they would like to hear it played back and we asked what they had been talking about.

"Nothing much. She ask where I come from and I been tell her, I come from up there."

We followed up by eliciting a few words. And ran into language difficulties again. Old Biddie seemed to mumble a bit, and it was harder to hear her through the noise of the fowls wandering around us. When I said: "I'm sorry, could you repeat that? I couldn't catch it because the cock was crowing", a funny look came over Biddie's face, "Cock, eh?" But she did repeat it. It was only later I discovered a male hen can only be called a rooster in Australia. Biddie must have found it hard to reconcile the word she heard with the polite context in which it was used. But, as is usual in these cases, the tone of voice was given precedence over the actual word, and I was granted the benefit of her doubt.

The next day we went back to Chloe Grant. I was eager to play the conversation recorded at Birdy Curtis's, get her reaction, and have her provide a translation.

"I wondered where you were going, when I see that orange truck drive past here yesterday," Chloe remarked. "I thought you might be going up to Birdy's place." And then she added, as an aside, "Silly old thing."

We played the tape of Birdy's three old crones. As Chloe sat on the verandah, listening to the two-word sentences and single-word replies, her lips pursed. When it was finished, she said to take that tape off and put a clean one on. Without any more ado, Chloe Grant told a fluent, flowing story in Jirrbal. A narrative about her youth, hunting for wallabies and scrub-turkeys, searching the jungle for grubs, fishing in one of the many rivers that abound in Jirrbal territory. When she had finished, we played it back to her. Chloe listened intently, plainly satisfied with the job she had done.

"That's one language for you. And now you'll be wanting Girramay, I suppose."

We just nodded acceptance and she was away into another reminiscence. Asking the white man for food, being refused. Searching for honey, avoiding getting stung. Digging up wild yams with a sharp-pointed stick. Bathing in the river for relief from the heat. Chloe carried on a dialogue with herself, adopting different vocal timbres for the two characters. One person remarks that she feels unwell. The other enquires what might be the matter and receives a high, singing reply, with the final syllable drawn out to a plaintive moan worthy of the finest revivalist preacher — *jarranggu gandanyu nganyaaaa* "oh, my leg is *that* sore". They seek out the native doctor, for curative massage.

Having started to record a narrative in each of the local languages, Chloe saw no reason to stop. Were we interested in Gulngay, the language that had belonged to the Tully River mob, of which Joe Kinjun was the last living member? You bet we were. Gulngay is in fact — from a linguistic point of view — another dialect of the same language as Jirrbal and Girramay, but it has a few words different and also one or two idiosyncratic bits of grammar. There is a verbal ending *-mi* which occurs only in Gulngay, indicating that something has happened and is truly finished. Chloe put this onto the end of almost every verb, as if it served as a mark of identification of the dialect. She assumed a resonant timbre, the voice sliding and falling to give the deep hollow sound that she felt characterised speakers of Gulngay.

Chloe told two more stories on that memorable afternoon of Wednesday 23 October 1963. Both were traditional legends she had heard from her grandfather, around the camp fire at Bellenden in the years before World War I.

Once upon a time the only water in the world was hidden away by Banggarra, the blue-tongue lizard. The other animals were able to assuage their thirsts only by chewing *gulbira,* kangaroo-grass, for the moisture it contains. They challenged the lizard — his moustache was wet, showing that there must be water secreted somewhere. No, you chew that *gulbira,* that's all there is, was the emphatic denial. The lizard, Chloe explained afterwards, spoke in Girramay, as if to emphasise his villainous nature. All the other animals, and the narration, used Jirrbal.

Gujila, the short-nose bandicoot, tried following him, and then Midin, the ring-tail possum, took a turn. But Banggarra spied them behind and took care not to venture near his private spring. Finally Galu, the mouse — the smallest animal of all — beat the cunning lizard. As Banggarra looked back to the left, Galu hid on the right; then when he looked back the other side, Galu jumped across to the left. As the lizard lifted the stone which hid his supply of water the mouse pushed it away — *mali, mali, mali,* "wonderful, wonderful, wonderful" as all the animals jumped into the water which burst out around them.

Then a legend which told of the origin of fire. Oblivious to the noise of Irene's children grumbling and crying in the background, Chloe explained that the rainbow snake once owned the only fire in the world. The birds — which had human form in those far-off days — tried one after another to snatch it away, but each one was knocked to the ground. Finally, the satin bird alighted so quietly that it was able to snatch the burning log. Everyone at last was able to cook his food, to the annoyance of the malevolent rainbow snake.

At the end of her story-telling marathon, Chloe sat back and lit another cigarette.

"There, you've got all the language from here now. Straight-out. Better than what those three old things up at Curtis's give you. They didn't say anything. They should have more sense. You didn't come all the way from London for: 'Where are you going? Oh, going up.' You wait till I tell them what I think of what they say into machine."

The next thing to do, Chloe decided, now that we had "got" Jirrbal, Girramay and Gulngay, was to search out the other languages of the area. There was Warungu, from up on the tableland beyond Kirrama station.

"Now that's a hard one. I couldn't tell you that. But you ask Peter Wairuna up at Garnet. He's the one who knows' that language."

Remembering the few odd, clipped words Norman Tindale had recorded in 1938 — and these constituted the main reason both Arthur Capell and AIAS had suggested we start work in the rainforest — I asked Chloe if she knew anything about Barbaram.

"Oh, that's up Mareeba way. My daughter-in-law, Edgar's wife, her mother Barbaram. Hey, Mavis," Chloe spoke to one of the girls who were sitting on the steps listening to us, "you go and fetch Mum over here."

Then, turning to us, "Mamie's mother is Barbaram. She never teach her nothing. But you go and see old lady. Old Mrs Simmons. She live in Garnet too. And she know Barbaram. I think she does."

Mavis came back with her mother. Tindale and Birdsell had said that the rainforest people were characterised by "short stature, crisp curly hair, and yellowish-brown skin colour" but Mamie Grant was the first really tiny person we had seen. She had woolly hair and a deep matte black skin. Mamie shook hands with us shyly, her natural reserve contrasting with Chloe's ebullience, and said she wasn't sure what language her mother spoke. But she was sure she would help us.

We stayed a week in Tully, visiting one or two speakers each day. The most important task was to get Chloe to translate the story texts already recorded. I played them back, stopping at the end of each phrase, while she slowly repeated and explained what she had said onto

Fig. 3. Joe Kinjun (Gulngay) enjoys a joke with Alison Dixon, enceinte, at his camp on the bank of the Tully River. (1963)

a second tape-recorder. She also dictated lists of names for plants and animals, body-parts and kin, and verbs and pronouns.

We returned to the Tully River to see Joe Kinjun. Their camp was deserted, but we found the Kinjun family spending the afternoon on the sandy shore of the river. Joe's sons were diving into the stream and spearing fish — barramundi and bream — which the women wrapped in ginger leaves to cook in the coals of a fire they had made on the sand. Joe was only too pleased to talk to us. But if we asked a specific question, he would go on about something quite different, talking for ten minutes half in English and half in Gulngay (without any translation for that part), so that we could only vaguely follow what he was getting at. What we could make out seemed to be partly at variance with what Chloe had told us, and sometimes Kinjun appeared to contradict what he had himself said a few minutes before. We had a friendly session with him, but it wasn't very productive.

It became clear that those Aborigines who were recommended to us by the white people were likely to be the least knowledgeable, and least useful for our purposes. The best informants tried to have as little as possible to do with whites, and were often branded by them as trouble makers. The Aborigines themselves laughed at sycophantic Uncle Toms like Joe Kinjun. *They* were welcome to waste *their* time talking to white people. They didn't know much anyway, and most of what they did, they couldn't keep straight. And at least it kept the others from being pestered with casual enquiries from whites.

Jimmy Murray could almost be put into the same category as Joe. He had been away for many years, and was also fairly simple-minded. It was all right him talking to white people, since there weren't many secrets he could tell them. (Although Jimmy was respected as a fine singer.) The Europeans looked askance at Chloe, certainly the most knowledgeable and intelligent person we met in Murray Upper; she was too sassy by far. And Mosley Digman was just a trouble-maker; no good would come of going to see him.

I went back to the mission on Friday afternoon to try to record some more texts. Paddy Biran, a thick-set Girramay man in his forties, was most obliging. We went through the names for points of the compass, some animals, and important local places. We then recorded some simple sentences describing gathering wood, making a fire, cooking meat, and then eating it. Most words were the same as the Jirrbal terms I had got from Chloe, but about one in five was different. "I'm hungry" is *ngayba ngamirbin* in Girramay, Paddy said, whereas a Jirrbal man would prefer *ngaja ngamirbin*.

Paddy also described some of the traditional foodstuffs, like black bean nuts, and scrub-hen eggs. The black bean tree *(Castanospermum australe)* grows very tall, its branches stretching up from the top of its long, straight trunk to reach the sunlight above the forest canopy. The nuts, with three or four kernels apiece, drop to the ground when they are ripe, towards the end of spring. The elongated half-shells are used by the children as boats, and raced down the river. To prepare the kernels for eating, they are first wrapped in leaves and baked in hot coals for five or six hours. They are then sliced very thinly, using a parer made from a snail-shell, and put into the river in a dilly-bag. A stream of water is directed onto them for perhaps twelve hours through a funnel made of rolled ginger leaves. Then they are roasted again, for at least half a day, and immersed in running water for a further period. Finally, they are ready to eat.

The whole process takes about two days. Ernie Grant, Chloe's third son, told us that when he was a boy he'd sometimes be hungry — and he might have to stay hungry for an awfully long time. He'd be told that food was being prepared, but it sure was a long time coming. It wasn't wise to cut short the preparation — leaching and roasting and so on are absolutely necessary to remove poison from almost all the vegetable food staples of this region. The zoologist Carl Lumholtz tells in his book, *Among Cannibals,* how he lived with the Warrgamay tribe, on the Herbert River, in 1882—83. He was very hungry one day and ate some black pine nuts that were only half-prepared — they had been roasted but not beaten out afterwards — with most painful results.

Scrub-hens, Paddy Biran explained, are too lazy to sit on their eggs as do other birds. Instead, they lay their eggs in a mound they build of earth and leaves. The heat from this pile of humus incubates them, and when the chicks hatch, they dig their way out. I had just read Dorothy Jones's anecdote, in *Cardwell Shire Story,* of how the early white settlers, puzzled by these scrub-hen nests, thought they might be Aboriginal burial mounds! Paddy explained that when wild tamarind fruit, *nyuga,* was ripe it was a sign that scrub-hen eggs would be ready to harvest. People would search out the mounds, dig into them to get the eggs, and then cook them in their shells. Each egg is as big as six hen's eggs, and provides a meal for several people.

Paddy was reluctant to record a text unless he had a mate to talk to. Mosley should be back soon — in fact he'd been expecting him all afternoon. Just as I was about to call it a day, Mosley Digman's truck rumbled up over the stones and round the potholes. Paddy went over to greet him and I followed, with the recorder switched on. Mosley was a short man in a wide-brimmed hat; he was full of vivacity and humour.

"Wagibin ngayba," Mosley explained that he'd been working all day for the white man, carting things about.

"Where shall we go tomorrow?" Paddy enquired, in Girramay. "Look for scrub-hen eggs?"

"No," protested Mosley, "too much chance of getting *gubarrnbanyu,* scrub-itch. Let's go fishing."

But Paddy was not to be deterred: "Scrub-hen eggs taste good, and it's the season for them."

"Wanya gugar, digurrigu jarruganda," Mosley exploded, "What do you think you are, a sand goanna, wanting to dig up scrub-hen eggs?"

Finally, they agreed to go upstream to see what fish they could find in a deep water-hole, and the children could bathe in a shallow part of the river nearby.

This pragmatic interchange, with its ready humour, was all captured on tape. It would nicely complement the monologue legends from Chloe, in building up a corpus that included all social varieties of the language.

The big event of that week was the corroboree on Saturday evening. Mrs Cowan called up her brother, Arthur Henry, who lived near the Tully, and he promised to bring across Joe Chalam, and Joe Kinjun and his sons. A full-scale singing corroboree hadn't been held for a year, and everyone was very excited about it.

Traditionally, there had been two kinds of intertribal meeting. I was told that the last fighting corroboree had been in about 1945, on the Cardwell flats. In these, a number of local groups would meet by arrangement, travelling from as far as Innisfail and Ravenshoe, and the adults would engage in a series of protracted fights to settle current or old disputes. There had been a fight involving just the Murray Upper people in about 1950, but on that occasion metal weapons had been added to the traditional wooden armoury. The original heavy, hardwood duelling swords were dangerous enough: up to five foot long, they were swung in single alternating strokes over the head against the opponent. But when they were finished with a metal saw-edge, the chances of anyone living to take part in another such battle were significantly reduced. One man had received a badly split head in that 1950 altercation — which had been about a promised wife — and the Tully police had broken it up on the third day.

Singing corroborees were a quite different matter. In precontact times, men, women and children from a number of nearby groups would gather at a place where food was in season (or they might bring supplies with them). They would sing and dance from dusk until early morning, and then spend the day resting and exchanging news and gossip, before launching into another night of song and revelry.

In North Queensland, just a few degrees south of the equator, the days vary in length by only an hour or so between summer and winter. This night, it was dark by seven, and soon the spectators began to arrive. A corner of a field near the Warrami homestead had been chosen as the site, and four or five white families parked their cars nose-in to the corroboree ground, got out groundsheets and thermos flasks and settled down to their own exchange of gossip and news. A couple of dozen Aboriginal children, and their mothers and aunts, took up position on the other side. They amused themselves with trying out their own dances, and with chasing and leapfrogging. I loaded tape onto the recorder and fixed up the microphone. Arthur Henry drove up with the Tully contingent in the back of his ute, to joyful greetings from black to black, and a more subdued Anglo-Saxon welcome of white for white. I walked round and talked to Marnie Digman, and Joe Kinjun and Joe Chalam. Jimmy Murray had been gargling to get his voice into shape, and Mary Ann was trying out the skin she would stretch over her thighs as a drum to accompany Jimmy's songs.

But time went by and still the main group of dancers had not arrived. There was no question of starting without them. Everyone else seemed to be having a pretty good time, but I got a bit impatient and worried.

"We start when they come," was all Jimmy would say.

Then I heard that they — Paddy Biran, Mosley Digman, Jack Murray and Mick Murray — might be up the road at the barracks where Mick Murray lived. So I drove up there and found Mick and Jack, two brothers who worked for the Cowans on their bananas and grass-seed. They were just sitting quietly in the gloom. I asked them to come on down so everyone could start — it was way after dusk, which was the agreed-on time to begin. They said, No, they couldn't come without their mates. They'd be coming. There was no hurry. We'd got the whole night ahead of us. And as soon as their mates came — maybe from Euramo, which was a good place to get a drink on Saturday night — then they'd all come down and the dancing could begin.

This was my first experience of "Aboriginal time" — something which I've come to envy, but which my nervous clock-watching European upbringing won't allow me fully to emulate. The principle is simple — start when everyone is ready to start, and stop once all the things that had to be done are done.

The best illustration I've come across of the difference between European and Aboriginal attitudes to time was at a conference the AIAS organised in Canberra in August 1971. Richard Gould had published a book, *Yiwara, foragers of the Australian desert,* which unwisely included a photograph of secret objects, knowledge of which is restricted to initiated men. An Aboriginal high school girl from a desert tribe had chanced to see this picture — and all hell had broken loose. She was to be ritually speared for having broken a taboo. AIAS tried to get in touch with Gould and his publishers to ask them to withdraw the book from sale, or at least remove this photo. Meanwhile,

Aboriginal communities in several parts of Australia, alerted by the wide media coverage, began banning anthropologists from entering Aboriginal reserves.

The people AIAS called together to discuss "Problems of field access" included directors of Aboriginal Affairs from the states, people from the federal Office of Aboriginal Affairs, anthropologists and linguists from all the major universities. And one token Aborigine. They had selected Phillip Roberts, a thoughtful and intelligent man from Roper River, in the Northern Territory.

The chairman, Black Mack (more formally known as Professor N. W. G. Macintosh, of the University of Sydney), moved through the agenda in a purposeful manner. After the opening remarks, we discussed "the formal and informal aspects of access to the field, in relation to Government and Mission administrations, including permits" until lunch. Then there was "relationship between fieldworkers and (a) administration, (b) informants in the field"; a break for tea, and then into "towards a definition of (a) 'secret-sacred', (b) the aims of field work".

Black Mack tried to get everyone to speak, and early on the second day he invited Phillip Roberts to put forward his point of view. He had one comment. He just couldn't understand the way we were running things. We discussed one topic for an hour and a half. Then, although we hadn't said all we wanted to on it, and hadn't reached any conclusions or consensus, we moved on to the next item. We talked about it for a bit. Then before we'd got that straight, we moved on to something else. Why? All these people had come from all over Australia and surely we should take things one at a time, and talk each one out? Wouldn't it be better to agree on just one thing, than to say a little about many? As I remember, the chairman thanked Mr Roberts for his most useful comment, and then moved on to the next item on the agenda.

At about nine or ten o'clock, Jack and Mick Murray came down with Mosley. Paddy Biran was ill and couldn't attend the corroboree; this was a great shame since he was a skilled singer. The men went behind the trees to decorate themselves with the white clay Joe Kinjun had brought from the Tully, and with yellow and red clay from the Murray. Jimmy Murray picked up the pair of boomerangs, cleared his throat, and then began, his high strong voice gliding through:

mulu bumima yilmbu mugarruga
mulu bumima yilmbu ganyjalganyjal . . .

The dancers emerged into the centre of the field, in single file, stripes of white, crescents of yellow, ribbons of red and broken circles of white dots across their chests and backs and arms. They cast themselves as fishermen, throwing a net into the coastal surf, pulling it in, marvelling at the mess of silver fish visible through the woven strands of lawyer-vine. Arthur Henry came across and whispered to me an explanation of the mime, as I held the microphone close enough to Jimmy Murray to catch his words and Mary Ann's steady rhythmic drum accompaniment.

A couple of minutes' rest, and then Jimmy Murray began again, intoning the same song, words sung with a regular metronomic rhythm, a deep breath snatched after every thirty-third syllable. As the dancers finished, someone said, in English, "Hey, I wouldn't mind one of those fish right now."

The dragnet song and dance were performed again. And then a fourth time. *"Yunggulan baya!"* the dancers now demanded, "time for a different song." Jimmy took a tremendous breath and began to sing of the pelican. The dancers spread their arms as he described it gliding over the waves on the lookout for fish, and then diving down to grasp a morsel to store in its capacious beak pouch. The dancers seemed so exactly to *be* pelicans, as their eager syncopated movements blended with Jimmy's narration.

Each song was performed several times, interspersed with discussion of how the dance routine could be improved.

"Ngana 'juuu' yalaman – we should call out 'juuu' when the fish is sighted," Joe Chalam suggested.

The next song also concerned a fish-eater, the whistling duck, flapping its wings as it dived down to land, plop, on top of a wave.

The moon went behind a cloud, and Arthur Henry suggested that we focus our car headlights on a patch in the middle of the field, the better to illuminate the dancers. There was another bird song, about the brolga, then one mimicking how white women comb their long tresses.

Mr Cowan cut half a dozen gigantic water melons into thick slices, for singer and dancers and spectators. Joe Kinjun took a slice in each hand and, playing his customary role of court jester, shouted across to the white enclave, "Two portion watermelon, just for one man."

A short break before Jimmy, his voice just beginning to get hoarse, described a girl in a red dress, looking like a butterfly, admired by everyone and revelling in the attention. Then a song about something that had been introduced into Aboriginal culture by the white invader — the bow and arrow. It had been assigned a name in Jirrbal, *bunarra*; this was a single noun, although plainly based on the English phrase. The dancers lined up, each in turn showing how clever he was by shooting off an arrow, with ostentatious aplomb, towards an imaginary target.

Finally, a song about the English bee. Buzzing around in procession, extracting nectar from flowers, going into an imaginary hollow log that was their hive, depositing the sweet honey. This had been performed only once when the rainclouds finally burst, streaking down on the dancers, making yellow paint run into red, and red into white.

The dancers would have waited until it stopped, but the whites had by then had enough of what was to them an occasional novelty — not a restatement of tradition and law and life, which is what the corroboree was for the Aborigines. Arthur Henry was keen to get on the road. "OK boss, we pack up now." The Tully mob crowded onto the back of the ute, with groundsheets and boomerangs and left-over clay, and went home in the rain.

3

"You never talk it to me!"

It was time to move on to Cairns, to pick up our mail, and then to survey the remainder of the rainforest region and see what other languages were still spoken. Tindale and Birdsell had listed twelve "negrito" tribes; four of them — Jirrbal, Girramay, Gulngay and Jirru — within the Murray Upper/Tully area. The others originally lived further to the north, up to and just beyond Cairns.

There was a short burst of rain as we left Tully, which is not at all unusual in an area with an annual rainfall of 180 inches — twice that on the Murray, although the distance is only a dozen miles as the crow flies. Three-quarters of it comes down in the wet season, which runs roughly from late December to late March, but there is still a good bit during the remainder of the year. Tully commonly receives an inch of rain in an hour, during any season. Drivers just have to pull in to the side of the road and wait — it is too hazardous to go on under such conditions. And if visitors comment, the people of Tully shrug, "Oh, that — it was just a little shower. You should be here when it really rains!" Appropriately, the envelopes that are supplied with picture postcards of Tully have a picture of a Cooktown orchid on the back, and on the front, "from Tully, the pretty wet place".

We crossed the railway line and turned onto the Bruce Highway, national Route 1. Past Bookalbookal Creek (its name derived from the word for "black bream" in Jirrbal) and through El Arish, a town of soldier settlements for veterans of the First World War. The sugar fields that fed the Tully Mill gave way to those of the Silkwood Mill, and then those for South Johnstone. Each mill can be spied from afar by its thick column of smoke, often a useful aid to navigation. We stopped for a cane train crossing the highway, its yellow engine pulling a hundred or more loaded trucks, moving slowly and steadily along the narrow gauge tramway to the crushing plant.

Then through Innisfail, with a population of around seven thousand, at the confluence of the South Johnstone and North Johnstone rivers. It is another town with a large Italian population, like Ingham, and its own weekly Italian newspaper. We drove past the Goondi mill, and across the long narrow wooden bridge over the Russell River, which was now just a gentle stream, wandering back and forth between sand banks. Like almost every bridge in North Queensland, it was only wide enough for one vehicle — people from the north give way to those from the south, and travellers from the east yield precedence to those from the west, on almost every crossing.

Coming up to Babinda, notable for an annual rainfall of about 170 inches, only fractionally less than Tully's, and also dominated by its mill, puffing dark shafts of smoke high above the town. Just before Babinda, we saw flames in the corner of a cane field. Worried, we pulled over to the side of the road. The flames leapt right across the field before we had time to take in what was happening. A number of small animals hopped or rolled or tumbled away, seconds ahead of the fire. The dry, crackling sound of the flames among the ten-foot-high stands of cane was like dozens of fortyfrappers on bonfire night. The flames joined together, way above the tops of the cane, merging into files of purplish smoke. Other drivers had stopped — not out of concern but simply to enjoy the spectacle. We learnt later that burning was a normal practice — each field would be periodically fired to get rid of the trash. The most spectacular sight was a field being burnt off at night, its red and yellow flames illuminating the sky for miles around. Then the fire died down, as quickly as it had arisen, with just a few stray patches still glowing and crackling.

Cairns was a delight. In 1876, the first direct route to the coast from the Hodgkinson goldfield had come out at Trinity Bay, and a city had grown up there. In 1963, before the introduction of jet flights from the south, it was not yet a holiday resort for tourists from the capital cities. Neither had television yet extended its tentacles that far. There was one air-conditioned store and one air-conditioned bar. But the heat, now in the middle eighties, didn't seem oppressive under the shade of the palm trees on the esplanade, in the banks on Abbott

Street, and in the department stores and cafes and bookshop on Lake Street.

Although without the benefit of an artificial fillip from the government — it had no army barracks, or university, or branches of state administration — Cairns had maintained a steady rate of growth; the population now stood at almost thirty thousand. It is the port and supply centre for the rich dairy country of the Atherton Tableland, and for the remote cattle stations and Aboriginal missions of the Cape York Peninsula. Although tinned food cost a little more than in Brisbane or Sydney, some fresh fruits and vegetables were cheaper — and better. Cairns is also a centre for big game fishing. Business tycoons and Hollywood stars match the strength of their lines and their limbs against giant marlin, and only take one back to Cairns to weigh if they think it might top the magic 1,000 pound mark. Sixteen miles to the east of Cairns is Green Island, a coral cay on the Great Barrier Reef. We made a note to take a day-trip there sometime to see the underwater observatory, and admire the rainbow splendour of fish and coral from a glass-bottomed boat.

We planned to live in Cairns during the coming wet season — when travel would be difficult and life in a caravan impractical — and so postponed looking for language speakers until then. I did go and visit the Police Inspector, who had authority over the whole region. He'd had a note about us from the Department of Native Affairs in Brisbane, to whom we'd had to apply for initial permission to undertake linguistic work. And we called on the Hookworm Man.

Hookworm can be debilitating within a few years if accompanied by a poor diet and low haemoglobin. It is prevalent in tropical Australia, especially where conditions of hygiene are poor. Especially among Aborigines. White settlers tend to eat a more varied diet, and to undergo periodic tests. I had been advised by people down south to wear socks, since that might help to avoid getting hookworm — it is hard now to recall the chain of argument that was put forward. In fact I didn't wear socks for very long in that heat.

The Hookworm Man was an employee of the State Department of Health. Based on Cairns, he toured the north, taking samples of faeces, checking them for hookworm, and administering doses of medicine as needed — one spoonful washed down with a draught of orange cordial. He visited every group of Aborigines — those on missions and cattle stations, and odd little groups that no one else had ever heard of, living in a tumbledown humpy by the mouth of a river, or camping by the workings of a deserted tin mine. I found him in his office down an alley just behind the post office, peering through a microscope at recent samples. The Hookworm Man gave me invaluable advice — where to go, whom to see, what roads to avoid, which cattle station managers were likely to be friendly and which not, and how to approach them. During the next few months, our paths criss-crossed, and people would often pass messages to one of us through the other.

"Tell that tall fellow to come back here," an old Aborigine would say to the Hookworm Man, "I've remembered another story about the dreamtime days, and I want to tell it to him."

The Hookworm Man had warned me about the Aboriginal settlement at Mareeba, one of the toughest there was. He'd been punched on the nose there when trying to give out medicine to hookworm sufferers. But it wasn't a place we could miss out. Barbaram — the strange monosyllabic language that looked quite unlike any other Australian tongue — had been spoken just to the west of Mareeba.

The road went north from Cairns for a few miles, up the coast. And then it turned west, ascending the steep mountains to the Atherton Tableland. It climbed a thousand feet in eight miles, twisting around spurs, turning back on itself a hundred feet higher. Our Land Rover chugged up in second gear, the heavy metal caravan swinging along behind. Alison counted how many times I had to turn the wheel full to the left, and then to the right, on the endless curves — and gave up at two hundred.

We went near the spectacular Barron Falls, with the railway line to Herberton passing right in front of it. (The line had been completed in 1910, just as the great tin boom — which had been the reason for planning a railway, a quarter of a century earlier — was finished. Such is the way of these things.) Then there were forty miles of fairly straight, narrow bitumen, through the forest, to Mareeba.

A small country town, the streets seemingly half-made and dusty, Mareeba only really comes to life once a year, at its winter rodeo. Roughriders and cattlemen converge on the town, and groups of Aborigines come from all directions, to camp in tribal groups positioned according to the relative locations of their homelands — a great time to do linguistic field work. For the first couple of days, that is — until the booze starts to take over, old grievances flare up, and fights break out.

Mareeba lived up to its reputation of being an unfriendly town. The policemen were curt and only minimally informative. And in the Aboriginal settlement – small wooden government huts next to the showground – we had a cool reception. People said that Johnny Grainger might remember some Barbaram, but he was quite senile and it wasn't clear that he had ever known any – he was just someone for the others to fob us off with.

Willie Richards was reported to be the last speaker of Jangun, but he said to come back the next day. We did. He wasn't quite ready and told me to take Alison and show her the town. I said I already had – Jack and Newell's all purpose store, the bakery, a few pubs, and that was about it. He said he'd be ready to talk in a few minutes. I sat outside and waited while he did his chores. Washed up and methodically dried a breakfast cup and plate. Swept the floor. Opened a window, swept a bit more. Closed the window. Finally, after about an hour, Willie Richards mysteriously led the way to the verandah of a nearby empty house and we actually recorded a little Jangun. Ten minutes – about forty words. Then two white Jehovah's Witnesses (or something like that) rolled up with a portable organ in the back of their pick-up, for an on-the-spot service. Willie said he was sorry, but I'd just have to come back another day.

It was possible to record a little Muluriji from Jack Cummings after he came home from work. We talked by candlelight in his hut at the far end of the settlement. And one apparently helpful man said that he didn't know any Jabugay himself, but he'd guide us to where the old people lived who did speak it. Mona Mona Mission – the place Ken Hale had worked at for a week three years earlier – had recently been disbanded, and the mission houses distributed to small settlements along the Barron River. We drove back along Route 1 towards Cairns and then branched right on a forestry track to Koah. No one was home. At Oak Forest there were three families fishing, but they didn't know anything – or so they said. Our guide said thanks for bringing him out, he might as well stay now he was there.

Then we made the gentle twenty-mile climb to Atherton, three thousand feet above sea level. In striking contrast to dusty Mareeba, Atherton has neat pavements, with large trees growing in strips of lawn down the middle of the main streets, their boughs overhanging the traffic lanes. It boasts several well-kept parks and a mildly sophisticated shopping centre with boutiques and "emporiums". It struck me as distinctly out-of-place in North Queensland; more like a bourgeois little town from southern England. Linguistically it measured up in much the same way. An old Aboriginal lady called — of all things — Esther Pink grudgingly asked us into her parlour. She could only remember a handful of words of Yidin, and didn't think there'd be anyone around who knew much more.

I thought Herberton would be worth a visit. The northerly branch of the Jirrbal-speaking tribe had ranged from the Tully Falls to the Wild River, upstream as far as Herberton. Leaving Alison in the shady Atherton caravan park, I headed off along a corrugated road to the south-west. It was as bone-jolting as working a pneumatic drill until I learned the secret — go fast, fifty miles an hour, and you skim over the tops of the ridges.

The main street of Herberton goes down a hillside, through a valley, and up again on the other side. Wrought-iron railings from prosperous buildings put up in the boomtime years of the 1890s look out on the boarding schools, which are the town's main industry today. But there was still an extracting plant working in the valley, crushing and stamping tin. And an Aboriginal settlement across the river, consisting of just a few scrappy government huts. I was only able to locate one ancient black lady. She at first mistook me for a local councillor, looking for distinctly non-linguistic favours. Disappointed at her mistake, the old crone affected not to know any language, and sent me up the hill to the hospital, to talk to old Tommy.

The hospital was easy enough to find. A few old people were dozing on the verandah and a few more sitting next to their beds — no one looked very ill. But there was absolutely no sign of any of the staff. After I'd been moseying around for a good twenty minutes, the door of matron's office opened and all of the sisters and nurses emerged, refreshed from their smoko. Yes, of course I could talk to old Tommy, who was over there next to the old white gentleman with a military moustache and demeanour.

Tommy had fallen in the fire and got burnt at Christmas time, but he was nearly better now. He'd done the same thing the previous year, and then, too, he'd been in hospital until November. Too much booze, he said. Tommy was deaf, and couldn't make out my polite request as to whether he'd mind if I asked him a few questions about his language, Jirrbal. I said it three times, pronouncing the words as slowly and clearly as I could. Then the old military gentleman cupped his hands to his mouth, put them three inches from Tommy's ear, and bellowed, "He wants your language."

"Oh, yes," said Tommy, "that good language. Jirrbal. They speak him all way back to Ravenshoe. All way down to Tully that language."

"Would you mind if I asked you some?" I enquired.

"Do you know any language?" my translator shouted.

"No more," replied Tommy, "my brother, he's the one knows all that language. He know all words for animal, and bird. They never learn me all that. My brother the one all right."

"Where could I find your brother then?" brought no response.

Again, Tommy's neighbour came to my aid, whipping out each word like a cannon shot. "Where. Is. Your. Brother?"

"Oh, my brother," said Tommy — appearing surprised that we didn't already know — "He dead. He die ten year ago."

Field work wasn't always so frustrating, but it could produce the most bizarre responses. I had wondered what the effect might be on Aboriginal children of being told in school that Captain Cook "discovered" Australia in 1770. This may relate to the comment of one elderly Aborigine who was glad I'd come to ask about his language, because of the fact that I came from England. It seems that an American anthropologist had been by a couple of years before, and my informant didn't approve of entrusting information to him.

"I'd rather give it to you," he confided, "because, you see, we all come from England in the first place."

The most useful piece of advice Stephen Wurm had given me, back in Canberra, was on how to approach the local policeman.

"First thing to do when you hit town, go and see the policeman. Act casual. Say something like, 'Pretty nice town you got here.' Doesn't matter if it's full of flies and bloody sand. He has to live there and he likes to think it's all right. Policeman will say, 'Could be worse. Where are you from then?' Tell him you come from Canberra, Institute of Aboriginal Studies. 'Oh,' he'll say, 'you want to talk to some of these black fellows around here, then? Have you got permission from Brisbane for that?' Now you'll have all the official rubbish from the Department of Native Affairs, but whatever you do, don't start pulling out documents and flashing them at him. Australians aren't impressed by lots of bits of paper, not like other parts of the world. They put up with bureaucracy, but they don't cherish it. Say, 'Oh, sure, do you want to see them?' and he'll tell you, 'No, that'll be all right.'"

Wurm stressed that the policeman should know almost everything about the town and is the ideal person to advise on where the most likely informants will be found. He said to ask, casually, in the policeman's idiom, "Do any of the old blackfellows around here talk lingo still?" "Oh yes," would be a likely reply, "you get the old yabber-yabber around town when they come in for their rations. Can't make it out myself." Wurm had a final warning – get the policeman to tell you who to go and see, but do *not,* whatever you do, let him take you there himself. If you arrive in company with the policeman, you'll be regarded with suspicion, and may well find it more difficult to gather the information you want.

When we arrived in Ravenshoe, thirty miles to the south of Atherton – Ravenshoe is so named because an early settler is said to have found an abandoned copy of Scott's novel on the site – I went to the police station. Only it didn't go exactly as Wurm had predicted. The sergeant was friendly enough, agreed it was an all right town, and didn't want to see my letter of authority. There were certainly a number of black-fellows around, but he'd swear they didn't know any of the old lingo. There was one way to find out – he'd take me over to old Willie Kelly. Willie was the most myall of all, and if anyone knew any language it would be him, but the sergeant was pretty sure we would draw a blank.

In vain did I protest that I could find my own way, that I didn't want to put him to any trouble. The policeman drove a few miles out of town, turned onto a track, through a gate, down a faint gap in the forest where the low branches banged on the cab roof, to a shack by the river.

"Hey, Willie, do you speak any Abo lingo? Fellow here from the south wants to make a recording of you."

"Yeah," said Willie, an alert white-haired, white-bearded man in a blue shirt and tidy long trousers, "I speak it okay. What do you want to know?"

"Well, stone the crows, you never talk it to me!"

"No, boss, you wouldn't understand it. Talk it to my own folks all the time." (Later, I found that there were a few dozen Aborigines in Ravenshoe, almost all of whom spoke fluent Jirrbal or Warungu; for some it was their first language.) The policeman left, shaking his head.

Willie Kelly was friendly and, in his way, helpful, but he provided a jumble of genuine information and bombast. When we arrived, he was

Fig. 4. Willie Kelly (Jirrbal) demonstrates how to make a fish-net, near Ravenshoe. (1963)

spinning his own twine, and was part-way through weaving a fish-net from it. He explained what he was doing into the tape-recorder, in his language and then in English: "... that's our tribal way to make net to catch these young fish."

Willie then insisted on presenting to us the half-manufactured net, and made it into a mini-ceremony, which I had to record: "This is a present I give you away, to you to take away with you, so to memory of how you come to met me and take this net to show the people."

Willie had an almost royal manner, handing over the present with a flourish and half a bow as I managed to mumble, "Thank you very much indeed." He could have been on the stage at Stratford, declaiming short sentences in Jirrbal, and then translating them into English.

"Wild yaaam" — he pronounced the vowel very long — "when they goes into ground, and deepity, and then use sharp-pointed stick so they can catch the yaaams out of the ground to eat, feed children."

The language he spoke I found afterwards to be Jirrbal, although for some reason known only to him, Willie had introduced it as Ngajan. We tried to get him to record a monologue text right through in language, and then go over it a phrase at a time on the other tape recorder. But Willie liked to be in charge. In his measured way, with careful tension-building pauses, he described how warriors would come together for a corroboree "in tribal way", stalk and sneak up and then fight. A phrase or two of Jirrbal, then a sentence in English, a little more Jirrbal, and so on.

During a break, we laughed again at the naivety of the Ravenshoe sergeant. Then Willie mentioned that he himself had been a sergeant in the native police at the Aboriginal settlement on Palm Island. We expressed wonder and then — when he insisted — admiration. (I mentioned Willie's claim when I visited Palm Island some months later and it turned out that he'd never been any kind of native policeman there, let alone a sergeant.)

Like Jimmy Murray, Willie Kelly had a wife (Biddy Clumppoint) who was older then he was, and who seemed to have a deeper and surer knowledge of the details of traditional life. He was forever excusing himself and going around the back of the hut, where she was preparing food, to ask her something. I suggested that she join us, but he said no, she wouldn't want to, she was too shy, and anyway she had jobs that must be done.

There was one thing at which Willie Kelly did excel, with no faking. He was a marvellous singer, who had the same easy, relaxed way of projecting a song as had — in their different genres — Leadbelly or Jimmie Rodgers. The first song related to what he was doing when we arrived, weaving twine into open-mesh fish nets. Then he sang one about a scrub-hen laying eggs, gathering up leaves and dirt over them until it had constructed a huge incubatory pile.

But the most haunting song — which for Alison and me somehow encapsulates life in North Queensland, Aboriginal customs, the bush, and the animals — concerned the willy wagtail, *jigirrjigirr*. This is a small bird, with sharp black-and-white marking, which wiggles its long tail as it walks. It is said to resemble an initiated man, decorated up in his finery, dancing on the corroboree ground. Indeed, in the Jirrbal "mother-in-law style", it is called *burulabarra*, literally "he who belongs to the fighting ground". Willie banged two pieces of stick together as his voice picked out the lilting words:

jigirrjigirr ngarru banggany
jindigara ngarru banggany

The first line was repeated three times, then the second, and then first, second, first. The end of this part was marked by a trilled *brrrr* from Willie, then, over the continuing clapsticks, *tsh-tsh, tsh-tsh, tsh-tsh, tsh-tsh,* crisp sibilant evocation of the bird's movements — before the song resumed. When we replayed the tape, Willie took on the role of corroboree dancer, sticking out his behind and wiggling it to the words, in perfect emulation of a nervous, proud little bird.

Willie Kelly knew he was a good singer, and wanted what he considered his proper reward. He suggested that we play our recordings in picture theatres down south, where white people would pay big money to hear a genuine Aborigine sing. We should then send the money — or a proportion of it — up to him. It was hard to strike a balance between being realistic and not being too cruel. We said we would investigate the possibilities but he shouldn't be too hopeful. We could have said that (from our observations) most of the white people in Australia wouldn't be interested in hearing Aboriginal songs, and certainly wouldn't be likely to pay much money for the privilege.

When we began our fieldwork, Aborigines did not have the full rights of citizens in Australia. Until the constitution was changed by a national referendum in 1967, the federal government did not have the power to make laws affecting Aborigines, and they were not included in censuses. Aborigines were entirely the responsibility of state governments.

Queensland had, in 1897, introduced an Aborigines Protection Act which gave the government dictatorial powers over the lives of Aborigines. Its introduction met with some opposition, but the state government of the day assured its critics that these powers were just, as it were, in reserve, and that it had no intention of changing the existing state of affairs. The government stuck to its word, for a few years. Then in 1913, the Aborigines were rounded up and taken, often in chains, to one of the government settlements. That on the Hull River, near Tully — to which many of the rainforest Aborigines had been sent — was destroyed by the 1918 cyclone. The people were moved to a new settlement on Palm Island, which was to attain notoriety as a repressive semi-penal institution.

Under the 1897 Act, it was an offence to sell or supply liquor to Aborigines. Whites and Aborigines could not cohabit or inter-marry without permission from the Chief Protector. Aborigines were not allowed to retain any money they earned — it had to be paid into a savings bankbook that was under the control of the local policeman. If an Aborigine wanted something from his bank account, he had to apply to the policeman and say what he intended to spend the money on. I heard many stories of an Aborigine asking for five pounds from his account and the policeman getting him to affix his thumbprint to a withdrawal form for ten pounds — a fiver for the Aborigine and a fiver for the policeman. In one town in western Queensland, the policeman became so affluent from tricks like this that he bought a big, flashy American car. The local Aborigines would point to it as he drove by and say, "There goes our car!"

There was a clause whereby particularly civilised and trustworthy Aborigines could be exempted from the provisions of the Act and accorded the same rights as non-Aborigines. A white person would have to put forward a strong case for an Aborigine to be granted exemption. This was mostly done — as far as my experience went — for people over sixty-five. Once exemption was granted, they would be eligible to receive the normal old-age pension, and the white family for whom they had worked all their lives — usually for a pittance — would thus be relieved of the responsibility of providing for them when they became too old to work.

We'd known something of the Queensland Act, and Willie Kelly had grumbled about it a bit, so it was fresh in our minds as we drove to the next small town, Mount Garnet. This was thirty miles further inland, beyond the rain forest, set in open wooded country. Garnet, as it is affectionately called, is the supply centre for the local cattle stations, and still has a couple of tin dredges that manage profitable operation.

The heat was overwhelming as we parked our caravan on the only available plot, next to a toilet that had one side open to the world and contained a bucket teeming with maggots. We went across to Lucey's pub. Alison sat in the lounge while I went through to the bar — into which women were not allowed, by Queensland law — to ask for a coke and a gin and tonic. The weatherbeaten, red faces of the cattlemen sitting on stools around the bar all slowly swivelled and surveyed me. "Pommy!" ejaculated one of them. I was made to feel that no one had ever asked for a gin and tonic in that pub before. Certainly they didn't stock tonic water, but could provide gin and lemonade.

Some helpful and interesting people lived in Garnet. After he came home from his work on the dredge, Fred Blackman and his brother-in-law, Peter Wairuna, spoke some of the tablelands dialect of Jirrbal. We were once more recording by the light of a candle. Fred's surname showed a certain lack of imagination — he had had to have one for social security purposes. Interestingly, his wife was known as Nora Fred or Mrs Fred, and not Mrs Blackman. (Mrs Blackwoman would, I suppose, have been more appropriate.) Peter Wairuna showed us a lump the size of a turkey egg on his thigh, the relic of a bite from a venomous snake from which he had, miraculously, recovered. I recorded him telling us about this in a few simple Jirrbal sentences. When it was played back, Peter almost fell off the log he was sitting on, in surprise. "So soon, so soon!" He'd expected that it would be some time before he could hear his own words, thinking perhaps of the time required to develop and print a film.

When I went back to Murray Upper and told Chloe Grant where we had been, she berated me for not having got Peter and his sister Nora to converse in Warungu, which they knew as well as — or better than — Jirrbal. But we'd missed our chance there. The news filtered through that Peter had hit Nora over the head during a drunken argument that Christmas. She died quite soon afterwards, and Peter only survived her by a few months.

Our main hope in Mount Garnet was to record some Barbaram from Lizzie Simmons, mother of Chloe Grant's daughter-in-law Mamie. We found old Mrs Simmons — eighty years old, toothless and cranky — sitting outside the cinema shack with her daughter, Chloe Day. They had a sack of groceries and were waiting for a lift home. Lizzie said that she spoke Gugu-Yalanji, from her mother, and told us a few words — *gaya* "dog", *mungan* "mountain", *buri* "fire". As we sat talking, a white man came in and out of the cinema, apparently on some errand or other, muttering to himself louder and louder each time. Naively, we couldn't think what was bothering him, and Chloe had to spell out that he didn't like white people talking to black, especially just outside his premises. The old lady said we could come out to her place — a couple of miles out of town — the next day, and she *might* tell us a word or two of Barbaram, which had been her father's language. But she wasn't promising, mind!

There was no rain about Mt Garnet just then and the dirt track to Lizzie Simmons' house was hard and dry, with ruts in it a foot deep. If the wheels of our Land Rover had slipped into them we'd have had a devil of a job getting them out again, so I took care to drive with one

Fig. 5. Lizzie Simmons after I'd tried, unsuccessfully, to get her to tell me some Barbaram, at Mount Garnet. (1963)

front wheel on the hill between the ruts and the other in the grass at the side of the track. The house itself was easy to spot from the glint of a huge pile of beer bottles. We'd never seen so many bottles in one place before. There must have been thousands of them; six feet high, the pile was just about as tall as the house.

Mrs Simmons sat on a chair outside, her stick grasped between her legs, looking for all the world like a witch. She wanted a pound note before she'd tell us anything. I wouldn't normally consider payment in advance, but since Barbaram was at stake, it was duly handed over. A few body parts were forthcoming: *guwu* "nose", *dirra* "teeth" and *jalnggulay* . . . "tongue," I prompted, since that was the Jirrbal word. Mrs Simmons smote her knee as accompaniment to a broken mocking cackle, "You make me laugh, you do make me laugh." Then *mara* "hand", *jina* "foot", and *bunggu* — what is *bunggu*? This was another I already knew, and I said it: "knee".

"What you asking me for? You know this already. You waste my time," Lizzie croaked, her eyes glinting at me from under half-open lids. I assured her that I only knew a few words, and that most of what she'd said was news to us.

Jalay "tree", *gandu* "dog". This wasn't Barbaram, of that I was sure. No, Lizzie agreed, she was talking Warungu, the language of her late husband, from the Garnet region. Her own language? Oh, that was too rough. And anyway she was feeling decidedly thirsty. *Jalun gari*, that means "got no more drink". It was one of the old lady's well-known failings — she'd once sold her granddaughter's favours to a white man for a bottle of beer, with the predictable consequences, Chloe Grant later told me.

Lizzie now decided that I was to drive into town and bring back two big cold bottles of beer for her. This was against the law, against the 1897 Act, but I agreed to do it.

"I'll keep your machine here," Lizzie indicated the tape-recorder, "to make sure you do come back."

And when we returned with the refreshment she was all compliments: ' Ah, you're a good boy. I'll be sure to send you a Christmas present."

Chloe Day, her daughter, was really helpful in trying to prise a few more words from the old lady, who now promised to stick to her *own* language. Chloe brought a variety of objects out of the house, for her mother to name — some matches, *wunju*, a dress, *gambi*, a jar of honey, *mula*, a huge spider pickled in a jar of methylated spirits, *jama*. We marvelled over this monstrosity and Lizzie decided to give it to us.

This was all very well, but Lizzie had now returned to Gugu-Yalanji, or a random mixture of Gugu-Yalanji and Warungu. *Nganjan* "father", *ngamu* "mother" — those were Gugu-Yalanji. *Gujila* "bandicoot", *gajarra* "possum" were Warungu, or maybe Jirrbal.

"You promised to give me some Barbaram," I pleaded. "The language from around Dimbulah and Petford. Other people know Gugu-Yalanji and Warungu. You're the only person who remembers any Barbaram. Couldn't you just pronounce a few words?"

Lizzie Simmons grasped her stick a little tighter, and directed her beady eyes at mine. "No," she creaked. "Barbaram too hard. Too hard for me. Far too hard for you."

The policeman at Millaa Millaa — back on the Atherton Tableland, half-way between Ravenshoe and the coast — plainly thought of himself as hard-bitten and tough. There were a number of Aborigines around town, and they did speak their own language. He learnt that I'd been in the area for a month, and enquired, "Have you picked up any of the lingo, then?"

It was a question to which there was no possible reply that could entirely please him. If I said "No", I'd appear to be incompetent. "Oh, just a little bit," I ventured, at which the policeman grunted, "Better man than me, then."

He recommended Biddy Tickler. If I looked lively I'd catch her up at the hospital — he'd seen the ambulance taking her up for the daily visit, and it hadn't yet returned. When I got to the hospital, Biddy was just getting into an ambulance to be taken home. I could follow it, and she would be happy to talk to me.

Tickler turned out to be an anglicised form of Digala, the Aboriginal name of Biddy's husband; it was based on *diga,* the name for the seed in any fruit that grows on a lawyer vine. Mrs Digala had leprosy and had lost the top joints from each finger and most of her toes; the stumps were freshly bandaged each day. All they could do about it, I was told, was to keep the sores as clean as possible. And luckily it wasn't contagious.

The ambulance pulled off the road alongside a field. I could see no sign of house or hut. The driver pushed down the middle strand of a barbed wire fence and pulled up the top one so Biddy could scramble through. Then he drove off and left her standing in the longish grass, among four cows and a bull. I followed Biddy through the fence, and she suggested we walk up the hill a little way and sit down in the grass there. She didn't smoke, and anyway she didn't really have the wherewithal to handle a cigarette. But she would be glad to share with me some words from her language, Wari.

We spent an hour going through the usual lexical list — mammals and insects, a few verbs, body parts, snakes, fishes, and a few adjectives and pronouns. Then, after giving Biddy a couple of pounds with many thanks, I asked if I could escort her home. We went over the hillock towards a large piece of corrugated iron, propped up on one side by two forked sticks, with a frayed piece of tarpaulin partially covering the gap. In the shelter was an old mattress directly on the grass, and a cardboard suitcase. As we walked down the slope, Biddy's husband, Harry, came from the other direction, at the end of his day's work on a local farm. I very cautiously circumnavigated the bull on my way back to the main road, thinking that our caravan seemed like a totally undeserved luxury.

The Atherton Tableland is the richest dairying country in Australia. There is a cheese factory at Millaa Millaa, a butter factory at Malanda, and the longest milk run in the world has huge tankers going regularly to Darwin, only a little short of two thousand miles away. Although it is situated squarely in the tropics, the high tableland yields rich pasture, all of it cleared from ancient rainforest within the last century. The hills and valleys are steep, but cows seem quite unconcerned at having to graze on slopes of forty-five degrees. The many small towns are joined by a network of bitumen roads, so that the whole area is more reminiscent of Sussex than of any other part of Australia — except that when the tableland hilltops are shrouded in mist, one might see a cow walk out of a cloud, with a kangaroo hopping out after it.

The policeman's other suggestion had been to visit the Brooks's farm, where a very old Aboriginal lady should be found. I went down the Palmerston Highway and then turned left onto another bitumen strip called Brooks's Road. This soon became a sandy track. After going through a patch of bush, it came out to a view of a magnificent valley, neatly planted with lines of fruit trees and square patches of pasture — in one direction were dairy farms stretching to Millaa Millaa, but on two sides there was virgin rainforest, reaching up into the mountains, with the peak of Mount Bartle Frere (Queensland's highest mountain) rising up in the north-east.

I drove down to the white house in the middle of the valley, stopping to give a lift to a young Aboriginal woman and two children. "Old Maggie should be home," I was told. "That's my greataunt. She's about eighty and knows all that Wari language. Maggie was brought up by the tribe and couldn't speak English until she was a woman. Me, I only know a few words here and there."

Mr Brooks, the elderly owner of the farm, was away taking his fruit to market in the tableland towns, but his wife made me welcome. Dressed in a loose, faded, floppy housecoat, she shouted out a welcome, urging me to speak up because she was deaf. Maggie Brooks was smarter, a squat figure with curly black hair, dressed in a coloured print frock. Maggie agreed to talk to me when the younger woman explained my errand, and we all sat around the table in the kitchen.

Maggie undoubtedly knew a lot, but it was hard to communicate with her. For one thing, she seemed to know only a little English, and that was pronounced without any s's or f's. She gave me a list of words in Wari — the names of animals, I later discovered — with no explanation or translation. The greatniece was a help — she explained that they would mean nothing to me without some gloss. Maggie then named a category, such as "snake" or "bird", and gave a dozen names, still with no further identification. Old Mrs Brooks — the white one — liked to join in, and her talk overlaid Maggie's on the tape. Something amused her, and one whole group of body part nouns was almost drowned out by a burst of high-pitched cackling laughter.

Mrs Brooks complained that her hearing-aid wasn't working. It needed a new battery and she couldn't put it in. I offered to do this for her, but it took a good deal of shouting from all three of us to convey the offer. When finally the message got through Mrs Brooks demurred. ' Oh no," she yelled in my ear, "I don't think I've got one."

Maggie was by now embarked on a list of place names. Just the names, one after the other, with no other information. Mrs Brooks was more concerned to tell me something by pretending she didn't really want to talk about it. "Don't you let on, Maggie. Don't tell him what's in those hills will you?"

I continued quizzing Maggie about the words for sun and moon and stars. But Mrs Brooks was not to be discouraged: "Don't you tell him about that gold down there, Maggie, he might go and find it."

The greatniece and I laughed, but it was a serious matter to the two old ladies. "Ah no," agreed Maggie, "we keep that for ourself. We go there by-and-by and find that gold. Gold up there someplace. Might be we find it."

Sensing my frustration, the greatniece suggested that if I could get Maggie together with her daughter Minnie, in Millaa Millaa, they would talk language together and it might be possible to record a real conversation in Wari. It seemed like a good idea. I contacted Minnie, who was staying in a tidy wooden house, raised on stilts, in the middle of town, and then went out to the Brooks' farm again the following day and brought Maggie back with me.

Besides Maggie and Minnie, there were three or four younger Aboriginal people in the room, and a gaggle of children. I switched on the recorder, said that they might prefer to talk without me there, and went out onto the verandah for ten or fifteen minutes. There was a lot of talking and laughing and shouting. When I tried the next day to transcribe the tape with the help of Harry Digala and Maggie's grandson, Tommy, I didn't have much success. In fact, it wasn't until I went through it slowly and carefully with George Watson, sixteen years later, that I fully understood what had been said that afternoon.

There was talk about what they might all do the coming weekend — go fishing maybe. Or they could chop out some witchetty grubs. Maggie stated quite emphatically: *"Jambun ngaja gulu janggany,* I won't eat grubs — just don't like them."

The most interesting comments, though, were about me, my going to fetch Maggie up to Millaa Millaa to talk language, and now standing out on the verandah.

"Mabi bayingala yawangga malagangu jangganany nyinany," Maggie said, "he's like a tree-climbing kangaroo sitting high in a tree eating malagan vines, that white man there. I'd like to throw him to the ground," she continued, "hit him when he's down there and the dog might bite him. Then peel his skin off, cook him in the fire and eat him. I'd eat the liver first. Cut his hands off, and his tail, and put him back in the fire to cook a bit more. Cut the carcass up with a knife and share pieces around to all the kids. . . . "

We were just packing up the caravan the following morning, preparatory to moving on, when the manageress of the caravan park came rushing up.

"Are you a professor of Aboriginal languages?" she asked, breathlessly.

Thinking it irrelevant in these circumstances to disclaim the promotion, I agreed that I was.

"There's a telephone call for you then, from the 4CA news."

Philip Wilson, who gathered, wrote and read the local news for the commercial radio station in Cairns, asked how long I'd been in the area, how many languages I'd recorded, how different they were, and how many speakers remained. It was the lead item on the six o'clock bulletin that night, I believe. He also invited me to come along and be interviewed when I was next in Cairns.

Philip was also an expatriate Englishman and we later became good friends. He told me that news items were sent in by correspondents in each town served by 4CA. They were paid according to the item's newsworthyness — generally ten shillings or a pound, although an announcement about a local play or sale-of-work might only merit two shillings and sixpence. Philip suggested that I keep my eyes open while travelling around, and call him up if I noticed anything that might make the bulletin. Just out of interest, I asked what was the most he could possibly pay. He thought for a few moments, and then said that if the Russell River were in flood and I saw six cars floating down towards the sea, with people standing on their roofs desperately shouting for help — well, that might be worth two pounds ten shillings!

News of our presence in Millaa Millaa hadn't been worth a phone call from the correspondent there. Young Tobin, the storekeeper's son, had written a letter that began (I was later told): "Dear Phil, There's some charlie in town trying to write down the Abo's lingo . . ."

We moved on up to Malanda, right in the middle of the dairying district. I never did get to see the Malanda policeman. He wasn't in the two times I called — a child said he was probably in the pub, but I was damned if I was going to seek him out there. Anyway, I reckoned I'd talked to enough policemen for one lifetime.

Two friendly old men sitting on a bench in the middle of town recorded a couple of hundred words in Ngajan. But the real finds were Jack and Nellie Stewart, speakers of Yidin. They lived with their daughter in a pleasant house not far from Lake Barrine, an eerie thousand-foot-deep lake in an old volcanic crater; the local tribes had regarded it as an evil place, to be avoided if at all possible.

Actually, I didn't find the Stewarts myself. They had been located the previous year by W. C. Wentworth, the provocative Liberal MP who had been at least partly responsible for the founding of the Institute of Aboriginal Studies. Mr Wentworth and his wife, Barbara, were in the habit of driving off each year to explore some remote corner of Australia. They had stayed at the Lake Barrine motel en route to the northern tip of Queensland, and a girl working there had said her father, Jack Stewart, knew all the old ways. Wentworth wrote down what the Stewarts told him of tribal organisation in the area, and AIAS passed it on to me. The Wentworths had taken us for a picnic the Sunday we were in Sydney, and had raced us up and down steep paths looking for Aboriginal rock engravings. (They had provided a bottle of Scotch in case − coming from Edinburgh − we might need a dram with lunch.) They'd suggested we could put up at the Lake Barrine motel for a week or two, but the AIAS people in Canberra had different ideas about the level of allowable expenses.

The Stewarts were charming and intelligent people. They explained everything most carefully and thought through in considerable detail what they should say. At last I had found some others who could measure up to Chloe Grant as a dream informant, able to reveal the complexities of lexicon and grammar in a way that I could immediately understand and record.

I spent two mornings with the Stewarts as they went systematically through the lexicon, prompting each other on the names of each species of lizard and frog, bird and tree, providing an account of colour and size and habitat, and, when they knew them, the common English names. Each artefact and type of trap was described in thorough detail, and its method of construction outlined.

When we were almost finished going through parts of the body, they insisted on including the verb *galnyjing* "have bilious attack, dysentry". Jack Stewart chuckled and added, "Tell that to the fellow in the parliament, he can laugh over that then."

"He wouldn't know?" Nellie queried.

But her husband insisted: "Yes he would, he all here."

To my great misfortune, I was never able to do any more work with the Stewarts. Whenever I went back, they were either not in, or − on the one occasion they were − Jack had fallen and hurt his head, which was swathed in a huge bandage, and they didn't feel like talking. By the time I returned to the field, in 1967, both had passed on.

When I returned to Cairns, the interview with Philip Wilson was quite good fun, and proved invaluable for later field work. We began by playing Willie Kelly's willy wagtail song, then talked for ten minutes − I said I'd been sent up by the government to record all the languages of the area − and finished with the scrub-hen song, again by Willie Kelly. As I travelled further afield over the next months, a recurrent greeting was: "Oh yes, I know you, you played that corroboree song over the wireless." It was perhaps the first time 4CA had featured any Aboriginal music. (When later I was interviewed in the Cairns studio of the ABC, the government radio station, my request to be allowed to play some corroboree music was met with the horrified response: "Oh no, I don't think that will be at all necessary.") One Guugu-Yimidhirr speaker whom I met up with at Deeral Landing said he'd heard on the radio about my coming around and had been carefully rehearsing his language for me; I was glad to sit down and record every single thing he had to say.

Philip Wilson couldn't pronounce his *r*'s very well, which lent a certain character to the newscasts. He was a tremendous journalist, although even he couldn't always find something new for a 7 a.m. bulletin after having been on the air until after six the previous evening. (But it was always possible to buy the *Cairns Post* on the way to work and retail a bit of that, if all else failed.) Sometimes there was no real local news and Philip was forced to begin the bulletin: "There are three rumours going around town today . . . " (only he pronounced it "three woomours").

In our interview he asked the sort of questions his listeners might have put.

"You really mean the Aborigines have a language? I thought it was just a few grunts and groans."

Then, "But they don't have more than about two hundred words, surely?"

I replied that I had collected over five hundred names for animals and plants from the Stewarts in a single morning, and that could only be a fraction of the total lexicon.

Many of his questions I had encountered before. At Murray Upper, one old white settler had asked what exactly I was doing. "Trying to write a grammar of the Aboriginal language" brought forth the unexpected response, "Oh, that should be pretty easy!"

When I enquired why, he replied: "Everyone knows they haven't got any grammar."

Philip Wilson followed the same line and I was able to assure him that Australian languages did indeed have a grammar, just as rich and complex as that of any other language. When he asked what language the local tongues most resembled, at the grammatical level, I took great delight in replying "Latin". The systems of case inflections and verbal conjugation, I assured the 4CA audience, were more reminiscent of the grammatical resources of the classical languages than of the simpler word structures found in English or French.

4

Full of Unforgettable Characters

We had now completed a preliminary survey of the surviving speakers of rainforest languages. It was clear that five of these "tribal languages" were mutually intelligible and could be regarded, from a linguistic point of view, as dialects of a single language. These were Ngajan (a few speakers at Malanda), Wari (Millaa Millaa to Innisfail), Gulngay (Tully River), Girramay (Murray Upper) and Jirrbal (Murray Upper, Herberton, Ravenshoe and Mount Garnet). I was later able to add Mamu (South Johnstone River) and Jirru (Clump Point). These seven modes of speech have almost identical grammars and a common lexical core, although just a few words do have more than one form over the language area — "woman" is *yibi* in Ngajan and Wari, *jugumbil* in Jirrbal and Gulngay, and *gumbul* in Girramay. The Aborigines insisted that each tribe had its own language, and that the odd lexical differences were indexes of political affiliation — *waju* for "nape" in Ngajan, while all the tribes to the south have *darra; gamu* for "water" in Girramay, while all the rest have *bana*; and a few more.

It is rather like the situation in Scandinavia, where Swedish, Danish and Norwegian are very nearly mutually intelligible and could really be regarded as dialects of a single language, on linguistic criteria. But language is an indication of political identity, and each of these separate nations prefers to say that it has its own distinct language. The Ngajan-Wari-Gulngay-Girramay-Jirrbal language was plainly the one I should study in depth. But it needed a name — for convenience, I chose Dyirbal to cover the complete dialect chain, although employing a single name is very much a linguist's artefact, which would not meet the approval of speakers. Dyirbal is another way of spelling Jirrbal, a central dialect that has the largest number of speakers (and in which I eventually became most fluent).

Nyawaygi, Warungu, Yidin, Jabugay, Muluriji, Jangun and Barbaram all appeared to be distinct languages. Barbaram remained the top priority — if ever I could locate a speaker — because of its apparently aberrant structure. But the other languages would now be given a lower priority; I would try to gather some further materials on them only as time allowed inbetween the intensive study of Dyirbal.

Murray Upper was, without doubt, the place to concentrate on. Several dozen people there used Jirrbal or Girramay as a first language, in every aspect of their daily lives. No other town had more than a handful of Aborigines, of which only the oldest spoke (or could speak) their own language. Everywhere outside Murray Upper, English had virtually taken over. We could fit in another couple of weeks collecting texts on the Murray before it was time to start looking for an apartment in Cairns for the wet season.

About sixty white people lived in Murray Upper, and about the same number of Aborigines. It was full of unforgettable characters, of both colours. There was one white farmer who used to play games with the trains. Queensland railways employ a 3'6" gauge, and the fastest speed at which I have clocked them was about fifty miles an hour — my Land Rover could always leave a train for standing. On a bit of a hill near Murray Upper, the coast express slows to a crawl. This farmer would jump on at the bottom of the slope, throw off whatever crates of cargo he could find, and then jump off before it started to pick up speed. Once he got umpteen tins of paint intended for stations higher up the coast. Soon his house, his sheds and his barns all appeared in bright railway red.

Old Mr Haydon, the postmaster, sold stamps and worked the manual telephone exchange. He couldn't be bothered with the Commonwealth Savings Bank, so Mrs Cowan in the store had taken that on. The exchange was open from nine to one and two to nine on weekdays, nine to one on Saturdays, and nine to ten on Sundays. Outside those times, if you could attract the postmaster's attention, there was a surcharge of one shilling and sixpence per call. It wasn't the extra cost that made people think twice before trying a call out of hours — it was the biting invective from Mr Haydon if he were called from his lunch or tea.

The postmaster was a deep-thinking, well-read man. When he proudly told people he was a member of the British Humanist Association, some of those at Murray Upper thought it was something to do with anarchy. He said he had read and understood the books written by his son-in-law David Armstrong, Professor of Philosophy at the University of Sydney, and I, for one, believed him.

Mr Haydon's brother lived quite alone in the bush, fossicking for precious metals. He'd normally get provisions every few weeks, but would often go for longer periods without seeing anyone. He had plenty to think about, he said, and borrowed David Armstrong's books to study them in peace. Every so often he'd come down for a week in Murray Upper – big metropolis! – but reckoned he couldn't take too much of it. One day we gave him a lift into Tully, and it would have been rude to refuse his offer of a drink. But I found I couldn't keep up with the straight gins. At ten in the morning! He said he reckoned he had to do a bit of catching up now and then.

The Aborigines at Murray Upper were (and still are) the largest group in Queensland living quite freely, outside the direct control of a mission or government settlement. But that wasn't really because they had been treated kindly during the hundred years of white settlement. In the early days, numbers had fallen rapidly – partly from introduced diseases like measles against which the Aborigines had no immunity, and partly from the influenza they caught when the blankets they were ceremoniously given each year on the Queen's birthday got wet. But quite a lot were shot – hunted in cold blood, like animals – and others were poisoned. There were several stories of dead Aborigines being found along the paths from their own camp to the white man's shack, where they had been given flour mixed with strychnine.

Out of the original population of perhaps five hundred members of the Girramaygan tribe, and an equal number of Jirrbalngan, just a few score remained. And these people were barely tolerated squatters on their own tribal land, despite the fact that they had been there for thousands of years before the white man came (in fact, for millennia before the Danes or the Anglo-Saxons, or even the Celts, arrived in Britain). Some white farmers would not permit Aborigines to live on their property. Others did grant this privilege, but only in return for the Aborigines doing some work around the farm. It was felt to be a real indulgence – letting an Aborigine erect his hut near a mountain about which he could recite creation legends, and to which he believed his spirit was connected.

That the Aborigines did survive to maintain a viable community in Murray Upper today is a tribute to their tenacity and resilience. It is also due partly to the backwoods situation. Most of the forest had not been cleared, especially on the rugged mountain slopes, and there was still plenty of native food around. Indeed, for many families, this was only supplanted by the white man's bread and beef as late as 1950. One group of Jirrbalngan had lived a traditional nomadic life around the upper reaches of the Tully River until about 1940 — three-quarters of a century after the start of white settlement. We were told that old Lorna, now living at Warrami, had been a member of that group.

There had been a school at Murray Upper since 1905, but it was intended for fully white children. (One black pupil is rumoured to have enrolled in about 1920; there were certainly no others during the next two decades.) Then, in about 1944, the enrolment dropped below nine, the minimum number set by the Queensland government as justification for a school. To forestall closure, a half-caste child was hurriedly admitted. Within a short time, all Aboriginal children were allowed to attend. The chain of history could be seen in Chloe Grant's family. Her eldest sons, Edgar and Les, had received no schooling at all; Ernie and Irene had had just four or five years' education, while Chloe's youngest daughter, Evelyn (born in 1948), had gone right through primary and secondary grades.

Admission to the school had turned out to be a mixed blessing. In 1963, about half the school-children were black; most would hear Jirrbal or Girramay as a main language at home. However, the principal threatened to cane anyone who was heard to speak in an Australian language within the school grounds, and this naturally tended to make more and more children stick to English at school and also at home. The future of the language looked to us rather doubtful.

Happily, things have improved since then. In particular, Rod Small, principal from 1976 to 1980, took a great interest in things Aboriginal. He set the children to interviewing their older relatives, recording stories in the local dialects, and started a project to document all the traditional foodstuffs in the form of an illustrated booklet with bilingual Jirrbal and English descriptions.

Even the most intelligent and industrious Aborigine was denied the opportunities for advancement that would have been automatically available if his skin had been pure white. Chloe's son, Ernie, was largely self-taught — to the degree that he had obtained a private pilot's licence. I used to work in the mornings and afternoons with Chloe on Jirrbal, and would sometimes help Ernie with an abstruse point in trigonometry during our lunch-break. Ernie was light-skinned enough to pass as a white man — which he did later when he spent five years in New Guinea as sawmill manager and timber salesman. But around the Tully, everyone knew which side of the fence he came from. When Ernie once tried to get a loan as downpayment on a property of his own, the bank was not interested. And even the Cowans — who had treated him almost as one of the family and helped in many small ways — felt, quite reasonably, that they were fully committed with setting their own sons up in the world.

Lindsay and Muriel Cowan were in fact the brightest spot in a bleak white landscape, so far as the Aborigines at Murray Upper were concerned. They employed quite a few of the men on their farm, providing fair wages and accommodation. They were happy to have a dozen or more old people and younger women and children living close by the Warrami homestead (in the house in which they had themselves lived until a few years before), and provided various sorts of assistance. Mrs Cowan allowed judicious credit at the store, and gave advice on questions of finance, social security payments and even moral dilemmas.

Yet things were far from easy, even for those Aborigines at the Cowans. The children might be bright and interested at school, but there were no facilities for doing homework. Electricity had not yet reached Murray Upper — it arrived the following year — and only the white people could afford kerosene-powered generators for lighting, refrigeration, and so on. The Cowans encouraged some of the older Aboriginal girls, who were now going by bus each day to the high school in Tully, to wash and iron their school uniforms at Warrami, and store them there, coming up each morning from their own houses to change at the homestead. This was kind and well-meaning. But how demeaning for the children! Scarcely surprising that they all left school at the earliest opportunity.

Since Murray Upper was to be the centre of our work, we jumped at Mrs Cowan's invitation to park the caravan at Warrami and use their toilet and shower. We got to know and like the Cowans, and their four sons and four daughters. It was good to sit on the porch, eating huge slices of watermelon and spitting the seeds across the grass, while we swapped ideas and experiences.

But there were even language difficulties here. One morning they invited us to come across for tea that day. So we went over to the house at about four, when everyone who happened to be around the farm stopped for ten minutes for a cup of tea and a piece of cake. But then at about six thirty, just as we were wondering what to cook for supper, someone came to ask where we'd got to. It was the first we knew that in Australia "tea" is the main meal of the day – a big slap-up feast with lots of meat, two or three vegetables, slices of bread and butter, and then a helping of pudding.

Lindsay Cowan was a slow-speaking, balding, firm-jawed bushman with more understanding and knowledge of the world than you'd find in a library of books. His opinions were delivered with a dash of crisp, laconic humour.

Lindsay had been brought up at Maclean, in northern New South Wales. His father's family had emigrated from Scotland and his mother's from Ireland, which led to huge arguments about religion and schooling. The father might appear at the convent one morning and whisk the children off to the local Presbyterian school, only for the mother to whisk them back when she heard what had happened. As one of a large family, Lindsay's opportunities were distinctly limited in the south, so he'd come north at the age of sixteen, in 1923, to seek his fortune. And by and large, he had succeeded. Lindsay loved to tell stories of the early days, when there was no coast highway, and the railway hadn't been joined up. To get to and from Cardwell – taking produce and fetching supplies – a fair number of steep gullies and creeks had to be negotiated. There was only one way to do it. The cart had to be completely dismantled each time, carried across piece by piece, and then reassembled on the other side.

The Cowans now had a thriving farm, which was being run more and more by their four sons. Lindsay had been concerned that each boy should do what he was most interested in. Alan had taken an agricultural degree down at Brisbane and then been a traveller for Shell Chemicals, based at Tamworth in New South Wales. But he'd become homesick, and asked if he could return. Kenny hadn't seen much point in schooling and hadn't been pressed to stay; he was the master-mind behind the bananas, which were sent down to southern markets in wintertime, when prices were at their peak. Lindsay recounted how he had once taken his youngest son, Ray, onto a hillock near the Murray with a view over most of Warrami, and said "Look there, son, what would you like to see on that land?" Ray had replied, "Cattle," and that's what he was now in charge of.

Mr Cowan and many of the other white farmers were angry about a contract the Queensland government had recently signed with King Ranch, an American pastoral company. They were most emphatically joined by the Aborigines. For most of this century, there had been useful grazing on the land between the Murray River and Davidson Creek, a tributary of the Tully. Many of the large trees had been left standing, but bushes and weeds had been cleared to make way for grass. Then the government suddenly decided that this land, which was leased to Lindsay Cowan and his brother-in-law Arthur Henry, had not been used to its maximum capacity. When the leases expired, the land was given – on a plate – to King Ranch. The charge, for free-hold land, was two dollars per acre for forest and five dollars per acre for scrub. Lindsay showed me the map of the King Ranch grant, its boundary weaving in and out to include every bit of flat land, but excluding all the rocky bits that could not be utilised. When we arrived, King Ranch had erected a high fence and was systematically clearing every tree and boulder with dynamite and bulldozers. They were destroying the country out of all recognition, in order to graze the maximum number of cattle.

Arthur Henry had had to sell most of his stock, but Lindsay had moved the Cowan cattle to a property he had just bought for this purpose, Princess Hills. It was only twenty-five miles away over the mountains but nearer a hundred by car – down to the coast road, up the mountains at Kirrama, then a long way round to cross the Herbert River and track back towards the coast. Ray, only twenty-one, was up there with a couple of stockmen, making yards and generally setting the place in order.

Lindsay Cowan had a fund of stories about local history. Naturally, those which interested me most concerned the Aboriginal tribes. He said that when he reached the Murray, the old white settlers reckoned there were no bad Aborigines left. All the trouble-makers had been shot. The most horrifying stories centred on a "pioneer" whom I shall call Lachlan. He became so enraged whenever he saw the Aborigines practise their age-old rituals and ceremonies, such as corroborees or initiation, that he was liable to start shooting at them. A fairly full traditional life-style was continued, but it had to be organised very cautiously, in places Lachlan was unlikely to frequent. The philosophical humour of the people in the face of this kind of interference is shown by the name they gave Lachlan — *Gubarrngubarr* "scrubitch", a parasitic mite that gets under the skin and causes severe itching and irritation.

Lachlan had a succession of Aboriginal concubines. There was one called Maria who looked after him particularly well, Lindsay said. But Lachlan grew tired of her. One day he took Maria off into the bush to a fresh mound built up by a scrub-hen and told her to dig down for eggs. When Maria had dug a deep enough hole, and was standing on the rim holding up an egg for her master — he shot her. She had just dug her own grave.

Lindsay Cowan told me he sometimes wondered about the virility of Aboriginal men. One would have a wife for a number of years, and she might bear no children. Then a white man would come and take her off, and she'd become pregnant at once. (If the black husband dared to protest he'd either be shot or sent off to the settlement at Palm Island as a trouble-maker.) I pointed out that Aborigines had purposely limited the size of their families by all sorts of means, to ensure there was enough food for all, and that they did have something approaching "zero population growth", which the rest of the world would do well to emulate. Lindsay went on to say that, although many half-castes were born in the Murray Upper area around the turn of the century, he knew of only two that were allowed to live — Chloe and her sister Lily. Their father, an Irishman named William Wade, was a sensible and compassionate man who took an interest in his daughters, as best he could. All the other white fathers had simply slaughtered their half-breed children soon after they were born.

Although Lindsay Cowan had a humanitarian concern for the Aborigines, he'd never been interested in learning anything of their customs or beliefs or language. His children had been to school with Aborigines and now worked on the farm with them. They knew how to say "time to eat" in Girramay, and a few more phrases. One put forward the idea that the Dyirbal word *yarraman* "horse" could be the conjunction of their word *yara* "man" and its English translation, because horses were associated with men. I explained that there are two contrastive *r*-sounds in Dyirbal (as in almost all Australian languages), a major point of difference from European languages. *Yarra* — with a rolled *r* like that found in Scots English — means "fishing line", but *yara* — with a liquid *r* more like the sound in English English or

Australian English — is "man". The word for horse is *yarraman*, with a rolled *r* like the sound in "fishing line" and unlike that in "man". In fact, *yarraman* "horse" comes originally from a language just south of Sydney where it may have meant "long teeth". It was adopted into the peculiar pidgin that early settlers used in communicating with Aborigines. When the first white men came into Queensland, they used the word *yarraman* "horse", thinking that they were speaking "*the* Aboriginal language". The Aborigines imagined they were being taught an English word, and it was taken over as the name in their own languages for this new animal.

White and black Australians pay scarcely any attention to a stranger's official rank or affiliation. They make their own observations of newcomers, and take their time deciding what sort of people they are. We were on good terms with the Cowans, but they couldn't quite work out what we were up to. I didn't seem to do any work, as they understood the term.

Then, one Sunday, everyone was away on a jaunt — except Lindsay Cowan and us. He came over for a chat and we offered him lunch — a tin of fish, a bit of bread, and some fruit. Beef is almost always the main dish in North Queensland, and he said how nice it was to get a bit of fish (we'd actually bought it at Mrs Cowan's shop). We had a good yarn, with Lindsay putting forward his theory of how white people evolved to their present level of civilisation because they lived in cold climates, where life was so hard that they had to strive, and be imaginative and inventive, in order to survive. Living nearer the tropics was too easy a life, and that was why the dark-skinned peoples had never progressed to our level. Lindsay also had another theory that, before long, all the coloured peoples of the world — black, brown, yellow and red — would band together and overcome the whites. It was only a matter of time, he felt.

Then at two o'clock I excused myself, picked up notebook and tape-recorder, and said I'd arranged to go across and spend the afternoon with Chloe transcribing a text she'd recorded the previous day. After I left, Lindsay said to Alison that he'd never seen anyone go to work on a Sunday afternoon before. He didn't rightly understand what I did, but he could see that I was very serious and keen on it. We decided later that this was the moment of acceptance.

Chloe welcomed us back. We played some of the tapes we had recorded on the tableland – Willie Kelly, Maggie and Minnie Brooks, and Peter Wairuna and Fred Blackman all talking in different Dyirbal dialects. She translated parts and told us what she thought of them. Not much! Those people had just said a few things over and over, or twisted them about too much. What we needed was to get the language straight-out – a proper story with all the details filled in, and everything properly explained.

Although Chloe had had a Girramay mother and an Irish father, she had been brought up in the Jirrbalngan camp at Bellenden. She'd been born about the turn of the century, and tribal life had continued pretty well intact until 1913, when the government had stepped in and taken many of the people away to settlements. After that, aspects of traditional life had continued in secret.

Chloe had a quick and active mind, and had taken note of everything that went on around her, absorbing all that was recounted around the camp-fire of traditional legends and beliefs. Absorbing, and also questioning those ideas. She learnt about a spirit called Dambun, a frightening creature, very tall with a pointed head and bushy hair, long tapering finger- and toe-nails, very skinny and emaciated, all bones and scarcely any flesh. One night Chloe heard a low moaning noise in the bush and was told it was a Dambun. She picked up a torch from the fire and went off to look for it, to the great consternation of the old people, who warned that Dambun would pin her chest with its long nails, then put her in a lonely cave in the forest and keep her there until she went mad. Ignoring all entreaties, Chloe went cautiously towards the source of the noise and found a curlew, as she put it "a poor unfortunately curlew", sitting on the ground, going "giwu, giwu, giwu". As she approached, the bird flew away.

A few nights later, another noise was heard and the old people, again diagnosing a Dambun, warned all the children to stay close to the fire and out of harm's way. Once more Chloe picked up a lighted torch and went in search of the noise. "If she shines that light on Dambun," the old people wailed, "it'll come here after us and we'll all have to move camp, away to the north." Chloe followed the noise, a low "mm, m, m" and suddenly saw two big eyes in the grass. She jumped back in fright, but returned, cautiously, to investigate. A mopoke owl was sitting in the grass, staring at her. When Chloe saw this, she burst into gales of laughter. The old people back in the camp were sure she had been caught by Dambun, and that the demon was now tickling her, producing those uncontrollable shrieks. That, at any rate, was the way Chloe told it to me.

Other people remembered how some of the Jirrbalngan elders had — when angered by her cheeky ways — chased Chloe out of the camp, shouting "half-white no good." They always allowed her back a few hours later — a child to be cared for and cherished like any other. She had worked hard in the white man's world, but her main delight lay in talking to her Aboriginal friends. However, Chloe's Jirrbal husband, Tom, had felt that their children would have more chance in the world if he spoke only English to them, so although they understood Jirrbal, they could only speak a smattering of it.

Chloe had the energy of someone half her age. She would be up at six in the morning, get Ernie off to work and the girls to school, clean and tidy the house, and be ready and waiting for us by nine o'clock. At first, when she yielded to our persuasion to tell traditional stories, Chloe apologised for each one, saying it was not true, just silly. This was the legacy from a century of psychological brainwashing by the whites — telling the Aborigines that they had no proper language, and reviling their customs. We assured Chloe that Jirrbal and Girramay myths were similar to many European stories and legends (including much of the Old Testament) which no one took as literally true.

At the beginning, whenever Chloe translated a sentence into Jirrbal she'd apologise that it was "back-to-front". I had to stress that each language had a distinctive word order, and that there was nothing sacred about the order of English. Jirrbal grammar and means of expression were every bit as valid and proper as those of every other language. Every language is a bit different from every other one, that's all.

We found the same sentiments all over North Queensland. Because of what white people had said to them, Aborigines were ashamed of their languages and legends, and they were at first wary of talking to us simply because they thought we would laugh at them. I had continually to combat this attitude and, indeed, to indicate points of beauty in their languages, ways in which they could say certain things more straightforwardly and clearly than could English. It is good to be able to report that things have changed a lot since them. In the late sixties, Aborigines all over Australia had a resurgence of pride in their own heritage, and in their Aboriginality. By and large, they have now stopped trying to become dark-skinned whites.

To counter the poor material she thought we had been given on the tableland, Chloe recorded more legends. One was about an old man who had been left looking after two grandchildren while his daughters went hunting and how he swallowed them; and of how the daughters got revenge on this Ngagi-bulgay "grandchild swallower". And then one about a dreamtime man, Murrngganu, who was so angry when his wives went off with another man that he rose up into the sky, roaring, and became a thunderstorm.

Chloe explained and translated these, and we also finished going over the five texts she had given on that memorable Wednesday afternoon in October. Each phrase was gone over – I had to pronounce it to make sure it was taken down correctly. Chloe explained the meaning of every word, and then mentioned alternative ways in which things could be said.

She also gave us more names of animals, each in three different dialects, Girramay, Jirrbal and Mamu. But Chloe wasn't too well up on trees. She suggested going to see Jack Murray, who had been married to her late sister, Lily – he'd be able to go through the Jirrbal names of everything in the forest.

Jack Murray was born after the tribes had been reduced to a fraction of their former size, and there was often no one of the right section available for a young man or young woman to marry. This may partly explain why (as I was told the story) his father was also his maternal grandfather, something that would never have been allowed in pre-contact days – they'd both have been put to death, Chloe averred. He was in his middle fifties, the youngest man in Murray Upper who had the deep tribal scars of initiation across his chest. (Jack Stewart had been the youngest initiated man I had met on the tablelands, and he was over seventy.) Jack worked on the Cowans' bananas, and I arranged to see him and his brother Mick one evening at the brick barracks which had just been built half-way between the Warrami turn-off and the homestead.

Jack was a quiet, introspective man and he spoke incredibly fast, in a clipped staccato manner. I was able to make out the names of individual trees, after a few repetitions – *wuyburru* "she pine"; *ngaya* 'silky oak", *wuray* "Davidson plum", *jiwurru* "swamp oak", *girruwun* "silver ash", and a couple of dozen more.

When I asked Jack if he would like to record a text, a traditional Jirrbal story, he offered the legend concerning the origin of fire. I already had one version of this, from Chloe, but it would be interesting to record another, and compare them. Jack started the narration at moderate speed, but with few pauses for breath. Soon he speeded up, mumbling and slurring the words together, his voice tailing off to an indistinguishable creak at the end of each sentence.

I just couldn't start to transcribe this by myself; it was impossible to make out the individual words. Chloe agreed to go through Jack's text, and so later did other people. But everyone heard slightly different things. I'd played other texts to different speakers and they had given me identical interpretations. In the end, I just had to give up on Jack's story. Only he could have said what exactly had been intended, and it's doubtful if I could have followed his explanation.

There was a rather pathetic old man at the "mission" — his name sounded sometimes like Joe Jamboree, and other times like Jonah Tambourine. Everyone said he was the last speaker of Jirru — which had been spoken at Clump Point, just to the east of Tully — so it seemed important that I try and record a bit from him. But Joe was so slow and dull that it wasn't very productive. His voice would drop to a scarcely audible whisper and several times he seemed on the point of falling asleep.

Joe Jamboree plainly couldn't work, or gather food for himself, and no one wanted to look after him. So Lindsay Cowan took him into Tully to get the policeman to grant Joe exemption from the Act, so that he would qualify for the old-age pension. There were, until recently, no birth records of Aborigines — there didn't have to be, since they weren't on the census and didn't strictly count as "people" — so the police had to get a doctor in Tully to estimate his age. A thorough physical examination convinced the doctor that he was at least sixty-five, and the pension was granted. But in fact Joe was no more than about fifty — Chloe remembered carrying him on her back, as a boy of four or five, at the time of the great cyclone in 1918.

Chloe continued to be our main adviser. She felt that the government people in Canberra had given me a hard job "trying to straighten out all this language", and that it was up to her to help as much as she could. Chloe answered my questions — which were prompted by grammatical and lexical points that had come out of her texts — and provided a commentary on material we gathered from Jimmy Murray, Jack Murray and Joe Kinjun.

A number of loan words from English had come in during the past century. The English words had, of course, been recast into the phonetic pattern of Dyirbal. Each Dyirbal word has at least two syllables, so *gown* became *gawun*, the term used to refer to any kind of dress. Dyirbal has no fricatives or sibilants, with the result that *f* or *v* is rendered by *b*, and *s* or *sh* by *j* — thus *naybu* "knife", *juga* "sugar", *juwa* "store". Our favourite borrowing was *mijiji* "white woman", which is based on *missus*. Chloe pointed out, though, that not every new artefact required a loan word. Sometimes an existing Dyirbal word could have its meaning extended to include some introduced object. "Shirt", for instance, is *maralu*, which also means "hollow log". When the Aborigines first saw a white man putting on a starched shirt, they were reminded of a bandicoot seeking shelter in a hollow log!

The most interesting thing about Dyirbal grammar was that it had genders. Each noun would select something which is a bit like the article in French, only there are four of them — *bayi yara* "man", *balan jugumbil* "woman", *balam mirrany* "black bean" and *bala diban* "stone". It soon became apparent that the genders were "masculine", "feminine", "edible" and "neuter". The third class covered just non-flesh foods — the rainforest contains hundreds of trees, ferns, vines, bushes and roots with edible parts, and these are all classified as *balam*. The same genders extend to loan words — sugar comes from cane and is *balam juga*. "White woman" takes the feminine article — *balan mijiji*. *Bala naybu* "knife", *bala gawun* "dress" and *bala juwa* "store" go in the fourth, residue, class, along with *bala jalgur* "meat", *bala yugu* "stick", *bala mija* "camp", and so on.

Chloe also explained that Dyirbal deals with time a little differently from English. *Janyja* "now" is the focus that divides up the day. *Janyjarru* "earlier on today" refers to any time before "now", while *gilu* is "later on today". The Jirrbalngan can talk of "morning" or "afternoon" or "evening" if they choose to — in terms of the position of the sun in the sky — but *gilu* and *janyjarru* are the normal words for placing past and future events within any particular day.

Jirrbal and Girramay were all very well, but we had to get some other languages too, Chloe insisted. Since Peter Wairuna hadn't supplied any Warungu, poor old thing (and the oddments from Lizzie Simmons were inextricably minged with Gugu-Yalanji), we should go to see old Alec at Kirrama, high up on the range behind Murray Upper. I arranged to drive up with Chloe the next day, and she suggested that Jimmy and Mary Ann Murray might like a trip too.

Jimmy said, Yes, he'd have to come along and help me out. He'd be needed to show the way, make sure I didn't get bushed. And to talk to Alec, explaining what was wanted. The way Jimmy put it, I'd scarcely be able to do anything without him along.

Mary Ann showed more noticeable excitement, enquiring *"Gilu waynyjiny?"* "Are we going uphill later on today?"

"No,' Jimmy told her, in English, "boss say we go tomorrow. Daybreak. You bring some tea and sugar to brew up on way."

There was only room for two in the cab with me and I'd thought of Jimmy, as navigator, and Chloe. That wouldn't do at all, Chloe explained. We'd have a fight on our hands. Mary Ann — although over eighty — wouldn't let her man sit next to another woman. It became apparent that amongst Aborigines sexual jealousies can be as strong at eighty as at twenty. In the end, both Jimmy and Mary Ann sat in the back, with Paddy Biran, who had also agreed to come along and help out. I just followed the road.

A narrow, winding forestry track zig-zagged up the range. After a couple of hours, we reached Kirrama cattle station, owned by Ruth and Doug Farquar. It is in traditional Girramay country, and the name Kirrama was an attempt to write down this tribal designation. (In Australian languages, unlike English, *k* and *g* are interchangeable, as are *p* and *b*, and *t* and *d*. This is the exact opposite of the *r* situation, where Australian languages distinguish between rolled *rr* and continuant *r*, two sounds that are interchangeable in English.)

Old Alec Collins, the man we had come to see, was past seventy and had been granted exemption from the Act so that he could draw a pension. But he still had to work. I could talk to him for half an hour before lunch if I liked. Jimmy explained at length — in a mixture of Girramay and English — what we wanted, and what he'd told me about his language, but Chloe interrupted and said we must get some Warungu quick. There was no time for the proper preliminaries, for Alec to size up who I was and how he should treat me. Alec spoke slowly, with an old man's drawl, thinking before each word. *Ngaya janay* "I stand up", *wagay* "climb", *ngaya yudi* "I swim", *ngabay* "bathe". We got a few dozen phrases and words on tape before I was called to join the Farquars for lunch.

Only I was invited to eat in the house. Chloe, Jimmy, Mary Ann and Paddy could munch the sandwiches we had brought, sitting under a tree. Alec and another Aboriginal stockman had their dinner, cooked by Ruth, in a separate hut. I was too taken aback to argue, too ashamed to make much conversation. I apologised afterwards to Chloe and the others, but they thought this quite unnecessary — it was what everyone did, and of course I had to follow convention in case I ever wanted to come back here. I didn't tell them one thing: that when Ruth dried the dishes, she used a separate dishtowel for the plates the two Aborigines had had. But they probably knew that too.

Jimmy Murray decided that another corroboree should be put on for us, again on a Saturday evening. It was similar to the first, and just as exciting. One or two of the songs were repeats — fishermen dragging their nets through the waves to snare hordes of silvery fish — but most were new. A song about poking a stick into a hollow log to dislodge the white-tailed rat — good eating. Then one about a kangaroo hunt. One dancer mimicked the animal: feeding, pricking up its ears, and then bounding away as a party of hunters crept stealthily up, spears at the ready in their woomeras, to let loose an attack once they were close enough. There were a dozen more songs — the one that struck our fancy most concerned an emu, strutting about so proud of its pretty stripes, followed by an offspring that was trying its best to imitate the parent's mincing gait. As far as I know, this was the last corroboree ever to be performed at Murray Upper.

Mrs Cowan had suggested that if we really wanted to hear some language, the thing to do was come along to the store on pension day. Old people converged on town from every corner of the bush every second Thursday, to draw their pensions from the post office and buy provisions for the next two weeks. This was a sort of ritual reunion — the exchanging of news and gossip and planning of future outings were conducted almost exclusively in Jirrbal and Girramay. I now had a fair collection of monologue texts, but was especially keen to record a bit of everyday conversation, which should show a quite different type of language from formal story-telling.

I first went to pick up Chloe and give her a lift down to the store. Mr Cowan drove up with old Lorna and half a dozen others from Warrami, and then went back for Jimmy Murray and Mary Ann. Birdy Curtis's three old ladies appeared. And Rosie Runaway, a diminutive old thing from the mission. Finally, Tommy Warren walked up the road with Joe Jamboree. Tommy was corpulent, his large stomach and developed breasts contrasting with Jamboree's inconsequential build. He walked heavily, with a stick, and his squeaky voice was especially incongruous coming from a heavy, bullish head with steady, piercing eyes.

Getting the pension money from Mr Haydon, thirty yards away, was not protracted. Then they came to sit on the concrete slab under the store verandah, talked, went inside two or three at a time to buy the needed stores, talked, swapped groceries, and talked some more.

Chloe got me organised: "You sit down here!" "He want to get your language in these machine. You got to talk proper. Jirrbal. Girramay. All same. Talk straight-out language. No more English. This machine pick it up all right."

Some of them were getting a bit edgy. Old Lorna wasn't going to have her voice in that machine. I might take it back to England with me and then she wouldn't be able to speak — she said all this very quickly, in Jirrbal, with her face turned away, and I had to ask Chloe to explain it.

"Don't be silly Jubula," she called, using Lorna's Jirrbal name (the word for black pine nut, a favourite food). "This thing not hurt you. You still keep your voice all right."

Then Jimmy wanted to hear some of the corroboree songs. That tape was in the caravan, but I said it wouldn't take long to drive across to Warrami and get it. I zipped the plastic cover up over the recorder and put it in a corner of the verandah, with the microphone in its stand on top. But, craftily, I did leave it switched on.

It picked up a conversation on the topic that was of most interest to the Aborigines at Murray Upper just then. It was the same thing that was upsetting Lindsay Cowan — the government's grant of land to King Ranch. Lorna complained that they were destroying the country. Banyjabanyja — that place is finished, the bulldozer's there now. Gurrungurru clearing — that's finished, there's a road lying across it. Yungigali (a rock that legend holds to be a transmuted dreamtime dog) — they're pushing that down now. People's conception sites (from which their spirits were believed to come before birth and to which they returned after death) — would be no more. If the trees were razed, rocks blasted away and swamps filled in, then places would become unrecognisable. They would cease to exist. This was worse than the white man coming in the time of our grandfathers. They killed some of our people and tried to stop some of our customs. But we still had our country. Cows on it made no difference. We could still go back to our own places. But now King Ranch has put up an eight-foot fence and said no one is to go over it. No good to go there anyway, the places are being destroyed. Nothing left. Nothing for us. Destroying the country is like killing us.

Chloe came in for some flack because two of her sons, Edgar and Ernie, were working with the Cowans' second son, Max, on a logging contract, felling some of the choicest timber from the King Ranch property and sending it to the Tully sawmill. Chloe disclaimed any responsibility. Then she said that, if it had to be done, why shouldn't her boys do it? But that only produced renewed mutterings.

There was also lots of miscellaneous chatter. One old lady was ribbed for being so mean. If she had a husband I'd take him away from her, Chloe joked. He'd rather come and live with me, to get away from such a mean wife. Mary Ann decided to get in on the joke too. Quite forgetting her eighty years, she declared that if she were married to the mean one's son, she'd take him right away, that he might never set eyes on such a mother again!

Interest was shown in every car that passed. Who's she got with her? What's she going up there for? Then they saw me returning, and discerned someone in the passenger seat. Who's that? Must be his wife. No, it's a dark person. Who is it? In fact I'd met Marnie Digman walking down to the shop with two of her children and had given her a lift. Only when I arrived back did anyone start talking English again.

We played the corroboree tape, to general satisfaction and Jimmy's pride. I put a fresh tape on for Chloe to organise some more material. Rosie Runaway enquired whether I'd been given the names of all the fishes. She embarked on an imaginary journey down the river, catching shrimps in a dilly-bag, cooking them in the ashes, and then stuffing them, cramming them into her mouth, to her great enjoyment — and also that of her audience.

Rosie continued on the imaginary walkabout. Cutting out a palm-heart, and some lawyer cane, and boiling them up. Looking for eels by torchlight at night. Getting walnut and green ginger. Chopping grubs out of an acacia tree. She was in a dreamworld of fifty years before. "Watch out for Lachlan!" Rosie warned. All the newly initiated men get up and hide in the bush for fear of that old *Gubarrngubarr*, although they're really too weak to move. The rainbow appears in the sky — a bad omen just after an initiation; people spit on the initiates and beat the ground to drive away bad luck.

Old Lorna had been enjoying the narrative at first. Perhaps she was

Fig. 6. Paddy Biran (Girramay), Mosley Digman (Girramay) and Joe Jamboree (Jirru) outside Mrs Cowan's store, Murray Upper, on pension day. (1963)

now feeling left out. Forgetting for a moment the fear that her voice might be sucked into the tape recorder and carried far away, she suddenly said in a loud voice: *"Wundu".* This, the crudest term for referring to the male sex organ, served as an effective swear word to mark her opinion of Rosie's line of talk.

I went into the store where Jimmy was getting his supplies — a big sack of flour, tea, sugar, rice, tins of corned beef, powdered milk, tobacco, and the usual fifteen packets of epsom salts. Tommy Warren was next in line and Mrs Cowan teased him a bit. "You know all the language, Tommy. Won't you tell it to Bob here?"

"No more," Tommy insisted, "I don't know nothing. Never learn it. Better ask them outside. No good ask me."

Mrs Cowan tried appealing to his better nature (assuming he had one), and then Tommy started on the other tack. "I tell him my price. Fifteen pound for my language. White fellow got to pay. That's *my* language. Not give it away for nothing."

It had been twelve pounds when I'd spoken to Tommy at the mission the month before. Somewhat taken aback at the 25 per cent increase (this was before the days of galloping inflation), I suddenly forgot all the advice Stephen Wurm had given about tact. "Well, if you don't know anything, you can scarcely expect me to pay fifteen pounds for it!"

This put paid to any hopes of working with Tommy. Seven or eight years later, he was happy to talk to me for free — in fact he demanded I come and see him, and write down what he had to say. I found then that Tommy didn't really know all that much, and was distinctly poor at explanation. He was much less useful than Chloe or the half-dozen other people I had gathered information from in Murray Upper.

Tommy, with his mixed sexual characteristics, was held in a certain amount of awe, but he could also be ridiculed behind his back. Chloe told me how she'd teased him when they were children together. And of how he had once married, to the girl who had been promised to him years before. But she had run away on the first night, calling out "That no good, that too small — can't satisfy me!"

Now, as Tommy gathered his provisions into a sack, slung it across his shoulder, picked up the heavy walking stick, and prepared to start off back to the mission with little Joe Jamboree, he wasn't included in the general conversation. His shouts were answered with a peculiar mixture of deference and contempt. And when he was — I think — just out of earshot, someone said *balan yara yanu,* using the feminine gender marker *balan* with the noun *yara* "man" (and *yanu* "is going"), a grammatical juxtaposition that exactly conveyed his equivocal status.

After a couple of hours, Mr Cowan returned to give lifts home to the old people — not only those from Warrami, but also to some who lived on other properties with less kindly owners. Chloe loaded her sacks into my Land Rover, and as we drove off, Mosley Digman shouted out to her: *"Guwal wurrba!"* ("Talk language!") The general consensus was that Chloe was the best person to teach me Jirrbal, and she was being adjured to do it well.

That afternoon I started, with Chloe's help, to transcribe the two reels of conversation recorded outside the store. I hadn't realised it would be so difficult. Three people might well be talking at once, and there were unfinished sentences, hinted allusions, and snatches of secret ribaldry. It took six times as long to work out a minute's conversation as it did a minute from a monologue text. But it was what I wanted — the language in its most natural form, being used in everyday conversation.

The store conversation had been in a mixture of Jirrbal and Girramay, with odd snatches of English from time to time. Because these two dialects are mutually intelligible, each person would tend to speak in his own tribal style. Except Chloe, who switched between them at will. But so far I'd only got one Girramay story, from Chloe. Paddy Biran had promised to help, and when I went across to see him on Sunday afternoon, Jack Murray was there as well.

Paddy announced that he was going to tell a story for the sake of the children, who were crowding around, so that they would learn something of their mythic heritage. *"Nganya nginda ngarilgani,"* he instructed Jack — you answer me back, keep the tale moving.

Then he described how *Yirrinyjila*, the dragon-fly, used in times gone by to be shaken by children. His hovering, quivering action is the result — and the people who shook him would get bad stomach-ache. The dragon-fly went over the top of a waterfall, watched by the rainbow, spirit of the falls, who was lying nearby in the form of a painted snake. The fly shook his wings, fanning the water and making a wide deep pool at the base of the falls.

A transistor in the next hut was blasting out pop music from 4CA, but Jack Murray, the gaggle of children who squatted beside Paddy, and I, had ears only for how *Yirrinyjila* moved to the north, extending the pool that way, and then came back down to the south. Paddy reached up for two boomerangs lodged in a trellis above his head, to clap together as accompaniment to a song about Yirrinyjila that he'd learnt long ago from Ngamijubaru (or Old Charlie King, as the whites called him):

The dragonfly fell by the splashdown of the falls,
He fell on the slippery part, by the splashdown of the falls.

Then Jack Murray merged the narrative into a related legend, about
the brown pigeon, which was sharpening a stone tomahawk ... Yes,
Paddy took up the storyline, the pigeon rubbed her bottom as she
ground the axe, calling out all the while *"Guguwuny, guguwuny"*
(which is her name). She rubbed a valley between two hills, and then
the axe blade flew off. It can still be seen, now a huge blunt stone, in a
swamp nearby. And the pigeon's nest and eggs were also turned to
stone — still there, in the foothills just beyond King Ranch.

We played the tape back. Paddy nodded in agreement with what he
had said and then summarised the stories in English. He told another
story in Girramay, about a bandicoot. And then the tale of the
cassowary — how he used to be a man, with a propensity for strangling
children. But his arms were cut off, as a way of stopping this heinous
habit, so that he assumed his present form.

"We give you song now, all right?"

"Yes, sure," I agreed. Paddy laughed as he gently tapped the
boomerangs together while rehearsing under his breath. One of his
boys was strumming a guitar inside the house, but that was drowned
out as Paddy suddenly launched into:

1. *wanyju nganya yanggul*
2. *ngamba jamu nyura*
3. *jirarri jarrbaru*
4. *mugal jirarrigu*
5. *yirayiragubi*
6. *banmangu warjangga*

This was a Jangala song. The lines, each of which had precisely six
syllables, were repeated in different orders: 1 2 3 4 5 3 2 1 6, 6 4 5 ...

Chloe had explained that there were two broad genres of song —
"dancing songs", and "love songs". The Jirrbal and Girramay dancing
style was called Gama; this described everyday events and was available
to everyone in the community. All the songs Jimmy Murray performed
at the corroborees had been Gama. A Gama song had just two lines,
usually of eleven syllables apiece. Sometimes the first seven syllables
were the same in each line, sometimes not. The lines were simply
repeated, in alternation, six or eight times.

Marrga was the dancing style of the Mamu tribe, and it was also a favourite among the tablelands group of Jirrbal speakers. The eight or nine songs Willie Kelly had recorded were all Marrga. These had eight syllables to each line. The first two lines were alternated, then Willie would play an instrumental interlude accompanied by an extravagant *brrrr* (the local equivalent of a yodel?), then two more lines, similar but not identical to the first two.

The first song Paddy performed that afternoon belonged to Jangala, which Chloe characterised as the "love-song style" of the Jirrbalngan and Girramaygan peoples. This was reserved for powerful emotional messages; it would seldom be danced to. Jangala was the vehicle for expressions of love, during courtship; or gestures of jealousy and anger.

Paddy's song could have been called "The Worn-out Penis", Chloe suggested when I played it back to her the next week. "Who's talking to me?" the words went. "There's something long and tattered, the head is all scattered, like the points of a fork — you ask me and I'll tell you about it."

Whereas the accompaniment for both Gama and Marrga was played on any old pair of boomerangs, Jangala required a special long stick, called *gugulu*. This was made from the hard Jidu tree *(Halfordia scleroxyla)* carefully shaped and polished smooth. It was hit with a piece of lawyer-cane, *baygal*. Paddy didn't have a *gugulu* instrument handy and was forced to make do with boomerangs that afternoon. But Jimmy Murray later fashioned one as a present for me "just so you'll know what it's like."

The Gulngay people from the Tully River had their own love-song style, called Burran, also accompanied by *gugulu* and a length of *baygal*. Legend has it that two women invented this genre, but it is now mostly performed by men. Each tribe features not only its "own" styles but also those of its neighbours, and Burran is popular all over the Dyirbal-speaking region, although everyone acknowledges that it really "belong to Gulngay".

Paddy enquired of Jack: "You want to follow-im me, or you just going to hit-im stick?" Jack indicated that he'd be content to accompany and listen as Paddy broke into a Burran song. It had four short lines — six syllables, three syllables, then six, then three again. His voice swooped powerfully through the words, building tension and then releasing it as the vocal volume suddenly dropped, stopped level, gently rose and fell, and then instantaneously doubled in force without change in pitch. Listening to the tape, one might imagine that the volume-control knob had been turned up, or that the microphone had been moved nearer to and further from the singer. In fact none of these things had been altered. But by an unusual vocal trick, an accomplished practitioner of Burran could achieve these sudden diminutions and increases in sound "in his throat", as it were.

It seemed to me a magnificent performance, and I couldn't understand why it was given a so much more restrained reception than that accorded the last number. Some of the other people from the mission, who had drawn near on hearing the Jangala number, moved off as if in embarrassment. It was only later that the words were explained to me. They were considered to be in the most shocking taste, even by the promiscuous standards of Jangala and Burran songs. A father seduces his daughter, the words recount, placing his organ inside her so that she conceives his child.

Then, to defuse things a bit, Paddy sang a couple of Gama songs. One described the humming noise made by little yellow native bees as they hurriedly dart in and out, looking for nectar. Then a song about snakes, moving fast, sliding across the ground in their striped skins, sounding like water in a spouting.

The final song Paddy gave us that day was another Jangala. He sang not of love, but of sorrow — at the tragedy that was encompassing the community, the senseless desecration of sites by King Ranch. It was appropriate that he should use the style that was reserved for feelings of the strongest emotional force. The words described a mist that was seen over his ancient country as it was cleared by the invading Americans. People again gathered close, from the corners of the mission, as Paddy's clear voice glided over the melody, gently rising and falling as he fitted together the six six-syllabled lines in different permutations.

"The mist lies over Guymaynginbi as the boom of dynamite disfigures it, as the nose of the bulldozer pushes it down. That was my father's father's country, and I had to make a song about its destruction."

Then Jack Murray took over, repeating the words in his inimitable slurred style, but with the same measure of despair.

Paddy was only in his forties, but he had a more intimate knowledge of traditional stories and ways than many older people. And he was the most versatile and accomplished singer I heard in North Queensland, advancing and enhancing an aeons-old tradition. A few months after we left the field, in 1964, a truck in which Paddy was travelling skidded on a dirt corner and overturned. Paddy, who had been standing in the back, was thrown out and killed. Without doubt a large part of the oral heritage of his people — in both legends and songs — died with him.

There were some more stories Chloe could tell, but she needed a mate to help her out with them, she said. We should go over to the mission and see old Jarrmay, otherwise known as Rosie Runaway. She could assist Chloe, answer her back, and prompt her with anything she had forgotten.

Jarrmay was a genuine example of Tindale and Birdsell's "tiny negrito people", being no more than four feet six inches in height. She had curly black hair, wore large glasses, and tended to cock her head on one side when asked a question, or when sizing up a stranger. She'd purse her lips and say "mm" when gathering her thoughts together. I've sometimes invited people to guess why she was called Rosie *Runaway*. Various suggestions are made — that it is a literal translation of her Jirrbal name; or the obvious one that she used to run away. No one has ever guessed correctly, although it should surely be easy enough. She was called Rosie Runaway because she was married to Tommy Runaway! (And he was the one who used to run away.)

The first story today, Chloe decided, would be about the very first contact between black and white. She called it, "The story of Captain Cook." There was only one slight flaw — Captain Cook didn't in fact set foot on shore anywhere along that bit of coast. But everyone knows about Cook. Every schoolchild is taught that he discovered Australia. (Can you imagine Aboriginal children — whose own heritage on the continent goes back over 40,000 years — being told that it was discovered by a white man less than 200 years before? And he wasn't even the *first* white man in Australia, for that matter.)

Chloe began with the title in English: "Captain Cook, first one". The last two words were the clue: she and Jarrmay were recapturing the first contact between the races, and the white tradition specified that the white man was Captain Cook. They had been told by their grand-parents that the Aborigines were at first cautious about drinking the tea they were offered, frightened of putting a smoking pipe in their mouths, and suspicious of the strange cake made with the white man's flour. It was no secret that here — as in many other parts of Australia —

they thought that the first white men were returned spirits of their ancestors. Partly because dead bodies are sometimes treated in such a way that the outer layer of skin peels off, revealing a white surface beneath. And partly because they were a strongly religious people who believed that the spirits of their parents and grandparents kept a kindly eye on them; what more natural than that they should return, in strangely-garbed corporeal form? (Aborigines have sometimes complained to me, rather bitterly, that they found out how wrong they had been about the white settlers just a little too late — when the pattern of invasion, murder, and purposeful destruction of social organisation was already well established.)

Jarrmay entered into the spirit of the story with infectious enthusiasm, evoking the scenes of apprehension, amazement, joyful dancing and sorrowful leave-taking. And she responded happily when Chloe suggested, after the Captain Cook saga had been replayed, that they should now tell me the story of Kennedy.

The 1840s was a halcyon era of Australian exploration. Edward John Eyre managed to cross the Nullabor from Adelaide to Perth. Charles Sturt followed the flight of birds into the arid centre, reasoning that they must be headed for water. Ludwig Leichhardt, who was said to have left Germany to avoid military service, went overland from Brisbane to Darwin, moving along the headwaters of the east coast rivers, across to those flowing into the Gulf of Carpentaria, and then into Arnhem Land. Leichhardt was burdened with a tent and heavy pieces of equipment — he may have succeeded as much by good luck as good management.

The most tragic tale concerns Edmund Kennedy, who disembarked in 1848 in Rockingham Bay, just north of where Cardwell now stands, hoping to travel overland to the northern end of the Cape York Peninsula. He began, in perhaps the most difficult bit of the whole Queensland coast, with two carts, which bore four tents, collapsible furniture, firearms, specimen boxes and the like. After negotiating swamps near the coast, Kennedy's party came up against thick jungle, where to cut a path for carts would take a day or more for each mile. Then there were steep mountain ridges that just could not be negotiated. It was only after wasting six weeks in the Tully area that Kennedy finally realised there was no alternative but to abandon the carts!

The exploring party arrived too late for the rendezvous with H.M.S.

Bramble at Weymouth Bay. Leaving the weakest members at a base camp there, Kennedy struggled further north, accompanied by Jackey-Jackey, an Aborigine he had brought from New South Wales who showed notable courage and good sense throughout the trip. Kennedy was eventually speared by hostile Aborigines from the far north. Only Jackey-Jackey, the botanist Carron, and one other member of the original party of thirteen were still alive when the rescue ship returned.

Chloe and Rosie told, in Jirrbal, how Kennedy had several *wilbarra*. This is a loan word from English *wheelbarrow*, used in Jirrbal to describe any type of wheeled vehicle. The party, they said, consisted of a number of white men and one blackfellow. They wandered around for ages, unable to find a path, searching for food. Eventually, one of the *wilbarra* fell down a crevice, scattering knives and forks everywhere. A big water tank rolled off a cart and is said to be still there today.

The story we were told showed marked resemblances to Carron's account of the journey. Some of the details could well have been handed down through the Aboriginal oral tradition. But the white people at Murray Upper knew about Kennedy — especially from Dorothy Jones's recent *Cardwell Shire Story* — and it is more likely that Chloe and Rosie were recasting what they had been told (or been asked about) from that source.

The torrential rain storm, which began soon after we entered Rosie's hut, eased off after half an hour, and the sun was beginning to shine again as they finished the Kennedy account, first in Jirrbal then in English. Chloe said she thought we'd had a good morning, and Alison and I agreed. I then took a picture of the storytellers, standing amidst the dirt and grime of the mission, and Alison took one of the three of us, Chloe coming up to my shoulder but tiny vivacious Rosie scarcely elbow-high (figure 1 on page 2 above).

The next day, when I passed the Cowans' open French windows on my way to take a morning shower, Mr Cowan called out: "Have you seen our baby? Come and meet her!" The Cowans' youngest daughter, Karlene, was just home from boarding school — she was a big girl for sixteen, tall and plump. Baby, indeed!

Then one of the boys called out from the breakfast table, "Hey, Bob, have you heard — Kennedy's dead."

All that went through my head was: yes, he was speared by a fierce tribe up north. But I couldn't understand why they should shout it out so early in the morning. Seeing my puzzled look, Alan Cowan gave more detail, from a radio bulletin. "Jack Kennedy, President of America. He's been shot in Dallas." I must confess (although I wouldn't have dared admit it to most people at the time, or for several years afterwards) that my feelings of sorrow were mingled with distinct relief. Kennedy's behaviour over Cuba had seemed the worst threat to peace for a very long time and I'd felt that his arrogant, impetuous nature was bound to bring serious trouble before long. But my main thoughts were for Edmund Kennedy. How could anyone be so stupid as to venture into impenetrable rain forest with wheeled vehicles? And at *that* point on the coast, where the rugged mountain range is clearly discernable from the sea. Kennedy had been a brave man, badly advised. A minor hero perhaps.

Now that the rains had begun, we were keen to get back to Cairns before bad floods came; we had been warned that roads were often out for weeks at the height of the wet season. But Chloe insisted that before we left, we must go through one other type of language: Jalnguy. A special language that a man had to use when talking to — or even when talking in the presence of — his mother-in-law, and the mother-in-law would use it back. Jalnguy was also used between a woman and her father-in-law, and between certain types of cousins. Every member of the Jirrbalngan and Girramaygan tribes would know Jalnguy, and had to use it with relatives from these particular kin categories. They were people who should be kept at arm's length in social dealings — one would not normally look them in the eye or be left alone with them without a chaperon — and the use of a special language, Jalnguy, was an overt index of this avoidance behaviour.

There was never any choice involved, Chloe said. A man would talk with his wife in Guwal, the everyday language style, but if a mother-in-law was within hearing, he had immediately to switch to Jalnguy. All the texts and vocabulary I'd collected so far were Guwal. Some of the old people had warned Chloe that it wasn't wise to divulge anything about Jalnguy, but she had decided to ignore them.

"Government sent you up here for language and we got to give you *all* different languages. You get into trouble if you go back, only got half of it."

Her rebellious spirit, a determination to make her own decisions (which had caused people to call out "half-white no good" in the old days), came to the fore. And afterwards everyone else agreed that she had in fact done right. I should be given the language "right through" if I was to be given it at all.

Everything, it seemed, had a different name in Jalnguy. "Water" was *bana* in the everyday style, Guwal, but *jujamu* in "mother-in-law". "Fire" was *buni* in straight-out Jirrbal but *yibay* in Jirrbal Jalnguy. "Man" was *yara* in Guwal and *bayabay* in Jalnguy, while "woman" was *jugumbil* and *jayanmi* respectively.

It appeared, though, that the grammar was the same — only the nouns, verbs and adjectives differed. Gender markers didn't change — "man" was *bayi yara* and *bayi bayabay*, "woman" *balan jugumbil* and *balan jayanmi*. "Black bean" took the "edible" gender marker in both Guwal and Jalnguy styles — *balam mirrany* and *balam dirraba*. Pronouns didn't change — *ngaja* "I", *nginda* "you", *ngali* "the two of us", and the rest. So in Jirrbal Guwal one would say *ngaja yanu* "I'm going" and that would be *ngaja bawalbin* in Jirrbal Jalnguy.

We went through a few score words, getting Jalnguy equivalents — body parts like "teeth", Guwal *dirra* but Jalnguy *ngunyangi*; animal names like "brown wallaby", Guwal *barrgan* and Jalnguy *yungga;* verbs like "laugh", Guwal *miyandanyu* corresponding to Jalnguy *yirrgunjinyu*. Then Chloe said that we needed some conversation in Jalnguy. It was always easier if she had a mate to talk to. We should go down to the mission, and once more enlist the aid of old Rosie Runaway.

It appeared that Jalnguy had not been actively used since about 1930. The gradual loosening of tribal bonds and the pressure of learning English as a second language may have been partly responsible. Since then Guwal had been used for everything, even when an avoidance relation was around. The traditional taboo relationships were still respected — a son-in-law would never look his mother-in-law in the eye, and he would talk softly in her presence, avoiding risqué subjects. But Jalnguy was no longer employed as a linguistic marker of these social attitudes.

In fact, only a few of the older people remembered much of the Jalnguy vocabulary. Rosie did, and although she and Chloe were not in a taboo relationship they were soon rattling on in a conversation that reconstructed old times. Walking in the bush, getting hot and sweaty and going for a bathe in the cool water of a nearby creek. Plaiting split lawyer vine into a dilly-bag. Then both ladies bewailed, in Jalnguy, the fact that they were the last ones who could speak it — children nowadays go to school and all they learn there is how to speak English.

Every single vocabulary word was from Jalnguy — not once did either Chloe or Jarrmay lapse into Guwal. Later on we went back to Chloe's and she translated the texts, phrase-by-phrase, into Jirrbal Guwal and also into Girramay Guwal.

Jalnguy was a revelation. I'd never heard of anything like this before, in Australia or anywhere else. Every member of the tribe had to know *two* distinct languages — or at least, two distinct vocabularies, for the phonetics and grammar were the same. Two names for every animal, two forms for every verb, two varieties of each adjective. But it was also something of an embarrassment. I felt I had quite enough to do, over the coming wet season, trying to work out the structure of Guwal. I decided to concentrate on the everyday style first, try to learn to speak it and fully analyse it. Further study of Jalnguy should be postponed until that object had been achieved.

5

"Time to get back to wife"

It wasn't hard to find an apartment in Cairns. It was a house really, raised up on six-foot high stilts, like many others in North Queensland. It had been a farmhouse, but the fields had now been replaced by streets of modern houses for the new suburb of Edgehill, in the lee of Mount Whitfield. Cassowaries were said to come down into the gardens, but we never saw one.

The old farmer and his wife had built some rooms for themselves by enclosing the stilts, so they could keep a good eye on their tenants. And an ear too, as they sometimes gave away. One day, for instance, we were discussing a possible trip to Cooktown and wondering what the road would be like. When Alison went downstairs a few minutes later to use the ancient clothes boiler, the old landlord sidled up to her and mentioned, as if by chance, that it wasn't advisable to take a caravan along the dirt road to Cooktown.

Australians back in Edinburgh had warned us about the flies. There are a huge number of species in Australia, and each seemed to have billions of members. They get in your eyes and hair and nose, and even in your mouth if you're foolish enough to open it for too long. Mosquitoes were bad, and their bites came up in angry red weals on newcomers like us; I once counted a hundred, all running into each other, on just one leg. At least there was no malaria for them to transmit. There had been at one time, but the American defence forces sprayed all the malarial breeding grounds in north Australia, at the end of the last war, and eliminated it. And at least you could hear a mosquito coming, and stand a good chance of squashing it, especially towards morning when it was sated with blood and slower on its wings. But the sandflies made no noise, and were almost too small to see — and their bite was as bad as a mosquito's. I was checking some proofs in Cairns one day, and it literally seemed as if the dots on the *i*'s were jumping up and biting me!

And the beetles. Beetles everywhere. Dozens of different kinds. It took a while to acquire the nonchalance of Kenny Cowan. When I said, "Hey, there's a beetle in the butter," Kenny's reply was: "Make sure he doesn't get too much of it."

One day Mrs Cowan had said to Alison and me — apparently divining our thoughts — "What do you think of the beetles?" I was embarked on a disquisition about how they weren't too bad once you got used to them — when it turned out that she was soliciting our opinion of a new English pop group whose records were being heavily featured over 4CA. I hadn't heard them, but the Aborigines had. When a day or two later Chloe was explaining the characteristics of the various local song styles she said: "Now Gama, that's the kind of music the Beatles play."

Cairns is a pleasant, lazy town with some good Chinese restaurants and a newsagency called The Korner Shop that seemed to be open all the time. While we were there, the Victorian state government decided for some reason to ban Mary McCarthy's new novel, *The Group*. All the shops in Queensland — which normally had the most repressive censorship — hurried to stock it. We bought our copy late one Sunday night in The Korner Shop. It was funny to read about the shenanigans of Vassar and New York — there among the palm trees in the hot, tropical summer.

In fact, the temperature in Cairns scarcely ever gets up to 100°F, but it is in the nineties all December, and so is the humidity. As I sat at a tape-recorder — going over and over the texts we had recorded, trying to transcribe them accurately, and to understand the grammatical constructions involved — I had a towel round my neck the whole time, to soak up the steady stream of sweat. Eventually our landlord down below asked me what I was doing. He was surprised — didn't think the Aborigines really had a language, or if they did there couldn't be much to it. But he was also relieved. "When I heard those strange noises all day I thought you were a Russian spy!"

The few weeks before the wet season properly breaks are the most uncomfortable of all. We could keep mosquitoes at bay by sleeping under nets, or by burning long spiral coils of compressed chemical, of

Japanese manufacture, whose smoke repelled the insects (and also somewhat irritated our eyes and throats). But then there were flying beetles. We had windows all around the house — without any screens — and they were all left open. At about dusk, the beetles started flying in — six inches long with elongated pincers. People told of the terrible things that happened if they got in your hair! They'd fly around, loudly banging against the walls, and then settle down — perhaps stunned — for a minute before starting off again. I tried putting the broom head over them to ease them out of the door, but they spat viciously and continuously from under it. And just as one was under control, three more would fly in. After an hour we couldn't stand it any more, so closed the windows and suffocated. It was weeks later that someone mentioned that flying beetles are only active for about an hour after sundown.

The wet season usually starts soon after Christmas. (But about one year in seven it sets in in early December, just to mock the statisticians.) By Christmas, it was like living in a turkish bath. We decided to go down to the beach on Christmas Day, for that's what we'd always imagined Australians were doing while we were huddled round a fire in Britain. When we got there, around noon, no one else was in sight — all the locals had enough sense to stay out of the searing midday sun. We walked down to the sea for a few minutes, and while we were there the ants ate the sandwiches we'd brought for lunch.

We'd been invited by Philip Wilson, the 4CA newsman, and Jane Wilson for Christmas dinner. Percy Trezise, a pilot for Ansett Airlines, was also there. He'd recently become interested in Aboriginal culture and painting (being an amateur painter himself) and was going off the next day for two weeks on Mornington Island. Percy-showed around a white pith helmet he'd bought for the trip. And as the sun set over Cairns, he pulled the cork from a bottle of sweet Australian sherry and threw it from the balcony. "We don't put corks back in bottles here in the north!"

Finally, just after New Year, the wet season really started. It rained for five days, about twenty-two hours of really heavy downpour each day. Just after it began, our daughter Eelsha was born. No, that isn't an Aboriginal name. It's simply a name I made up. (After all, if a linguist can't invent names, who can?) I'll swear that when we met she winked at me. I winked back. We've got on well enough ever since.

I suppose it's a common failing to begin by being over-ambitious and later to set more modest sights, in the light of what is practically possible. Before leaving Britain, I had asked AIAS to provide a cine camera so that I could simultaneously film and record daily events. Conversational exchanges had to be placed within their situational setting in order fully to comprehend the pragmatic effect – so the argument went. The Institute had eventually acquiesced, and we had left Canberra with a bulky camera and half a dozen reels of film. Only when I got to Murray Upper did it become apparent that tape-recorders were quite enough to handle. If I had started messing with a camera as well, it would have worried the people (how much would Tommy Warren have charged to be filmed?), and would have taken too much time away from language analysis. AIAS wanted me to move on and survey the greater Cape York Peninsula during the second half of our year's field work, and I could see that a full statement of the grammar of Jirrbal was going to take all of six months. (It was in fact eight years before a typescript was finally despatched to the publisher!) I waited three months, so as not to lose face, and then sent the cine camera and films back to AIAS, untouched.

I was making progress with going over the dozen good texts we had recorded. But there were lots of queries, and I'd be able to work faster if some of them could be cleared up. When a break came in the rains, I set off at dawn to drive down to Murray Upper for the day. It took about three hours – narrow, winding bitumen, caution over the single-lane bridges to Innisfail, a straighter road to Tully, and then ten miles of dirt from the Murray Upper turn-off. Chloe was doing her house-work, in an old dress with the sleeves pulled up. She gave me a great welcome, asking for news of Alison and the baby. And, happily dropping what she was doing, settled down for seven hours of intensive linguistic work.

We went through some of the texts again, checking that my trans-criptions were accurate. There was one phrase I just couldn't place in the Gulngay tale. I heard it as *jilaway,* but no word like this occurred elsewhere.

"Oh," said Chloe, when it was replayed, "I talk in English there – 'Shut up Irene!' is what I said, because Irene she giggling and making it hard for me to concentrate."

Chloe described the verbs for different kinds of stance. As with probably every other language in the world, Dyirbal has words for "sit", "stand" and "lie". *Nyinanyu* "sit" also has a general sense meaning "stay", "settle (at a place)". The verb "to marry" is *nyinay+man,* literally "stay with —", "settle down with —". Then there is *wanggurinyu* "crouch down on heels with knees off the ground". And a word that made Chloe dissolve in peels of bell-like laughter: *wugumbanyu.* This refers to someone sitting huddled up, very still, with arms grasped around the legs which are pulled up so that the knees touch the chin. Old people had sat like that in the middle of winter to keep themselves warm, Chloe remembered from her childhood. Whenever after that *wugumbanyu* came up, Chloe would laugh and laugh — so funny were the memories.

One of her friends called around, an Aboriginal lady who didn't really know very much about languages. And Chloe the showman explained what she was telling me, describing all the different things we were doing so that the Government people "will have all this language right, down there in Canberra".

When we began, in October, Chloe reckoned to know two tribal languages well — Jirrbal and Girramay. Within a couple of months she would give the number as four, having added Gulngay and Mamu. Now, in February, Chloe described herself as knowing something about seven languages. She had included Warrgamay, to the south of Girramay (and a quite different language, on linguistic grounds), Ngajan, the most northerly dialect of Dyirbal, and Yidin from Cairns (again a quite different language).

She would go through the seven languages for the sake of her audience, saying a short sentence in each with the appropriate vocabulary and grammar. But a most important contribution was the way she demonstrated differences in voice quality, speed of articulation, breathiness, nasalisation, and the like. Each dialect or language was primarily characterised by the different vocal postures of its speakers. For Mamu, Chloe would adopt a deep voice, slowly drawling the words; for Ngajan lots of the vowels would be grossly lengthened; and for Yidin — of which she admitted to knowing only a few words — Chloe adopted a sharper, nasalised timbre.

After lunch I suggested taking a photograph of Chloe and her daughter-in-law, Mamie — but this wasn't to be countenanced unless they could first change into their best dresses. A yellowy-green print for Chloe, the design showing different kinds of tropical fruit, and a blue-and-white dress for Mamie. The pose was at first stiff and self-conscious, but the last picture was of Chloe walking towards me, laughing, just as she thought I had finished. (See frontispiece.)

Then, before it was time to drive back to Cairns, Chloe cleared up one of the areas that had been really bothering me, by explaining the complex system of locational indicators in Dyirbal. I already knew that each noun should be accompanied by a gender marker — masculine *bayi*, feminine *balan*, edible *balam*, and neuter *bala*. Now, Chloe explained, something else could be added to this marker showing where the thing referred to is located. *Balan+bayji jugumbil bajinyu* would be "woman a little way down the hill fell over", *balan+dawu jugumbil nyinanyu* would be "woman a fair way up river is sitting down".

I discovered that there are more than a dozen different forms that could be added to a gender marker. They indicate whether the thing being talked about is uphill or downhill; upriver, downriver or across the river; or just a long way away. And they indicate whether it is a long, medium or short distance up or down. The ending *-u* (pronounced like English *oo*, as in *boot*) means "long distance", *-a* is "medium distance" and *-i* (like English *ee*, as in *feet*) is "short distance". So *-bayju* is "long distance downhill", *-bayja* "medium distance downhill", and *-bayji* "short distance downhill"; and so on.

Dyirbal is spoken in the well-watered mountainous country between the Great Dividing Range and the coast. The grammar of the language mirrors the geographical terrain in which its speakers live. (If the Dyirbal-speaking tribes should be moved to flat country, this system would surely drop into disuse in a short time.) I felt, as Chloe explained these dozen forms and their meanings, the overpowering beauty of Dyirbal — how it had evolved a grammar that was such a fine blend of elegance and pragmatic power.

One day, our landlord in Cairns called me down to help corner a snake that had strayed in from the nearby canefields. He soon despatched it, with one blow from a sharp caneknife, and identified it as a green tree snake. Not really dangerous, the snake book said, but it could be harmful to small warm-blooded mammals. That seemed an accurate enough description of baby Eelsha, who was at last gaining weight amidst the heat and rain and sweat.

Snakes are the only really dangerous things in Australia. And they *are* bad. We got friendly with Iain Ramsay, a doctor at the Cairns Base Hospital who had come out from Scotland just before us and who had been in charge of Alison's pregnancy, and he recounted some horrifying tales. A taipan bite is lethal within twelve minutes — no chance of rushing to a hospital and looking around for the right serum. Iain had heard tell of a cane cutter who one day bent his left arm around a clump of cane preparatory to cutting it — only to be bitten on the hand by a taipan. As the story goes, he knew that desperate measures were called for, and cleanly amputated the hand with one stroke of his knife. This saved his life. But, as Iain said, you'd need to be pretty certain that it was a taipan — and not a green tree snake — before doing something like that.

Iain's wife, Margaret, was a delightfully prickly character who added a bit of spice to our lives in the wet season. She'd decided that she didn't much care for Cairns or its people. When Margaret went on about she didn't like this, or they didn't have that, I tried to interpose that theirs was a different culture from Scotland's, and should be judged as such. "Culture!" she expostulated, "they don't have any culture at all up here."

One day Margaret interrupted a policeman in the middle of writing her out a ticket for a parking offence. "Call yourselves policemen?" she taunted. "You're just a lot of little boys playing at being policemen."

Margaret Ramsay could be fun, but the most rewarding white person we met in Cairns was Douglas Seaton (whom I'd looked up at Philip Wilson's suggestion). Douglas had been a sign painter in Cairns all his life; his hobby was the study of Aboriginal culture and artefacts. He'd spent untold weekends with the Jabugay people, listening to their traditional stories and writing them down (in English), visiting sites that have religious significance for them, learning how implements were made and used, and studying Aboriginal designs. He and his wife were soft-spoken and shy, old before their time, but they had a tremendous amount of lore and wisdom to communicate.

Douglas told us that, once, when he went into the bush, his Aboriginal guide asked to be allowed to go first. If he came behind, the temptation to plunge a knife into a white man's back (in retaliation for past wrongs to his tribe) might be too strong, and since Douglas was a friend he wanted to avoid this.

The passing of the older generations of Aborigines saddened Douglas, as if he were losing his own kin. He told me of how a couple of years before he had met one of the last Yirrganyji people at the

Cairns wharf, waiting for a boat to take him back to Yarrabah Aboriginal Mission.

"There aren't too many Yirrganyji left now, Tommy," Douglas had commented.

"No, Douglas," had come the reply, "only old Joe, and me and you left now."

Percy Trezise — the Ansett pilot who was getting a local reputation (soon to be expanded into a national one) as an expert on things Aboriginal — had great respect for Douglas Seaton. It was he who had first aroused Percy's interest when he heard a lecture Douglas gave. But Douglas had little time for the extroverted Trezise, "going around letting off his mouth about things he knows hardly anything about."

Both the Seatons had failing eyesight and, although they were only about sixty-five, were selling their house and most of their possessions to move into a masonic old-folks' home in the south. Douglas passed on to me some old maps, a copy of Lumholtz's *Among Cannibals* (only with difficulty did I make him accept payment for it), and his old bush-knife. After we'd left the field, he wrote to say that two weeks in the old-folks' home had been enough — there was nothing to do! So they went up to Cooktown to think things out, then came back to Cairns to build themselves another house. Douglas's wife died four or five years later, and he followed her within a couple of months. As Percy put it, "he sang himself to sleep, blackfellow fashion."

I did what field work I could around Cairns, but there wasn't much to do. A couple of people who knew some Yidin weren't awfully interested and gave me nothing very useful. I went up to the Jabugay encampment at Redlynch, seven miles out of Cairns, but it was — as the Hookworm Man had warned — pretty raw and tough. Although I recorded a few words, no one was interested in giving texts. And, really, I had enough on my plate with Dyirbal. (I've always preferred to do one thing properly, rather than dabble.)

Ken Hale is a sort of legendary figure to linguists. He went to a one-teacher school in Arizona, then had a Navajo room-mate at the University in Tucson and learnt to speak that language from him. He has done a lot of work on American Indian languages and can speak half a dozen of them quite fluently. Just after finishing his doctorate, in 1959, Hale came out for two years' field work in Australia. Most of that time he spent in the Centre, on Warlpiri, but he did tour right round Western Australia with the Australian linguist Geoff O'Grady, and also went all round the Cape York Peninsula as far as Mornington Island in the Gulf of Carpentaria. On his way down from Cairns to Sydney, Ken had done about an hour's Jirrbal with Joe Chalam at the Tully River, and then had called in briefly at Murray Upper and (when Tommy Warren wouldn't talk to him) had recorded an hour of Girramay from Mosley Digman.

Out of the dozens of Australian languages he had gathered data on, Ken Hale admits to being able to carry on a conversation in seven or eight. He'd spent one week on Jabugay, while at the old Mona Mona mission. When Ken heard I was in Cairns, he asked me to follow up his work and try to get information on how relative clauses are formed in Jabugay. He sent a tape in which he spoke to his old informants in Jabugay for twenty minutes, telling them what he was doing now and asking their help. A twenty minute address, after one week's field work on the language! I took the tape up to Redlynch post office on pension day and found half a dozen Jabugay, including Gilbert Martin, with whom Ken had worked. When I played Ken's message — twice over — they shook their heads in astonishment. "Very well pronounced", was the considered verdict.

My approach to linguistic field work was to try to get at the structure of a language from the inside, as it were. I aimed first at recording stories and conversation, and then I looked at the structural patterns in these texts, generalising from them to a full statement of grammatical rules and structures.

This approach contrasted with the method of asking long sets of questions in English to try to build up paradigms, somewhat on the pattern of traditional grammars of Latin. In Canberra, I had read an account by Father Worms of how, in the thirties, he and Father Nekes had tried to elicit verb forms in Nyol-Nyol, from speakers living in West Kimberley in Western Australia. They would grind through things like, "I will have seen you, I will have seen him, I will have seen them, You will have seen me", and then "I had seen you, I had seen him . . ." and so on. Small wonder that Worms should report:

> much patience was also required in dealing with the natives . . . the endless repetition of conjugations especially made them tired, listless and disinterested. The authors had to be very careful in order to receive correct information, as some women tried to "make it easy", as they confessed later when found out, by simplifying complicated grammatical forms so as to shorten the sessions and lessen enquiries.

Just asking from English may reveal similarities and likenesses to English patterns, but it is unlikely to uncover things in a language which *do not occur* in English — for example, the complex set of forms for uphill, downhill, upriver, downriver and across the river. The method I chose focussed first on constructions that occurred most frequently in Dyirbal, and then gradually extended to all the important grammatical contrasts.

I did, of course, supplement the information from texts by asking a few questions, but this was always a secondary step. When the time came to work on relative clauses, for instance, there were a hundred examples available in the texts already processed. I could make tentative generalisations from these, and from them predict other types of relative clause construction. I could then check with speakers as to whether they were good Dyirbal sentences, modifying the generalisations as necessary.

But this technique immediately got me into trouble, in an unexpected way. I collected all instances of verbs from the texts and began by examining the verb of which there were the most examples: "to go". But, unfortunately, this is the *one* irregular verb in the language — and its forms don't correspond to those for any other word. Once I had got over this, it was plain sailing. It was clear that there were two classes of verb; one has the non-future ending -*n* (e.g., *buran* "see, look at"), and the other has the non-future ending -*nyu* (e.g., *nyinanyu* "sit, stay, settle"). There are hundreds of verbs in each of these classes. And there is just one verb with the non-future ending -*nu, yanu* "go". Of course I should have realised that if a language has any irregular verbs, these are usually amongst the most frequently occurring words. I should have remembered the irregular verbs in English — like *give, see* and *take.*

I made a few more quick trips to Murray Upper between the rains, taking advantage of the Cowans' generous offer to stay at Warrami overnight. Chloe was completely absorbed in our project, and always eager to work at it all day.

"If only I been to school and learned how to read and write," she mourned, "I could write it all down for you."

But she did check quite thoroughly that things were taken down correctly by getting me to read them back to her.

Chloe's daughter, Irene, helped in many ways. She had had a couple of years' schooling, which had included a little grammar.

"Come on mum," Irene decided one day, "we've got to find out your tenses. Future and present and past."

Once you look for a thing, you'll probably find it, and Irene decided *burali* was future of "see", *buran* present and *burangu* past. In fact the plain future "will see" is *burany,* contrasting with the "should" or "must" form *burali.* And both present and past are covered by *buran* (non-future was the label I chose for this). Irene's "past tense" *burangu* actually marks the verb in a relative clause, such as "the man, *who had seen me,* went off." It is a fine example of the dangers of trying uncritically to apply the grammatical categories of one language to study of another!

Difficulties of quite a different sort can arise in asking questions from one language to another. In English, reference to future time is shown by *will* or by *be going to* – *he will cross the river* and *he's going to cross the river* have almost the same meaning. One day I unwisely asked Chloe how to say "He's going to cross the river" and she gave *bayi yanu mabili,* literally "He's going so that he can cross the river", treating "go" as a separate verb. (The future tense I was looking for is *bayi mabiny* "He will cross the river".)

Chloe and I usually worked for about three-quarters of an hour, and then took about a fifteen-minute break. This would happen quite naturally. Someone would walk or drive by and Chloe, inveterate gossip, would wonder what business they had which could take them up that way. I'm a pretty good gossip, too, and we'd swop scandal for a while. Then Chloe would say, when she felt we'd had a long enough rest, "All right, what's next then?" and work would continue.

Whereas English has just singular and plural pronouns, Dyirbal has three varieties: singular *ngaja* "I", dual *ngali* "we two", and plural *ngana* "we all (three or more)". And while English has just "you", Dyirbal again has three forms: *nginda* "you (singular)", *nyubala* "you two", and *nyurra* "you all (three or more)". From my examples of each of these in the texts, I could see that each had different forms, depending on whether it was subject, object, indirect object, possessor and so on (like *I* and *me* and *my* in English, only more complicated). I asked Chloe a few questions to fill in the gaps in this pronominal matrix.

Chloe's main dialect was Jirrbal, but she was also fluent in Girramay, and had picked up a fair bit of Mamu, the dialect spoken south of Millaa Millaa. For most words, Chloe could tell me whether it was the same in Mamu, or else what the Mamu form was. Now she mentioned that Mamu had a seventh pronoun, *nganaymba,* which could be used by a man or a woman and meant "me and my spouse". But Chloe wasn't too certain of Mamu. The person to tell me everything I wanted to know about it would be George Watson, over on Palm Island. And if I went across to Palm, there was also Alf Palmer, who would be able to put me right about Warungu, the language we hadn't got much of from old Alec at Kirrama.

We talked one day about all the tribes from the old days and how those from the coast had almost completely died out. "Chinaman did that," explained Chloe, and when I expressed surprise, she told me that at the end of the last century, there had been tens of thousands of Chinese in North Queensland. Some had joined in the gold rush — and had been known to smuggle gold dust back to China inside the bodies of compatriots who were being sent home for burial. Chinese had also worked with bananas and sugar cane down on the coast and had paid Aborigines with opium charcoal, making them hopelessly addicted to this killing residue. Many of the Chinese had been sent home when the "white Australia" policy came into force around 1900 — but by then the damage had been done.

Then gossip turned to the early white settlers on the Murray. All of them had been given names by the Aborigines, although they weren't themselves aware of this. The names were evocative of their nature and habits. There was *gagara* "moon", the name given to Hughie Henry because he had a fat body and a bald head, looking just like a full moon. Ikey Anderson, a kangaroo shooter who came out from Germany in about 1910, was known as *yugu-nyirrga-bara,* alluding to his tree-like penis, which he was wont to ram in (and there was also a song about him). Brice Henry had been called *jabu-janggay* "fish-eater" because he used to wolf down seafood.

It had started raining an hour before and was getting worse all the time. Chloe broke off and looked out of the door. "Time to get back to wife," she advised. "Six hours more and the water come down these river and block road. You go now you'll get through all right. Don't leave it any later."

When Ken Hale sent the Jabugay tape, he'd urged me to try to find a speaker of Barbaram, the apparently aberrant language that Lizzie Simmons had declined to speak to us. Certainly Dyirbal and Jabugay had very normal Australian grammar and vocabulary, not radically different from the Western Desert language, almost two thousand miles away. But from the few words that Norman Tindale had published of Barbaram, that language looked really different.

People at Mareeba had mentioned Albert Bennett, at Petford, and early one Sunday morning I set out to try to locate him. I followed the winding bitumen road through Mareeba to Dimbulah, a small Italian-dominated town whose main crop was tobacco, usually with a few fields of marijuana hidden away round the back. From there it became a faint sandy track with no signposts at all. There was a farmhouse right next to one T-junction, and I was able to find someone to ask which was the right road. (A signpost was put up there the following year — just before the council election.) Then I was on my own, over the Divide. The rainforest had given way to lots and lots of tea-trees, whose roots stuck up into the path. I came to Emu Creek, a tributary of the Walsh River, which flows west into the Mitchell River, a stream that itself empties into the Gulf of Carpentaria. The creek was in flood. But it only came two or three feet over the concrete causeway, and I was just able to edge the Land Rover across.

Petford had a population of several thousand when the mines were working, but by 1963 it was down to just a few dozen. It was served by the railway to Chillagoe and Forsayth, with trains three times a week. And the town was also almost entirely supported by the railway — the men in Petford were mostly fettlers, keeping that stretch of the line in repair. There was just a post office, and a shop selling everything you could imagine, run by Mrs Doreen McGrath (a couple of years later she took on the post office as well). Mrs McGrath told me that Petford had once been a bustling town with five pubs. She was cautiously helpful and explained how to get to Albie Bennett's. Over the railway line, round by the old schoolhouse — it had closed a couple of years back when the number of students fell below nine, and now Mrs McGrath's children and Albie's daughter got lessons by mail from Brisbane — then about a mile down the track — steering clear of a six-foot pothole in the middle of the road — and there would be Albert Bennett's corrugated-iron shack, among the tea-trees just a stone's throw from Oakey Creek.

Albert was an oldish, square-framed man with curly grey hair. He was sitting stolidly on a bench just outside his open front door. I introduced myself, but he really wasn't very interested. He didn't remember any Barbaram language, but who'd want it anyway? What good was it?

Now Stephen Wurm had prepared me for questions of this sort. Don't talk about universities, Wurm had said, they won't know what they are. Tell them you come from the museum in Canberra. Everyone knows what museums are, and everyone thinks they are good things. Say you want to put their language in the museum because it's something important. So that it can be preserved — one day their grandchildren can come and listen to it, and see how the old people spoke.

I tried this line on Albert Bennett and he seemed to soften a little. But he still sat quietly chewing on a piece of grass, on the end of the wooden bench, just in the shade. I stood in the sun and hoped. Finally he volunteered a word.

"You know what we call 'dog'?" he asked. I waited anxiously. "We call it *dog*." My heart sank — he'd pronounced it just like the English word, except that the final *g* was forcefully released. I wrote it down anyway. And then he volunteered another word: *mangarr* "grey kangaroo".

Over the next hour I squatted there in the sun, going through several hundred parts of the body, mammals, birds, insects, fishes, kin terms, and the like. And got twenty-eight Barbaram words (including *dog*). Some of them were as interesting as those Tindale had collected. Every word in Dyirbal (as in most Australian languages) begins with a single consonant, but Barbaram had some commencing with a vowel, *aru* "wallaroo" and *almen* "forehead", and others with two initial consonants, such as *mba* "belly". In the other languages, every word has at least two syllables, but Albert Bennett gave *we* "mouth". No word in Dyirbal, or in most other Australian languages, can end in a stop consonant (*b*, *d* or *g*) but Barbaram had *mog* "man" and *gog* "water". It was certainly unAustralian in its forms.

Albert said he didn't remember very much and recommended me to go and see Mick Burns who lived in Edmonton, just a few miles to the south of Cairns. He was older than Albert, and he'd know more. I said I would, and drove back to Cairns in good spirits. At least I'd got *some* Barbaram. Recorded on field tape number 38 — which seemed like a lucky number.

6

"Drink this!"

Although I had blanket approval from the Director of Native Affairs in Brisbane, it was still necessary to get permission from the Superintendent at Palm Island before visiting that settlement. I wrote, explaining my linguistic project. And waited. Finally I was able to get through on the telephone. Yes, certainly I could come, whenever I wanted (they seemed surprised they hadn't replied). There'd be room for me in the male guest house but no, I really couldn't bring Alison and Eelsha.

Bush Pilots flew a plane three times each week from Townsville to Palm Island, leaving at seven in the morning. It took six passengers and there was room for a seventh — me — in the co-pilot's seat. At least the plane had two engines. The pilot hadn't been to Palm Island before, and as a bad storm had come up over to the east, he decided to fly up the coast some way and try to cut in round it. Eventually we came to a straggle of islands — the Palm group — but the pilot wasn't exactly sure which was Great Palm. There it was — it must be that one down there to starboard — comparing the shape with that on the map. No, it can't be, there's no landing strip. One of the other passengers had been there before, and he came to our aid. Now the landing strip was plain to see, across the south-east corner. Only it was occupied by a number of cows, and by some small Aboriginal boys. The pilot flew the plane low over the strip, buzzing them out of the way, and then came in to land, bumping to a halt in the furrows. The storekeeper was there with an old open truck for the three-mile drive into the settlement. We sat up on the back, bits jolting off my tape-recorders as I tried to avoid being hit by tree branches when I was tossed in the air by a particularly deceptive pothole or protruding root.

Palm Island had a notorious reputation. The Queensland government tried to break up tribal groups by sending some members to one settlement and some to another. Far away from their traditional territory, separated from relatives and friends, many people simply lost the will to live. But a few fought on. Those who tried to stir up trouble were shipped off to other settlements. And the worst trouble-makers finished up under the harsh regime on Palm Island.

The AIAS librarian in Canberra had shown me an article by Colin Tatz, in *The Australian Quarterly* for September 1963: "Queensland's Aborigines; natural justice and the rule of law." Tatz had described a horrifying situation in Queensland Aboriginal settlements. Rules laid down for the conduct of courts were not ideal; but even these were not followed. The superintendent (who usually had no legal training) might often be effectively prosecutor and clerk of the court as well as judge; there was no appeal from his sentence. (He was also — theoretically — the defence, by virtue of the fact that he was a gazetted "Protector of Aborigines"!) Scarcely any of the accused realised they could plead "not guilty"; or perhaps they didn't dare to do so for fear of reprisals. Anyway it would scarcely have mattered. Of 275 people brought before the court in a two-year period at one settlement, *all* had been found guilty. Some of the offences were real enough — arson or assault. But, mingled with these, were jail sentences for gambling, swearing, or for two adults who were not married to each other having "sexual intercourse" in the privacy of a house.

But, however badly the courts might be run, Palm Island really was a beautiful place, fully as nice as I'd imagined it in that grey Edinburgh winter. It has a high, wooded hill in the middle, set in silver sands and the bluest imaginable sea, just a dozen or two miles from the Great Barrier Reef (with some of the finest fishing anyone could wish for). The main street was lined with tall palms, and although the roads were a bit dusty there were grass lawns with fruit trees — mangoes, oranges, pawpaws. The air felt fresh and relaxing.

The truck dropped me off at the guest house, where I was just in time for breakfast. White bread brought in on the boat from Townsville, for the white people. The Aborigines ate rough black bread, baked on the island. There were two male schoolteachers, fresh out of college, where they'd never been told anything about the special problems of teaching Aboriginal children, and without even any experience in an easier situation on the mainland. The government optometrist, on his annual rounds, explained that he could — he really could — stand coming to a "dry" place like this once in a while, although in Brisbane he had three large bottles of beer each evening. He always brought three bottles home with him and his wife had his glass keeping cold in the fridge. A fellow who'd come over to service the island cine equipment reminisced about the Torres Strait islands, where they usually provided a girl for a stranger or — if there were no girl available — then a sweet young boy might come along instead.

I walked down to the office to be told the conditions under which I might work. The first rule was that no Aborigine was allowed in the white part of town, unless employed there as a domestic servant. White people were not permitted to walk around in the Aboriginal section and were most emphatically forbidden to enter an Aborigine's house. If I wanted to talk to anyone, I should give his name to an Aboriginal policeman who would find and fetch the person concerned. I could then talk to him in the courthouse, under the supervision of a native policeman. Terrific! I could see I was going to get on like a house on fire — develop a really warm relationship with the people!

As luck would have it, the superintendent, Bartlam, had just left on two months' accumulated leave. His deputy, Tom Murphy, was a sensible and humane man who listened to my expostulations and agreed that I could have a bit of latitude because of the sort of work I was doing. He wouldn't insist on the courthouse if I could find some other suitable place, but — mind you — no going into an Aborigine's house or asking an Aborigine to the guest house.

The first person I wanted to see was an old, white-haired cannibal called Pompey Clumppoint. He did odd jobs for Pat Ellnor, the white boatbuilder, and I talked to him in Ellnor's garden. Pompey, who came from Clump Point, was the only person left — except poor old Joe Jamboree — who knew any Jirru. Pompey had been sent to Palm Island for eating people. Soon after he'd got there — sometime in the twenties — he and another two men had killed and eaten someone there on Palm, so the story went. There was nowhere else Pompey could be sent.

The Dyirbal-speaking tribes had not, traditionally, ever killed people *just* so as to eat them. A person who was judged to be a hopeless criminal might, by consensus, be condemned to death, and could then be eaten. Sometimes one tribe would retrieve the body of a

Fig. 7. Pompey Clumppoint (Jirru) holds woomera and boomerang he has made, on Palm Island. (1964)

recently-dead man from a neighbouring group and eat his remains. (They might have had a spy at the funeral ceremony, to tell them when and where to come.) It was hard to find anyone who actually admitted to cannibalism — it was always "the next tribe" who did that, or "sometimes people from around here, but I never done it myself."

Pompey gave me some words in Jirru. He took a long while to think about each one and said that he couldn't tell any stories. But he gradually thawed out. The second time I saw him, he started talking a bit about his early life, and sang some fine songs. And, as a parting present, he provided a quick gourmet guide.

"Chinaman, he taste best. Then Aborigine. And Englishman worst of all, too tough and bitter."

Alf Palmer worked at boat-building, but he was able to take a couple of hours off now and then, and we talked in the boat shed. Alf was a tall, resolute Warungu man. He'd been born back of Kirrama and worked all around the cattle stations as well as on farms on the coast. Although over seventy, he still chose to work full-time. Besides Warungu, Alf also knew Jirrbal and Girramay, and Warrgamay, the

Fig. 8. Alf Palmer (Warungu) in the boat-shed on Palm Island. (1964)

language from the lower Herbert River (between Dyirbal and Nyawaygi), and as we went steadily through all the types of nouns, Alf gave me each in these four "languages". When we started on sentences, four versions were again given of each, with every word correctly pronounced according to the phonetic system of that language. All of the languages had two *r*-sounds, but they were pronounced a little differently in Warungu from what I had learnt for Jirrbal and Girramay. Alf made me say the word for "woman" in Warungu about six times — *warrngu, warrngu, warrngu* . . . and then he sighed and said that I still hadn't *quite* got it, but we'd come back and have another try later on.

Norman Tindale, the anthropologist from the South Australian Museum, had been on Palm Island the previous year, and he'd worked a lot with George Watson, the man who had been so strongly recommended by Chloe. George was a sergeant in the Aboriginal police force. Although he was — I believe — born around 1900 (about the same year as Chloe), he gave his age as fifty-seven. George's hair had only an edging of grey and he was turned out smartly — neatly pressed long creams and a white shirt, sleeves evenly rolled up. George's father had been a white storekeeper and carrier, but he had been brought up in the tribal way by his Mamu grandfather, on Jordan's Creek, a few miles from Millaa Millaa. He was every bit as intelligent as Chloe, but had a more deliberate, thoughtful manner. While Chloe would rattle things off faster than I could write them down, George would think carefully through every question before giving an answer and it would be cogent and very much to the point. While Chloe's English was merely good, George's was well-nigh perfect. Over the telephone, I don't think it would have been possible to tell George apart from the average white farmer. This made it all the more sad that he'd never had the opportunity of learning to read and write.

The first day, I talked to George and his wife Ginnie, a member of the tableland group of Jirrbal-speakers, from Ravenshoe, on a bench in the public part of the settlement, outside the hall. We just got to know one another, and went through some vocabulary areas. The kids playing around, listening and laughing, worried George a bit, so we arranged to walk out along the beach the next day, when he would record some traditional tales.

George carried one tape-recorder and the tapes, while I had the other

Fig. 9. George Watson (Mamu) on Palm Island. (1964)

and an armful of notebooks. Finally we found a fallen log on which it was possible to balance ourselves and the machines. We were bitten by mosquitoes *and* by ants from the rotten wood. But they became of little consequence as George told me the absorbing Mamu legend concerning the "first man", Ngaganunu.

Ngaganunu came across the sea from the east, and went up the Herbert River. He built a camp there, and then a boil formed on his leg. Ngaganunu squeezed the boil and a child came out — the first child. The child was also called Ngaganunu, literally "thigh-from". His father went off each day spearing kangaroos and wallabies; he gave their hearts to the baby, to suck the blood for sustenance. So things continued until one day, while Ngaganunu was out hunting, two sisters came up the river, saw his tracks, and followed them to the camp. They found the baby hanging in a cradle, took it down, and fed it from their breasts. When they heard the man returning, the women hastily replaced the child in its cradle and hid up a tree. The baby was given a suck of wallaby heart but, being already sated, vomited. The father saw something white in the spew.

"Who's been feeding my child with breastmilk?" he cried.

Ngaganunu then prowled around the bush with a massive erection, searching for the women.

The youngest woman found this sight so funny she had difficulty in restraining her laughter. But the bigger sister solemnly warned her: "Ssh! we must stop quiet lest he find us. Goodness knows what he might do."

Finally, the younger sister could control herself no longer and let out a loud guffaw. Ngaganunu looked up, then climbed into the tree and brought down the two women, one across his thigh and the other over his shoulder. He jumped down to the butt of the tree, placed the women on the ground and tried to copulate with them, one after the other. But he had no success; there was nothing there.

I could see why George had wanted to tell the story away from town, with no children around. Against the noise of the sea gently lapping the sandy beach, he explained the way in which Ngaganunu provided the women with sexual organs. He first got two sharp pieces of quartz and put them sticking up where the women habitually sat, the points covered over with leaves. After the women had sat down, and been pierced by the quartz slivers, he tried again to have intercourse. But there was no satisfaction at all. Ngaganunu next attached a kangaroo heart to each woman, to make a vulva, and two lungs as vaginal lips. But again, when he tried to make love, there was no satisfaction. Finally he picked a wild cucumber, split it in two, and pushed the two halves in through each sister's anus to make the vaginal orifice firm and tight. Now, at last, Ngagangunu found satisfaction.

But after a while the women became tired of his continual attentions, and hatched a plan. They heated a yellow walnut in the fire, so that it would explode at the right moment. And they told the walnut not to go off until the opportune time, when Ngagangunu was covering them with his body, copulating. All went according to plan. The walnut exploded, burning and frightening Ngagangunu. He ran away to the west, leaving the women in peace.

The story had been so fascinating that I had forgotten to watch the machine, and the tape ran over the end of the reel while George was retelling it in English.

"What happened to the child?" I asked.

George thought. "They never tell me that. I don't know what happened to the child. He just goes out of the story after he spew up."

We arranged to meet again the following day. George said I should look up Jack Doolan, a clerk in the settlement office. Jack was the only white man on Palm for whom the Aborigines had any respect, George added. He'd been recording some legends from George to send down to Tindale, and generally making notes on the language and culture.

I found Jack Doolan in his cool, verandahed house in the white section, just under the hill. He was in his late thirties, of medium height, spare-limbed, and an ex-boxing champ. Around 1950, Jack had worked as a patrol officer for the Native Affairs Branch in the Northern Territory, exploring unknown parts of Arnhem Land and opening a supply post at what is now Maningrida. Now, after war service in Korea, he was working for the Queensland department. Some years after our meeting, Jack returned to the Territory to work as liaison officer with Aborigines who were breaking away from the white yoke and starting up their own cattle stations. From this, he went on to be an eloquent and effective member of the N. T. legislative assembly. On the Labor side, of course.

We sat yarning late into the night, long after Myrna Doolan — who also worked in the office — had put the six children to bed and then decided she needed some rest herself. Jack talked about girls in Japan and crocodiles in Arnhem Land, but mostly about the totalitarian regime on Palm Island. George Watson had mentioned sample "crimes" for which Bartlam had sentenced people to time in jail (a small wooden stockade out towards the airstrip). One man had been given a week in jug for not having his shirt tucked into his trousers. And two women had got a week apiece for arguing too loudly across their side fence.

Jack told me a story about George's son, Ralph, who had one of the most important jobs on the island — he was the bulldozer driver. At one time, Ralph worked seven days a week for six weeks. Then there was a football match he wanted to play in. The white overseer said Ralph could take the Saturday afternoon off. But apparently the super-intendent chose that day to prowl around, and was infuriated to find the dozer lying idle. The overseer, having regard for his own skin, denied having given Ralph Watson permission to play in the match. So Ralph got six weeks in jail for being absent from work, and was demoted to a lowly job.

The people on Palm Island — numbering about a thousand in all — came from scores of different tribal groups, from every part of Queens-land. None of the people who'd been brought up in the settlement spoke any indigenous language — just a kind of pidginised English. This was because of the dormitory system, Jack said. Children had been taken from their parents at about eight years old and placed in single-sex dormitories, where they had to stay until they were married. Limited home visits were permitted on Saturday afternoons only, which gave little opportunity for instruction in traditional lore and skills. In the dormitories they would often be laughed at — or even whipped — for speaking their parents' language.

By 1963, dormitories were being phased out. Young children and boys were allowed to stay with their parents, but a close guard was still maintained over the teenage girls. Sometimes a group of ten or twelve would break out and flee up into the mountain with some teenage boys. But this hadn't happened for a while. The native policeman made sure that order was maintained. And yet the girls still — unaccountably — got pregnant. Doolan told me Bartlam almost had apoplexy when someone suggested that perhaps his trusty dormitory policeman might be to blame.

It was getting towards two in the morning when Jack got out *Whispering Wind* by Syd Kyle-Little, his partner in those early exploits in Arnhem Land. We looked at some of the photos — of man-eating crocodiles, of the tough escarpment country. Jack told a few stories

which made my hair stand on end. On page 190, Kyle-Little had
written of Doolan: "I never worked with a better all-rounder, or a more
congenial companion."

"There," chuckled Jack, as we decided to call it a night, "I've told
my kids they should learn that by heart."

I had several more good sessions with Alf Palmer down in the boatshed,
during that April week on Palm Island. And over at the old men's home
were a couple of people from the far west of Queensland who were
eager to record songs. And a white-haired old fellow called Tommy
Kangaroo, who spoke Lama-Lama from high up in the Cape York
Peninsula. This was a strange language with odd-sounding vowels and
more consonants than in the rainforest tongues. I recorded a bit from
Tommy, but he was so senile that it didn't make much sense. George
Watson came up as we were finishing and got quite concerned.

"When you ask him something he talks about something quite
different."

"I know, but what can I do about it?"

George just shrugged.

Monty West, the offbeat American who so fascinated Capell, had
spent a couple of months on Palm about 1961. He'd taken down
material from some of the oldest and most senile inmates of the old
folks' home — I was shown the tree where Monty had sat, day after
day. Unfortunately he didn't transcibe the material very well, and he
didn't try and work out any of the grammatical patterns. But the old
men loved him. As soon as Monty left the island — so I was told — a
couple of them just lay down and died.

Jack Doolan said that he'd urged Monty to work with George
Watson, whose knowledge of traditional life and language was extraordinarily sharp. But Monty wasn't interested. George was a native
policeman, far too tidy and precise. I mean, he didn't *look* ethnic.

I gained tremendously from George's keen, insightful mind. He was
able to explain, quite explicitly, things that other people had only been
able to talk around. The verbal affix *-man* had been bothering me, to
take just one example. There was *yanu* "go" and *yanuman* "take", then
nyinanyu "sit, settle down" and *nyinayman* "marry". George explained
that it conveyed something like English "with". "He goes" *yanu*, "he
goes with her" *yanuman;* "he settles down" *nyinanyu*, "he settles down
with her", *nyinayman*. Suddenly, the penny dopped and all the data I

had, all the things other people had told me about this — everything fell into place.

On the last afternoon I requested another narrative, perhaps an account of some recent historical event. George hesitated. After a few moments he said he could tell the story of the last cannibalism. He hadn't been there, but he'd heard all about it. There was just one condition: I mustn't play it to anyone who had been involved. I agreed, and only ever played it to Chloe, after swearing her to secrecy. Chloe confirmed that that was what *did* happen, as the story had reached her.

The victim was Mick Bulbu (Burrbula), who'd been messing about with other people's women, and with young girls who'd been promised in marriage to others. Despite ample warnings, he'd persisted in this misconduct and everyone agreed that an influential Wise Man called Tommy Springcart (Jumbulu) should put an end to it.

Jumbulu went up to Tully to draw some of his money from the policeman, and then met Burrbula in the Euramo pub. They drank for a while around the back of the pub. (Aborigines were never allowed in the main bar.) Then Jumbulu started accusing Burrbula of the many misdemeanours. Burrbula responded with counter-accusations, and the two of them began to fight. Some of Jumbulu's accomplices were hiding in the sugar-cane nearby with an axe. Jumbulu took this and hit Burrbula with the reverse side. He aimed the blow at the back of the neck, in between the two muscles which lie just below the base of the skull. Hitting someone in this place — called *rudu* in Dyirbal — causes almost certain death and leaves no mark. I was told that even a European doctor with the full resources of post-mortems couldn't find out how someone died if they'd been hit at *rudu*.

Jumbulu and his helpers then carried the dead body over the railway line to a secluded spot. Others came, as Jumbulu drained the victim's blood off into a bottle, and cut out the kidneys. Then he picked out two young men, whom we can call Charlie Jericho and Frank Lawson, and offered them blood and kidney.

"Drink this!" he instructed them, "and it'll make you into a wise man."

Charlie took a drink of the blood, but spewed it up again. He tried once more and this time was able to keep it down. The bottle went to Frank and he too vomited up the first mouthful. But, urged to try again, he did succeed in keeping down the second swallow. "His stomach caught and retained the blood," as it is described in Dyirbal.

They threw the mutilated body into a swamp, for crocodiles to feast on. But, George remarked, this was a mistake, because crocodiles don't like dead meat — they prefer something they've killed themselves. So the body remained there, floating in the swamp.

Meanwhile, a friend of Burrbula's, anxious about him, asked at the pub, then followed the tracks across the railway line and up to the swamp. On seeing the body, he ran to Tully and returned with the policeman.

Justice took its course. The sergeant rounded up Jumbulu and Charlie, and then went up to the farm of Hughie Lawson, a corpulent old white settler, to apprehend Frank. Hughie was astounded at the accusation. He'd brought Frank up almost as his own son, and *he* wouldn't do a thing like that! There must be some mistake. Frank denied it at first but then, under questioning, admitted his complicity. Old Hughie fainted dead away.

Jumbulu was given a long sentence. Charlie and Frank got off with a caution, mainly because of the lawyer Hughie Lawson hired. George told me the killing happened in about 1941; Jack Doolan checked the records on Palm Island and found that Jumbulu's jail sentence had extended from October 1940 until 1956. Eventually Jumbulu returned to Murray Upper, where I worked with him once, in 1970. I found Jumbulu to be extraordinarily knowledgeable and intelligent. Jumbulu died in the mid-seventies, as did Charlie.

For George, the lesson of the last cannibalism was clear.

"Look at Charlie, he's got thick red lips — that's because of the blood he drank then. And Frank, he's had TB, been up to Cairns for treatment. That's where it came from."

"You really think so?" I asked.

"Must be," said George, "but one thing certain, nothing good going to come of it."

The rains had now eased off, and we were able to take the caravan down to Murray Upper for a week or so at a time, gather more material from Chloe and the others, and then return to Cairns to analyse and digest it. It was pleasant at Warrami. The Cowans had a grove of orange trees just by the house, and there were also melons and mangoes. At night, we were wakened by the shrill cries of flying foxes, large fruit bats which swooped in to sample the wares. Flying foxes are good eating, Jimmy Murray told us, but they have a terrible stink and not many people can get past that. Mrs Cowan and Chloe — and everyone else — were quite delighted by Eelsha. Both black and white Australians value children very highly, much more than is the case in Britain.

"Just the first one," Chloe lamented. "Poor things, you won't know what to do with it. First two I had, didn't really know what to expect. Then next two I getting a bit better. And when numbers five and six come along, that's when you really *are* a good parent!"

I told AIAS that it was highly desirable for me to spend a few more months in the rainforest region, and they didn't protest. But I would explore the hinterland, partly to investigate the languages that surrounded Barbaram, with its monosyllabic words and other oddities. To the east and south were Yidin, Dyirbal and Warungu, which are on the normal Australian pattern, with every word having at least two syllables. Now data were needed on Wagaman and Jangun, which were originally spoken to the west and north of Barbaram.

One Saturday at the end of April, I set out on a journey to the west. Mrs McGrath, in the store at Petford, said Albie Bennett had gone off fishing for the weekend. He'd told her about me, she said, and mentioned that he'd been thinking back and could now remember a few more words of Barbaram. I promised to come and see him again very soon.

A few miles beyond Petford, the track loops round to Lappa Junction. Only it wasn't a junction any more — the branch line to Mount Garnet had been taken up the previous year when a bitumen road had been put in from Ravenshoe to Garnet. Lappa's main building was the pub, with an irregularly lettered sign on its crooked iron wall. The publican was foreman of the gang that kept the railway line in repair (this was where Albert Bennett worked). He used to pay them on Friday night, in the pub, and everyone was expected to drink a certain proportion of his wage before leaving. He had to get a bit of trade somehow!

The Hookworm Man had warned me that the road from Lappa to Almaden was the worst he'd met — I should go very slowly and cautiously or I'd break an axle. It was a steep descent down the west side of the range. Then from Almaden — eight or nine houses, a store, a pub and a railway station (but no Aborigines) — the road went flat and straight twenty miles to Chillagoe. The thick bull dust on the track could produce alarming skids. I tried once to keep pace with an emu that was running through the trees on the left — thirty, thirty-five miles an hour, and then it veered off to the south.

In the heyday of mining, Chillagoe had a population of many thousands, with at least ten pubs. Now there were only a hundred people, but still two pubs. The houses looked as if they had been set down at random in the bush, but closer scrutiny showed an ancient pattern of streets. King Street, Queen Street, and so on, were barely visible tracks, and nine out of ten of the original house blocks were vacant and overgrown.

In 1964, Queensland still had a law that no women were allowed in a public bar (and no unaccompanied men were permitted in a lounge bar) but that was one of the laws which seemed to be suspended in Chillagoe. Among those propping up the bar was a brawny female station boss mixing her beers — and her oaths — with those of stockmen who had ridden half-a-day to wet their whistles.

The policeman said there really weren't any Aborigines in town — just an old lady down by the creek — but there were mobs at a cattle station some way to the west. The road was just passable after the wet — he'd been on it himself a couple of days ago. I went down and recorded a bit from Mabel Callaghan, but she spoke Olgolo, from way up on the Alice River. Yes, she'd heard tell of Wagaman, the language of Chillagoe, though there was no one here now who knew it.

The road went along by the side of the railway to Mungana, which had once been a largish town. Not a soul lived there now. The last house — the station house — had been trucked away the previous month. The railway line just ended at nothing — well, at a big cattle yard. It was kept open for transporting cows to the meat works in Cairns. Tumbledown houses were scattered over a hillside around the deserted mine workings. But no people. (Five years later I saw a poster to encourage immigration, in the window of the Queensland government office in London. It featured a large map with Mungana boldly marked on it. I wonder if anyone thought of going to live there?)

A few miles further on, the road seemed to disappear into the swollen bulk of the Walsh River. Well, the policeman said he had forded it, so I should be able to. Half-way across I opened the Land Rover door to see how deep the water was, but shut it again quickly — the water-level was just above the bottom of the door. For relief, I sat and had lunch on the sandy river shore, to the annoyance of a yellow-crested cockatoo who insistently proclaimed from the top branch of a tea-tree that this was *his* territory.

My first view of the cattle station was of a wide lake spotted with ducks, surrounded by green pastures; the track bending round it to an old, white-roofed homestead, shaded by high trees; a plane just landed from Cairns with mail and supplies, and the manager's yellow truck driving towards it. I stopped for a few moments to take in this verdant scene, an absolute contrast to the dry, brown country I had been driving through for the past hour.

The manager welcomed me routinely, and said I'd be welcome to stay the night. Dinner would be at six-thirty. The cattle station, owned by a large national or perhaps multinational pastoral company, covered ten thousand square miles. Most of the stockmen were Aboriginal. There were about a hundred dark people living at a camp over there — he pointed to a group of huts a hundred yards behind the homestead — but he'd prefer that I didn't go down there myself. When I tried to argue, he said that *the people* wouldn't want me there. We could send a messenger for whoever I wanted to talk to. (But how was I supposed to find out who I wanted to talk to?)

There was no question of my working in the homestead, of course. So we all sat in the shade of my Land Rover, just outside the garden gate, and moved round with the sun. Dust got into the tape-recorder, and even though we all wore wide-brimmed hats the sun was still a nuisance. But if white wanted to talk to black, that was how it had to be done.

One old man, Jack Brumby, knew the Wagaman language. That is, he remembered a few bits of it. "Eye" *mirra*, "hair" *dangu*, "neck" — no, he couldn't remember that.

"Of course you do," prompted his wife, whose own language was Gugu-Mini, "Wagaman say *manu* for 'neck'."

"Oh yes," agreed Jack, "we call it *manu.*"

All the words seemed to have two syllables, on the regular Australian pattern, quite unlike Barbaram. After an hour, Jack declared that he really didn't know any more. So I started taking down Gugu-Mini from Mrs Brumby. Although her white hair made her look older than Jack, she was quick-witted and helpful, where he was slow and lethargic. We were in full swing when the jackeroo — white lad training to be a manager somewhere, someday — came and said we'd better break it up; it was time to get dressed for dinner.

So I found out, the hard way, that some of the larger cattle stations far from the mainstream of Australian life preserve nineteenth-century customs that have disappeared in other parts of Australia. I didn't have any long trousers with me, or socks or shoes. But I did put on a clean shirt, once I'd been shown my bedroom.

The jackeroo took me up the stairs in the old part of the homestead, built ninety years before by the first white man to bring cattle into this country. He pointed down the corridor. "Your room's the third one on the right." He didn't actually come down the corridor with me (his own room, shared with the book-keeper, was located right by the top of the stairs). I later learnt that that part of the house was considered structurally unsafe and that people generally weren't game to go into it too much (except for the Aboriginal girls who made the beds and dusted, but they scarcely counted). The manager lived in a modern single-storey building a few yards off.

The Aboriginal cooks had prepared a good meal — beef, of course. All meals there were beef — roast or grilled or fried or broiled or stewed. The manager carved and served the meat while his wife added vegetables. Usually they showed a film on Saturday night, and the nearest neighbours often drove the forty miles across for it, but it hadn't arrived on the plane today. So after dinner, we drank Scotch and water while the book-keeper played the piano. Then everyone went to bed about nine o'clock.

I was up at dawn the next day and found the jackeroo in the tool shed. He told me a bit about how things went. Although the Aboriginal stockmen were the most important workers on the station — they would search out stray cattle in a way that no white man could and they worked willingly and well — they were treated quite poorly. The Hookworm Man had told a similar story. He'd made the long trip out to gather his samples and found that almost every Aborigine had hookworm (which is what you'd expect with the sort of unsanitary conditions they had to live in). He didn't have time to go all the way back, so he'd sent the medicine to the manager with a list of who should take it. But he doubted whether the manager or his wife would have bothered to give it out.

After breakfast we sat again in the shade of the Land Rover and continued with Gugu-Mini. Jack Brumby was feeling sick, and he didn't know any more anyway. But there was a slight-framed old man with the engaging name of Peter Flying Fox who was willing to record some Olgolo. This was a language in which every single word began with a vowel (I found later that the initial consonants had just dropped off through an historical change — every one of them). *Ikatha* "shoulder", *abuba* "breast", *ele* "eye", *ulbmbula* "nose".

Then Peter Flying Fox asked if I'd like any songs. Accompanying himself by tapping two tobacco tins together, he sang in a style quite unlike those on the coast. Unlike anything I'd ever heard before. He achieved an echo effect from somewhere in the back of his throat, and the songs themselves consisted apparently of gliding vowel sounds broken up by incredible glottalic closures. The sound was more arresting and bizarre than anything the electronic gadgetry of recording studios can produce today. Two of the spectators contributed a rhythmic grunt, as dancers would, adding more beat and excitement to the haunting message of the songs.

It was some of the most beautiful music I'd ever heard, and seemed oddly out of place in the oppressive atmosphere of this cattle station. The manager's wife sat on the verandah all morning reading a fat paperback by someone like Harold Robbins. The Aboriginal domestic staff came to ask her what should be cooked for lunch. Once she looked up from her novel and called out: "Rosie, see that red hen – take it away and wring it's neck, it's annoying me with the noise it's making." I was getting edgier and edgier. None of Peter Flying Fox's songs were recorded correctly – he'd start before I was ready and the first few bars didn't get on to the tape. I suddenly felt I couldn't stand a minute more of it. I thanked the manager's wife, who was very civil – wouldn't I wait for lunch, until the manager returned from inspecting the fences to the north, did I have enough petrol for the trip back? Really thanked Peter Flying Fox and the dozen or so other people who had helped. And drove away, trying to blot the nineteenth century out of my mind.

Barbaram was still a major priority. Following Albert Bennett's suggestion, I'd located Mick Burns, living with his daughter's family in a house on tall stilts at the south end of Edmonton. He was a tall, light-skinned man, very old. He hadn't thought about his language in years, and didn't think he could help me. But I persisted, mentioned a few of the words Albert had given, and he grudgingly thought a bit. Mick Burns sat on the top step, leaning against the door frame, and I squatted on the step below. He remembered twenty-seven words. And I paid him a pound.

Paying people is a tricky matter, and Stephen Wurm had given me useful advice about that too. Never make it too formal, with anything like clocking-on and clocking-off, he'd said. People won't work with you for money – they'll do it because they want the language written down, and as a gesture of friendship. But of course you must give some financial reward for all the hard work and effort put in, only don't make it look like a boss paying a worker. Go into the bank to draw some money out and then say, "Here's a bit for you and a bit for me". Share it out like the Aborigines do themselves.

I always avoided getting out my wallet and counting notes when paying anyone. I kept a pound or five-pound note in my shirt pocket so that when shaking an informant's hand, and thanking him for all the help he or she had given, I could pass a suitable note over "to help you on your way." Nothing could be more destructive of good relations than to insist on each informant signing a receipt for money received, as AIAS did in the late sixties when it got into its full bureaucratic swing. And the fact that scarcely any informants could write their own name — no matter, get them to affix a thumbprint!

Anyone who demanded payment in advance — as Tommy Warren and Lizzie Simmons had done — was unlikely to be much good, I discovered. People had to *want* me to record their language. But I did pay everyone I worked with, except on Palm Island where this was expressly forbidden. Sometimes, though, it might have been better not to. Mick Burns didn't want the pound note for his twenty-seven words. He felt he hadn't really remembered anything — he might try and think a bit more that night, to see if his mind could move back in time. But I pressed it on him, pretty much against his will. When I did go back the next week, he declined to talk at all. He'd done a bit of thinking, he said, and could remember nothing else. I'd have to go back to Albert.

At her suggestion, I had telephoned Mrs McGrath and asked her to pass on a message to Albert about when I was planning to come, so that he wouldn't go out fishing. Albert seemed quite happy — if not pleased — to see me, and made room for me to sit on the bench with him, out of the sun.

"I don't think I can help you much more," he said, when I told him about Mick. "I did remember three more words, but I can't think of them now. Oh, heck."

I met the third and last living member of the Barbaram tribe, Jimmy Taylor, who had walked down from his barracks near the store. Jimmy seemed to remember less than either of the others, but he had an eager, excited manner, in contrast to Albert's lugubrious introversion. Jimmy also had a terrible stammer (unusual in an Aborigine). With his staccato prompting, Albert remembered *ga* "east", *wo* "west" and then *liborr* "eye", *anyag* "sit down!", and so on.

We had a good session, getting another seventy-five words, and — even more important — bits of grammar. I'd ask for a sentence using the words they'd given, and they rarely hesitated. "Man" was *mog* and "wallaroo" *aru*. "The man shot the wallaroo" was *mogul aru ndare,* the verb coming last (as in most Australian languages). There was no ending on the object noun but — just as in Dyirbal — the subject of a transitive sentence (describing someone doing something to someone or something) had a special ending, here *-ul*. (Linguists call this *-ul* 'ergative case inflection', although I didn't know this was the appropriate term until I returned to London and Halliday told me about it.)

Most exciting of all, I could see a relationship between Barbaram and the other languages I'd studied. "Stomach" is *bamba* in Dyirbal but *mba* in Barbaram; "we two" is *ngali* in Dyirbal and Wagaman but *li* in Barbaram; "east" is *naga* in Jangun and Yidin but *ga* in Barbaram; and "fish" is *guyu* in Jangun and Wagaman as against *yu* in Barbaram. Barbaram had simply dropped off the initial vowel and consonant. If the word originally had a long vowel, then a short vowel remained at the beginning of the word — "boomerang" is *waangal* in other languages but *angal* in Barbaram.

So Barbaram *did* seem to be a language of the Australian family, only it had undergone a quite regular change that had produced odd-looking words. Stress probably shifted from first syllable (as in Dyirbal) to second syllable — *bámba* to *bambá*. Then the first syllable was gradually dropped off in pronunciation, yielding modern *mbá*.

I became quite superstitious about Barbaram. The first recording I'd made from Albert Bennett had gone into tape 38. I decided that 38 was the lucky Barbaram number, and all other tapes were numbered in multiples of it. At the beginning of tape 76, I asked Albert to say the name of the language. "Mbabaram". He said it again: "Mbabaram". Tindale had missed the initial consonant cluster, and there was no *r* after the first vowel.

I called in to see Mrs McGrath, to buy an ice-cream and tell her what a successful morning we'd had. She introduced me to her husband, Bill, a tall, gangling farmer who ran a few cows on the unpromising land around Petford.

"You know, Robert, when you first came here," said Mrs McGrath. (I'd introduced myself as Robert — I don't know why since everyone else knew me as Bob. Maybe it was just part of the Mbabaram mystique.) "When you first called in, we weren't sure what to make of you. You know, you used long words that no one round here would ever say. But now we've got to know you a bit more, we can see that you're all right." Goodness knows what words I used. I'd always thought I was able to modify my language to the situation I was in. But Doreen McGrath certainly made me self-conscious about it. Several times after that I'd find obscure Latinate words coming into my head when standing chatting in the Petford store, and hastily suppress them. There must have been something about Mrs McGrath that brought out the long words in me!

We went back to visit Albert several more times during the next few months. It had to be on a weekend, because he worked on the line all week. Talking for an hour and a half was pushing Albert's concentration and patience, and then it was wise to leave it for a couple of weeks before the next session. So a lot of miles had to be driven for quite small reward — marked contrast to Chloe, or George Watson, who could work for six hours at a time, day after day. But the Mbabaram corpus gradually built up. By August I had 200 words, all of them used in a variety of sentences.

Each time I went back, Albert would begin by saying that he had nothing new to tell me (although he was friendly enough). Following Doreen McGrath's advice, I'd begin by chatting about railways — he'd explain the logistics of replacing sleepers, tamping the track, and reorganising the timetable. Then I'd say: "Look, there were just a few words you gave last time that I may not have got down right. I wonder if I could just go over them again?" "All right," Albert would reluctantly agree. And he'd be good for an hour or so of Mbabaram.

During the first weeks in the field, I tended to record everything — using the tape recorder like a rough notebook. But then it took an awfully long time to transcribe it all afterwards. Gradually, when I was working with a language that I was getting to know reasonably well, like Dyirbal, I would just take most things down directly into a notebook. Texts had to be recorded, of course, and phonetic queries. But questions about vocabulary or grammar and commentaries on texts didn't need to be immortalised on tape; it was just too time-consuming.

I did, however, record almost every minute of the brief Mbabaram sessions. Not only did the language have short words, but there were strange vowels. Dyirbal and all the surrounding languages have just

three vowels *i, u,* (pronounced like *ee* and *oo* in English) and *a.*
Mbabaram had these and also *i̵,* that sounded half-way between *i* and *u.*
Besides *li* "we two" (relating to *ngali* in other languages) and *yu* "fish"
(corresponding to *guyu*), Mbabaram also had *yi̵* "I" (probably relating
to an original form like *ngayu,* which is "I" in modern Yidin). And it
also had *e* and *o,* as in *neg* "stand up!" and *dog* "dog".

Four years later, when I was spending a year at Harvard and first met
Ken Hale, he pointed out that the *e* and *o* had developed in Mbabaram
in the same sort of way as in some languages he had worked on from
further up the Cape York Peninsula. An *a* in the second syllable of a
word had become *o* if the word had originally begun with *g.* So from
guwa "west", Mbabaram had derived *wo.* We were sitting on a beach
near Gloucester, Massachusetts one Sunday in September when Ken
suddenly saw the etymology for *dog* "dog". It came from an original
gudaga, which is still the word for dog in Yidin (Dyirbal has shortened
it to *guda*). The initial *g* would have raised the *a* in the second syllable
to *o,* the initial *ga* dropped and so did the final *a* (another common
change in the development of Mbabaram). Ergo, *gudaga* became *dog* –
a one in a million accidental similarity of form and meaning in two
unrelated languages. It was because this was such an interesting
coincidence, that Albert Bennett had thought of it as the first word to
give me.

The last time Alison and I went out to Petford that year, Doreen
McGrath had been thinking up ways to assist us. She recommended
calling in to see an old white man – all the people left in Petford were
old – who had known some of the original Aborigines before they had
passed on. He lived in the last house out of town on the Irvinebank
Road, Mrs McGrath told us. It took us quite a few minutes to find it,
simply because we hadn't got used to the scale of things in Petford.
The last house was, in fact, next door but one to the store. We had a
yarn, but didn't learn very much from him.

Albert and Jimmy actually invited us *into* the house that last time,
to work at the table. Although cooler, it was a mixed blessing, for the
corrugated iron walls gave the worst possible acoustic effect, imparting
a dull quality to the recording. Albert's wife also invited us to stay for
lunch – curry and rice, with fruit and custard.

Albert explained how the white man had changed the country since
he was a child. Felling all the forest around Atherton had altered the
pattern of rainfall, the whole ecology of the area. At one time, the river

had flowed in all seasons, but now one had to dig down in the sand to find water at this time of year, and even then it wasn't too good. I did drink a tumblerful of the brackish liquid Jimmy brought, to dubious looks from everyone else.

There seemed always to be a mysterious quality to Mbabaram, as if it were a language that belonged to the country and was returning to it. Besides the 38-fetish for numbering tapes (now up to 114), I dedicated each Mbabaram notebook (in Dyirbal) to the rainbow serpent, prime spirit of that part – and probably all other parts – of Australia. That night, in the caravan at Malanda, I was seized by terrible stomach cramps and couldn't move for two days. It may have been the water. But I prefer to believe that it was the land, and the spirits of its people, protesting against the treatment they had received. Against the mining, against the rape of the forest, and against the invaders who had – directly and indirectly – ensured that the Mbabaram tribe had dropped from perhaps five hundred members to three old, tired men.

7

"Of course we'll keep in touch"

We played Chloe a bit of the Mbabaram tape and she wondered at it. She'd never heard any of those words before. Fancy that! That old man up there still knowing a bit of Mbabaram, poor old thing. At least he'd been able to help me out when that cranky old Lizzie Simmons wouldn't. Wait till Chloe saw her, she'd give her a piece of her mind.

Chloe was more interested in the half-dozen Mamu texts I'd recorded from George Watson.

"He really knows that language. And what he tell you there — that's right. He got it right all through, that old man."

It gradually came out that Chloe and George, both half-castes, had been at one time destined to marry each other, according to the Aboriginal system of "promising". Chloe said she hadn't really fancied the idea, and she took good care to keep out of George's way. (It seemed that George had had a fairly lively life. About half the old ladies I met became unnaturally coy when his name was mentioned, and admitted that they'd been "girlfriends" of George Watson many years before.)

The four genders of Dyirbal were attracting my interest. At first it seemed that they were "masculine", "feminine", "edible" and "neuter". "Edible" was clear enough — all fruit and vegetables took the gender marker *balam*. There was *balam gubungara*, a palm tree, whose "heart" was eaten, and *balam bangginyu*, a tree fern that was ground and roasted. And honey belonged in this gender class too, since it was made from the nectar of flowers — *balam girnyjal* "honey". "Meat", though, was *bala jalgur*, in the neuter class.

Words describing human females took *balan* — *balan jugumbil* "woman", *balan nayinba* "teenage girls" — and words denoting human males took *bayi* — *bayi yara* "man", *bayi rugunmi* "teenage boys". But *bayi* and *balan* also occurred with non-human nouns and I couldn't see any order here at all. Some fishes were *bayi* and some *balan*. Most birds were *balan* but a few were *bayi*. "Sun" was *balan* but "moon" *bayi*. "Stars" were *balan* and "thunderstorm" *bayi*. I tried hard to look for some principle that determined which gender marker a noun took, but couldn't find anything. Perhaps it was just arbitrary, I ruminated, with speakers simply have to *learn* the gender of each noun, rather than deduce it from any general rule.

But then I found that I *did* have intuitions about the gender of a new noun. Although I wasn't right all the time, my guess was correct much more often than randomness would predict. And I observed that some of the children who were learning Jirrbal didn't have to be told the gender of each noun, but appeared to be working in terms of some general principle.

Chloe was interested in exploring this topic. In addition to nouns referring to human females, we worked out that all nouns referring to water and fire took *balan*. Thus *balan buni* "fire", *balan nyara* "flame", *balan yingginy* "spark", and *balan bana* "water", *balan yuramu* "river", *balan burba* "swamp". But why was the moon *bayi* and the sun *balan*? Oh, that was easy — in Jirrbal myth the sun is a woman and the moon her husband. So "sun" takes *balan* because of the connection with human femininity and "moon" is *bayi* through the connection with human masculinity. "Stars" are like pinpricks of fire (they are not personified en masse) and so they are *balan*, like fire. "Thunderstorm" is believed to be a mythical man, making loud noises across the sky, and takes the masculine gender marker. Chloe reminded me of the story of *bayi murrnganu*, a man who turned into a thunderstorm.

Most animals, it seemed, took *bayi*. But why did almost all birds take *balan*? Because birds are believed to be the spirits of dead human females, Chloe explained, and so they take the female gender marker. *Balan dundu* is the generic term "bird", and then there are *balan guguwuny* "brown pigeon", *balan gurugu* "diamond dove", *balan gugu* "mopoke owl" and many more. But *bayi gurrijala*, the eaglehawk — he's a bird that eats other birds and so he's in a class of his own — he's *bayi*.

If some members of a certain class were harmful, I inferred, they were put in a different gender from the rest of the class, to emphasise their dangerous nature. Most fishes are *bayi,* but the stone-fish and the toad-fish — which can inflict injury on a person — are specially marked by being *balan.* Trees with no edible parts are, as a rule, *bala,* the neuter gender. But the dangerous stinging trees are also *balan.*

So there were some general principles that decided which gender a noun belonged to. One had to know a good deal about the properties of things, and about the system of beliefs of the Jirrbalngan — such as sun and moon being a woman and her husband, and so on — to understand and formulate the principles.

Whenever we came across a new noun, I would ask its gender marker. "Cricket" was *jiday,* Chloe said. Is that *bayi jiday* or *balan jiday*? Chloe thought for a moment: *balan jiday.* Oh, *balan jiday,* I repeated, as I wrote it down. My voice rose slightly at the end of the phrase, a tinge of surprise that a non-human animate should have *balan* not *bayi.* This gesture of a question was enough for Chloe to add an explanation.

"Yes, she's *balan* because our old people they think cricket is old woman spirit making that noise. So it has to be *balan.*" The gender assignment seemed "special" to her, too, but there was — as there usually was — an explanation, in terms of the belief system of the Jirrbalngan. (The explanations Chloe gave were nearly all confirmed — or given spontaneously — by other speakers, showing that they did have a general currency.)

Chloe was a natural linguist. Given the proper educational opportunities she could well have been doing my job. Chloe had a theory that all languages must be related — only one had to get below the surface, as it were, to see the links. She gave a lot of attention to the hidden similarities between Dyirbal and English, as part of her contribution towards "helping me out". In fact she used to lie awake at nights thinking up correspondences. The Dyirbal word for "shallow" is *jala* and its comparative "shallower" is *jalabara.* This was one of Chloe's favourite examples; certainly if *jala* had been a loan word from English *shallow* (which it wasn't), it would have had exactly this form. Then there was the verb *digun* "dig". But *digun* is used only to describe raking or shallow digging with the hands, on the surface; there is a different verb, *nadan,* for really digging down. That didn't worry Chloe, though — Jirrbal *digun* and English *dig* seemed to her good enough examples of ultimate connection. (Goodness knows what she'd have done if she'd had Mbabaram *dog*!)

One day we were going through one of the texts Paddy Biran had recorded. It was about the cassowary — who was then a human, as were all animals and birds in the dreamtime past. He wasn't a very pleasant person and had the habit of sneaking up on children when they were playing, and wringing their necks. He kept on doing this until there were scarcely any children left. (There is a Girramay verb *wuyan* "keep on taking bit by bit from a group, or from a pile of objects, until scarcely any remain", that perfectly describes this.) So the other dreamtime animal-people put their heads together to see what could be done about it.

The cassowary was afflicted with head lice and the scrub-wallaby called out to him: "Come over here, and we'll pick the lice from your hair." After a fair amount of persuasion, the cassowary agreed. But he'd forgotten that having lice picked from one's hair can have a soporific effect. As he slept, the scrub-wallaby cut off one arm with a tomahawk, and then the other. Chloe took over the story: "That wallaby he cry *'Juyi, juyi,* now cassowary can no longer strangle our children.' " And it was that act of amputation which is said to have turned the dreamtime person into a cassowary, as he is today.

Juyi was a new word. It was clear that it belonged to the set of exclamations, rather like *wow, ow, phew* and *oops* in English, but I wanted a bit more on its meaning.

"You know!" said Chloe, as if I was suddenly being very stupid. "You got the same word in English — *joy*. Scrub-wallaby say *juyi, juyi* in Jirrbal, but it's the same thing. It's *all* the same really!"

Irene's husband had come and taken her and the babies off to where he'd got a job, so just Chloe and I were talking together most days. We did have visitors, though. I remember one day when the Jehovah's Witness man called.

There was, as far as I could see, one main reason why Chloe and some of the other Aborigines at Murray Upper had joined the Jehovah's Witnesses: because they were the first white people to treat them as peers, to call them "brother" and "sister" and tell them all were equal in the eyes of the Lord. (The eyes of the Lord were obviously, on these grounds, to be preferred to those of the policeman, or the Tully bank manager.)

Anyway, the Witness arrived one morning when Chloe was in full swing, and she put on her most consummate act of showmanship. Scrapping the traditional story we had been about to record, she launched instead into the Creation story. The Old Testament plot, mingled with an odd bit of geology she had picked up, told in Jirrbal. A long time ago a man was created. Now he must in fact have been God (Chloe always liked to have an ultimate cause), because the next thing was that the earth was made, and it was boiling hot. This heat was funnelled off in smoke, and then he set to clearing the planet up, making it nice and clean. Once the world was shipshape enough, *janyja banggul yugu jarran.* Chloe translated it for the benefit of our visitor: "he plant the tree." *Janyja banggul yidir nalngin* — "he plant the grass." She now provided a translation for each sentence, which she normally didn't do, but after all the story was especially for the Witness. God made all the fish, and then some water to put them in. And alligators, and bullocks with their horns. Then birds were made. And elephants — simply described as *guwu jalnggay,* animals with "long nose".

The Jehovah's Witness — a man of far less intelligence and imagination than Chloe — sat uneasily, fidgeting and looking for a chance to go. She was telling the story *for him,* but I don't think he even took in the bits of translation. Finally, he thanked "Sister Chloe", and me (or he said he did), and looked forward to seeing her on Sunday.

Chloe's theory of ultimate relationships extended to religion as well. The mythic creator in Jirrbal legends was called Jujaba; dreamtime stories concerned "Jujaba-time". To Chloe, the similarity between Jujaba and Jehovah could not be coincidental: they were certainly variants of the same word, the same person.

And her natural scepticism extended to both religions. As a girl she had asked the old people about the origin of things.

"And I asked them once before — old people — I said: 'How did this mountain and water come to be?' *'Juru, jujabagu wayuman.'* they told me, 'don't know, Jujaba might have made it.' Same thing in this Jehovah's Witness — *just* the same, no different."

In each instance Chloe felt that she was being fobbed off. Jujaba made it. God made it. What did that tell her? Nothing. They're just the same — no difference at all.

Chloe was quite determined that I should have adequate information on all the languages surrounding Dyirbal (and of course she did enjoy the odd trip to see old friends). Warrgamay, next to the south, I'd got from Alf Palmer on Palm Island. Nyawaygi, further south again, was the language spoken by Willie Seaton, the first Aborigine I'd ever spoken to (when Alison had had to bundle me out of the car). I'd been back to see him since, and got quite a few words and a few simple sentences. But there was one other speaker of Nyawaygi I must visit − Long Heron. Jimmy Murray agreed, and thought I'd need him along too to help out with questioning. So early one morning, Jimmy and Mary Ann (in the back together), and Chloe and I (in the front) set out for Warren's Hill, a short distance to the south-east of Ingham. The journey there was uneventful − we stopped once to pick some ferns growing near the road, and another time to watch a flock of brolgas dancing on a flooded field.

Long Heron lived up to his name. He was very tall, and only a little bent despite his great age. He was reputed to be about a hundred years old and I believe that he was − at the least − well over ninety. That would mean he may have been born before his tribe had ever set eyes on a white man. Yet now here he was, with Willie Seaton (twenty years his junior), one of the last two people who had any real knowledge of traditional language and customs.

Heron was friendly, and willing to talk about whatever I wanted. While Chloe buzzed away in the background, swapping quickfire gossip with the womenfolk, Jimmy and I went through all the usual lexical domains. I started off mentioning the Girramay names for fauna and flora and body parts, enquiring after the Nyawaygi equivalents. But this turned out not to be the best tactic. Heron would sometimes say the Nyawaygi word was "the same" as Girramay when in fact there was a slight difference. Many words were, of course totally different. Some, like *jina* "foot", really were the same in both languages. But there could be subtle differences, as with "beard", Nyawaygi *jalba* corresponding to Dyirbal *jalbar*. I found it better to ask the English names; that way I could be sure of getting the exact Nyawaygi pronunciation.

Heron wasn't able to tell any stories in Nyawaygi, but he gave some simple sentences. We had been through a fair amount of material and he seemed a bit tired, so I turned to Chloe for a while. Later, Jimmy told me that he didn't really know Nyawaygi and Heron wasn't all that familiar with Girramay, so they had spoken a bit in the intervening language, Warrgamay, of which each had a smattering. But Jimmy didn't mention this until we were driving home. I said I wished he'd told me at the time for it would have been fascinating to get it on tape.

The journey home was much more eventful. A mile from Heron's we were enveloped in clouds of steam − a gasket had blown. I had a thirty-gallon watertank and quickly filled up the radiator. Then I had to fill it up again. And again. Every half-mile, or oftener. It was only four or five miles to the garage at Ingham, but it seemed like a hundred as I kept running from tank to radiator and back. My three companions ignored the whole affair; they behaved as if stopping every few hundred yards to fill the radiator were a perfectly normal way of travelling.

It would take a couple of hours to repair, the garage said, so we had time to go to a cafe in Ingham. The food was good, but there was just one difficulty — Mary Ann had never in her life used a knife and fork. Jimmy and Chloe embarked on a complicated course of instruction, but it really seemed to me scarcely worthwhile learning such a skill at the age of eighty, if she'd got on all right without it up till then.

We still had time to kill, and there was a cool seat on the main street, half-way between two hotels. (There are hotels every hundred yards on each side of the main street in Ingham.) Now Jimmy had one weakness, which he shared with many other Australians, both white and black. Mary Ann was afraid that if he got a single sip we'd never get him away — the bender would go on for days. Whenever Jimmy wandered off, ostensibly to look in shop windows, Mary Ann would summon up all her English and urgently whisper at me: "Watch him. See where he go. Might be *gunyjarrigu*. You stop him!"

I wandered after Jimmy and he turned to chat — admiring the ten-gallon hats in the clothiers' display. When I went back, Mary Ann got even more desperate.

"You watch out," she warned me emphatically, "he start drinking we never get him home. You make him afraid. Say to him you tell policeman if he get a drink. He not 'llowed to drink by Act."

I was at a real loss to know what to do, but so persuasive was Mary Ann that I did what she said. I lamely told Jimmy not to get a drink or I might tell the policeman. He looked nonplussed only for a moment. Then, "No, you wouldn't do that," he said. He was right — of course I wouldn't have. We were all glad when the Land Rover was ready. We did get home safely — and quite dry.

We had quite a lot of other bother with the vehicle, and AIAS were their usual inconsistent selves. One day the cylinder block cracked and — knowing how AIAS felt about money — I had it welded rather than buying a new one. "I think it'll probably be all right," I wrote, "and it only cost £40 instead of £80." They wrote back sorrowfully that thinking it would probably be all right was really not good enough, and they wished I'd done it properly and bought a new block. (In fact it lasted perfectly well.)

I never quite knew where I stood with AIAS. I would receive one letter telling me that I was their best field worker (really!) because I'd sent in the expense statement on time and a quarterly progress report. Then there'd be a letter berating me for writing on both sides of the paper. Getting a prompt statement of expenses to AIAS didn't cause me much worry. For the first quarter, we recorded our actual expenses under each category. For the next quarter, I put the total sum accurately at the bottom of the page. And then I just varied the entries under the subheadings – this one up 5 per cent, that one down 10 per cent, so that they added up to the correct total. It satisfied them and it certainly left me a lot more time free for linguistic work.

It seemed like a good idea to plan my next trip to Palm Island while Superintendent Bartlam was still on leave. I found I could travel across for free on the Hayles launch that went from Townsville at half-past seven in the morning (twice a week) with the settlement supplies. The only difficulty was that Tattersall's Hotel insisted it was no bother at all to fix me an early breakfast – and the two poached eggs didn't enjoy the trip overmuch. The social atmosphere on the boat was razor sharp. The score or so Aborigines returning to their personal South Africa didn't have a glance, let alone a word, for the few whites making the trip. As I leant over the side, in agony, retching, I felt someone could easily have crept up behind and tipped me in.

Palm Island had no jetty (or there was one, but it wasn't long enough, or something). A group of Palm Islanders appeared alongside with rafts to take off the supplies. A group of American day-trippers, were on the boat but were not permitted on shore. Paterfamilias commented on the strength of the raft party, at the top of his voice, about a yard away from them. "Hey! Look at that big buck nigger there! Look at his muscles! Hey, look at the way he picked that up. Gawd, he's a primitive specimen if ever I saw one!"

We were taken off in a rowing boat, and then waded the last bit. The water was thigh-high and I had to hold aloft the two tape-recorders, one in each hand. Our bags followed on the raft.

Palm Island was officially "dry", although sometimes yeast mysteriously disappeared from the bakehouse and was put to a higher purpose than that for which it was originally intended. A blind eye was turned to the white staff importing some booze, but it had to be done discreetly. The Townsville supplier knew to take the beer out of its marked carton and pack it instead in a baked beans box. But the Palm Island wharfies could hear the "slop, slop" of the liquid as the cartons were carried ashore, and it was reckoned fair game to lose about a third of the cans from each consignment.

Jack Doolan was invaluable at organising things in advance so that I could get the most benefit from every minute of my time on the island. He'd arranged for George to have the afternoon off work, and for me to see Alf Palmer the next morning. Jack had regretfully to report that the two speakers of Mbabaram who Albert Bennett told me were sent to Palm Island in the thirties had died a few years back. But he had uncovered Mitchell Dodd, who spoke Wagaman. Mitchell gave quite a bit of information that corresponded well with the little I had gleaned from Jack Brumby at the cattle station out west. It was certainly a normal Australian language, which had *not* lost the first syllable of each word, as had its neighbour Mbabaram.

I'd omitted to bring any cigarettes with me. No matter — I should be able to buy some at the store on Palm Island. In fact trying to shop there turned out to be quite an experience. A wide counter ran the length of the shop, with ceiling-high wire mesh down the middle. The goods and Aboriginal assistants were on one side, and customers on the other. You started at the end of the line, told them what you wanted, and the assistants put it in a pile on the shop side of the grill, moving it down as you progressed in the queue. The white storekeeper was on the cash register at the end; customers were not allowed to touch their goods until they had paid for them.

I stood in the line, which seemed to move very, very slowly. The cashier kept the cigarettes — the assistants weren't trusted with them. When I eventually reached him, he regretted he couldn't sell me any: it was child endowment day, and the superintendent had ordered that no cigarettes were to be sold on that day. The sort of mothers you got here, he said, would be likely to spend all their endowment money on smokes rather than on food for the kids. They had a point, but so — I thought — did I. I wasn't a mother, I wasn't getting child endowment. I was a visitor and I really did need cigarettes for my work. The cashier was sorry, but rules were rules.

I went back the next day and stood in the line once more, for about three-quarters of an hour. When I got to the cashier, he said: "Sorry, we're out of them."

"Were you out of them yesterday?"

"Probably."

"Why didn't you tell me *then*, save having to queue up again?" As far as I can recollect, he just grunted a reply.

George Watson appreciated a smoke while we talked, but he did have a half-packet of his own tobacco left. The first thing I wanted to do this trip was to go over a story. Father Worms had recorded a "Djirbal" text from someone called "Moidja" while he was doing a locum as Catholic priest on Palm Island for a few weeks in the late forties. I started reading Worms's transcription, but George stopped me. "Hey, I told him that!" Muyija is one of George's names, and all the material Father Worms had gathered was given him by George and his Jirrbal wife. The story was actually in the Mamu dialect, with one distinctively Jirrbal word interpolated. Father Worms' transcription and translation were so bad that George said he'd tell it to me properly, from scratch.

It was a most important legend, George reckoned, containing the explanation for the origin of death. There were in the dreamtime, two brothers. The elder, Muyungimbay, had two wives, while the younger one, Gijiya, had none. One day Muyungimbay was out in the forest, chopping out witchetty grubs, when he encountered one odd-looking grub. He cut it open and it smelt of semen. A taste confirmed that it *was* semen. From this, Muyungimbay knew that some funny business was going on back at the camp, and he returned home post-haste. (When I later recounted the story to Jack Doolan, he was intrigued as to what word George had used for semen. "Spunk", of course.)

Muyungimbay saw his wives coming up from the creek with semen dribbling down their legs. Although Gijiya denied his accusations, Muyungimbay had no doubt what had happened. The next day he invited Gijiya to accompany him on a food-getting expedition. They came to a rotten log, full of grubs.

"You go to the bottom end and chop there, and I'll start at the top," instructed Muyungimbay. The two brothers got closer and closer to each other as they chopped out grubs nearer and nearer to the middle of the log. Then, suddenly, Muyungimbay chopped his brother, who fell down as if dead.

Muyungimbay was only part-way back to the camp when Gijiya caught him up, remarking that he must have fallen asleep. The younger brother picked up a short piece of wood, for the fire. When they got home Gijiya asked their mother to cook his grubs for him, since he was feeling unwell. The piece of wood burned shorter and shorter, and still Gijiya had bad pains, much to his mother's concern. The shorter the log burned, the sicker he became. Then the last of the log burned away and, when this happened, Gijiya died. His mother buried the body, but cut off his head and kept it in a dilly-bag, so that she could gaze on it and remember her dead son.

A few days later, the mother was sitting in the camp when she heard the kookaburra call out its characteristic laughing cry, "ga, ga, ga, ga, ga, ga." Then she saw Gijiya returning from the land of spirits.

"Oh, it's you," she said, "sit down here in the camp." Gijiya sat there.

Then he asked: "Mother, there's a bad smell here, what is it?"

"Oh, it must be that rotten walnut over there," mother replied. Gijiya went over to sniff the walnut, but he wasn't satisfied that that was what had attracted his attention. Soon, he left the camp.

The next day the kookaburra's laugh once more heralded Gijiya's return. Again he sat down in the camp, and again he sniffed, and complained of a strange smell. This time mother put it down to the grubs the two brothers had brought home. This answer failed to satisfy Gijiya. Soon he left the camp.

When Gijiya returned for the third time, to the kookaburra's call, his mother simply put her head out through the side of her hut. Gijiya would not sit down this time, but remained standing. Once more he complained – more loudly now – of a nauseous smell. His mother lost her patience.

"This is what you can smell," she said, pulling his decomposed head out of the dilly-bag in which she had secreted it. "Here, gaze upon your own head!"

"Oooooh!" cried Gijiya, staring in horror, *"Gugu-galbu, yaliyali nyurray gijiyagarru burunggaru marri, yunggul yunggulba, gugu-galbu.* Farewell, you will all follow me, along the road I lay down to the land of spirits – one-by-one, when your time comes."

"He was the first one to die," said George, "because he seen his own head. And, just like he said, we all follow him in death. One by one. When our time comes."

Years afterwards, whenever we heard the kookaburra crying out – especially around dusk – George would say: "Listen to that, he calling out that Gijiya coming." And even when I'm far away in Canberra, that inane laugh brings back to mind the younger brother and what he started.

Father Worms's version of the story was very short and omitted all sorts of important detail. When I took this up with George, he gave a plausible explanation: "He was a Father, you know, so I couldn't tell him that bit about the spunk in the grub or about the wives misbehaving. I had to miss those parts out." So Father Worms had been given a bowdlerised version, in deference to his cloth.

However badly all the other white staff on Palm Island behaved towards Aborigines, Jack Doolan got on well with them. Indeed, it could be almost embarrassing. Jack mentioned that the week before he'd been sitting on the beach with a couple of Aboriginal friends, waiting for the boat to come in, when one of them had asked him for a smoke. Jack said, No, he had only a few left and he'd need them for himself.

"Oh, come on," his friend urged. And then he used the plea that can scarcely fail between one Aborigine and another: "Don't be mean to your own colour!"

Jack wasn't perfect, of course, and his particular Achilles heel was the same as Jimmy Murray's. That's perhaps one reason why Jack's wife didn't mind Palm Island so much, although sometimes Jack and a couple of mates would take a boat across to the nearest pub, at Lucinda Point near Ingham, and there were hair-raising stories about the wild journeys back.

Everyone on Palm Island who did a "job" got paid. This was supposed to provide something like pocket money, since they had a weekly issue of rations. Jack told me the basic weekly entitlement for everyone over five years old: 1 lb sugar, 2 oz tea, 4 oz rice, 3 lbs flour, 1 lb salt, 6 oz peas, 8 oz barley, 4 oz sago, 1 lb rolled oats, and 4 oz soap. The weekly meat ration was 5½ lbs for men over 16, 3½ lbs for women over 16, 1 lb meat for children from 10 to 16, and 1 lb mince for children aged 5 to 10. But, as Jack added: "The meat contains a hell of a high percentage of bone and fat. The mince, from my own observation, is almost all fat with a liberal dosage of preservative added."

Wages varied from about ten shillings to — so far as I remember — about ten pounds a fortnight for the bulldozer driver and for the chief sergeant of the native police. Jack "borrowed" the pay list from the office one night, and we averaged out the wages over the whole settlement. Typically, a man on Palm Island could expect to get just on twenty-five shillings per week (two dollars fifty in decimal terms). That had to cover cigarettes, admission to the picture show, sweets for the kids, butter or margarine, jam and honey, and any other food additional to the basic ration. It could scarcely be said that the Queensland government was being too generous to the people it had so savagely dispossessed, and from whose traditional territories over on the mainland it was now raking in a fortune through grazing, dairying, sugar, tobacco, mining, and the like.

Life on Palm Island did have its redeeming features, though. One man told me that he'd rather stay there than move to Townsville, for one principal reason: safety. There was a high chance of his kids being knocked over by a car or lorry on the mainland roads, he maintained, a risk that was almost absent on the island. And it was a beautiful place, where one could find real peace (if the administration would let you).

One afternoon George and I walked across to the other side of the island to visit his daughter and her family. On the way, he told a story about how a superintendent called Robert Curry had run amok, and showed the place where he'd been shot. It was an involved tale. After Curry's wife died, he'd taken up with a half-caste girl called Rosie. But his children wouldn't accept this, and neither would Rosie's Aboriginal lover (whom Curry had jailed). One night, Curry doped his two children and set out to burn down most of the settlement and blow up his enemies. He set fire to the school and the store, and blew up his own house with his children fast asleep inside. Then he shot at the doctor, and knocked the doctor's wife unconscious before running out of the settlement. But the storekeeper let two men out of jail, armed them — and one of them shot Curry from the cover of a huge mango tree over by the jetty. Or something like that. It sounded rather like one of the more gory bits of the Old Testament.

George then talked about the famous strike on Palm Island in the fifties, when most of the men just refused to work, in protest at the poor quality of food. Bartlam had had armed police sent over from Townsville and the leaders were simply transferred to another settlement, as far away as possible. In the seventies, a small team of filmmakers from Sydney — Alessandro Cavadini and Carolyn Strachan — made a moving film, called *Protected,* about this strike, but it has never received a wide distribution.

A movie was showing in the hall that night, but there was no way I could attend it with George and Ginnie. Aborigines sat downstairs, and the whites up in the balcony. Even Jack Doolan advised me not to go against this convention — it wouldn't do anyone any good, he said. At the start of the film, Burt Lancaster warned that we shouldn't believe everything we saw in it. When he calmly walked across the floor of the ocean, escaping from a wreck, it brought the house down (the upper house and the lower one).

The next day, I took up what could well be a tricky topic. I'd picked up a lot of names for various types of "private parts", as people called them, but I wasn't quite sure what each referred to. I needn't have worried — George wasn't at all embarrassed. We didn't really have a common language for talking about them but eventually, with a lot of description, it was all sorted out. George taught me the various Mamu and Jirrbal terms and told me which were the more polite ones. He was, in turn, intrigued to learn the words I knew: vulva, clitoris, and the like. "Fancy, I've lived all this time and never knew that", and he went off home repeating them to himself.

I hadn't thought much about Jalnguy, the special "mother-in-law language" since Chloe had first mentioned it in November. But now that I had a passable understanding of the everyday speech style, it seemed time to go into Jalnguy in more detail. George had heard it spoken in the presence of taboo kinsfolk during his youth, and remembered a great deal from then. Just as there were separate everyday styles for the various tribes, so there was a Mamu Jalnguy distinct from the Jirrbal Jalnguy which Chloe was familiar with. Most words were the same — "fire" was *buni* in each everyday style and *yibay* in both Jalnguys. But there were a few differences. "Foot" is *jina* in all everyday styles, but where Jirrbal Jalnguy has *jurumbur,* Mamu Jalnguy has *winarra.*

George explained to me the different words for "go up" in everyday speech. I already had *wandin* "go up river" and *waynyjin* "go up anything other than a river, for example, up a hill, up a cliff, up a tree, or (fly) up in the air." There is also a more specific verb *bilinyu* "climb a tree, using just one's legs and hands to pull oneself up." And there is *bumiranyu,* to describe climbing a tree with the help of a long rope of lawyer vine. The climber throws the rope around the tree, holding it with both hands to support his body at right-angles to the trunk. By alternately jerking the rope a bit higher and moving his feet up the trunk, a skilled practitioner can virtually run up a tall straight tree-trunk, *bumiranyu*-fashion.

George explained that, although there were three distinct words for tree-climbing in the everyday language, these were all translated by a single word in the mother-in-law style. All of *waynyjin, bilinyu* and *bumiranyu* would be rendered by *dayubin* in Jalnguy. It was possible to specify the mode of ascending by adding something to the Jalnguy verb — *bilinyu* would be *dayubin dalmbirarru*, literally "go up along at a tree" and *bumiranyu* could be *dayubin galgulba*, literally "go up with a lawyer vine". (*Dalmbirr* and *galgul* are the Jalnguy equivalents of everyday style words *yugu* "tree" and *gamin* "lawyer vine" respectively. The grammatical endings *-rarru* "along at" and *-ba* "with" are the same in all styles).

The form *dayubin* was interesting in itself. *Dayu* is one of the dozen or so forms that can be added to a gender marker to indicate position up or down hill or river. *Dayu* itself means "long way up hill or up a tree". *-Bin* can be added to any adjective to make a verb, rather like *-en* (or *become*) in English — *gundun* is "short" and *gundunbin* "shorten, become short". Here the Jalnguy verb *dayubin* is made up of these two grammatical bits (which could not be combined in this way in the everyday style). Similarly, the everyday verb *wandin* "go upriver" is rendered in Jalnguy by *dawubin*. *Dawu* comes from the same grammatical system as *dayu*, and it means "long way upriver".

It was becoming apparent that the mother-in-law style, Jalnguy, did have most interesting linguistic properties. I had never before heard of any speech-style with this sort of social role — for communication within earshot of a relative of a particular kin category, to whom a proper degree of deference was due. And the structure of Jalnguy seemed as novel and interesting as its conditions of use.

Before we left North Queensland, I wanted to get some more information on Jangun, the language originally spoken to the north of Mbabaram. The only speaker left appeared to be Willie Richards in Mareeba. Back in November he had given me a few words, after a lot of bother, before we'd been interrupted by the arrival of a travelling church group. I'd have to try him again.

Willie was just as elusive as before. "Too busy this afternoon, you try come back tomorrow," was his first response. The next morning, he attempted to defer conversation until later in the day. But we had to move on, I insisted, couldn't he just spare me half an hour now? Well, all right, Willie grudgingly agreed, but he'd have to wash the dishes and tidy up his hut first. I sat outside and waited, for an hour — while windows were opened, the floor swept, plate and dish washed, windows

adjusted once more, then a chair moved, then the floor again . . .
No, he still wasn't quite finished. It was his game, but I decided to
modify the rules a little. Standing in the doorway, I shouted out words
to Willie as he puttered around inside. He was so far away that the
microphone didn't always pick up his responses very strongly but I
repeated them after him, loudly and clearly, into the recorder. It was
a language of the regular pattern — without the odd vowels and clipped
monosyllables of Mbabaram — and this procedure succeeded tolerably
well. It was the only way I could get Jangun equivalents for most of the
Mbabaram words Albert Bennett had given. The following year, the
Mareeba policeman deemed Willie Richards too old and senile to
continue living by himself, and George Watson was sent over from Palm
Island to escort him back there; he died soon afterwards.

I now saw that Mbabaram was unique, among languages of this
region, in having lost the first syllable from most of its words and
having developed new vowels. All of the languages surrounding it had
conserved disyllabic forms, similar to those found over most of the
continent.

When we got back to Cairns — after talking to Willie Richards in
Mareeba, recording a little more Ngajan in Malanda, and unsuccessfully trying to find Jack Stewart's present whereabouts — we found two
telegrams waiting for us. One was from Dr Capell, at the University of
Sydney, asking if I was interested in a lectureship there. The
Department of Anthropology had been allocated a new position, and
they wanted to appoint another linguist, to assist Capell. It's lucky I
didn't accept this offer, because it turned out to be a mirage — the
administration later told the department that it wasn't to appoint a
linguist; it had to appoint an anthropologist!

The other cable was from AIAS, offering a further year's grant. It
mentioned that an increase in stipend could be discussed; it would have
to be, since we'd found that living in Canberra might cost a lot more
than I was getting paid. Originally, I had thought of perhaps spending
eighteen months in Australia, a year in the field and six months writing
up the results back at the Institute. But, having seen AIAS (and
Canberra), the second part no longer held much appeal. The Institute's
headquarters at that time could scarcely have provided an atmosphere
less conducive to serious academic work.

Although I was getting lots of data on Dyirbal, and gaining a fair
understanding of how the language worked, I felt unable to write up

the grammar until I could return to the right sort of stimulating academic atmosphere – a department of linguistics with colleagues who were working on similar topics, and with the facilities of a first-class library. So when a telegram came the following week, offering a lectureship in linguistics with Michael Halliday – who had moved down to University College London just before we left Edinburgh – I accepted, thankfully.

The more I worked on Dyirbal the more I got out of it. Each month seemed to bring twice as many insights as the one before. Although we'd been looking forward to a few weeks in Torres Strait, it did appear most sensible to spend August on a final fling at Murray Upper. AIAS, who seemed to be eating out of my hand at this stage (I may have been the only field worker to send in quarterly expense statements on time), agreed.

Never having received any instructions on how to go about field work (apart from the half-hour conversation with Stephen Wurm), I did have a number of funny ideas, which were only discarded the hard way. For a reason that I cannot now recall (if indeed there was one) I had a thing against file cards or slips. This meant that all my vocabulary had to be put into a foolscap notebook, and then copied into another book when there was no room for further additions. Extraordinarily time-wasting. I finally succumbed, and made out a card for each word, in 1966. And my Dyirbal lexical information was so spread over dozens of miscellaneous notebooks that – in 1983 – I am *still* trying to tie it all together. (When I began intensive work in Yidin, in 1971, everything was totally streamlined from the start. The Yidin dictionary took far less work than the Dyirbal one.)

Dyirbal has no monosyllabic words, and in fact most words have just two syllables. There are, all told, just thirteen consonants – b, d, g, j, l, m, n, ng, ny, r, rr, w and y – and three vowels – a, i and u. Disyllabic words have the structure CV(C)(C)CV(C) where C indicates a consonant and V a vowel, and parentheses, (...), enclose an optional element. Only eleven of the consonants can appear at the beginning of a word, and only seven at the end. In the middle, between vowels, there are seventy-five possibilities of one, two or three consonants. The total number of disyllabic words is thus 11 x 3 x 75 x 3 x 8 = 59,400.

I got the idea of saying each of these possible words to Chloe, and asking her whether it was in fact an occurring Dyirbal form. I knew there'd be a fair number of "accidental gaps" – possible word

structures for which there just wasn't any existing vocabulary item, at
that stage in the language. (English has a fair proportion of "accidental
gaps" — things like *dit, tras, ipem.* Advertisers sometimes make up a
new name by exploiting one of these gaps — *bik, persil* and the like.)

I ruled a book with one square for each of the 7,425 CV(C)(C)CV
possibilities (leaving off the final C). Then I wrote in all of the
vocabulary I had already collected. The book was arranged so that
words that were phonetically similar occurred next to each other, to
help distinguish between things that sounded almost the same. *Barmba*
was next to *bamba* and some way away from *bara,* for instance. The
words in a conventional dictionary or lexicon are in alphabetical or
"lexicographic" order. Since my words were phonetically ordered, I
labelled the book a "phonicon".

I started going through the phonicon with Chloe in July. There seemed
to be a lot of words in certain parts of the book — beginning with *b* or
g, or with *-mb-* or *-lg-* between vowels. I went quite slowly through
these sections when saying the 7,425 forms one at a time to Chloe, and
then said each with the possible final consonants. There were many
fewer words beginning with *d* or *n* or *r,* or with *-nb-* or *-lw-* between
vowels, and I went rather faster through these sections.

Chloe agreed it might be quite a good idea, a way of getting down as
much as possible of the language. I'd read out each form and she'd say
whether it was a Dyirbal word or not. Some of the words she
recognised I already had, but many of them were new items. If the
word was a noun, Chloe indicated whether it took gender marker *bayi,
balan, balam* or *bala.* She thought about which of the three dialects
(Jirrbal, Girramay or Mamu) each word occurred in, and if it wasn't in
all three gave the corresponding forms from the other(s).

Then Chloe gave one or two typical sentences for each word,
showing the sort of circumstances in which it could be used, and the
other kinds of words it might typically co-occur with. *Burrmbun* was
a verb describing how the old people would wipe off illness with a
snatch of the hand off the skin — *balan bajingu banggul burrmbun gayga*
"he brought her round after she'd fainted by *burrmbun* at her eye."
Bayi bujimburran, a stinking beetle which might squirt some fluid at
you — "he's danger to eyesight". *Buyju,* Chloe explained, was a
crawling man, someone who keeps coming back asking for something
even after having been rebuffed several times.

About every hour, after we'd done a couple of pages of the phonicon, I'd switch on the recorder and then go back over them, Chloe pronouncing each word and giving a couple of sample sentences (often different from the ones she'd said earlier, which I'd written down). We'd then have a short break before doing the next page. When I got back to London, it took about a year to transcribe all those phonicon tapes. But I did have fairly rich data on most words, enough for a presentable dictionary entry.

One tape-recorder was already out of order and the second one broke down as we started on the letter *G*. The result is that I only have half as much material on words that begin with *g-*, written notes, but nothing taped. Phonicon data are most useful for verbs and adjectives — which are less "exactly translatable" between languages than are most nouns — and, as luck would have it, words in Dyirbal beginning with *g-* contain a slightly higher proportion of nouns than any other letter. So it wasn't as bad as it might have been.

We went back to Cairns for a week's solid work on field materials (without the distraction of someone knocking on the caravan door every hour or two to offer another myth); and to get the recorders repaired. Then we gave up the flat there, wishing our landlord happy listening, said goodbye to Phillip Wilson and the other friends we'd made, and went back to Murray Upper for a final dose of checking and questioning.

Chloe greeted me with the announcement that they had a surprise. I must stand in the middle of the yard and close my eyes. I heard a distantly familiar cackle in the background, and was suddenly poked in the middle of the back with a stick. Quite firmly. There was old Lizzie Simmons, come down for a visit with her daughter Mamie, who lived in the patchwork shack behind Chloe's house. I think she did remember me, although she had grown more senile over the last nine months. Her thirst hadn't gone with her wits, though. The old lady still demanded a nightly bottle of beer. Chloe told me with a mixture of disgust and admiration that they had to store the carton of beer in her house, so that Lizzie couldn't get at it in the daytime. Lizzie Simmons finally died in the Tully hospital on Christmas Day 1968, never having told me a word of the Mbabaram which I'm pretty certain she did know.

Over the next three weeks, Chloe and I continued to go through the phonicon page by page. She made the vocabulary of Dyirbal live, as the

most mundane words were imbued with gossip and rascality. *Dalnga*
was used to describe a "dry tree", half-dead and withering. As with
many other words in Dyirbal, it had a second meaning, rather risqué.

"When you see Jack Murray, you tell him that word. His thing
dalnga now, since his wife die. My sister Lily. He don't have any woman
now, so he *dalnga*. That old man come round here and want me to
marry him but I wasn't having any of it. I got enough to do bringing up
these girl. I tell him go look for woman somewhere else. No good
coming here. I'm not interest in him."

Our impending departure was alluded to when Chloe explained the
meaning of *guyngay*. This adjective described someone who is upset
because, say, a favour wasn't repaid him. If we should fail to write to
Chloe after returning to England she'd feel distinctly *guyngay-bin!*
You mustn't say that, *of course* we'll keep in touch, I insisted.

Going through the 7,425 possible CV(C)(C)CV forms was, all in
all, only a limited success. I did gather some hundreds of new words —
my vocabulary probably had between a thousand and fifteen hundred
words when I began, and over two thousand at the end of the phonicon
check. But many words from the first half of the alphabet only came
up in the explanations Chloe gave for words from the second half —
they hadn't been recognised when I'd pronounced them at their place
in the recitation. It was an interesting thing to try, and was by no
means a waste of time. But I don't think I'd do it again, nor would I
recommend it to any other budding field worker.

We kept going around and talking to plenty of other people in the
Murray Upper area. I remember one visit to Joe Kinjun's camp on the
Tully. Joe came up, full of bonhomie, and began talking to Eelsha. He
held up his thumb for her to play with. What a thumb! I can still see
it quite clearly. The nail at the top was blotched and broken. Rivulets
of scars transversed the lower part. Old, worn-in dirt filled up the cracks
and folds, and blobs of fresh dirt adorned some of the clear spaces.
I think there was a thorn somewhere. The thumb appealed to Eelsha
and, as she reached out, Joe wiggled it, making the bits of dirt dance
but not quite fall off. Alison and I could only look on, with fascination
and horror.

Joe was the last member of the Malanbarra tribe, which spoke the
Gulngay dialect of Dyirbal. This was the only group on which
historical information was available. Dr Walter E. Roth, the northern
protector of Aborigines at Cooktown, had visited the Tully River in

1900 and written a hundred-page "ethnography" of the tribe, mostly based on information given by Ernest Brooke, a local settler who was Roth's host. It has never been published in full, but Roth used many bits of it in his *Bulletins* on *North Queensland Ethnography,* published between 1901 and 1910. One of the things Douglas Seaton had passed on to me in Cairns was a copy of Bulletins 9 to 18.

Alison had been through these, picking out information on the Malanbarra. She gave me some linguistic extracts to clarify with Chloe. And she asked people like Jimmy Murray about some of the customs and ceremonies described by Roth, such as how before burial a corpse might be tied up, the knees pulled up to touch the chin, and the flats of the hands at the side of the head. Jimmy was quite taken aback to be confronted with questions about things he vaguely remembered from his boyhood, and which neither he nor anyone else had discussed with us. They'd always thought very highly of Alison for her ability to pronounce words accurately, and now she acquired a semi-mystical quality through having somehow acquired such accurate knowledge of half-forgotten practices. When I made a short return field trip to North Queensland in 1967, leaving Alison in England with the children, Chloe and Jimmy and the rest told me they had assumed that the framework for the investigations had been mapped out by her, with my task being essentially just to fill in all the boring grammatical and lexical details.

I had a number of queries, arising out of the texts George Watson had given me, which demanded another quick flip to Palm Island. I left Murray Upper at four one Saturday morning and drove down to catch the seven o'clock plane from Townsville. After a white-breaded breakfast at the guest house — where a visiting nursing sister lectured the other lodgers on how she didn't like people who said "Christ!" or "Oh Lord!" when they cut their fingers ("if you aren't friends with Jesus, then just keep quiet about him") — I went down to the office. Bartlam was back. Very much as I'd imagined him — large, bull-headed, red-faced, an ample belly, and gruff. Tom Murphy took me cautiously into the sanctum. "Mr Dixon had two trips here while you were away and he's just come back to clear up a few points. Came in on the plane this morning and he'll leave on the early plane Monday." Bartlam grunted, clearly indicating that he didn't believe linguists or anthropologists should be allowed in in the first place, but if they did have to come — well, short trips at the weekend would be the least disruptive to settlement routine.

Tom Murphy said that since I'd been working with George Watson — a sergeant of police and thus someone to be given at least a measure of trust — he'd thought it was all right for us to work on the beach, right away from the settlement, rather than in the court house. Bartlam grunted again, partly in disbelief, partly in vehement confirmation of how he knew important rules would fall into disarray once his back was turned, and partly in ungracious acquiescence.

George was waiting outside the store. As we set off to find a suitable log to sit on, he suddenly suggested that we go to his house. It'd be easier there, since there was a table, and it was nearer. I pointed out to George that this would get us into deep trouble. It wouldn't worry me, but George had to live on Palm. Surely it wouldn't be worth the trouble it would cause? George seemed unconvinced, but we went along and found a log. One without too many ants in it.

The last time I'd been there we'd discussed whether it would be a good idea for George and Ginnie to leave Palm, and go back to live on the mainland. We were pretty sure Bartlam couldn't stop George leaving if he wanted to, although he could no doubt be difficult about it. I'd encouraged George in the strongest possible terms to leave. He was sure he could get a good job around Innisfail. How could he stand Palm Island?

Jack Doolan told me, that evening, that George had mentioned his thoughts on leaving to Bartlam as soon as he'd returned from vacation. Bartlam had told him it was a silly idea — that he didn't know when he was well off. The way he'd put it to Doolan: "George Watson fits in all right here, got a responsible position, but he'd never make out on the mainland, you know — doesn't have what it takes to fit into society out there, none of these blackfellows do."

It rained that night, and the next morning George was quite firm that we should go and work in his house. I demurred, simply because I feared what the consequences might be for him. George lost patience. "Look, I'm inviting you into my house. Are you coming or not?" So we made a rude gesture in the direction of Bartlam's house, and for my last day on Palm Island, we pretended we were somewhere — anywhere — else in the world, and behaved like normal human beings. George cleared the table in the kitchen, Ginnie made a pot of tea, and we were able to chat and laugh together like friends. We checked my transcription of some of the texts recorded on earlier visits and then I played some of the songs from the Murray Upper corroborees, and a couple of

Chloe's stories. He hadn't seen Chloe for ten years. She was sharp all right — knew that language. George explained a few grammatical points that had bothered me, and the meanings of some difficult words. Then he and Ginnie came with me to the door, and we shook hands on the threshold.

(Bartlam was told about our scandalous behaviour, and I believe it tipped his mind against trying to stop George leaving. Luckily he didn't dare put him — a sergeant of police! — in jail. But if that was how George was going to behave, then the sooner he was off the island the better.)

Alf Palmer was, as always, willing to answer my questions. But I never have liked getting information by simply asking questions in English. Alf didn't feel he was ready then just to talk by himself in Warrgamay, or in Warungu. But he suggested I should leave some tapes with Jack Doolan. Alf would think what he had to say, get his grandson to write it down for him, and then record it with Doolan when he was ready. Sure, that was all right by me, and Jack was more than willing. After I left, Alf recorded one tape in each of these two languages — saying a sentence, then what it meant, then another one, and so on. It wasn't exactly running text, but it was useful material.

In fact those tapes took a long, long time to reach me. When Jack wrote at Christmas, he referred to the tapes as if they were something in the distant past, but I hadn't seen them. At my suggestion, he'd sent them down to AIAS to make a copy and send the originals on to me. At first the Institute lamely maintained that they hadn't known they were for me. Then they couldn't find them. I was so embarrassed, I had to write to Jack and assure him the tapes were fine, before I'd ever heard them. I felt too ashamed — for AIAS — to tell him what had actually happened.

Jack also recorded for me another story by George Watson. This was a legend of which I'd recorded a snatch from an old Ngajan lady near Malanda. It was about the origins of Lake Barrine, Lake Eacham and Lake Euramo, three volcanic craters on the Atherton Tableland.

As George told the story, two youths had just been initiated. Until their scars healed, they were not permitted to leave the camp except with a chaperon who would clear a path for them, sweeping all the leaves and sticks out of the way with a bramble broom. Well, these two initiands were left alone in the camp while their elders went out for food. One of them wanted a shit, so they just *had* to go a short distance into the bush for this purpose, breaking the taboo. They saw a wallaby a short way ahead of them through the trees. Disregarding the taboos, one boy sent his companion back to the camp for a spear while he watched the wallaby. He threw the spear at the animal, but it missed and impaled itself into *giwan,* the flame tree, which is sacred to the rainbow serpent, prime spirit of Aboriginal Australia. Even worse followed: when he withdrew the spear from the tree, it had a fat grub on its point.

It would be difficult to imagine the established taboos being more comprehensively broken, all in one go. When the old man who was guardian of the initiands returned from hunting, he knew something was wrong. The sky flared with a shade of blackish-red never seen before in the middle of the day — a colour that appears at sunset — and the earth began to crack and heave, spilling out a liquid that engulfed the camp and all the people in it, and formed the three modern crater lakes.

Now this was — it seemed to me when I heard the text, and George's discussion of it in English — a plausible description of a volcanic eruption. But how long ago had these lakes been formed? I wrote to the International Geophysical centre in Rome, and they put me in touch with Professor Donald Walker in Canberra. He said the volcanic craters were probably formed about ten thousand years ago.

Was the Mamu/Ngajan legend really founded on fact? Had it been handed down — a real historical event interpreted in terms of the local religious system — for ten millennia? In the last century, anthropologists had found historical "truth" in everything, often reaching quite ridiculous conclusions. Then the pendulum had swung the other way: myths were myths, nothing more, and had no historical basis — that is the modern doctrine.

I remembered the story of Captain Cook, who'd never been anywhere near Murray Upper. If this could be made up within two hundred years, what chance was there of an accurate account of the eruption being handed on for ten millennia? But there are important differences. The "Captain Cook" bit was made up by Chloe — no one else at Murray Upper would have approved; it had no tradition. She was telling of the first white/black contact experience, and had called the first white man Captain Cook because the white people said he was the first. The Lakes story, however, was an established legend, known to several tribes.

At the end of the tape, George remarked that when the lakes were formed, there wasn't thick jungle in that country, as there is today, but "just open scrub". This was recorded in late 1964. In 1968, Peter Kershaw, a scientist at the Australian National University, constructed a dated pollen diagram from the organic sediments of Lake Euramo and showed, much to everyone's surprise, that the rainforest in the area is only about seven and a half thousand years old. So it probably *was* "just open scrub" when the volcano erupted and formed the crater lakes some three thousand years earlier. And George had recorded this legend several years *before* Kershaw started work there. Aborigines have, of course, been in all parts of Australia for at least forty thousand years. A strong case can be made for the Lakes story having been handed down, from one generation to the next, for something like ten thousand years.

August was the busiest month of the year at Warrami. New South Wales banana growers fed the southern markets for ten months of the year, but in August, their supplies dried up, and prices were high for Queensland bananas. The Cowans worked right round the clock — picking, grading, packing and dispatching. The Cowan boys did most of the harvesting, assisted by Jack and Mick Murray. The bananas were graded according to their length (in inches) — eights and sevens and sixes. Then they were packed in the boxes, which had been nailed together from pieces of wood cut to length by the sawmill. The bananas were arranged in neat rows, all of the same size, with no bruising and no gaps.

Most of the packing was done by the women. The Cowan daughters — Bev, married to Graham Haydon, a sawmiller and son of the crusty old postmaster; Dorelle, on leave from her nursing course at Innisfail; and Karlene when she was home from school. They were assisted by other white wives from Murray Upper, and a number of Aboriginal girls. Alison helped too, while Eelsha dozed in an old pram under a shady tree. The Cowans insisted on paying her at the regular rates, which was generous of them since we felt we owed them quite a bit for hospitality over the past ten months.

We were feeling sad at the thought of leaving, and so was Chloe. But she was determined that I wasn't to go away without as full an understanding of the language as she could impart. When I suggested getting a bit more of the "mother-in-law style", Jalnguy, Chloe agreed it was high time we came back to that. Let's do it properly. Go through all different sorts of words, and see what the Jalnguy name is for each. An interesting pattern emerged. All the lexical words — nouns, verbs and adjectives — are different in Jalnguy, but Jalnguy doesn't have as many forms as does Guwal, the everyday style. There are different names for every species of lizard in the everyday style: *banggarra* "blue-tongue lizard", *biyu* "frilled lizard", *buynyjul* "red-bellied lizard", *giyabay* "stripey lizard", and so on. Guwal does not have any generic term "lizard". But Jalnguy has *only* a generic term, *jijan* "lizard". All of *Banggarra*, *biyu*, *buynyjul* and *giyabay* would be translated by *jijan* in Jalnguy, Chloe averred. If one wanted to distinguish between different kinds of lizard in the "mother-in-law style", then one would have to add an extra specification to *jijan*, describing the colour or size or habitat or behaviour of an individual species.

This kind of relationship — a single Jalnguy term corresponding to a number of Guwal words — recurred in other parts of the vocabulary. *Jamuy* is the Jalnguy term for "grub", relating to the specific Guwal terms *jambun* "long wood grub", *mandija* "milky pine grub", *gija* "candlenut tree grub", *gaban* "acacia tree grub", and so on.

How did people learn the "mother-in-law style", I wondered. Of course, the tribes used a classificatory kinship system, whereby every person in the community is given one of about twenty kin labels, based on their relationship to you through your parents. The preferred pattern is for a man to marry a mother's elder brother's or father's elder sister's son's daughter. Now, any person who is in a relationship of mother's elder brother's son or father's elder sister's son (or equivalent) to a given man is said to be his *nyubi*. I had translated *nyubi* as "father-in-law", but it is really "any potential father-in-law". Half a dozen or more people may be in *nyubi* relationship to a man, and he will be expected to marry a daughter of one of them. Which one he marries will be decided by the parents, and the marriage may be "promised" many years before it can actually be consummated. But he should use the Jalnguy speech-style in the presence of anyone in *nyubi* relationship — whether he be his actual father-in-law, or just a classificatory (potential) father-in-law.

So the set of kin to be treated with particular respect was already known when a child was born: all *nyubi*, and the wives of all *nyubi* who would be *waymin*, potential mothers-in-law. The child would gradually become aware of the circumstances in which these relatives would use Jalnguy to him, and he would be expected to start using it to them when he was about eight years old. By the time he was an initiated man, it would be absolutely obligatory for him to use Jalnguy whenever a *nyubi* or especially a *waymin* was within earshot; absent-mindedly to use Guwal in these circumstances would be a matter for profound shame. The rather vague level of reference in Jalnguy — working almost entirely through generic terms — was thus plainly appropriate to the "social distance" that had to be maintained whenever a taboo relative was around.

Chloe treated us as if we were members of her family. And so did the Cowans. The nightly "tea" at Warrami, although it was a highly informal meal, followed its own ritual. Mr and Mrs Cowan had their places at the head of the huge table. Mrs Cowan's sister, Joan, who looked after the Warrami homestead, sat down first, on Mrs Cowan's right. Then everyone else — often as many as a dozen — sat themselves anywhere along the sides. There were always important things to discuss — the cattle, spraying the next crop of bananas, the shop, odd bits of gossip. During a lull, Lindsay might toss off in my direction a fascinating snippet about the Aborigines. "Those black fellows had something like our old age pension, did you know? Just the old people were allowed to eat bandicoots. They're easy to catch, but it was forbidden to the youngsters. So the grey-haired folks, who couldn't move very fast, had a supply of meat all to themselves."

And then, after tea, Lindsay and Muriel Cowan might wander off towards the barn, perhaps for a private talk about a worry concerning one of their children. The house was always full of people, and sometimes they needed to find a place where there was no chance of being overheard.

Usually, films only came to Tully when they were past their best. But now the lower cinema had *Tom Jones,* which had only just opened in Sydney. Almost everyone from Warrami was going in to see it. "And that includes you two," said Mrs Cowan. "Go on, it's time you had a night out. Eelsha'll be quite all right here with me."

The Aborigines from Murray Upper made an expedition to the Tully cinema the following week, but not to see a film. Slim Dusty was in town. Perhaps the most popular singer in Australia, Slim gives American country-and-western treatment to an entirely Australian repertoire. Songs about the Mount Isa Rodeo, about cattle duffing, and pubs with no beer. He is an especial favourite with the Aborigines. At just about every settlement I visited, I'd hear *Middleton's Rouseabout* or *The*

Drover's Lament playing in the background, and a group of boys on guitars, starting their own Slim Dusty tradition. Each year, Slim tours right round North Australia with his show, stopping for a performance in every little town.

A couple of taxis were ordered from Tully, and six or seven people piled into each one. Not quite as expensive as you might think — the Tully taxi drivers had a special rate for Aborigines, about three-quarters of what they'd charge a white person. This wasn't done out of charity; it was simply that the Aborigines were their best customers, deserving a discount. People who had been traditionally nomadic naturally tended to spend a good deal of their wages on moving around the place. In the old days, it had taken a week to walk through the forest to Ravenshoe in order to visit relatives. Now a taxi could make the journey in three or four hours.

The only one who didn't patronise the Slim Dusty concert was Chloe. She'd just bought herself a new cardigan for the winter mornings, and it had been much admired.

"They ask me, 'Where you get the money for that nice cardigan, Mum?' I tell them: 'I don't give my money to Slim Dusty. I keep my money for myself. This keep me warm. You all go to Tully and give your money to Slim Dusty. *He* won't keep you warm.' Silly things . . ."

We finished off the phonicon, and checked a few more points from Roth's *Ethnographic Bulletins*. He had maintained that the Tully River people were ignorant of the physiological basis of conception. Anthropologists had labelled this as a belief in "virgin birth". According to Roth, although the Malanbarra knew that for animals, copulation was necessary for conception, they did not know it was also true for humans! This seemed very unlikely, and Chloe maintained he was quite mistaken. "They know all right," she said, "only they never talk about that."

A stranger to our society might be similarly misled. He'd hear stories about storks and blackberry bushes and he might — certainly before the modern, permissive society arrived — have found it quite hard to get anyone to actually talk seriously about the nature of conception. Chloe's statement seemed to be supported by a word that had come up in our progress through the phonicon: *bulmbinyu* "to be the male progenitor of" specifically refers to a father's role in the making of a child.

Finally, our last day arrived. Chloe had found that batteries which were too spent to power the tape-recorders still had some useful life in her torch. By the time we left, a long line of them was ranged in her living room, along a horizontal beam that supported the outside wall (there was no inside wall). When I returned, two and a half years later, Chloe said that they'd used the last battery only a few months before.

Chloe wanted to make one last recording; a message for me to play to the government people in Canberra. She gave a short autobiographical sketch, first in Dyirbal, and then in English.

"I was orphan girl, orphan baby. I had no mother. So they 'dopt me. One old lady she had her son, about nineteen-year-old boy, and she come to river, she pick up a bit of rubbish under the water, and she rub it on her breasts, she made the milk come. That's how she came to feed me on the breast and she reared me so good. . . . And so I came to twelve year old and they let me know that my mother was died and I wouldn't believe them. And at the same time after they told me and I look at myself on the face, see that I am look bit like her. But no, I look at her boy, he is look like her a bit but I look at my auntie, she look different — like me. So I must be look like her. I begin to realise it that my mother is died, and they showed me her grave. And there she is."

Chloe's voice became blurred, heavy with emotion, as she turned now to address the government. "And that's how I come to learn about these language, and luckily, and here they are, your people will learn some of this language from me, because it's true. Everything I say is true, in this news today for Robert Dixon, out from England to learn about our language. And there they are, people. Thank you for sending this young fellow to learn some of our language." And then we added eight more batteries to the line along Chloe's shelf.

That night, the Cowans gave us a memorable farewell party, inviting almost all the white people in Murray Upper. (Only white people, of course — for it to have been otherwise would have been inconceivable at that place and time.) As we drove off the next morning, Mick Murray appeared on the road, flagging down the Land Rover. I'd tried to record some stories from him during the year, but he'd been too busy, or not interested. Now he said he was keen to tell us a story about a stone pigeon nest, up in the forest behind Davidson Creek. But it was too late. I could only say that we hoped to return some time.

8

"Doing all these Jalnguy"

It was a long drive down south, but we did it a lot quicker than on the way up. Dropping off the caravan in Brisbane, we had a day on the beach at Surfer's Paradise, and then popped in to see Dr Capell in Sydney. He took us to lunch, but didn't say very much when I talked about the mother-in-law style, the loss of initial syllables in Mbabaram, and the texts we had got. When he left, I mentioned to his research assistant (whom he'd invited along as well, confounding tradition) that Capell didn't seem at all pleased.

"On the contrary," he assured me, "he was very pleased indeed. You've got to realise that his scale of emotional reaction is rather narrower than other people's — the average person might range from 0 to 100 but with Dr Capell it's 49 to 51. Take it from me, he was very pleased indeed."

In Canberra, the AIAS was just the same as ever. I wondered whether I should play them Chloe's final "message to the government", but decided against it. (They got a copy of the tape for their archives, of course.) We met Fred McCarthy, the executive member of the AIAS Interim Council, who was on his fortnightly visit up from Sydney.

"Did you record all the legends of the area?" he asked.

"Well, no, not really," I hesitated, "although we did get a lot."

"And vocabulary — did you get a pretty complete dictionary made?"

"A fair-sized one, but there must have been many more words that didn't come up," I admitted.

"I don't know why linguists never do things fully," Fred sighed.

But he was friendly and helpful. We were pleased when, a few months later, AIAS was made a permanent statutory body and Fred McCarthy was appointed its first full-time principal, moving up to Canberra from his job at the Australian Museum in Sydney. At last the institute seemed to have someone who cared.

On the way back to London, we stopped off for a week in Mexico. Bob Longacre, who I'd met at the International Congress of Linguists two years earlier, showed us around the field headquarters of the Summer Institute of Linguistics, at Ixmiquilpan. The institute is a missionary body that expects its members to acquire a full understanding of the structure of a new language before starting on Bible translation. Longacre had a week before the beginning of the next linguistic workshop for missionaries, so he took us to see a Mexican village, down some caves, and around pre-Inca temples. The dry, cactus landscape was a striking contrast to the knotted vines and creepers of the rainforest we had just come from.

Then London, and down to earth with a bang when Halliday gave me all the introductory lectures to a postgraduate diploma course. He was director of a bizarre thing called the Communication Research Centre, which was a ploy for getting linguistics into University College by the back door. The next year he was made a professor, and the new Department of Linguistics consisted of just two people — him and me. We were a two-man show until I left, in 1970. Or rather less some of the time, since Halliday took a year off in 1967–68. And I didn't see why I should be left out, so I went to Harvard as soon as he got back, for 1968–69.

At first, preparing lectures took up all of my time. Writing up Dyirbal would obviously be a rather lengthy task, so as soon as I got some free time I began work on Mbabaram, on which I had gathered much less material. I knew that — the academic rat-race being what it is — I'd need to get some publications out before I could attract any further support for my research. By the summer of 1965, two papers on Mbabaram had been accepted by reputable journals.

Then it was time to really settle down and work intensively on Dyirbal; transcribing the phonicon tapes, going over each of the thirty-one texts I had recorded, and working out the grammatical constructions and how they interrelated. Things used to echo through my head for weeks on end. One word in particular, *gurawarrabajanmigurru*, has been going round and round in my brain on and off for nineteen years. It is rhythmical and mellifluous, and it has a fascinating meaning. Gurawarrabajanmi is a place on the Tully River named from an odd event that is said to have taken place there. *Gura* is a noun, "vaginal lips". *Warra* is a particle that indicates that an action is performed on an inappropriate object. *Bajanmi* is the perfective form of the verb "to bite". The place name means "where the man bit the woman's privates when he shouldn't have done", as George Watson put it. Then *-gu* is the allative case ending, "to", and *-rru* is a post-inflectional clitic "along". The whole word from text XXV, *gurawarrabajanmigurru*, is "along to the place where the man had bitten the woman's vaginal lips when he shouldn't have". Certainly something to conjure with.

When I explained something of the structure of Dyirbal to Halliday, he said: "Lovely, I like ergative languages." I hadn't heard the term "ergative" before. It hadn't come up in any of the lectures I'd had in Edinburgh, or in the books I'd read.

Dyirbal has, like every other language, two basic kinds of sentence. Those that must involve two nouns, where someone does something to someone (or something) else, are called "transitive" — *he hit me, she saw him, you carry it,* and so on. Then there are sentences that only demand one noun; these are called "intransitive" — *he went, she laughed, it fell,* and so on. The interesting fact about Dyirbal is that nothing is added to a noun either when it is the subject of an intransitive verb, or when it is the object of a transitive. But the ending *-nggu* is used when it is a transitive subject. So *yara yanu* is "man is going", *yibi yanu* is "woman is going". Then *yara-nggu yibi buran* is "man sees woman", with *-nggu* on the subject noun *yara* "man", but no ending on the object noun *yibi* "woman". This *-nggu*, which is used just for transitive subjects, is an example of the "ergative case inflection", Halliday said. The significant point is that transitive subject is treated differently from intransitive subject — intransitive subject is in fact dealt with in the same way as transitive object, in receiving no marking at all.

Halliday told me that ergative marking is also found in Eskimo, in Basque and in many of the languages of the Caucasus. I added that it occurs in many Australian languages, but only on nouns. Pronouns are quite different. They have one form for both transitive subject and intransitive subject (*ngaja* "I", *nginda* "you" in Dyirbal) and a different form for transitive object (*ngayguna* "me", *nginuna* "you"). Thus we'd say *ngaja yanu* "I'm going", *nginda yanu* "you're going" and *ngaja nginuna buran* "I see you". Pronouns in Dyirbal (and many other Australian languages) are just like English and Latin and French; *ngaja* and *nginda* could be called "nominative", and *ngayguna* and *nginuna* "accusative" forms. Halliday admitted he'd never seen anything like this: ergative on nouns and nominative-accusative on pronouns — in the same language.

Unlike in English, words can occur in any order in a sentence in Dyirbal, since what is subject and what is object is always apparent from the endings (or lack of endings). The verb most frequently comes at the end of a sentence, but it can occur anywhere else. Thus *yibi buran yara-nggu, yara-nggu yibi buran, buran yibi yara-nggu* and *yibi yara-nggu buran* all mean the same thing, "man sees woman".

While this mixture of ergative and accusative patterning made Dyirbal fascinating at the level of grammar, the data on the mother-in-law style were equally important for the semantics. I'd only begun to work systematically on Jalnguy in the last few weeks in the field, and didn't realise the full significance of it until I came to mull over the data back in London.

The many-to-one correspondence between Guwal and Jalnguy vocabularies was a key to the semantic structure of Dyirbal. If one Jalnguy word was given as the equivalent for a number of distinct Guwal terms, it meant that the Guwal words were seen, by speakers of the language, to be related. For nouns, it revealed the botanical and zoological classifications which the Aborigines perceived. For instance, *bayi marbu* "louse" *bayi nunggan* "larger louse", *bayi daynyjar* "tick" and *bayi mindiliny* "larger tick" were all grouped together under a single Jalnguy term, *bayi dimaniny*.

It could be even more revealing with verbs. The everyday style has four different words for kinds of spearing, and also such verbs as *nyuban* "poke a stick into the ground (testing for the presence of yams or snails, say)", *nyirran* "poke something sharp into something (for example, poke a fork into meat to see if it is cooked)", *gidan* "poke a stick into a hollow log, to dislodge a bandicoot". All seven of these Guwal verbs are rendered by just one word in Jalnguy: *nyirrindan* "pierce".

Sometimes Jalnguy grouped together verbs in a most surprising fashion. For instance, *gundumman* was given as Jalnguy equivalent of *julman* "squeeze, for example, squeeze a boil, knead flour", and also of *bugaman* "chase, run down, as in catch a runaway steer". What did these two verbs have in common? It was only when I had a chance to discuss it with Chloe that she explained *gundumman* means "bring together". Hands come together in *julman,* while *bugaman* describes a pursuer coming into contact with what he is chasing.

But I'd only got Jalnguy equivalents for a selection of the Guwal vocabulary. The more I worked on this, the more imperative it became to return to North Queensland and work quite systematically on Guwal-Jalnguy correspondences. Grammatical analysis was also throwing up a number of points that required checking or further exemplification.

So I applied to AIAS for the return air fare to Townsville, the hire of a vehicle, and some money to live in the field for a month and to pay informants: £600 in all (=$1,500 in the newly introduced Australian decimal currency). They refused. This took me by surprise, since AIAS had seemed so impressed by my first year in the field and had offered a year's extension. I wasn't asking for any salary – if I had that would have made the total sum much higher.

I discovered the reason for their refusal: AIAS weren't happy about my only spending a month in North Queensland – couldn't I make it three months? I couldn't get away from University College for that long, didn't want to leave my family for more than a month, and, most importantly, needed no more than a month to get answers to my questions. AIAS suggested that I send them my questions, and they'd get someone in Australia to ask them. But what would take me a month would take another linguist six months, since he would have to learn the language first, and understand the grammar as well as I did.

Luckily, Arthur Capell was chairman of the AIAS linguistics committee, and he wrote a letter that injected a vein of sanity into the affair. Although AIAS hadn't said so to me, he confided that they had decided that if I could raise some of the money from elsewhere, they'd put up the remainder.

At last I had a clue as to what I should do. The University of London doesn't have much money for things like this, but they gave me the maximum grant allowed by their Central Research Fund, £200. When I informed AIAS, they immediately supplied the remaining £400.

I'd written to Chloe and George, but had received no reply. I hadn't really expected to. Neither had had the opportunity to become literate, and although they could have got someone to write for them, it wouldn't have been easy. Jack Doolan had given me George's new address on the mainland before he himself left Palm to become superintendent of Snake Bay Settlement on Melville Island in the Northern Territory. But Bev Haydon, one of Mrs Cowan's daughters, came to the rescue. She wrote to say that Chloe was now living in Tully, and then she rang up George's employer to check his present whereabouts.

The flight from England is never pleasant — sitting in one chair for thirty-six hours (and this was before in-flight movies). But Alison had bought me the first volume of Bertrand Russell's *Autobiography,* which made it a bit less tedious. I was put next to two English ladies, both married to Australians and both returning from their first trips home in a decade. We got on Christian name terms at Teheran, and then at about Karachi, they asked me what I did. "Anthropologist" is the answer I sometimes give to such a question, since "linguist" is often taken to describe a polyglot. They obviously conferred while I was out of my seat — around Singapore — and then one asked: "Bob, what exactly is an anthropologist?"

"What do you think?"

"Well, we decided that it's someone who's kind to people and animals." . . ! (I should have said, "No, you're thinking of a philanthropologist.")

We landed for an hour in Darwin, at three in the morning. There was just time for an ice-cold beer in the transit lounge. And a Slim Dusty record was going round on the jukebox. I suddenly felt as though I'd come home. This was such a refreshing, exciting, relaxed country after the pedantics and puns of grimy, class-ridden Britain.

During the two and a half years I'd been out of the country, the Council of AIAS — academics, members of parliament and a few public servants — had decided to do something about the language situation. Scarcely any linguistics was being studied in Australian universities, and the obvious move would have been to endow a chair, or a number of permanent lectureships. If good people had been appointed, this would undoubtedly have led to further appointments, and also attracted good students. But AIAS didn't think this way. They decided to establish eight temporary research fellowships and eight postgraduate scholarships — and wrote around to the universities asking how many they'd like. The less it knew about linguistics, it seemed, the more positions in linguistics a university would ask for — and solemnly be awarded, by AIAS. The only professional linguists were Stephen Wurm and his assistant Don Laycock, at the Australian National University, and

Arthur Capell, still soldiering on alone at Sydney. Capell got just one of the new scholars. But one department of English (in a university with no professional linguists) got no less than four! A student who knew no linguistics was given an intensive one year's training in Old English (!) and then sent into the field for two months. Just two months' field work as the basis for a Ph.D! One AIAS scholar decided there were thirteen significant sounds (phonemes) in the language he studied, whereas there are in fact twenty-two. His grammar was published by AIAS before it had been submitted to his doctoral examiners. It was failed for the degree — twice. And it was someone like this that AIAS had thought could ask my questions for me, to save me the trip out!

Probably more by good luck than good management, the AIAS linguistics appointees did include one or two people who had already had some training and were capable of working on their own. Steve Boydell, recently-appointed secretary of AIAS, was an enterprising organiser, and he suggested I might like to look in on Margaret Cunningham, the AIAS Research Fellow at the University of Queensland. It was a happy thought. We had breakfast together on Sunday morning in Brisbane while I was between planes. Margaret had been trained by the Summer Institute of Linguistics, had worked on languages in the Philippines, and had just come back from field work on Alawa in the Northern Territory.

It was terrific to have someone to talk to about Australian languages; I got a lot out of that breakfast. When I wondered why Australian languages borrowed vocabulary from their neighbours at such a rate, Margaret suggested this was due to the taboo on the name of any dead person. Not only was the proper name of the deceased not to be pronounced, but also any common noun or adjective or even verb phonetically similar to the name might be proscribed, for a length of time. It would often be replaced by a form borrowed from a neighbouring language, Margaret said. Of course, that was it! Although I'd been aware of some of this, I hadn't been able to put all the bits together before.

The slow plane up the Queensland coast finally reached Townsville at four in the afternoon. I checked into Tattersall's Hotel and slept for twelve hours. The question then was whether the Land Rover I was picking up from the local depot of the Commonwealth Department of Works would be able to get through to Murray Upper. London newspapers had reported the worst floods for years, although the day before I left they were said to be receding. It was *just* all right — the water was only lapping the top of the bridge over the Herbert River at Ingham. The day before, it had been impassable.

Murray Upper had been under water for a week, and the Cowan boys had gone around in a boat delivering supplies. But now there were just gigantic washaways, and holes all over the track. The Cowans welcomed me like a long-lost nephew — it was good to be back. Alan was now married, and Ray was still at Princess Hills. Dorelle had married, but she and her daughter were staying at Warrami while her husband worked on the bauxite up at Weipa to try and make some quick cash. He was called Peter Fox, which conjured up for me a vision of Peter Flying Fox, the white-haired old Olgolo man who had sung haunting songs, full of glottal catches, at the cattle-station west of Chillagoe, in 1964.

Jimmy and Mary Ann Murray came up to the house as soon as they spied the Land Rover. I'd bought a carton of duty-free cigarettes at Singapore airport, and unwisely opened it in front of them to give Jimmy a packet. When Mary Ann asked him for a cigarette, she was directed to me: "Boss got whole heap, got them cheap he say. You ask him, he give you packet for yourself." And as more old friends came up to say "hello", the cigarettes that I'd thought might last a week, all melted away within half an hour. It was silly of me to have forgotten one of the basic moral principles of Aboriginal society: if anyone has a lot of some commodity, then it should be shared around equally, without any delay.

I went straight into Tully, that afternoon of Monday, 20 March 1967, to find Chloe. It was tremendous to see her again — effervescent, on top of the world, words tumbling over each other as she said how glad she was to see me, what a hard time she had "bringing up all these girl all on my own", what terrible floods there'd been, and how were Alison and the children — now we had a baby son as well, fancy that!

Chloe had a small flat in Tully, and was still looking after her youngest daughter and two grand-daughters. "Better here than out at the Murray. Too danger out there. Strange men hanging around. My boys get worried about me at that lonely place all by myself." But the flat was too small for serious work, she said, and when I came back the next day we went to Ernie's house, three miles up the road towards El Arish. He had married a part-Aboriginal girl from Mount Molloy, just beyond

Mareeba. ("Don't take this the wrong way, but I do think it's better if they marry their own kind," as Mrs Cowan had told me, putting forward a sincere view with which many people would no doubt agree.) Ernie and Enid let us use the table in the cool kitchen space under the house, which provided ideal working conditions. Enid even cooked lunch for us, which seemed too good to be true!

I started going through all the nouns, verbs and adjectives in my accumulated vocabulary lists, asking how to say each one in the mother-in-law style. *Bayi midin* "ring-tail possum" was *bayi jibuny* in Jalnguy. *Balan mawa* "shrimp" came out as *balan dunguy*. The information given by Chloe, and later George, correlated well with what they had told me three years earlier. Jalnguy had not been actively used since about 1930, but it was clear that it was being remembered quite accurately.

I asked about each verb within a simple sentence. A gender marker used alone functions something like a third person pronoun in English. *Bayi bajinyu* "he falls down" (or "he fell down") was *bayi dagarranyu* in Jalnguy. There were three tense choices, according to my analysis of Dyirbal: future ending -*ny*; immediate future -*ngurra*; and the most common one, present-past, which was -*nyu* with verbs of one type and -*n* with the other class. Verbs are nearly always cited in the present-past form.

Some grammar had to be checked as well. Back in London, I'd worked out what I thought were the rules for putting clauses together, and tried to predict complex sentences from these. Now to try out the predictions on Chloe to see whether they were good sentences of Dyirbal (if they were, it would show that I'd deduced the right grammatical rules).

For nouns, transitive object and intransitive subject have the same form — with no case ending. Two clauses could be put together if they have a noun in common and it is transitive object or intransitive subject in each clause. *Yibi-nggu yara buran* "woman saw man" and *yara bajinyu* "man fell down" could form a single sentence (said on one intonation tune) — *yibi-nggu yara buran bajinyu* "woman saw man and [man] fell down". Yes, Chloe agreed, that was right — that was good Dyirbal.

But pronouns have a different pattern. One form of each pronoun is used for both intransitive subject and transitive subject — thus *ngaja* "I". So *ngaja nginuna buran* was "I saw you" and *ngaja bajinyu* was "I fell down". Surely, since these two sentences had *ngaja* in common, I could say *ngaja nginuna buran bajinyu* and it would mean "I saw you and [I] fell down". Chloe thought a minute. You could say that, but it meant something different "I saw you and *you* fell down". If you want to say "I saw you and (straightaway) I fell down" it would have to be *ngaja nginuna buran bajingurra*. Oh! This was something new.

The next day I drove up to find George and Ginnie Watson. They lived in a two-room wooden shack on the highway at East Palmerston, belonging to Gordon Gaynor, George's employer. Mr Gaynor had a cattle farm, and a butcher's shop in Innisfail. He seemed a good boss, giving George a few days off with pay to talk to me. If we needed more time, that was all right, George was happy to work at weekends to make it up. They were glad to be away from Palm Island, no doubt about that. And it made for much pleasanter working conditions. Ginnie spoke the tablelands variety of Jirrbal — she and George conversed in the language if no one else was there — and she was a great help while we went through the same points I had discussed with Chloe. (I always try to check out everything with at least two different speakers.)

They gave me exactly the same answer as Chloe had when I tried to put together *ngaja nginuna buran* and *ngaja bajinyu* — there must be a *-ngurra* in there. That night, back at Warrami, I looked through all my texts for instances of *-ngurra*. Sure enough, it had two functions. Firstly, *-ngurra* added to a verb indicates that the intransitive subject (or transitive object) of that verb is identical to the transitive subject of the verb of the preceding clause. And it also indicates that the action of the clause follows immediately after the action of the preceding clause (I'd known this, which was why I'd been calling *-ngurra* an "immediate future" tense.) It worked the same way with pronouns and with nouns. *Yibi-nggu yara buran* is "woman saw man" and *yibi bajinyu* is "woman fell over"; putting these together gives *yibi-nggu yara buran (yibi) bajingurra* "woman saw man and then she immediately fell down". To coordinate two clauses in Dyirbal, the intransitive subject and transitive object (the non-ergative functions) in the clauses must normally refer to the same thing. The verbal ending *-ngurra* is used when transitive subject occurs, in the first clause. Coordination works on an "ergative" basis, whether nouns or pronouns are involved. Nouns have ergative case marking and pronouns don't — but this doesn't matter for the rules of coordination.

All this was a great surprise to me. Dyirbal really was a very ergative language, totally different in this from English and other European tongues. It was a fair while before I accepted this, but there was really no doubt about it. Chloe and George provided exactly the same corrections to all the sentences I tried, showing that the nominative-accusative form of pronouns was irrelevant to the way clauses were combined together. The syntax of Dyirbal is, quite simply, ergative through and through.

Ernie and Enid invited me to stay, so I divided my time between there and the Cowans. Ernie was now working as scrub-boss for the Tully sawmill, deciding which trees should be felled and in what order. His desire to set up in business for himself was thwarted not by the actual colour of his skin — which was lighter than that of some of the Italians in Innisfail — but by the fact that he was known to be an Aborigine. He took Chloe and me into the bush to study traditional foodstuffs; and we all went to the pictures together in Tully.

It was a couple of hours' drive up to George and Ginnie. I'd have one long day with them, tire them out, talk with Chloe all the next day and tire her out, and so on. Really, pace AIAS, I had never in my life got so much work done as during that month. One day Chloe decided that she should come with me, to "help out" with George. This would have been embarrassing, since I was going to be asking him the same points I'd been through with her the previous day, and she wouldn't have taken that at all well! But Ernie and I persuaded her that it might be too exhausting. I did get them together later on, when I was good and ready to do so.

Chloe and George both had extraordinarily intelligent minds, but used them very differently. I could get through things more quickly with Chloe — her responses were immediate, almost instinctive. George, on the other hand, would always think a question through and give a measured, deliberate answer. Chloe would sometimes go back and correct what she had just said, or think a thing through in the evening and tell it to me from a different angle the next day. George rarely did. As a result, I got two quite different kinds of view on each grammatical and lexical point; putting them together provided a sound overall perspective.

Chloe knew the Jirrbal dialect best, although she was also competent in Girramay and knew a fair deal about Mamu and Gulngay. She once warned me that she had a bit of a tendency to muddle together things from several dialects. I said that I had noticed that, but thought I'd been able to sort them out all right. George spoke pure Dulgubarra Mamu. Ginnie spoke Jirrbal, a different variety from Chloe's, from up on the range. The dialect differences were not great, but they were looked upon as vital social indexes.

Jirrbal was the dialect I knew best, and I sometimes forgot to make adjustments when asking something of George — using *banaganyu* "return home" instead of the Mamu form *ngurbanyu,* or the "with" affix *-bila* in place of the shorter Mamu variant *-ba.* George would give me a steady look.

'Do you want me to teach you Mamu, or do you just want to do Jirrbal?" he'd say, with the patient near-contempt almost every speaker has for dialects other than his own.

"I'm sorry," I'd say, "I do want Mamu." And I'd rephrase my question with the necessary adjustments.

One thing that never failed to fascinate about George and Chloe was how they stated their ages. I'm pretty sure that they were almost exact contemporaries, born within a year or so of 1900. In 1963, Chloe told me she was sixty-three, while George said he was fifty-seven. When I returned three years later, Chloe was sixty-four and so was George (he'd decided, I think, that he'd like to retire and draw the pension the following year). Only by the time he was eighty did George give what I think was his true age.

We went over the story of the Crater Lakes, which George had recorded with Jack Doolan, to make sure I had it transcribed correctly, and George told another story. Then some more Jalnguy. George kept on teasing Ginnie that she was always one step behind us — talking in English when I wanted the everyday style, and in everyday style when we were doing mother-in-law. If George said something that she didn't agree with, she'd berate him as a no-good white man (Ginnie had no foreigners in her pedigree) and retire to a corner, ignoring us.

The arguments George and Ginnie had were sometimes more revealing than their straight answers. There was the verb *darrbin* "get crumbs or dirt off a blanket by shaking it", for instance. George sugges-ted that the Jalnguy equivalent of *darrbin* was *bubaman,* which I knew corresponded to the everyday style verb *baygun* "shake, wave". Ginnie said — No, he was quite wrong, *darrbin* went into Jalnguy as *nayngun* (the correspondent of *madan* "throw"). It turned out, as they argued back and forth, that George maintained it was the action of the blanket

which was criterial — the blanket is shaken — while Ginnie said it was
the motion of the crumbs off the blanket — the fact that they are
thrown off.

I usually picked up a cooked chicken for lunch on my way through
Innisfail, so that we wouldn't have to interrupt our work too much.
Otherwise, George had a tendency to send Ginnie off to cook, which
could provoke a furious argument. Ginnie liked to be in on things, and
I did find her contribution valuable.

I'd written a very tentative grammar with illustrative sentences,
taken from the materials I'd gathered on the first field trip. I'd changed
some of the words in sentences — but not the grammar — so as to use
only a limited vocabulary in the explanation of grammatical points. All
these had to be checked with Chloe and George. It turned out that
almost all of them were all right, but some had a double-meaning (it
sometimes seemed to me that every second word in Dyirbal also had a
risqué metaphorical sense). *Yara-ngu yugu* could mean "man's stick"
as I had intended (as an illustration of the possessive ending *-ngu,*
rather like English *'s*), but *yugu* "tree, stick, wood" could also have a
phallic connotation. Better change it to *yara-ngu wangal* "man's
boomerang" to be on the safe side. I agreed. Thus it is that my grammar
of Dyirbal is — I maintain — not only linguistically correct, it is also
completely expurgated, and could be read in mixed company with
never a hint of a snigger.

On the way back from a productive day with George and Ginnie, I
was brought with a start out of Aboriginal Australia into the real world
of present-day Queensland. Policemen, who I hadn't had contact with
for a long while. Just coming into Mourilyan, I overtook another car
where there was a broken white line. The line went solid, and a
35 m.p.h. sign came up, just before I was able to pull in, so I couldn't
slow down until I had finished passing. A police car was coming from
the other direction, but I had plenty of time to get in before it reached
me.

That wasn't their opinion, however. They turned round and came
chasing after me, through the thirty-five mile speed zone, at about
seventy. A couple of thugs, they scowled when I said I was out for a
few weeks from England.

"Do you realise you could have caused damage to this valuable
police car? Not to mention your own vehicle. And endangered our
lives." I loved the order of priorities (and the fact that my life didn't

figure in the list at all). They issued a ticket for $10 to be paid at the Court House in Innisfail and warned me not to try to leave the country without paying it. (I didn't, although I seriously considered doing so.) They didn't actually kick me, but made it quite clear they'd have liked to have done so.

When I complained about this to Lindsay Cowan, he had an answer typical of the bush philosopher. "You ought to count yourself lucky. If you'd been in Nazi Germany, a couple like that'd have had your life. Since it's Queensland, you've got off lightly with a $10 fine."

I also wanted to record some more of the most northerly dialect of Dyirbal, Ngajan. Working in London on the material I'd gathered in different dialects, I'd noticed that Ngajan had undergone an interesting change. "Push" is *biimban* in Ngajan as against *bilmban* in Jirrbal and Mamu. "Many" is *gaabu* in Ngajan but *garbu* in the southern dialects. For "large fig tree", Ngajan has *gibaa* and the rest *gibar*, and for "beard" the forms are *nyumbuu* and *nyumbul* respectively.

Where the other dialects had a vowel followed by *l* or *r* (or *y*) before another consonant or at the end of a word, Ngajan has replaced this sequence by a long vowel (none of the other dialects had any long vowels). There were some examples of the rule applying twice in a single word. "Meat" *jalgur* became *jaaguu* in Ngajan, and "road" *yalgay* was *yaagaa*. I wanted more material in Ngajan, to check out this rule in more detail. And I also wanted to investigate whether Ngajan had any "mother-in-law" speech style.

I knew there weren't many speakers left. In November 1963, I'd recorded a couple of hundred words from Tommy Land and Jimmy Brown on a bench outside the Malanda Hotel. When I went back in July of the following year, Tommy Land was dead and Jimmy Brown rather senile. He'd tried to tell me the story of the origin of the Crater Lakes, but had slipped into English half-way through each sentence. An old lady called Mollie Raymond had been in the group, and she'd taken over, but still with a fair admixture of English. George told me that Jimmy Brown had since died. He recommended Mollie Raymond or Ginnie Daniels, both around Malanda somewhere.

Ginnie Daniels lived in the Aboriginal Reserve by the reservoir. (A pleasant change. In most Australian country towns, the Aboriginal reserve is out near the rubbish dump.) Near the reservoir, I asked again and was told it was "the last house down the dirt track there — but mind that black dog, he's a fierce one that, he'll bite soon as look at you." My hopes rose. I'd long ago arrived at the inductive generalisation that the more dogs an Aborigine has, and the fiercer they are, the more likely he is to have a good knowledge of traditional ways and language. Almost every Aborigine has at least one dog. George Watson always had three, and sometimes as many as five.

Not that I like dogs myself. I don't, and was always scared of them as a child. But I'd learnt, from George, a special sort of blood-curdling Aboriginal cry that will stop even a man-eating dog in its tracks, and make it retreat, whimpering softly (or perhaps just growling under its breath). Ginnie Daniels' dog was terrifying. But I put on a brave front and was able to reach her front door. In response to my knock, there was a twitch of the curtain and then a scrambling noise and the sound of a bolt being shot. I knocked again, louder, only to hear a cry coming from the back of the building.

A couple of younger women from next door finally came along to help. Ginnie Daniels had thought I must be a policeman and locked herself in the toilet. She was finally coaxed out. I was able to get close enough to offer her a cigarette and we both relaxed a bit. I delivered best wishes from George Watson. No, *I* wasn't George Watson, he was down in Palmerston, but he'd asked me to give his regards. Didn't she know George Watson? Oh yes, she knew him all right. (It was getting more and more confusing.)

Ginnie said she'd tell me a bit of language, as far as she remembered it, and the neighbours stayed to help out. I asked a few words for animals and implements, that I hadn't got on the previous field trip — "parrot" *biimbiran,* "water bag" *duguba.* And then I ventured to enquire about the mother-in-law style. Yes, they had a Jalnguy all right. What would *marraba* "bird" be in Jalnguy? "Let me think, that's *jarii.*" What about *guda* "dog", what would that be in Jalnguy? Ginnie couldn't remember. To give her a bit of time, I mentioned that I was going out to see Mollie Raymond afterwards; she was supposed to know a lot. Everyone laughed, a bit self-consciously, which seemed a little curious. Had she thought of the Jalnguy for "dog" yet? Again Ginnie hesitated. Then, to my surprise, a voice came from beind the closed door of the back room: *"Nyimbaa."* Yes, Ginnie agreed, that was it.

So we continued. Ginnie was able to answer some of my questions, and most often when she couldn't, the voice from the bedroom would fill in; sometimes it would correct her. After a while I wondered, rather diffidently, if the person from the other room wouldn't like to come out and join us. It really seemed more sensible for her to be in the centre of things. Everyone looked a bit doubtful about this. Then the voice said, wait a minute, it had to put its slippers on. And Mollie Raymond joined us. She immediately took over, and we were able to go at about four times the pace.

"*Bagan* that's the word for 'spear him' in Ngajan, same as Mamu. But 'hit him', they say *balgan* but we got it a bit different, *baagan*. See, they got *bagan* 'spear', *balgan* 'hit' but Ngajan says *bagan* and *baagan*. And Jalnguy — *bagan* he's *nyirrindan* and *baagan* is *duyin* in Jalnguy."

Mollie Raymond is small and thin, with lightish skin and match-stick legs. She has a retentive memory and a quick mind, almost in the same class as Chloe and George. Mollie could scarcely give two sentences without a word of English creeping in, and my attempts to record texts from her were singularly unsuccessful. But she is very good on vocabulary, and remembers speaking Jalnguy herself, as a girl. Mollie's father was one of the first white men on the goldfields, a Russian geologist. She must have been born ten or more years before the turn of the century and was brought up in a totally tribal way. Now she has outlived her husband, her son, one of her daughters, and everyone else who had any real knowledge of Ngajan.

It took a long time to persuade Mollie to really talk to me. In 1964, she was only goaded into action by the half-formed material others were putting out, and it was the same in 1967. There was no invitation to return. In 1971, I was concentrating on Yidin, but went to see Mollie a couple of times to get some more Ngajan, because I really thought she couldn't live much longer. She was, at last, glad to see me and ransacked her memory for the Ngajan names of bush plants and trees. Again in 1974, still fully occupied with Yidin, I popped in to see Mollie again and record a bit more. Only after having completed a grammar of Yidin, did I come back in 1977 to work up a complete dictionary of all the dialects. George Watson and Mollie and I went out into the bush with a botanist to identify native plants, each year from 1979 to 1982 — and old Mollie, ninety if she was a day, spindle-legged, walked us all off our feet, pointing with excitement at each new plant she found, giving its name in the everyday style and in Jalnguy, explaining what it was used for, how it was cooked, and breaking off a piece to show us. She is truly indestructible.

From Malanda I went on up to Petford. A red kangaroo jumped out of a field of lush grazing grass and hopped up the road ahead, as if showing the way. The Petford postmistress had moved away, and a couple more of the dozen or so houses were empty. Now there was only one telephone: "Petford 6 – McGrath, D. M., Strkpr".

Mrs McGrath was as friendly and helpful as ever, and I tried not to use too many Latinate words. Her husband Bill popped in, looking more gaunt and thin than ever, still trying to run cattle on that unpromising country. Doreen had passed on my telephone message to Albert Bennett and he was waiting for me. Albert lived alone now, in the solitary house by the river, since his wife and daughter preferred the more cosmopolitan round in Mareeba. Old Jimmy Taylor had gone a bit in the mind, from drinking too much beer and metho, and was now in a home down at Charters Towers. Albert had retired from the railway. He spent his time doing a bit of fishing. And thinking.

Albert thanked me for the cards I'd sent each Christmas. He didn't think he had anything else to tell me, though. I'd got it all last time. But Albert seemed to be uttering these words rather half-heartedly – because he always said them. As he'd got older, and had more time to think, he'd gone back to his youth and in fact Mbabaram *was* coming back to him. (When I saw Arthur Capell in Sydney a couple of weeks later, I mentioned this and he said, with a dry laugh, "Yes, it happens to all of us." I'd forgotten that Dr Capell was just about the same age as Albert Bennett.)

I'd thought before that the sounds *i* and *e* were variants of a single vowel (and I'd written this in the papers I'd published on Mbabaram). But with the new words Albert recorded onto tape 152 (the next multiple of 38, my lucky Mbabaram number), it became plain that they were contrasting vowels, which did carry a difference in meaning – *nig* is "take it!" while *neg* is "stand up!." The same applies to *o* and *u*. Ah, well! I wouldn't – had I had a choice – have published the Mbabaram analysis until there'd been a chance for further field work. But I'd felt I had to get something into print in order to get a grant for more field work (the world being organised the way it is). I sent a postcard to Halliday saying that I'd gained two vowels, but lost a tense. This was *-ngurra* in Dyirbal which I'd thought was an "immediate future" tense, but which now turned out to have an important syntactic role.

Philip and Jane Wilson had invited me to stay with them in Cairns. He'd left 4CA and was now running a weekly newspaper, *The*

Northerner, that specialised in local news and views. But it wasn't working out too well. A main difficulty was that Phil was too honest. A restaurant owner would promise a lucrative half-page advertisement if the paper would put it next to an "article" praising his establishment. Philip would have none of this — it was against all his journalistic ethics. However, the local businessmen who had put up the capital to start the paper didn't see it like that — they wanted the paper to show a profit, and they didn't give a hang for the Wilson principles. (Quite soon after this, Philip Wilson got a job in the state-run ABC network; he is now one of the main interviewers for television news in Brisbane.)

I hadn't put much time aside on the 1967 trip for Yidin, which is a totally different language from Dyirbal. I felt I really had all I could handle with an in-depth study of one language. But I did want to find out whether Yidin had a special "mother-in-law" speech style. Jack Stewart would be the best person to ask but, as usual, he wasn't easy to locate. Half-way up the Gillies Highway, I met an old Aboriginal man walking down the road, a long way from anywhere. He identified himself as Alec Morgan, Jack Stewart's brother-in-law. He didn't know where Jack was but, yes, he could speak Yidin himself. I turned the vehicle around and took him to his destination in Gordonvale (which would have been about a three-hour walk). We sat on a bench in the town centre while Alec filled in some of my Yidin gaps. He also gave me the equivalents in his "mother-in-law" style (still called Jalnguy) for a few score words.

But, as I discovered five years later, he'd been fudging it a bit. Something I'd noticed was that occasionally the term for some object in the Jalnguy style of one tribe was the same as the term for the same object in the everyday style for the next tribe. "Back, backbone" is *juja* in both Mamu everyday style and Yidin Jalnguy (as against *ngabil* in Mamu Jalnguy and *bawuu* in everyday Yidin). Alec Morgan had obviously noticed this too. He knew a few words of Mamu, one or two of which were the same as Yidin Jalnguy. When he didn't know the Yidin Jalnguy equivalent of something I asked, he just gave me the term in everyday Mamu. There were some genuine Jalnguy forms among those he said, but they were muddled up with words that were not Jalnguy at all. I always do take care to check everything as thoroughly as possible, with several different speakers. Checking has confirmed the consistency and correctness of the Jalnguy I got from Chloe and George and Mollie Raymond. And later checking with other people who knew some Yidin Jalnguy revealed the patchwork nature of Alec Morgan's responses that day.

I didn't know when, if ever, I'd get back to Australia, and so it seemed a good idea to get a bit more on the languages to the south and west of Dyirbal. Willie Seaton — the first Aborigine I ever spoke to — was still around in Ingham. I spotted him while driving up from Townsville the first day — a tall man with an upright stance, made even taller by the pork-pie hat he wore, walking across the Trebonne Creek bridge. He couldn't talk just then, so I arranged to call in when next I passed through Ingham, on my way to Palm Island. We had a good couple of hours, but Willie said the best thing would be to take him to Long Heron's, so that the two of them could talk together. This seemed like an excellent idea, and we planned it for the Monday, on my way back from Palm.

Palm Island was as beautiful as ever, and there had been small but significant improvements in the settlement. Most important was that Bartlam had been "promoted" sideways, to the Townsville office of the Department of Native Affairs. (This was later renamed the Department of Aboriginal and Island Affairs and then changed again to the Department of Aboriginal and Islander Advancement. Advancing *who?* The mining companies who had been given carte blanche over Aboriginal land?) Two Aborigines were staying in the guest house (eating white bread): Henry Four-Mile and Keith Reynolds, both from the Yarrabah settlement near Cairns, being trained on Palm to be clerks. Keith was an accomplished country and western musician who had toured with Slim Dusty for several years until (I was told) Slim dropped him because he was jealous of the acclaim Keith was getting. He used to do the song Slim wrote about Albert Namatjira, the famous Aboriginal painter from Alice Springs: "Oh, hushed are the voices and grey are the skies, and many the tear-drops fall from dark, saddened eyes; and many fair brothers will stand with bowed heads — for the message came this morning, Namatjira is dead."

Keith played tennis with one of the school teachers. Black playing white, on a public court! That would never have been permitted three years before.

As usual, the Palm Island superintendent hadn't replied to my letter, so I'd had to phone up to get permission to come over. Yes, Alf Palmer was still there, the superintendent had discovered after having to ask quite a few people around the office. I was only planning to be there for two days, so I asked him to pass a message to Alf that I'd like to see him on Saturday. "Will do." But he didn't. By the time I looked for Alf, after flying in on the early plane, he'd already gone off for a day's fishing on the reef. I really missed Jack Doolan, who'd have had it all organised for me if he'd still been there.

So I had a day free on Palm Island with nothing particularly to do. It was not an opportunity to waste. I walked on over to the old people's home, to see what interesting languages might be going a-begging. Only a few people were there — many had had the same idea as Alf Palmer — but they included Jim Gunnawarra (named after the cattle station he'd worked on), a white-haired old Olgolo man. He seemed happy enough to smoke my cigarettes and go through a few words. Olgolo had more complicated phonetics than the languages I was used to, and I had to concentrate to pronounce each word correctly after Jim. He had a very breathy articulation, puffs of air like *h*'s all through each word, and I wasn't sure whether this was a characteristic of the language or of his speech. It's hard to know where to draw the line between following the general phonetic conventions of a language, and copying the idiosyncrasies of accent of an individual speaker. Going too far over the line, one runs the risk of appearing to mock. But with just one speaker, it's almost impossible to distinguish between language-general and speaker-particular factors. Luckily we were joined after lunch by Jim's sister Nellie Ketchup (I never enquired, but I assumed she liked it a lot). She had none of Jim's breathiness, so I dropped mine — to Jim's approval, I think.

This was the same language I'd recorded a little of from Mabel Callaghan at Chillagoe and Peter Flying Fox at the cattle station out west in 1964. It was only when I came to listen to the tapes and put it all together, a few years later, that I realised what an interesting language Olgolo is. It has dropped the first consonant from every word — so that *every* word begins with a vowel, the only language I know from anywhere in the world like this. *Guda* "dog" has become *uda, guyu* "fish" is in this language *uyu,* while an original *minha* "animal, meat" is now *inha.*

As with many other languages in North Australia, Olgolo often puts a generic term before a specific noun. It would say *uyu urrba* "fish barramundi", or *inha albmba* "animal possum". On Peter Flying Fox's tapes, he'd pronounce a word in two or three ways — "barramundi" would be *uyu urrba,* or *urrba,* or *yurrba,* and "possum" would be *albmba* or *nhalbmba.* It seems that generic forms like *uyu* and *inha* are reducing to be something like gender-class prefixes *y-* and *nh-* on specific nouns — just like the gender prefixes in Swahili and other Bantu languages from East Africa. And this grammatical change was yielding words that *did* begin with a consonant, moving Olgolo away from its aberrant phonetic structure!

So my Saturday had been pretty well spent. There was a dance that night which both blacks and whites attended — something else that would never have been allowed in the Bartlam days. Alf Palmer was there, to watch the young people enjoying themselves. It was a pity I hadn't come the previous week, he said, when there'd been real corroboree music. Tonight it was going to be "island dance" — music from Torres Strait with a Hawaiian lilt and flavour — which was growing in popularity among young Aborigines in North Queensland. As I helped Alf lift chairs away from the dance floor, I asked whether Warungu or Warrgamay had any "mother-in-law style", like Dyirbal Jalnguy. Warrgamay had certainly had one, Alf remembered, but he could only recall three words of it — *binyjubarra* "foot", *guygarra* "water" and *mandila* "hand" (the forms in everyday style are *bingany,* *ngalu* and *mala,* respectively).

The next day, Alf helped me fill out some gaps in the basic grammatical paradigms for Warrgamay and Warungu. He still wouldn't give any connected texts. When Monty West had been at Palm Island in 1961, he'd taken down a bit of material in Warrgamay from Jimmy Johnson (although, unknown to West, it contained a liberal admixture from the Girramay dialect of Dyirbal), and had recorded some Warrgamay texts from Johnson. West had lent me his notes and I'd eventually been able to extract a copy of the tape from AIAS. The quality of the recording was awful! West had hired a cranky old recorder from Townsville and run it off the erratic home-made power supply on Palm Island. When I played the tape to Alf Palmer, he said he couldn't make out a word, and I didn't blame him. I'd tried, with my head against the speaker, and finished up with an ear like a waffle but — with the help of West's notes — I had gained some idea of what was being said. At least I was able to ask Alf a few questions about words and grammar that I'd heard in the texts, and clarify some points that way.

And so to Nyawaygi, and getting the last two speakers together. Actually, that turned out not to be as straightforward as it sounds. Willie Seaton wasn't at his house in Toobanna. His wife was there, and she said she'd take me to him. Roy Heron, Long Heron's grandson, came along as well, for the ride. We found Willie at his daughter's, and from there he guided us to Heron's place on Warren's Hill.

On the way we ran into a tremendous thunderstorm, which made driving and navigation pretty tough. I drove up as close as possible to the corrugated iron hut in which Long Heron and his family lived, so that my passengers wouldn't get too wet. Seeing them into the shack, I cut my foot quite badly on a protruding piece of rusty iron that was scarcely visible through the rain. When I climbed into the back of the Land Rover to get the tape-recorder, I had to make a hurried search for a piece of sticking plaster to try to bind the two halves of my big toe together and staunch the flow of blood. I didn't want to mention it to Seaton and Heron since it might have taken attention away from the important language work ahead.

Long Heron was now feeling his hundred years. His mind was clearly as keen as ever, but his tall frame was a bit hunched and his speech so slurred that I couldn't really make out anything he was saying. Heron and Seaton sat on a stretcher bed in the dark shack while I squatted on a block of wood, tape-recorder on the earthen floor beside me. This was a unique chance, unlikely to be repeated, so I tried to string English sentences together into what I hoped was a plausible story of traditional life, Seaton translating sentence-by-sentence into Nyawaygi.

Heron's Nyawaygi was solider than Seaton's — it should have been, he was at least twenty years older — but he could hardly articulate. For the hour we sat in that gloomy hut, with the rain banging on the roof and drops trickling through the joins and onto us, I would ask a sentence, Seaton would attempt a translation and then Heron might add to it, or correct something, slurring his words so that no one but Seaton could understand him. Seaton would then repeat what Heron had said.

I couldn't write much down — it was too dark to see. And I was so absorbed in trying to catch the responses above the rain that I let the tape run over the end of the reel.

"About finished now, have you?" asked Seaton.

But I stammered a request to go over the last dozen sentences again, since I hadn't recorded them and they did have useful examples of dual pronouns. They were tired, and the rain started up again just as we left.

Fig. 10. Willie Seaton, with hat, and Long Heron, aged about one hundred (Nya-waygi) outside Heron's hut on Warren's Hill near Ingham, just after the rain had stopped. (1967)

I was right. That was the best material I ever got on Nyawaygi. I never saw Long Heron again — he died in hospital in Ingham in 1970, something over a hundred years old. Roy was reported to know a little Nyawaygi, but the old man and Seaton had laughed at his few suggestions that day. He died of alcoholic poisoning, at about the same time as his grandfather, aged about fifty.

By the time I returned to work seriously on Nyawaygi in 1973, only Willie Seaton was left. He is an intelligent man and was unfailingly helpful with words and most sentences. But those slurred corrections from Long Heron include the only instances of really complex sentences in Nyawaygi.

It was good, amidst my exacting schedule, to be able to return to the homestead at Warrami where, as Mrs Cowan said "there's always a bed for you". They didn't mind if I shut the door for a couple of hours after tea and tried to wrestle with some analytic problem, planning a further line of questioning to pursue next day. But most of the time at Warrami I just sat and chatted or listened to Lindsay's anecdotes about the pioneer days and the troublemakers then — both white and black.

If he couldn't find a son around, Lindsay drafted me to help with jobs around the farm. It was time to slaughter a cow, which would provide meat for the whole Cowan clan for a fair number of weeks. After Lindsay shot it, we used my Land Rover to hoist it up by a pulley so that the carcass could drain overnight. Next day a flurry of Cowans cut up the beast, inserting labels like "joint" or "soop" inside the individual polythene bags, and packing them into the freezer.

Now it was time to get back to the serious business of gathering the Jalnguy words that corresponded to all the Dyirbal words I had collected, to discover the semantic structure of the language. Chloe decided she wanted some mates to help her think through some of the hardest words, so one day we went up to Murray Upper and assembled a sort of committee on Jalnguy, outside Jimmy Murray's hut at Warrami. There was Jimmy, strutting about with his fat belly, organising people and telling them all to "talk over there, tell it to boss, now" but not actually contributing very much himself. It was the old ladies who knew Jalnguy best — Rosie Runaway, Jimmy's Mary Ann, another old Rosie, Chloe herself, and a couple more.

We sat on upturned kerosene tins and bits of wood, and I think someone had a chair. The general tendency just to chat and gossip was cut short by Chloe, as chairman.

"We been sitting up in Ernie's house in Tully, Robert and me, doing all these Jalnguy. But it too hard for one person by herself. You got to help me out. Together we be able to give Dixon what he want." Then she turned to me, "What next, then?".

"Rawurray," I ventured an adjective with a meaning something like "lazy".

"Same," someone opined.

"No way," contradicted little Rosie Runaway, "got to be different, all Jalnguy different." A couple of suggestions were put forward and discussed before a consensus was reached. *Malu,* that was the Jalnguy for *rawurray.*

The most knowledgeable one of all was old Lorna (Jubula), who had been a member of the last group living in the bush, until about 1940. She had been the one who in 1963 hadn't wanted her voice put on record in case it took away her speech. I wasn't recording that day, but Lorna still sat ten feet away from the rest, her back turned to us. She was listening to everything and would comment on most words — fast-spoken Jirrbal, verbs chock-full of affixes, so that I couldn't pick it up (especially when I could scarcely hear it). But Chloe or Jimmy would often repeat it for me, more slowly.

Everyone concentrated for a couple of hours that morning, and again in the afternoon. Even the dogs lay around quietly, as if they were trying to remember back. It was a veritable Dyirbal academy, examining obscure verbs and adjectives in the everyday style and deciding exactly how this or that could have been said in Jalnguy, if one had wanted to discuss the topic when a taboo relative was within earshot. It was a real intellectual challenge — a search for the most appropriate usage, and for the reasons why one suggestion should be preferred over the others.

There was a bit of food around for lunch, but something cool to drink would be nice, Chloe suggested. I drove down to Mrs Cowan's shop for fifteen bottles of soft drink. (Some of the younger people had been sitting there, listening and learning, and they were thirsty too.) We had a break for lunch and everyone chattered away in Jirrbal or Girramay. It may have been a break for them, but I couldn't afford to relax. My mind was already swimming, but I tried to follow what was going on, to see if there was anything new I could pick up. It wasn't every day that I could eavesdrop on such an animated set of conversations.

All sorts of things fell into place that day. For many verbs I'd originally been given a one-word English gloss. *Nudin* was "cut", and so was *gunban* — and so was *banyin* — I was told. But they didn't all have the same Jalnguy correspondent. *Nudin* and *gunban* were both *jalnggan*, but *banyin* was *bubaman* in Jalnguy; all of the committee agreed on that.

Now *bubaman* I already knew as the correspondent of the everyday style verb *baygun* "shake or wave something, or bash something on something else, for example, pick up a goanna by its tail and bash its head on a tree to stun it." The concept seemed to be "put something in motion, holding on to it" (and it might or might not impact on something else).

Further detail was needed. *Nudin,* I discovered, means "cut deeply, sever", while *gunban* is "cut to medium depth, cut a piece out". Fine, both are further specifications of the general Jalnguy verb *jalnggan* "cut". Now for *banyin*. Every language has a few words like this, which describe an important everyday activity but which seem a bit bizarre to people from a different cultural background. *Banyin* means "get a stone tomahawk and bring it down on a rotten log so that the blade is embedded in the log, then pick up both tomahawk and log by the handle of the tomahawk and bash the log against a tree so that the log splits open and the ripe grubs inside can be extracted and eaten". It involves a tomahawk, which is the major implement for cutting or chopping. But the criterial action is seen to be the bashing of the log against a tree to split it; this can be inferred from the fact that the Jalnguy correspondent is *bubaman* "shake, wave or bash" rather than *jalnggan* "cut".

That evening, Alan and Glen Cowan had invited me for tea at the house they were renting just the other side of the school. Glen's parents, Mr and Mrs Clarke, came along as well. Sturdy country folk who'd lived all their lives in Tully, they were sensible people, who knew how to make a living from the land and didn't trust politicians from the south. Talk turned to what I was doing there. They couldn't really understand what I could find to do all day with the Aborigines – and I'd been working on it for three and a half years! It didn't seem the moment to try to explain Jalnguy or the gender classes or the *-ngurra* construction.

These Aborigines weren't even married properly, I was told. They just lived with someone and didn't have any rules or laws about marriage. This couldn't be let pass. Maybe they couldn't match us in material possessions, I expounded, but they did have a more complex kinship system, with more finely articulated social roles.

"Don't believe it."

OK, give them some facts. "There are four sections. Each person belongs to just one. They are called Jigungarra, Gurgurru, Gurrgila and Garrbawuru. Now a person belonging to Jigungarra must take a marriage partner from Gurgurru – no two ways about it, that's what he's got to do. The children of a Jigungarra man are Gurrgila and they in turn must marry someone from Garrbawuru. Then a Gurrgila man's children are Jigungarra again. And so a boy will belong to the same section as his father's father (and a girl to the same one as her mother's mother), and so on."

They *did* believe me in the end, but they were astounded. To think that they'd lived all of their lives in Tully, in closer proximity to a group of Aborigines than almost anyone else in Queensland, and they'd never had the shadow of an idea that the Aborigines had *anything* like this.

(I thought it wise not to go further and mention the distaste that Aborigines had for marriages that were "too close". Alan's brother Max had married his first cousin, something that was anathema to the Jirrbalngan. They even had a word for it, *nyirririmu,* Chloe told me. "No good'll come of it, you'll see," was her warning.)

A few years later, I met a young white schoolteacher at the Yarrabah Aboriginal Settlement, who came from Tully. He was just then learning that Aborigines were people, and interesting people at that, who had their own cultural perspective and conventions, which were just as valid as ours. He was ashamed, he said, when he looked back at his schooldays in Tully. There were black children in the class, but the white kids had never mixed with them. He'd been literally scared silly of the black kids – he'd really thought they were devils and that they might get him and do awful things. He couldn't really be blamed – that was the way his parents (and teachers?) had taught him to regard Aborigines.

George and Ginnie felt like a trip to Murray Upper. They hadn't been there for many years. So George put on a clean pair of long trousers and Ginnie put her shoes in the car – she didn't actually put them on – and gathered up some blankets. We stopped off in Tully for a couple of hours while Chloe and George put their heads together over some tricky points in Jalnguy and then yes, of course they'd record a text for me. It's not an easy thing, when you haven't spoken Jalnguy or heard it spoken for over thirty years, to stick entirely to Jalnguy vocabulary and not lapse into the more familiar everyday-style idiom – but my two reliable teachers succeeded.

George asked Chloe where she'd been living before and which of the girls in the house belonged to her. Chloe said she'd moved down from Murray Upper because too many of the men there were trying to marry her. They should be too old for that – they ought to look at themselves in the mirror, George suggested. They both laughed and stopped.

Chloe and George were enjoying themselves, so that when he suggested "Shall we do another one for Robert?", Chloe agreed enthusiastically. Ginnie didn't join in, but she approved of the banter (so long as it remained on a fairly intellectual level). The next Jalnguy conversation was longer, about the people George and Ginnie would see at Murray Upper, and their traditional places.

It was getting late, and time to move on. We stopped at Mrs Cowan's shop to say hello — everyone always went first to Mrs Cowan's in Murray Upper, to find out what was what and because it was always nice to chat to her. I bought a few provisions for George and Ginnie — two tins of corned beef, a loaf of·bread, some tea and sugar, a packet of tobacco and some papers — and we then went on out to see Mick Murray. Mick lived in "the pocket", right at the end of the Cowan's property under the mountains — it was dark and cold and a little eerie with the grim peaks looking down from three sides. The house Mick lived in had originally belonged to the Cowans' eldest daughter, Val May, but she hadn't liked it out there. No one did, except Mick.

We worked on a little more Jalnguy, chipping away at it bit by bit, and then George and Ginnie were tired. Mick was already cooking supper in a billy-can over some smouldering coals just outside the back door, at the top of the steep bank which overlooks the northern branch of the Murray. "We'll see you again tomorrow, Robert," they said, as I drove back to my billet at Warrami. All the Aborigines in North Queensland call me either Dixon, which is fine, or Robert, a name I never use and normally dislike. I have always introduced myself as Bob (except to Doreen McGrath), and the white people use this name. One reason why Aborigines address me as they do could be that all words in Dyirbal have at least two syllables, and Robert fits this preferred phonetic pattern better than Bob.

As I drove back to the pocket the next morning, the legend about the origin of fire started going through my head. George had told me the Mamu version back on Palm. At one time, the only fire in the world was guarded on a high mountain ledge by the rainbow, who had taken on the form of a snake. All the birds, who were dreamtime people, had to eat raw food, and it made them sick. So they decided to try to grab the fire from the rainbow serpent.

The eaglehawk had painted yellow clay on the scrub-turkey's neck (which explains its present colour). When the scrub-turkey flew towards the ledge, the rainbow saw her and knocked her back. Other birds tried to snatch the fire, but with the same result. Finally, the eaglehawk asked Bajinjilajila to try. (This is *Dicrurus bracteatus* or "spangled drongo", although George called it "satin bird" in English.) No, she had a stomach ache and couldn't go. But the eaglehawk cured this ailment by rubbing her with armpit sweat, *ngamurray*. Still Bajinjilajila demurred, but eventually persuasion won her over. She was painted black, with charcoal, so as to be inconspicuous (which explains her present colour). Bajinjilajila flew up and landed on the ledge so quietly that the rainbow serpent did not see her come. To this day, Bajinjilajila does just this — no one sees her approach or land, but there she suddenly is, sitting on a branch nearby.

Only the wind from Bajinjilajila's wings, as she alighted, alerted the rainbow. He looked around the top of the piece of burning wood, but the bird hid behind the bottom end. Then the snake lifted that end up, but by now the intruder was around the top. The snake turned his back on the fire to have another sleep. Then Bajinjilajila picked up the glowing fire in her beak and flew off with it. The snake turned round, a fraction too late. He lunged after the bird, but missed her, just snicking the end of her tail — which explains why the Bajinjilajila today has a split tail. The bird flew on, bashing the fire against the Moreton Bay tree, against the bonewood tree, and against the crowfoot tree — and that is why wood from these three trees burns so well today.

The road went up, past Birdy Curtis's place, across the river, and then turned in to the pocket, under the mountains. There was Mount Smoko — and then Dowse Rocks, called in Jirrbal Dirrabigal. It is pyramid-shaped except at the top where there are two small peaks, a bit like the humps on a camel. George was sitting on the steps yarning with Mick. "It's a funny thing here, Robert," he began, gesturing towards Dirrabigal.

I knew what he was going to say, because it was just what I'd been thinking. The Jirrbal people at Murray Upper also had a legend about the origin of fire, which Chloe had told me on that second afternoon in October 1963. It was the same as George's Mamu story, detail for detail, except at the end. In the local version, the snake had struck out at the bird but had missed her completely, and had instead hit Dirrabigal, making the split top at its peak.

"Didn't you know that before, George?" I asked.

"No, never heard of it. I know our way — I tell it to you on Palm — but I never hear tell of their way."

"Which is the oldest, which is the original version, do you think?"

George thought for a few moments: "Must be ours. That bird got a split-tail everywhere but this the only place where a mountain got a split top. Must be ours is the oldest and then Jirrbal take the story and change that bit of it. That's how I think it must be. But I might be wrong. What do you think about it, Robert?" I said I couldn't see any flaw in his argument.

We went around Murray Upper saying hello to everyone. Lorna, old Jubula — I got the idea that there'd been something between her and George in days gone by, but she wasn't overfriendly now. In fact George complained that no one at Murray Upper except Mick Murray was very welcoming to them. Maybe it was a legacy from the old days when there'd been bitter tribal enmity between Jirrbal and Mamu. Going through the phonicon had been revealing of inter-tribal attitudes. When we'd come to *nunggan* "large lice, denizens of armpits and the like", Chloe had said derisively that Mamu had had them, dirty lot that they were. And there were oblique hints that the Mamu were the real bad cannibals and grave desecrators. In the late seventies, when I came back to complete work on a dictonary of Dyirbal, George sometimes declined to come down to Murray Upper — or if he did accompany me there, he preferred not to stay overnight. The journey he liked was up to the tableland to see Mollie Raymond and her friends; those were his real kinfolk, he maintained.

On the way back to Palmerston, we stopped off with Chloe again and I was able to clarify verbs of hitting. Which verb to use depended on the type of blow, and whether or not the implement was let go of. *Balgan* is "hit with a long rigid implement (such as a stick), held in the hand" whereas *minban* is "hit with a long rigid implement that is thrown". This also covered being struck by lightning — the bolt of brightness that can have such lethal effect is just like a long rigid implement, and it is certainly thrown. Recently *minban* has been extended to cover "shoot", which Dyirbal speakers saw as similar to the action of lightning. Then *bijin* is "hit with a rounded implement, for example, punch with the fist, hit with a stone, a woman banging a skin drum stretched across her knee, heavy rain pounding on one". The same verb is used whether the rounded implement is held on to or let go of — hitting someone with a stone held in the hand or with a stone that is thrown are both *bijin*. Finally there is *bunjun* "hit with a long flexible implement, for example, spank with the flat of the hand, whip with a belt, hit with a bramble stalk"; this sort of implement would always be held in the hand.

Balgan was glossed sometimes as "hit" and other times as "kill". This was the blow most likely to kill, and killing was most frequently done this way. It could really be rendered "hit, with the strong potentiality of killing". In fact Dyirbal has no verb exactly corresponding to English "kill". There are two appropriate adjectives — *buga* "dead, stinking, rotten" can be used of an animal or a human, and also of fruits and meat, whereas *guyi* "dead spirit" is restricted to humans. Both adjectives can be made into transitive verbs by the suffix *-man* — *bugaman* (of anything), *guyiman* (only of humans) "make dead, kill".

On that sombre note we returned to Palmerston. Ginnie had left her shoes up at the pocket, but she didn't miss them for a couple of days. Mick found them there, and I took them back the following week.

I had intended that my Jalnguy questioning should fall into two parts. The first was now as complete as I could get it that trip — going through everyday language words and asking their Jalnguy equivalents. I took a day off to go down to the motel at Mission Beach to prepare for the second stage.

A six-by-four-inch card was made out for each Jalnguy verb, and on it were listed all the everyday-style verbs for which it had been given as correspondent. Since there was a many-to-one relation between everyday and mother-in-law vocabularies, I expected to finish up with a fair number of Guwal forms on each Jalnguy card. A couple had just one — Jalnguy *yirrgunjinyu* had only occurred as equivalent of Guwal *miyandanyu* "laugh" — but most had four, five or six Guwal verbs for the one Jalnguy item.

The *jubumban* card was fairly typical. This Jalnguy verb had been given by Chloe, and by George and Ginnie, as the equivalent of *bijin* "hit with a rounded object", *jilwan* "kick with the foot or shove with the knee", *dudan* "mash food with a stone", *dalinyu* "deliver a blow to something on the ground, for example, fall on". One Jalnguy verb and four Guwal equivalents.

I finished going through all the stage one material, arranging it by Jalnguy verbs, and in mid-morning set off back to Tully for my appointment with Chloe that afternoon, to start on stage two. This was to ask things the other way round — for a given Jalnguy verb, what were its Guwal equivalents? It would be interesting to see how the results of stage two correlated with those of stage one.

It had rained heavily during the night, but most of the dirt road back from the beach was pretty firm, and I could drive comfortably along at forty. The road ahead seemed a different colour, which was nothing unusual in that part of the world, with its many different types of soil. What I didn't realise until too late was that it was the colour of mud — thick gooey mud, some eight inches deep. I tried to turn into the skid, but only succeeded in moving further over to the right where — just at that point, and nowhere else along the track — there was a highish bank. Although I had slowed down, it was not enough to avoid slamming into the bank. The impact turned the Land Rover onto its side and I fell against the door, on top of the tape-recorder, amidst a shower of broken glass from the side window.

I just lay there a few minutes, making sure everything was all right, that all I had was a couple of big bruises. And wondering what the appropriate Dyirbal verb would be to describe the bump into the bank. I went over all the possibilities and decided on *bijin*. It was certainly hitting something with a rounded, blunt object — the Land Rover. I'd have to check with Chloe when I saw her.

Then I climbed out and walked to a farm that was, luckily, only about two miles back down the road. Well, the farmer said, he didn't like not to help someone out, but it cost a lot of money to put petrol in the tractor, y'know. I was happy enough to offer $5 for the fuel. (When I told Ernie of this, he was scandalised — that anyone should take, or demand, money for helping out in such circumstances!) The farmer gave me a pull to get upright and I drove off, only slightly shaken, to keep my appointment with Chloe. I was a bit cranky for the rest of the day. Except for one thing: Chloe confirmed that *bijin* was the correct verb to describe the impact.

Old Lindsay Cowan had the last word, as he often did. I was describing the accident to him — the mud, the skid, the bank just at that point — as one chance in a hundred. Lindsay heard me out. He agreed that it was one chance in a hundred that I'd turn the vehicle onto its side there. "But you've probably had the other ninety-nine chances, when nothing happened," he added. I thought back to the times I'd met huge timber-trucks on narrow, winding range roads at the one place where I could squeeze by. Yes, I agreed, he was right. I probably had had the other ninety-nine chances.

Then into stage two. *"Jubumban,"* I asked Chloe, *"Minya guwara?* What would that be in Guwal?"*. I had four Guwal words on the card for this Jalnguy item, verbs for which *jubumban* had been given as equivalent in stage one, the Guwal to Jalnguy elicitation. I wondered if she'd give them all, or just a selection, and which would be named first. The answer was simpler than that. *"Bijin,"* Chloe said, "that's what you'd say for *jubumban."* That was all. I enquired if there were any more Guwal words that would translate *jubumban*, but she said "No, just *bijin."* After trying everything else, I finally just read out the other words on the card. What of *dudan?* Oh yes, that was *jubumban* too. Same for the other two. These were all correct, but *bijin* was the only Guwal word that had occurred to Chloe when I said *jubumban*.

The same thing happened with every other card. Chloe gave just one of the list of Guwal words, ignoring all the others that had been given as equivalents of the Jalnguy word, in stage one. And then, when I went up to put the same questions to George, he gave exactly the same responses. *Jubumban* was, for him, just *bijin,* and again I had to prompt to get him to agree that the other words on the card were also equivalents. For every card, Chloe and George picked out just one verb. And they selected the same one.

The next thing I did was to focus attention on *bijin* "hit with a rounded object" and *jilwan* "kick with the foot or shove with the knee", two words from the *jubumban* card. How would this distinction, shown by two separate words in the everyday style, be rendered in mother-in-law, if it were needed? *Bijin* would be just *jubumban*, but *jilwan* would be *winarra-gu jubumban* or *wangabay-ju jubumban* — adding *winarra* "foot" or *wangabay* "knee" in instrumental inflection to the basic verb *jubumban*. *Bijin* is, like *jubumban,* just "hit with a rounded object" but *jilwan* is "hit with a specified type of rounded object, namely a foot or a knee".

The same thing happened when I contrasted other pairs from the cards. Nothing was added to the central correspondent, *bijin* — that was always left just as *jubumban* — but for each of the other words something could be added to *jubumban* as a further specification. Again, exactly parallel answers were obtained from Chloe and George, for this card and for all the other cards.

These results in stage two took me totally by surprise. I'd had no idea this was what could happen, no working hypothesis that these facts could confirm. But they did suggest an idea about the semantic structure of a language. Maybe the verbs of any language fall into two types — let's call them "nuclear" and "non-nuclear". The nuclear verbs are the most frequently-occurring items and have wide, general meanings — like "give" and "tell" and "look". Nuclear verbs could not generally be defined in terms of other verbs. Non-nuclear verbs, on the other hand, are more specialised and could be defined in terms of a nuclear item. So *stare* would be non-nuclear in English, and it could be defined as *look hard*.

Dyirbal Jalnguy has the minimum number of words necessary to say in Jalnguy anything that can be said in the everyday style. Guwal has both nuclear and non-nuclear verbs, as have all other everyday-language styles. But Jalnguy just has nuclear verbs. And when a Jalnguy verb is put to a speaker, he will just give the nuclear Guwal verb as equivalent (*bijin* for *jubumban,* and so on). Jalnguy can do without any non-nuclear verbs because it simply creates a "definition" by using the nuclear verb and adding a noun or adverb. For *jilwan,* Jalnguy will simply spell out "deliver a blow with the foot" or "deliver a blow with the knee".

This seemed a real breakthrough. The relation between the two speech styles of Dyirbal revealed something about the underlying semantic structure of the language — and perhaps of all languages.

I said goodbye to Chloe and George with sadness and the most genuine thanks. The Cowans gave another party for the white people of Murray Upper to say farewell; I was sad to leave them, too.

I spent a day in Sydney where — observing his reactions quite sharply — I seemed to detect a glimmer of approval when I told Dr Capell of the Jalnguy results. It seemed to me that I was really doing another bit of field work in Sydney — a list of questions about Australian languages to ask Arthur Capell, at the back of the book of questons about Dyirbal grammar for Chloe and George. Then, sad to leave Australia, back to London.

9

Lots of Linguistic Expertise

I'd written a draft grammar of Dyirbal during 1966, but was now dissatisfied with it. It tried to make a contribution to linguistic theory, using all sorts of neologistic terminology — in effect putting the language second to the theory, referring to aspects of the grammar only as needed for linguistic model-making. When I got back, in May 1967, I decided to start all over again. I now had a better understanding of how the language worked, and my aim would be to try to describe it as clearly as possible, with the minimum of pseudo-scientific jargon. The ergative structure of Dyirbal was different enough from the grammars of familiar languages, without the added complication of an obscure presentation.

I've never been fond of collecting degrees and had up to this time subtly managed to avoid doing a doctorate. But it was becoming increasingly clear that it would be a useful thing to have — a Ph.D. would make getting a visa to work in the U.S.A. very much easier to obtain, for one thing. I was writing a grammar of Dyirbal anyway so — why not submit it for the degree?

As I worked through the mass of material from that productive month in the field, and wrote the thesis, some points emerged that really required further clarification or checking. When, in mid-1968, my grammar of Dyirbal was accepted by Cambridge University Press for publication in their new "Studies in Linguistics" series, I suggested to Michael Black, the editor of the press, that the final revision should be delayed until after another field trip. I wanted to get the grammar absolutely right, since it was unlikely to be the sort of thing which would go into a second edition. He emphatically agreed.

How right we were! The press did not, at that time, know how many copies of a book on an obscure languge were likely to be sold, so they printed 2,500. When sales were slow, a number were issued in paperback, almost as a sort of "remaindering". Although this grammar attracted wide attention and has probably been referred to in print as often as any language description, worldwide sales, hardback and paperback, were only 1,483 in the nine years after publication!

I spent the academic year of 1968–69 as a visiting lecturer at Harvard University, where I taught a course on semantics, with a big chunk on the nuclear/non-nuclear distinction inferred from Guwal-Jalnguy correspondences; and a course on the native languages of Australia, with heavy emphasis on the grammar of Dyirbal. These attracted a small but high-powered audience, who gave me lots of stimulating feed-back and a number of new insights into the grammatical structure of Dyirbal.

I also went down the road to the Massachusetts Institute of Technology to learn from the lectures of Noam Chomsky and, particularly, Ken Hale. It would be difficult to list all that I gained from Ken during that year (quite apart from his and Sally's hospitality and friendship) – facts about Australian languages, ideas about their structure and development, and just a general way of looking at language and culture.

Back in London in September 1969, I started to plan another quick field trip before finally revising the Dyirbal grammar for publication. It seemed reasonable to assume the mixture would be as before – one third of the money from the University of London (as much as they could grant) and the remainder from AIAS. London came through all right. But AIAS? (You've guessed!)

At the time of my previous application, in 1967, I'd had just two publications on Mbabaram. Now I had a book contract from Cambridge, as well as several papers in leading international journals or anthologies. But AIAS simply said "No". Unfortunately Arthur Capell was no longer linguistics chairman, so I missed the advice he had passed on two years before. I investigated charter flights and was able to cut the estimate a little. AIAS said they'd put the proposal to council again, but the whole thing seemed rather doubtful.

Luckily, something else came up. I'd become pretty depressed on returning from America to a department that still consisted only of Halliday and me. Americans often get excited about things that are not really worth getting excited over, but at least this produces a stimulating atmosphere. And in MIT and Harvard, I'd been in contact with the finest collection of linguists gathered together in any one city in the world.

⸱ A Chair of Linguistics had just been established at the Australian National University. It had been advertised months before and I hadn't applied. Then the gossip network came through with the news that no one good *had* applied. I wrote a letter of interest one afternoon, just to try to shake myself out of depression. We'd long fancied living in Australia, and it would be nice to be in an expanding university rather than constrained by the English economy. I could do more field work, have contact with the few good Australians working on the languages, and perhaps have students in the field (it was awfully lonely being the only Australianist in Europe). After a flurry of telegrams I was, to our considerable surprise, offered the job.

I hadn't cared for Canberra at all in 1963. Since then, it had doubled in size and acquired a lake. And my own priorities had altered. After five years in the crowded centre of London, Canberra would be a change, and it was probably a rather good place for children to grow up in. So we went out there in July 1970, and I immediately plunged into a demanding — but exciting and satisfying — round of planning and teaching courses, administering, politicking, and trying to do a bit of research round the edges.

It wasn't until late November, when the end-of-year examinations were over, that it was possible for me to take off. I spent a couple of days at the first cricket Test in Brisbane — the beginning of a fascinating series in which Snow and Illingworth won back the Ashes — and then flew up to Townsville to pick up a vehicle — and into the field.

The first person I went to see, of course, was Chloe. She was feeling her age a little, but her mind was still as bright and sparkling as ever. The girls had now left home and Chloe was living with Edgar (her oldest son), Mamie and family, at Bellenden, just by the coast highway north of the Murray Upper turnoff. Bellenden has an interesting history. Charles Eden relates in *My wife and I in Queensland* how he and John Davidson began a sugar plantation there in 1868, worked by Kanaka labourers imported from the South Sea Islands. Some of the first racial hostility began then. Eden's Kanakas would go for a walk in the bush on Sundays to kill (and eat) any Aborigines they chanced to encounter. The sugar was badly affected by floods, and the plantation appears to have been mismanaged — the venture folded within five years.

Old Isaac Henry had Bellenden for many years. He was a portly white man, whose gait amused the Jirrbalngan. Chloe sang for me a lilting song describing the pigs, he kept, and their resemblance to their porcine owner: *Bigibigi yiniringu, bayingala yawara, jananyu bigibigi.* The property was inherited by Isaac's bachelor son, Hughie, and then on down to Hughie's nephew, George Henry, who was now employing Edgar to help with the cattle, fencing, and other farm work.

Chloe greeted me like a long-lost son. How were Alison and the children? We now had three, so it was getting on to be what Chloe considered a reasonable-sized family. I wanted to go through all the chapters of my thesis, making sure I had everything absolutely right and getting more examples of some critical things. Chloe approved of this — we must be sure to get it right, then the government would be properly pleased. (I never had the heart to tell her the government didn't really give a damn!) But she didn't know where we could work — Ernie was in New Guinea and there was no room in Edgar's house, "too much children there".

Gladys Henry, George's wife, had always taken an interest in the local Aborigines. A couple of dozen of them were living in a camp on Bellenden, including my old friend Rosie Runaway, who had moved down from the old mission at Murray Upper. A sign on the highway announced "Aboriginal artefacts for sale" and Mrs Henry sold dilly-bags, boomerangs and eel-baskets, passing all of the price on to the craftsmen who made them. She had also accumulated an interesting museum of old Aboriginal artefacts (which was later sold to the James Cook University at Townsville).

I was staying with the Cowans again — it was nice to be back (and now we were looking forward to some of them coming down to stay with us in Canberra). But Gladys and George Henry were also most hospitable and friendly. It was all right working in the garden — although Chloe was a *little bit* on edge. When it rained, Gladys invited us to work in the large, cool, nineteenth-century living room, but that wasn't at all successful. Gladys was sitting at the other end of the room, paying bills, and sometimes listening to what we were doing, peering at us over the top of her spectacles. Chloe was torn between the sort of front she wanted to put on for Gladys, and the quite different self that came out in her working relationship with me. She was alternately being helpful and showing off, so that I didn't know where I was.

A major project on that trip was to check that I hadn't missed any grammatical generalisations. Gender markers with a noun are masculine *bayi*, feminine *balan*, edible *balam*, and neuter *bala*. They also show the same case as the noun they go with — so *yibi-nggu*, with ergative ending *-nggu* marking the agent of some activity, would be accompanied by gender marker *ba-nggu-n*. The final *-n* shows feminine, and the *-nggu-* is ergative suffix, the same as that on the noun itself. "The woman saw the man" would then be *Bayi yara banggun yibinggu buran* (literally "man woman-by saw").

The first element in these gender markers can be *ba-*, meaning "there (and visible)" or *ya-* "here (and visible)" or *nga-* "not visible but audible (or remembered)". *Balan yibi miyandanyu* "woman is laughing there" would describe someone you could see, but *ngalan yibi miyandanyu* would be used when you could hear a woman laughing but couldn't see her, or if you were remembering some event from the past when a woman laughed.

All that had been clear since 1967. And also the adverbs that began with *ya-* and *ba-*. There was *yalay* "here" and *balay* "there". Then *yangum* "from here" and *bangum* "from there". And *yalu* "to here (to this place)", *yali* "to here (in this direction)"; *balu* "to there (to that place)", *bali* "to there (in that direction)". My question was whether there could be any adverbals beginning in *nga-*, as there are gender markers in *ya-*, *ba-* and also *nga-*; that is *ngalay, ngangum, ngali, ngalu*. No, said Chloe, after a bit of thought. There was a different word *ngali* "you and me", a pronoun. Of course there was, and to have an adverb of the same form might cause great confusion.

The next day, Gladys Henry was going with a group of Aboriginal ladies (Ida Henry, Daisy Denham, one-arm Rosie and old Biddie) on an expedition up Davidson Creek to find a traditional site that was said to have a large pigeon nest and two eggs, all transmuted into stone in the long-ago dreamtime. Paddy Biran had told me the story of this, in Girramay, back at the Murray Upper mission in 1964. Chloe excused herself — her legs weren't too good and she had an asthmatic chest. But she encouraged me to go along, then I could later tell her all about it.

My four-wheel-drive Land Cruiser was useful in getting within a few miles of where the site was thought to be. "I'm going to take one of those eggs away, Ida", Gladys kidded, and the ladies looked at her, and at each other, very doubtfully. But how they walked! We kept having to wade across the river, which seemed to be bottomed with sharp quartz. They just sped across in bare feet, and provided a heavy stick to help me lurch from rock to rock, each one seeming about to pierce through my sandals. Time after time they *just* steered me away from touching a stinging tree, whose hairs are said to inflict a pain that takes three months completely to disappear.

Then we encountered a big black goanna, *gugar (Varanus varius)*, six feet long. On seeing us, it ran up a tree and then looked down, tail-up, watching intently. I'd heard stories about what good food they were, and mildly commented on this. *"Bajalbila,"* was sufficient reply — don't monkey with him, he's "liable to bite".

I finally got scrub-itch that day — a plague of tiny red mites that get under your skin and itch like mad. Gladys and George said the best cure was to rub oneself all over with kerosene, so I did. Then the Cowans said, no, I should rub myself all over with methylated spirits, so I did that too. One of them cured it (and I didn't go up in flames).

We never did find the stone nest. Gladys said later that after she'd threatened to take away an egg, the women had probably decided not to show us, and I agreed. Jack Murray heard about this and said he'd take me there, no worries. But we didn't have an opportunity that trip, and by the time I returned Jack had passed away. Then, in 1979, I was looking for Mick Murray one Saturday, but was told he'd gone into the bush to show Mrs Jones — the other local white woman who took an interest in things Aboriginal — a stone nest belonging to a chicken-hawk. In the intervening nine years, it had been upgraded from pigeon to chicken-hawk. I saw Mick the next day and he said, No, they hadn't been able to find it.

Gladys and I were talking in English (she couldn't speak a word of Dyirbal, despite many years of association with the people) and the old ladies underestimated how much I could understand. What they were saying was so interesting that I kept quiet for a while. In fact it had more than gossip value. I could swear that when talking about going to the stone nest, they used an adverb *ngalu*. The next day I confronted Chloe with this. Yes, that would be correct, she acknowledged, *yalu* is "to this thing", *balu* is "to that thing", and *ngalu* is "to something remembered from the past". There's no adverb *ngali*, because of the pronoun *ngali* "us two" (and anyway, "in a remembered direction" is a bit odd). It was a useful reminder of the limitations of asking questions over a desk — it is no substitute at all for living with a language, observing it being used, and using it oneself.

The big event in Chloe's life since I'd last seen her was a trip to Melbourne for a Jehovah's Witnesses convention. She'd travelled the two thousand odd miles by bus. It wasn't so much the city of two and a half million people that Chloe remembered, as the countryside around. She'd stood with her daughter by the Yarra river wondering what it must have been like a hundred and fifty years ago when blackfellows ruled the roost. Chloe added that she was now too old to be bothered with the Witnesses any longer. "They keep coming here with their 'Sister Chloe' but I tell them 'I'm old lady, you leave me alone'. I don't want nothing to do with them now."

Gladys Henry had finally published her book on Aboriginal legends of the area, including a map of the Murray River with many place names. They were only fragments of longer stories, written in English with some proper names in Dyirbal; unfortunately the transcription was very poor. It was called *Girroo Gurrll, the first surveyor.* Chloe decided to give me a full version of the title story, which was about a dreamtime hero called, properly, Girugarr. Coming from the south, Girugarr was the first person to explore the present-day tribal territory, naming each place after something he encountered there.

As always, Chloe and I had a good gossip. The person who was at this time both amusing and annoying the other Aborigines was Joe Kinjun, laying on his Uncle Tom act even thicker than before. He was the only person who was always ready to talk to white people, but on his terms. He'd talk in a mixture of Gulngay and English that was difficult for anyone to follow, and would always dictate how any conversation was to go. A direct question — and an insistence on a straight answer — was something he did not appreciate.

One well-meaning white lady had recently been taking Joe around the local schools, having him demonstrate traditional crafts and skills. He would have little games at her expense (knowing that she understood very little of his language). One school had some Aboriginal kids in the class, who understood what he was saying, Chloe reported. The white lady introduced Joe, who picked up a spear, looked her in the eye, and said *"Nginda ban gura bulgan."*

"What's that Joe?" she enquired politely in her posh white voice, quite unaware that he'd just complimented her on the size of her you-know-what.

Joe continued: *"Ngaja nginuna gura warjumany."*

Our hostess responded to this quite obscene suggestion in the same sweet, encouraging tone. "Good, tell them some more, Joe."

I suppose in a way Joe was getting his own back – on behalf of the late Malanbarra tribe, of which he was the sole survivor.

Joe used to make baskets for Mrs Henry to sell to tourists and he often walked over from the Tully, sometimes helping her demonstrate items from the museum to visitors. One afternoon, Gladys asked me to be on hand to translate, to bring out the full flavour of what Joe was saying. I did just that. Small boys from the Cardstone school were scared enough when Joe picked up a sharp-pointed spear, pointed it in their direction and said something rather vehement in a strange language. But when they learnt that *Ngaja nginuna bamba jurrganyu guyibili* meant "I'm going to spear you in the stomach – until you're dead", they quivered, white-faced.

Joe was a help, though, in confirming a vague idea that I'd had for a long time. This concerned the qualities necessary to be a Gubi, a word which can only be rather inadequately translated as "wise man" or "Aboriginal doctor". Right at the beginning of this field trip, before Joe realised how much Dyirbal I could understand, I asked him, in English, if he were a Gubi. His reply was a typical blend of languages. "No more, I not Gubi, but *gilu ngaja nginuna balgali, waguli gunyjali, gubibilmbali.*" This means: "Later on tonight I'm going to kill you, and drink your blood, and that'll make me a Gubi." (My response was a half-scared "Oh no, you won't.")

It was exactly as I had suspected – a Gubi must be a good hunter, he must have a sound knowledge of traditional lore and legend, and (sine qua non) he *must* have partaken of human blood!

Lindsay Cowan again included me in the family circle, and used me as a farm helper when no one else was around. Some young foals were due to be gelded, but in truth I must have been more of a hindrance than a help with lassooing the frightened animals, then holding them tight in a narrow pen while Lindsay's knife did its work, the discarded testicles being chucked across as titbits for his dogs. It was pleasant, though, once more to have a home to return to, and good friends to chat with about the rain, and politicians, and local gossip.

On the second day of the 1970 trip, I drove up to renew acquaintance with George and Ginnie. The house they had lived in was deserted, but I found George working with Mr Gaynor, putting up some posts for a new cattle yard. He had sad news: Ginnie had passed away two months before. She'd been around when they got my letter saying I'd be coming soon, and had been looking forward to it, George said, after the good times we'd all had a couple of years ago.

George hadn't fancied living on in the old house, so Mr Gaynor had allowed him the use of another one, a mile or so further up towards the mountains. He was living in it with Dicky Briggs, another old Mamu man, and a couple of younger fellows who worked on farms nearby would come over at weekends. It had been a white folks' house, a good wooden frame, with four or five rooms, and electricity. But apparently someone had started dismantling it, from the middle out. There was a large hole — perhaps six feet square — right in the middle of the floor, with a drop to the earth four or five feet below. One had to be very careful when walking about the house at night, or after a heavy drinking bout (or both).

As usual, I plied George with the same questions I had asked Chloe, checking and extending the grammar chapters of my thesis, making sure the example sentences were all right (we were still eliminating double-entendres), and doing a bit more on Jalnguy. This time I was going through all the everyday-style adjectives to get their Jalnguy equivalents.

George's Mamu and Chloe's Jirrbal have about eighty-seven per cent of the words in common, and their grammars are almost identical. But there are a few interesting differences. I'd known that Mamu (and Gulngay) had a verb ending *-mi,* which Jirrbal and Girramay did not have. Now, for the first time, it became apparent that it marked a kind of relative clause, referring to something that had already happened, *before* the event described by the main clause. *Yara yibi-nggu buran* is "woman sees man" and *yara miyandanyu* is "man laughs". To make a relative clause, *-mi* is simply added on to the verb: *yara miyandanyumi yibinggu buran* "woman sees the man who had laughed". The other sort of relative clause — something that is happening at the same time as the event of the main clause — is shown by *-ngu* on the verb: *yara miyandangu yibinggu buran* "woman sees man laughing". In contrast, Jirrbal has only one kind of relative clause, the *-ngu* sort. For Chloe, *yara miyandangu yibinggu buran* would cover both the meaning "woman sees man who had laughed" and also "woman sees man laughing". So at last I'd been able to place the verbal ending *-mi* within the complete system of the grammar.

The second time I went up, George asked if I would like to stay with him for the weekend. Sure, I'd love to. So on Friday, I first went to

George's place and did some language work there, and then we drove into Innisfail to go to the bank, buy provisions and so on. There's a very good Italian restaurant in a basement in Innisfail, but George maintains he doesn't care for spaghetti. So we ate in the cafe he always chooses, and we had fish and chips, which we almost always do.

A television set in the cafe was showing the second Test from Perth. I soon became glued to it and George, who had played cricket on Palm Island, was interested too. But he was really fascinated when I told him the story of Basil D'Oliviera who was batting, effortlessly, with majestic sweeps and cuts. I told him how D'Oliviera could never have played for his native South Africa, so he emigrated to England and made the national team there. Then when he was picked to tour South Africa with the English team, the South African government had called off the tour at the embarrassment it would cause them to have a coloured South African play against its all-white team. I explained how South Africa had always declined to play cricket against India, Pakistan and the West Indies. George kept on asking me more questions about Dolly, and how he had had to move half-way around the world to get picked for international cricket. "Well, he made it," George concluded, as D'Oliviera slammed another ball into the boundary fence, second bounce.

We'd need some beer for the weekend, George said, when we were having a drink after lunch, I suggested half a dozen stubbies, but he demurred. There'd be two people coming in from farms, and they'd want some. We bought a carton of two dozen which seemed to me ample — four or five bottles each — although George still appeared quite doubtful.

George always had an insatiable appetite for work. On the 1967 trip, we'd start at nine or ten in the morning, have half an hour off for lunch, and then at about six I'd close my notebook and suggest that that might be enough for one day.

"Haven't you got anything else to ask?" George would enquire. I'd admit that I did have, but was saving it for another day.

"Do it now!" George would demand, "We're not tired, are we?"

And Ginnie, who was, would agree that she wasn't. I was usually dead beat by then, and my mind was spinning round with no place to go. But we usually did another half hour before George would allow us to stop.

He hadn't changed. While waiting for the others to arrive, George broached the carton of beer and we began on particles. These are words in Dyirbal which, unlike nouns, pronouns, adjectives and verbs, don't take any endings at all. They serve to modify the meaning of a complete sentence. Some are quite straightforward – *gulu* "not", *yamba* "maybe". Then there is *yanda,* which means that someone tried to accomplish something but didn't quite succeed – *bayi yara yanda baninyu* "man tried to come (but couldn't quite reach this place)".

By now Dicky Briggs had returned, and Robert Major and Barney Brooks arrived from the farms on which they worked during the week. I hopefully enquired about tea, but no one wanted to eat – just drink. The carton was gone in an hour and more was urgently required. It seemed to me that we'd all had quite enough – everyone was nicely drunk without having become dangerous or violent. Dicky Briggs didn't agree, and disappeared. When I asked George where Dicky had gone, he said he'd walked up the road to the phone kiosk to ask an Innisfail taxi-driver to bring out a load of beer. This was quite a normal procedure – the taxi charged nine dollars, plus the cost of the beer. Dicky was absolutely determined. There was no way I could let him give nine dollars to a taxi-driver when I had a car there – so I had to give in and drive down to the nearest pub, about fifteen miles away at Wangan. Three cartons was what they wanted – seventy-two stubbies – and a couple of bottles of sherry. I was beyond arguing.

The rest of the evening can be imagined. George wanted to do a bit more work, but that only lasted ten minutes. Then he suggested I put on a tape of corroboree music, of Jimmy Murray singing. We all enjoyed it, except that Robert Major insisted the singer was Davey Douglas from Lake Eacham, who he knew well and could recognise anywhere. I pointed out that I'd never met Davey Douglas. He might sing in the same style but this *was* in fact Jimmy Murray. I wasn't inclined to press the point, but George was, and the fight looked as if it might get a bit nasty. Dicky Briggs became worried, and he kept imploring George to send me off to "stay in a boarding house" (although where I'd have found one open at midnight I don't know).

Suddenly, everything was quiet. George decided that we should do some more work. He was not to be dissuaded, and so there we were, at one in the morning, talking about particles. The beer hadn't quite gone, but during the fight I'd picked up the last half dozen bottles and chucked them out of sight under the house. We went to bed at about two o'clock, George insisting that I take his mattress while he put a blanket on the floor. In truth I'd have preferred the floor, since the mattress was a bit dirty, a bit holey, rather smelly, and not a little lumpy. But I did sleep, fitfully, until the first hint of dawn, three hours later. Now, apparently, was the time to eat. George had a huge hunk of bread plastered with corned beef, but I couldn't face it. A couple of bottles of beer were found (not those I had hidden).

It was decided that a trip to Lake Eacham would be a good way of spending Saturday, and we were off as the sun peeped over the horizon. Wallabies were dancing all over the empty road, before turning in for the day.

The morning was crisp and beautiful as I drove slowly towards the tableland up the Palmerston Highway — said to be the road with the most bends in Australia. George was sitting in the cab, and he told stories about each clearing and creek — how and why they were named, where corroborees had been held when he was a boy, and so on. The rest were in the back (I had an open truck that year), and when we came into Millaa Millaa they banged hard on the cab roof. "They want some beer," explained George, and my heart sank. So, at seven on Saturday morning, Barney Brooks and Robert Major knocked on the back door of the Millaa Millaa Hotel and negotiated part of a wages cheque they had received the previous day for another two cartons of stubbies.

We had quite a good morning at Lake Eacham. I'd mentioned that I'd never tasted a scrub-turkey egg, and so everyone hunted around the lake for a fresh mound that might contain a ripe egg, leaving George and me to work on the bench outside the kiosk. More particles. *Mugu*, a fascinating word that indicates that it is impossible to avoid doing something that is, in fact, quite unsatisfactory. *Ngaja balam mugu jangganyu* "I had to eat that food — it was stale, but there was nothing else". *Ngaja bala mugu galgan* "I had to leave it behind — it was too heavy to carry." My notebook from that weekend contains material of very mixed quality. Most pages bear a notation at the top "GW drunk" or "me very tired" or both. Almost every point had to be checked over again when we were in better form.

Then Dicky suggested going to see the show put on for the tourist bus, at the Malanda jungle. We stopped off at a couple of pubs on the way (we stopped off at *every* pub we passed that day) and got there just as the Pioneer coach drew up. There were three elderly Aborigines — Paddy Moran, Robert English and Davey Douglas — with a young white man, Mr English, in charge. As the cameraed and sunglassed Americans and New South Welshmen got off the bus, Robert English threw his boomerang in a long, high curve. And it did fall back just by his feet. We walked along a path, past a row of trees planted in the thirties by the members of an Australian cricket team, including one by Don Bradman. As we sat on benches in a clearing in the patch of jungle, Mr English described the traditional weapons – spears, woomera, shield and the big heavy sword – to Paddy Moran's demonstration. Davey Douglas sang a couple of corroboree songs. And finally Paddy Moran climbed a tree *bumiranyu*-style, looping it with a lawyer-vine rope and then speeding up the trunk, tossing the rope out one step at a time above him. Our party sat on one of the side benches, chatting away in Dyirbal and chucking off at the performers. It was a good show.

I decided it was definitely time to go home. As we drove past the Millaa Millaa pub, there was again a furious thumping on the cab roof. I ignored it and drove straight through town, but the noise intensified. "You'll have to stop," said George, and I did, half a mile past the cheese factory. Robert Major announced that he wanted another drink, and that I wasn't going to stop him. I said he could do what he wanted, but I wasn't going in one more pub that day. So Robert got off and announced he'd find his way back himself. Later, as the rest of us were negotiating bend after bend on the Palmerston Highway, I said to George I supposed he'd be able to hitch a ride.

"No, Aborigines can't do that," George informed me. "White man can hitch all right, but an Aborigine might stand there all day, no one will pick him up."

"Why?" I wondered.

"That's just the way it is," George said.

We got back to the house and, thank goodness, George didn't insist on doing any more particles. We just sat around and chatted for an hour or two. I "discovered" the beer hidden under the house, and it was very welcome. "Good job we didn't have this last night," someone said, "I think maybe we drank too much then." We'd had a good day all round. They hadn't found a scrub-turkey egg, but when I came the next week Dicky produced one and fried it up – a meal for three or four men. I calculated that over the twenty-four hours, five of us had drunk 144 stubbies of beer and 2 bottles of sweet sherry, in addition to a couple of gallons consumed over the bar. (I'd had maybe 5 stubbies in all.) But then he wouldn't touch any booze for another week, George told me. When he drank he liked to do it properly, and then he'd need a rest.

I was completely exhausted, and at seven o'clock excused myself and made for a motel in Innisfail. The proprietor switched on the television and there was still an hour before close of play in the Test match in Perth. But all I really wanted was a shower and a long sleep.

The previous year I'd found, in an 1899 book called *Eaglehawk and Crow*, by the Reverend John Mathew, a short vocabulary from the "Walsh River" that was plainly Mbabaram. For "dog", Mathew had put down *tok(?)*, the question mark presumably meaning that, like me, he wondered if he had really been given a true Mbabaram form. Many of the words coincided with those I'd already got from Albert Bennett (and Mathew's transcription wasn't too bad), but there were a few new words.

I hadn't been able to get a message to Albert Bennett, and our vehicles met along the track half-way between Mrs McGrath's store and his house. Albert was off to spend the day with his friend, the old white man who lived in the last house on the road to Irvinebank. He wasn't keen to go back home, but I persuaded him to spend a few minutes with me there on the track. So we sat on the sand, the tape-recorder on the tailgate of Albert's ancient truck.

He hadn't got anything new to tell me, Albert began, as always. But then I produced the 1899 vocabulary, and that did interest him. I read out some of the familiar words first. "Yes, he's got that right," Albert complimented. Then some of the words we hadn't had before, and a number of them came back. It was a short step from that to asking new sentences — trying for tenses on verbs and cases on nouns. How to say "she hit me with a stick", "he cut the tree with an axe".

We had an hour and a half by the roadside. Albert's recall of Mbabaram seemed better than it had been in '67, and far in advance of that in '64. I arranged to make the long trip back to Petford again the following week, and then got as far as the sixth tape of Mbabaram — number 228 (they were all multiples of 38, the lucky Mbabaram number).

Mrs McGrath greeted me as a real old friend. She was writing something while we chatted, but didn't say what it was. A couple of days later, there I was written up under "Petford notes" in the *Cairns Post*. The paper's local correspondents sent in details of everyone going on

Fig. 11. Albert Bennett, last speaker of Mbabaram, outside Mrs McGrath's store at Petford. (1970)

holiday and every visitor to each hamlet. I was worth a whole column-inch! The news was sad overall, though. Bill McGrath had become very ill and had been shuttled back and forth to hospital in Mareeba until finally he was sent to Cairns. Doreen asked me to pop into the Base Hospital and see him. He remembered me, although he couldn't recall my name, and seemed glad of a visitor. He died a few weeks later.

I'd hoped to have quite a lot of time on this trip to investigate whether it would be worthwhile coming back the following year to start an intensive study of Yidin. But the work on Dyirbal and Mbabaram took longer than I had anticipated (as things often do), so that I had only one day spare. Jack and Nellie Stewart had both died, I was told. Yarrabah settlement, across the bay from Cairns, was where most of the Yidinyji tribe had been sent, and that was plainly the place to look.

Cape Grafton peninsula, on which Yarrabah is situated, is separated from the main coastal plain by the Murray Prior Range, which rises to 2,700 feet. Access had been only by sea, but a road was being built, and the manager said over the phone that I'd be all right in a four-wheel-drive vehicle. I just made it — though it took three tries to get up a slippery hill that the Main Roads people were trying to get into shape before the rains came and washed it all away again.

I had to look up the manager first (the name had been changed from superintendent when the 1897 Act had been replaced by one in the mid-sixties that was marginally less bad, but still about fifty years behind the rest of the world). He took me to see the chairman of the Aboriginal Council who suggested Dick Moses might be able to help.

Moses, as he called himself (the Dick seemed to be an appendage — he often said Moses Dick in place of Dick Moses when asked for his full name), was a quiet, white-haired old man. He was prepared to listen to me, but obviously wanted to consider carefully whether he would cooperate.

I had only one day available, and it was important to make as much headway as possible. To start with, I played Moses a short text in Mamu by George Watson, as an example of what I'd been doing, and of what I wanted. He didn't understand Mamu (which is why I picked a short text), but he could recognise some words, and George had also told the story in English. It was about a big turtle in the sea, who had a hot cooking stone placed in her stomach and then ran inland to warm the water at Innot Hot Springs. She then commanded that all the other big turtles should remain in the sea — only small tortoises would be allowed to live on the freshwater rivers.

I asked Moses if he knew any Yidin stories on that pattern. Yes, there was the tale of Damarri and Guyala, he said. They were Yidinyji creators, who made all the wild tucker and things. He obviously couldn't tell it off the top of his head, but I asked if he might think about it over lunch, and perhaps record the story for me that afternoon.

The rest of the morning we spent getting Yidin nouns — body parts, flora and fauna, parts of the environment, artefacts and so on — and then a few pronouns, and some verbs in simple sentences. Moses had chosen a spot on the beach, just a few yards from the water's edge, under a shady, long-leaved tree, its leaves a bit like a banana plant's. Moses sat with his legs crossed, heels tucked in behind the knees, while I alternately crouched and knelt and sat on the sand, and tried to write down correctly the long vowels, and the placement of stress.

Lunch was a great embarrassment. I'd brought a couple of sandwiches, but the manager took me up to his house, on the hillside, and I was given a meal of stewed steak and two vegetables while the rest of the family (including mother-in-law) just had salad. I could do little but eat it, and thank them.

After lunch, I didn't immediately press Moses for a text but went through a few adjectives for half an hour or so. Then I asked whether he could now tell the story of Damarri and Guyala. Another story should come first, Moses decided, about shells — olden-days money — and what happened to a messenger from the coast to the tableland who wouldn't surrender his consignment to three acquisitive bird-people. I switched on the recorder, and for five minutes Moses told the story in fluent Yidin, with no intrusion from English, against the sound of the sea lapping on the shore. I played it back while he nodded in agreement. And then Moses told it in English, following the pattern of the George Watson tape he'd heard.

He was, like George, a specialist raconteur, who told each story carefully and thoughtfully, in a rich, fairly formal prose style and with every point explained. Transcribing the text was no problem — it took about an hour to play it back phrase-by-phrase, with Moses repeating a phrase more slowly if needed. I wrote down the text in phonetic script and read out what I'd put to check if it was correct, noting the meaning of each bit. Towards the end, I remembered some of the words that had come before and could translate simple phrases before he did. Moses complimented me: "You know this language already!" I said it was because he was a good teacher.

Now we were ready for Damarri and Guyala. This was a longer story, twelve minutes, and the small crowd that had gathered around us during the afternoon listened appreciatively. We replayed it and then recorded the English version. By then, it was four o'clock, and I decided it would be pushing things too much to attempt any more transcription just then. That could be the first thing next year, for Dick Moses was now plainly keen for me to come back.

I think it was just about the most productive single day I've ever had, and certainly the most productive first day with anyone. Moses clearly had an unparallelled knowledge of Yidiny (I'd found it had a final palatal nasal, like Spanish ñ and Yidiny would be a better spelling than Yidin). He was intelligent, and a good, patient teacher with the gift of being able to explain things in a way I could understand. Certainly way up at the top, in the Chloe/George league. I was looking forward to next year.

A lot of linguistic expertise was gathered in the Aboriginal camp at Bellenden. After we'd got the grammar checking under control and I broached the subject of Jalnguy equivalents for adjectives, and some fairly obscure verbs, Chloe decided that she needed some help. So we walked the two hundred yards across from Edgar's house.

"Mind that long grass there!" Chloe made me jump. "Brown snake live there. I won't go that way — too much danger. This way here longer but more safe."

Jarrmay (Rosie Runaway) and I greeted each other like reunited cousins. She pulled up a block of wood and sat attentively, chin cupped in her hands, elbows on knees, waiting for us to begin. Spider Henry, his wife Ida, and a couple more old ladies were there, too: a real committee on Jalnguy, much like the one we'd had at Murray Upper three years earlier. Some of the words needed a lot of thought and discussion — it could be fifteen minutes before a consensus emerged as to the most appropriate Jalnguy correspondent. *Jami* "fat", that would by *nyunjan* in Jalnguy. What about *manyjay* "full up"? Several ideas were half-advanced until Rosie cried out *"wungun"*. Of course, everyone smiled at each other, that was it.

Joe Kinjun appeared, fleetingly. He wondered what I was doing there at the Bellenden camp, why I couldn't be satisfied with talking just to him, as all the other white people were. But Joe knew no Jalnguy at all and he soon left, to ribald comments from the others. Mrs Henry said later she'd heard he'd been down and that must have been a great help — he was so much more articulate than the others, wasn't he? She wasn't at all pleased with my answer.

"Oh, anything the others know I'm sure Joe would know too," Mrs Henry insisted.

But Chloe supported me — "That Kinjun he doesn't know one word of Jalnguy" — and Gladys had to accept it, reluctantly.

A pattern of work was established. When I was at Bellenden, we'd do an hour or so on grammar in Gladys's garden, and then walk down to the camp for a bit more Jalnguy. One man there knew more than anyone, Chloe said. That was Tommy Springcart, Jumbulu, who'd been initiator of the last cannibalism in 1940, the story George had recounted on Palm Island (which I had to pretend I didn't really know anything about). He'd spent a good few years in jail and had then lived on Palm Island or worked on a cattle station out west. Jumbulu made periodic visits back to the Murray, but I'd never managed to catch up with him before.

There was dirty business afoot, Chloe told me. A young Jirrbalngan fellow had recently been found dead near Mount Garnet. The police didn't know how it happened, but the Aborigines did — a sharp blow in *rudu,* the hollow at the back of the neck (the same kind of blow that had been used on Mick Bulbu, in 1940). Accusations and counter-accusations had been flying, and several young men were going around in fear of their lives.

Jumbulu was very much mixed up in this (I never got all of the details clear) and was away on some wizardry during the first Bellenden session on Jalnguy. But the second time he was there, Chloe whispered, in that small hut over there. I should go over and talk to him to see if he'd join us. Jumbulu didn't emerge from his hut when I introduced myself and wasn't interested in a cigarette. "No," he couldn't come.

But then when we started, discussing the Jalnguy equivalents of *yurjun* "slip down" and *bilbanyu* "grow up", he could hear what we were saying and became interested. Jumbulu came out and started talking to me while the others were busy thinking. He was Warungu, he said, not from here at all — which was a lie. He may have been trying to test me in some way, but after I'd pointed — tangentially — to a number of inconsistencies in what he'd been saying, and noted his very slight knowledge of the Warungu language, the pretence was suddenly dropped. We became the best of friends, and from then on he cooperated fully and frankly.

We had three or four really good sessions when Jumbulu joined the committee. He'd sit on a log while we were talking, weaving long eel-catching baskets, *yinggar,* for Mrs Henry to sell in her little shop. He truly was a Gubi — Jumbulu probably had the deepest knowledge of anyone I worked with in North Queensland — and was highly intelligent, with a knack for explanation. Jumbulu put up a front of stupidity to white people in general (I think I was the first white fellow he'd ever really talked to), as a convenience. The local whites tended to dismiss him as a pretty useless old man.

Jumbulu wanted to know when I was going down to Townsville. Not till the end of the week, but I'd be glad to give him a lift then. He accepted, but meanwhile wanted me to run an errand for him. When I went into Euramo to get a couple of loaves of bread for Chloe, could I also fetch him some groceries? Sure. Jumbulu dictated the shopping list. It was a lot of items, running to twenty dollars in all. The store-keeper seemed a bit doubtful about booking up so much to Tommy Springcart, but I stood by him — he'd shown me his savings bank passbook and it had over a hundred dollars in. All right then — I was given the goods. We just about made out all the items. I had down "Wolbrook sauce" and that would be Holbrook's Worcester Sauce. And "Golden eye tea" — it could surely only be Goldenia tea.

Jumbulu accepted the groceries and thanked me. He began stuffing them into a gunny sack. During the night he slipped away, unseen, without a word to anyone. Chloe told me he feared for his life. A bone — a pointing-bone — had been put on his bed, and if he hadn't seen it before lying down it would have been the end of him. So he'd got out, quick.

I never had the privilege of meeting Jumbulu again. He came back to the Murray a couple of years later and died there about 1976. He was buried in the old cemetery at Warrami. I never had the nerve to ask whether the Euramo storekeeper got his money, but I'd be rather surprised if he had.

George Watson wanted a lift to Townsville on his way to spend Christmas with his daughter on Palm Island. I arrived at Palmerston early in the morning, hoping to do a day's work — some more Jalnguy — before we drove down to Murray Upper for the night. But George had been drinking the previous night, and again since the crack of dawn. I saw little point in writing down a lot of half-thought stuff, so I suggested we drive off at once, to the Murray. As we travelled, George insisted that he could work just as well when drunk as when sober. He'd proved to me he could. I said no, he couldn't. And I quoted an example — the simple answer he'd given to one question I'd put to him when he was drunk and the detailed, thoughtful reply he'd given to the same question when his mind was functioning more clearly. Oh, said George. Then he said he didn't know why I kept on asking all these questions anyway — a bit of this and a little of that. What I needed was stories,

stories and more stories. That was the language straight-out. Not questions about odd words and sentences. True to this precept, he began again to tell the tale of Gijiya and the origin of death. Until he fell asleep, before getting to the death bit.

George intended to camp the night at the house next to Warrami, lorded over by old Lorna. They didn't seem particularly pleased to see him (he was reasonably sober by this time), but could scarcely say no. Jimmy Murray had died since my last trip, but Mary Ann was still around — she lived on for another decade, quite senile. Tommy Warren, the expensive old hermaphrodite, had moved to Warrami when the old mission buildings were taken away. He gave George — and me — a hearty welcome.

Tommy had grown fatter and fatter. He was now so corpulent that he couldn't stand up, but just sat in his little hut — open at two sides — poking the fire and listening to a transistor radio. If he needed to go to the toilet, Tommy just crawled away a short distance, with his little shovel. He couldn't get in a normal car and it was a tough job, requiring several men, to manoeuvre Tommy into the back of a ute.

But he seemed happy enough, sitting there in a pair of shorts not done up at the top — his belly was too wide — and a shirt flapping over his ample breasts. Tommy crawled outside to talk to us. I was now on to onomatopoeia. Speakers of Dyirbal have institutionalised versions of each bird call (just like our *miaow,* only on a much larger scale). Some calls are like the name of the bird — *balan bubunba* "pheasant" says *"bu-bu-bu-bu"* and *balan jiwunyu* "pink-chested kingfisher" goes *"jiwu jiwu jiwu".* But others are quite different — *balan windan* "yellow mountain-bird" calls out *"jaru-jan-jan"* and *bayi gayambula* "white cockatoo" has a cry *"gurrunggarra gurrunggarra".* I was going through all the birds, asking for imitations of their cries and the verb that would be used to describe the call. Tommy found this great fun. His high-pitched, girlish laugh punctuated George's careful descriptions and uncanny imitations. I asked how *bingay* (a kind of ibis) sounded.

"He was calling out just now over in that tree." Tommy shouted up to where the bird had been: "Hey, you, sing out again then this fellow catch you" and dissolved once more in a shrill explosion of mirth.

The following morning, as we drove through Ingham, George was singing a Burran-style song to himself: *jaburr banda burul, bunggugu, jinbi yagundayi, nayili.* There was a few minutes silence and a chat. And then he started on a quite different tune. *I'm thinking of you tonight, old pal. Wishing that you were near. I'm dreaming of the time, and the days gone by, when you filled my heart with cheer* ... It seemed vaguely familiar.

"Who's that by, George?"

"That's a Jimmy Rodgers song, Robert."

"Not Jimmy Rodgers, the American singer who made a lot of records in the thirties?"

"That's the one. I had more than twenty of his records. Bought them in Townsville. Used to play them on my gramophone over on Palm. Then I went away to the mainland to work on a farm for six months and left my brother to look after them. When I got back, they were all broken."

I'd picked up a few second-hand seventy-eights by Jimmy Rodgers that year and my particular favourite was *Gambling Polka Dot Blues*. Did George know this? He sang it through for me, from beginning to end. *I thought a was a gambler, broke every shark in town. Until I met a rounder, who called all I put down* ... George recreated every vocal nuance from the original record, although it must have been all of thirty years since he had last heard it. *And lost my money like a man. I've got them Polky Dot Blue-ee* – a rippling blue yodel – *Blues, oh them Polka Dot Blues*.

I asked a few more questions. Did he have any records by other American artists, such as the Carter Family? Yes, one or two, but he didn't like them as much as Jimmy Rodgers. What about Gene Autry? No, bought one once but didn't like him at all. George wished he could hear Jimmy Rodgers again. Were any of his records available? Certainly, and I'd send one up. There was an LP, *The Best of the Legendary Jimmy Rodgers*, with lots of George's old favourites on. I sent it a few months later, addressed to George care of Mr Gaynor. Mr Gaynor didn't in fact pass the parcel on to George for six months (!). He told me he knew George would want to play it on the Gaynor's record player and he waited until he'd got it fixed. But George eventually got to hear his old favourites again, and he said he did enjoy them.

In Townsville, we had to go first to the Department of Aboriginal and Island Affairs Hostel, to obtain permission to catch the plane across to Palm. A sordid place, dirty, with the people lying around with bottles of wine and metho. The white manager asked me what I was doing there. It was doubtful if George could get across to Palm that day – everyone was going there for Christmas – but he should be all right in the morning. He could stay the night. On a metal bed base (someone had taken the mattress), or on the concrete floor. George said he'd be all right. But I bought him a six-pack of stubbies before catching my plane to Canberra. I reckoned he'd need them there.

10

"This way be bit more better"

Revising the grammar section of my thesis for publication took up most of 1971. I rewrote every section, to improve the explanations, generalisations and exemplification. (The semantics part had already been summarised in a long article so a complete discussion of that was postponed until I had time to finish a cross-dialectal dictionary of Dyirbal, which would give me more data on Jalnguy correspondences.) A few grammatical points still needed checking, but I sent the typescript to Cambridge University Press in September, organising it in such a way that bits could be expunged, added or changed at the end of a paragraph, if necessary, after I had done a final check in the field.

We left Canberra in late November, planning a nine-week field trip over the summer vacation. There was a small tent, borrowed from the Department of Geography, for Alison and me to sleep in, and our station wagon — with the back seat folded forward — should do for the kids. Eelsha was now seven, Fergus five and Rowena four. Leaving home before dawn, we made good time, covering the five hundred odd miles to Moree in northern New South Wales by four in the afternoon.

About fifteen miles beyond Moree, we heard a big bang under the bonnet and then another one. Inspection revealed an egg-shaped hole in the side of the engine, with oil pouring out. I caught a lift back into Moree with a lorry, and when I told my story at the garage they laughed. "You don't need a repairer's," they said, "you need a new-car showroom!" But we got it towed back, and the local Repco agent had a reconditioned engine. (They told me what had gone wrong with the old one: a piston, instead of moving up and down, had started going from side to side!) Unfortunately, it was Friday night and the job would not be finished until Monday. With no car to camp in, we spent three nights in the Moree motel; not a very encouraging beginning to the trip.

The town had a swimming pool and a spa with hot mineral springs, heavy with sulphur, so that was something to do. We were told that a few years back, there had been a big furore because Aborigines were banned from the hot pools. That had been settled, though with a lot of acrimony, and all the pools were now open to everyone.

Trying to make the best of things, I went to the police station and enquired if there might be anyone who remembered Kamilaroi, the original language of that region. They gave me a couple of names down at the Aboriginal settlement, way over beyond the other side of town. There was only one way to get there — to walk. It was three miles of dusty track, and just as I turned in the gate — hot and sweaty — a police car drove up. I remembered Stephen Wurm's advice: never let the policeman take you out to the settlement or you'll be viewed with suspicion. Just my luck. The policeman greeted me and the Aborigines looked on thoughtfully.

"Hey, they think I had a cushy ride out with you. When I've just walked all the way from town," I called back.

"You tell them," said the policeman.

Nobody actually used Kamilaroi any more, but I was able, by going back two or three times, to record almost a hundred words that had been remembered by Tom Binge at the settlement and Charlie White in the hospital. It was something. The phonetics of the words were clear, which could be a help in explicating some of the fuller materials on Kamilaroi taken down by missionaries in the last century. The following year, one of my students, Peter Austin, did more work around Moree and then in 1976 another student, Corinne Williams, did an honours sub-thesis on the Yuwaaliyaay dialect of Kamilaroi, at Walgett and Lightning Ridge. Peter and Corinne were able to rescue all that was left of this important language.

We got to Murray Upper without further incident. It was good to be at Warrami again, but also sad. Lindsay had died quite suddenly the previous April (aged sixty-four). Still, Mrs Cowan gave us a warm welcome. It was the first time Alison had been there since 1964, and the Cowans had never met Fergus and Rowena. Eelsha was taken for a ride round the yard on a horse and we inspected the new banana shed and the melon field.

First of all, I had to check the few outstanding points in the grammar of Dyirbal, and for this only the keen minds of Chloe and George would do. Chloe was living up at Silkwood (half-way between Tully and Innisfail) with her granddaughter Eunice and her husband; Mamie and Edgar were also nearby. She was her usual ebullient, extrovert, plain-spoken self. Alison had brought a dress for her.

' Oh, that's nice. I like a print, pretty colours. I wonder if it'll fit me," said Chloe, holding it up against herself. "Oh no, what a shame, it's too small in the waist, no good at all."

When we went back next day, Chloe said Eunice had told her off for being so ungrateful after Alison had gone to all that bother. We said it was all right. That was just Chloe.

We rented a caravan at nearby Kurrimine Beach for a few days.

'I'm not as young as I was," warned Chloe. "Shan't be able to work all day, like we used to. Just half a day, maybe."

That was fine, I said, I'd go and see George in the afternoons.

"I don't know if he be any good, that old man," expounded Chloe, getting into her gossip-monger stride. "He just drink all the time since his wife die. Drink himself silly. I don't think he be any good to you. Not able to think from the drink."

I found George living in the same house with its big hole in the middle of the floor, quite sober, bright as ever, and perfectly able to work all day and half the night if need be. He was now retired, but still did a few odd jobs for George Gaynor. I double-checked the grammar with both Chloe and George, and on returning to Canberra sent nine pages of alterations to the sub-editor in Cambridge, catching the book just before it went off to the printer.

We chatted about old times over lunch with Chloe — what her children and grandchildren were doing — the terrible things that were happening in the world. Then, the last day, George came to spend the night at Kurrimine Beach. He insisted that we talk in Mamu, which was a good thing. Did Alison have time to learn much of the language? he asked. I tried to say she was kept pretty busy with the children, and used the adjective *burrun* "busy" together with *nyalngga* "children". George knew what I meant, but that wasn't quite how you said it. There was a single word in Mamu, *wayngu,* that meant, simply, "busy with the children". Beautiful. This was something I'd never have obtained in a thousand years through asking questions; there was no substitute for actually *using* a language, and studying it that way.

We thought we'd have a bit of a holiday and see a few new places before the rains came, and then settle down to serious work on Yidiny. First we visited the caves at Chillagoe — splendid grottoes with their stalactites and stalagmites now lit up by a string of electric bulbs. There were two pubs in Chillagoe: the one by the station served Aborigines, but its beer tended to be a bit warm; the other one was better, but people with dark skins were not welcomed. I had a drink there, in error, and I could see why Aborigines avoided it. One fancy stockman, in town to wet his whistle, declared that there should be an open season on Boongs, just like on ducks.

"You mean that you could shoot any Aborigine you could find between such a day and such a day?" someone asked.

"Yes," came the reply, "except that I'd have an opening date but no closing date."

On the way to Chillagoe, I stopped off to see Albert Bennett, for what turned out to be the last time. We got a few more words and put some of the old ones into new sorts of sentences. I'd gone about as far as I could with Mbabaram by then and had case forms for almost all the nouns, and tenses for the verbs, and a vocabulary of about two hundred and fifty words all told, which we had put together in sentences in most possible ways.

The work on Mbabaram had just been completed in time. My 1972 Christmas card brought a letter from Doreen McGrath:

C/- P.O., Petford
30.12.72

Dear Robert,

I must apologise for not writing to you earlier about Albert. I intended to but only realised I hadn't when I saw your card to him. I opened it of course and would like to keep it. It is a nice picture.

Albert passed away in July. Very sudden. He came up to the shop on the Saturday afternoon and got a few things. Was well and in good spirits. On Tuesday he didn't turn up for his bread and meat so I asked Sharron if she would look after the shop while I went down to see why he hadn't come up. Just as I was about ready to go, my son Bill came home unexpectedly and insisted on going instead of me.

He found Albie dead in his bed. Bill said he'd torn his trousers away from his tummy as the pain must have been there. Bill thought he'd only been dead a day or a day and a half but a postmorten showed he died Saturday night, not long after he came up for the order. Heart failure.

He was buried a couple of days later in Mareeba and it would have done your heart good (an Aussie saying) to have been at his funeral. There were sixteen cars, several families to each car, proportion being half black and half white. Of the whites attending, one was a pensioner, the rest of us representing families of substance all with businesses, properties, etc.

The Church of England minister officiated and gave one of the best and most moving services I have ever attended. Particularly as he knew "he was only an old blackfellow" by most people's standards . . .

The other place we'd always been meaning to visit — but had never quite got to — was Cooktown. It was a dirt road all the way from Mareeba, and some caution was needed. There'd been a bit of rain in some of the creeks, so we followed the safe course of disconnecting the fan belt before fording the worst ones, and then tightening it up again on the other side. That way the fan couldn't spray water all over the engine.

Cooktown was, of course, named after the famous explorer, who had been forced to spend six weeks on shore repairing the *Endeavour* after its encounters with the reef. He recorded a bit of Guugu Yimidhirr, including the word *kangaroo*. During the mining boom a hundred miles inland, in the 1870s, a town of 10,000 people had grown up at the mouth of the Endeavour River. Now there were only 500 there. A couple of fine old brick buildings survived. The Catholic Girls' School was now a useful museum, its collection covering both the town and its Aborigines, and the old bank building was still used for its original purpose. The bank must once have had a staff of dozens, but now the sole teller for the Bank of New South Wales had all the room he needed. Withdrawals were done at one counter, deposits at another, foreign business over there, and loans at this desk in the window. And he had the whole of the upper floor to live in.

The streets were wide and underused. There was a baker's shop, then a couple of empty lots, then a house, and some more empty space, and so on. But it has a beautiful, relaxed, tropical atmosphere. A few retired people, a bunch of hippies (it was hard for the single policeman to check all the places one might grow marijuana), a couple of good cafes. And lots of sandflies and mosquitoes! We camped at a caravan park on the beach where we were savagely bitten.

We met up with the Havilands in Cooktown. I'd known John Haviland at Harvard and then, when he got a NATO Fellowship, he persuaded NATO that the only place he could study the sort of linguistics he wanted was Canberra. This was at least partly because John and Leslie (an anthropologist), and daughter Sophie, fancied a trip around the world. He had planned just to work on the linguistic material he'd gathered in Mexico on Tzotzil, a Mayan language, but when everyone else started going off for a summer of field work, John and Leslie decided to do a bit themselves.

I'd suggested they study Guugu Yimidhirr, spoken around Cooktown, since they could drive there from Canberra, and it was in urgent need of professional linguistic attention. John had obtained the necessary permission from Brisbane, so the morning after we arrived, he drove the twenty miles out to the Lutheran Mission at Hopevale to introduce himself, and I went along for the trip. There'd been intelligent and sympathetic German missionaries at Hopevale — notably Pastor Schwarz, who had begun in 1887, at the age of 19, and had spoken the language fluently. As a result, quite a lot of traditional culture survived, and the language was still actively spoken by most of the community.

We had to go through the usual bureaucratic routine, waiting around in the office until the mission superintendent had time to say "G'day" to us. (John had been making a sociolinguistic study of the way in which "Good day" was pronounced in Australian English. Some migrants overemphasised the reduction, he decided, but by careful study John thought he'd got it just about right.) Then we had to see a Ph.D. student in anthropology, in her caravan, and one of the school-teachers who had worked a bit on the language. All this before we could actually get to talk to the Aborigines themselves! The school-teacher mentioned that, unlike some other languges of the area, Guugu Yimidhirr had dental sounds, made by putting the tongue against both top and bottom teeth, *dh* and *nh*.

"I know," I said.

"How?" enquired John.

"I was listening to the girls talk, back in the office, while you were with the superintendent."

Although he has a regular WASP pedigree, John Haviland is dark-complexioned and wears a moustache. In Mexico, people thought he was a dago, and at Hopevale they were convinced he was a half-caste. This may have been quite useful, but he didn't really need that sort of assistance: John is a natural language-learner — quite in the Ken Hale class. His fame soon spread over the North, and down at Yarrabah I was asked if I'd heard of the linguist up at Hopevale who lived with the people and spoke their language fluently. He played good country music on the fiddle and even translated some standard songs into Guugu Yimidhirr, to everyone's great delight.

It was agreed that all the Havilands could move out to Hopevale as soon as they wanted. But before they did that, and we made our way back to Cairns, John and I visited the small Aboriginal Reserve in Cooktown itself — a dozen prefabricated huts on a hillside overlooking the town. It was a useful afternoon, for we recorded material in three languages, each of which was down to its last few speakers: Mary Ann Mundy had a good command of the Flinders Island language, off the coast to the north; Joe Musgrave told us a bit about Gugu-Daiban; and Bobby Kenny knew a little Gugu-Warra, about eighty words of which we got down, though they were hard to transcribe because of the sequences of unusual vowels. Bobby had broken his upper arm sometime in the past and it had never been properly set. The two parts had mended together at right-angles, giving him two elbows and a three-dimensional limb.

A little piglet kept running between our legs, rooting into the tape recorder and squeaking wildly. One of the participants talked to it as if it were a baby, so we scarcely liked to kick it away. John told me that when he went back four months later, the pig was full-grown and an even worse menace, but its owner still addressed it with endearments that would have been more appropriate to a child, or a fluffy little kitten, or a lover.

Cooktown is in fact the pig centre of Australia. Captain Cook had released a couple in 1770 — for food in case he or anyone else should return — and they had quickly bred and spread. In the immediate vicinity of Cooktown, there are the most powerful wild boars with long tusks, which can be really dangerous. The further one travels, the less dense and less fierce the pig population gets. They are occasionally seen around Murray Upper, but I never heard of one hurting anyone down there.

Our recording was almost complete when a woman sitting on the concrete step outside one of the huts started a long, mournful lament. She'd just come back home and been told that an uncle had died. As soon as she had time, she'd sat down to sing, to wail, as a way of expressing her sorrow. It was a profoundly moving song, laden with grief, and it was likely to continue for several hours.

Cooktown was on the rim of white civilisation; to the north, were no hardtop roads, no towns. Aboriginal people here had been less swamped by western ways than those on the Atherton Tableland, or even at Murray Upper. There was something at once incredibly ancient, but at the same time strong and vibrant, about the funeral dirge that echoed around us, growing all the time more intense and more abandoned, as we drove away, back into town.

Yarrabah was something between Hopevale, with its healthy, open bicultural aspect, and the prison-camp atmosphere of Palm Island. There were fewer rules and less regimentation at Yarrabah than at Palm, but the same dead feeling. Aboriginal culture had been almost destroyed; and there was nothing to take its place.

It had been founded as a Church of England mission by the Reverend J. B. Gribble, who had had similar establishments in New South Wales and then in Western Australia (he had been literally hounded out of the latter state, for speaking too plainly about mistreatment of Aborigines.) Six months after founding Yarrabah, in 1892, he had been taken ill and was succeeded by his son, E. R. B. Gribble. The younger Gribble had no real understanding of, or sympathy for, Aboriginal life. The extent of his ignorance is revealed by a word list Gribble completed for an amateur anthropological journal in 1897. For "to live" he gave *gobo* which is actually "leaf", and for "to know" Gribble wrote down *gnudju*. Surely he should have been able to recognise that *nguju* is "no", one of the commonest and most important words in Yidiny.

Yarrabah had a more homogeneous tribal population than Palm Island. I reckoned that of the thousand or so people there in 1971, about a third were Gungganyji (from the Cape Grafton peninsula where Yarrabah was situated), about a third were Yidinyji (from the Cairns and Mulgrave River area), and the remainder were a mixture of tribes from other parts of Queensland. The early missionaries had been very strong on the "dormitory system", whereby young boys and girls were separated from their parents and actively discouraged from learning tribal skills and from speaking their own language. When I began work, there were just two people at the settlement who knew much Yidiny – Dick Moses and Richard Hyde. And Gunggay, the dialect of Yarrabah itself, was gone. The last speaker had died a few years back, and no one now at Yarrabah remembered more than twenty words of Gunggay.

The Queensland government took over from the church in about 1960, with the provision that the only minister allowed would be Anglican. (Palm Island had three — a Catholic, an Anglican, and someone who represented a medley of the free churches.) Attendance at the Sunday services had for many years been compulsory, but this was dropped when the state took over, and a good Sunday now might see twenty people in church. It was plain that although the traditional beliefs and religion had been forcibly suppressed, they had been replaced by nothing.

Yarrabah seemed to be a more relaxed place than Palm Island, but it took only a short while for us to realise that some of the big-brother-ness was still there, under the surface. Let me quote one example. One of the white schoolteachers missed a period and called in at the settlement hospital for a pregnancy test. When the result came in — positive — it was communicated first to the manager, although he had no authority over the school, before the girl herself was informed. This was a personal matter, over which the hospital should have maintained confidentiality. But not at a Queensland Aboriginal settlement. The hospital had simply been told by Brisbane to communicate such matters to the manager. And they had to do so.

I didn't expect that our whole family could immediately descend on Yarrabah, so we rented a flat in Cairns for a few weeks. Alison drove me across to Yarrabah (an hour's run, over the mountains) for half the week; the other half I worked on the materials I'd gathered, back in Cairns.

The manager who had provided such a kind, but embarrassing, lunch the previous year had been moved on. His replacement, Joe Rogers, was really pleasant and helpful to me. He was somewhat taken aback when I arrived at the office, for Brisbane had written introducing "Professor Dixon", and Joe had expected a rather elderly gentleman! He showed me a one-room bachelor flat down by the creek and said that he'd arranged for me to take meals with the elderly Anglican pastor and his wife, thinking we'd be much of an age! But that suited me, for I'd have all the more time for linguistic work if I didn't have to worry about shopping and cooking. And in fact Father and Mrs Brown were most charming and gracious hosts.

Father Brown was eighty-two. He'd got married for the first time just four years before, perhaps because he was feeling a little lonely. Father Brown (I never found out his full name) was an Englishman who had come out to Australia in about 1930, disappointed at not getting a post he'd set his heart on back home. He had joined the Bush Brotherhood, a group of Anglicans dedicated to taking the church into outback regions (and this involved a vow of celibacy). Father Brown told me how they used to travel through the far west of Queensland, in a Model T Ford, at sixteen miles an hour.

"And if we got a really flat, straight stretch we would go at eighteen miles an hour. We thought that was quite something!"

He'd been superintendent of Yarrabah from 1939 until 1949. Now, irked by retirement, he'd been allowed by the Bishop to return to Yarrabah as pastor.

Father Brown was a kind and feeling person, but he lived in his own world. He'd conduct services each morning and evening, every day of the week. When I made the mistake of asking if he'd had a good service, if many people had attended, I received a gentle reprimand.

"I have an obligation to the church to conduct services twice each day, and if anyone wants to come then that's their business."

He had an impressive theological library from which Mrs Brown would read to him, each morning and evening.

Neither Father Brown nor any of the other missionaries had ever learnt to speak Yidiny or Gunggay, or taken any interest in Aboriginal ideas and values. What a contrast with Pastor Schwarz at Hopevale! Father Brown told a story about Schwarz. During the last war, he said, he was in Cairns on some business that took him to the police station. There he saw a familiar face behind the bars of a cell. It was seventy-four-year-old Pastor Schwarz. He'd never got around to applying for naturalisation and so, despite the fact that he'd been running the mission at Hopevale for no less than fifty-five years, he was now to be interned as an enemy alien! A crazy example of blind bureaucracy. (After the war, Schwarz returned to live in Cooktown, but he was never permitted to return to the mission he had spent his life building up.)

Although there were no official restrictions on white people going into Aborigines' houses, or vice versa, Yarrabah was, like Palm Island, effectively split into two halves, black and white. On one side of the central town square were streets of Aboriginal houses, and on the other were administrative offices, the hall, school, hospital and some larger houses, almost all of which were reserved for such people as schoolteachers, the storekeeper, the white policeman, the pastor, and administrators. Just a few housed Aboriginal families.

The manager's house was in the best position of all, high up on the edge of the range that rose sharply just behind the settlement. Its site turned out to be a mixed blessing when television came to Cairns – it was the only spot where you *couldn't* get good reception.

I'd sent Dick Moses a card saying how much I was looking forward to renewing our brief acquaintance, and he was waiting for me. He had chosen a tree, a large shady fig, a bit further from the sea than the one last year, and we settled down under its shade, Dick cross-legged, heels under knees, chewing on his pipe. With George and Chloe, we'd usually had a table or chair or something to sit on. But for the next four years, I sat on the ground with Dick Moses. It took some getting used to – I'd stretch out, leaning over the notebook, for half an hour, and then sit up with it on my knees for a while. Moses never varied his position, except to take one heel out from under and place the other one there instead.

He was keen to get straight down to business. The first thing, of course, was to transcribe the story of Damarri and Guyala, which we'd recorded last year. This was the most important story for the Yidinyji

Fig. 12. Dick Moses (Yidiny) at Yarrabah. (1972)

people, Moses told me, since it explained their way of life and their social organisation — where everything came from. Whereas the Jirrbal have four sections, Yidinyji have just two moieties — Gurrabana and Gurraminya. Each person must marry someone from the opposite moiety, and children belong to "the same side" as their father. Guyala and Damarri began the moieties, Moses explained. Guyala was the sensible brother, and Gurraminya belonged to him. This is the moiety associated with the dry season when flesh food can easily be procured. *Minya* means "edible animal"; *gurra* appears to have no meaning outside the two moiety names. Damarri, the silly brother, began the Gurrabana moiety which is associated with the wet season (*bana* "water"), when food is scarce and life is harder.

In the legend, Damarri and Guyala travelled from the north into what is now Yidinyji territory, encountering a group of people who offered them hospitality. The two brothers planned to run off in the middle of the night with two women from that camp, but when they attempted to do so, the women screamed out, "No, leave us, we belong to those people."

The brothers dragged them away: "No, you belong to us now, we'll fight over you and be your guardians."

Guyala took both women. When Damarri asked for his, Guyala promised him one by-and-by, when they reached their camp. But, despite this avowal, "he never give him one," Moses maintained.

People in that country were hungry, since there was little flesh food. The brothers set out to provide them with vegetable foods. Guyala, the helpful brother, demonstrated one type of root: "Just soak this for a short time and it will be ready to eat."

But Damarri, the contrary fellow, disagreed. "No, it must be soaked all day to get rid of the sour taste."

Damarri finally wore down his brother in a long argument about the vegetable, and to this day it requires lengthy leaching before it can be eaten.

Next they turned to yams. Guyala wanted to place the yams just below the surface of the soil, so that they could be harvested by just pulling on the vine, but Damarri insisted the yams should be sunk way down in the ground, so that they could only be obtained by hard digging, with a yamstick. Again an argument ensued, and again Damarri won — the *jimirr* yam is today found a long way down. Next they made traps — holes in the ground, covered with bushes, into which animals would fall. And nets, for turkeys.

Guyala began to name places. Damarri suggested that just a few names would suffice, well spread out, but Guyala maintained that there must be many names, one for each place along a route, so that people would remember the sequence of places along a path, and the name for each, and would not get lost. This time, Guyala won – there is a name for every corner and clearing, and one named place can usually be seen from the next.

Next Damarri took *mundimay,* a long vine, and *badil,* rickety nuts, and made them very bitter so that they would require lengthy preparation before being eaten. But Guyala arranged *gubuum,* black pine nuts, so that very little needed to be done to them. Again Damarri argued the necessity of lengthy soaking and roasting, but Guyala overruled him and *gubuum* can either be cooked or eaten almost raw, after just a few minutes' roasting and soaking.

The two men had to fight an inland group, which they arranged to do the following morning. Guyala said he would wake his brother at first light, then they could reach the fighting ground on time. When he looked for him, Damarri was gone, and Guyala thought he must have gone on ahead to the agreed location. But Damarri had walked in a different direction, gone on until he found *danba,* the Bougainvillea tree, with sharp prickles. He'd run up against the tree, impacting on the prickles so that he got what looked like spear wounds.

When Damarri eventually turned up at the fighting ground, Guyala asked where he had been. "Here, at the side, fighting with you. Look at all these wounds!" Damarri pretended. But Guyala knew, despite all his brother's protestations, that he had not been there.

Finally Guyala took the boat and returned to the north, from whence they had come. Damarri was left by himself. He crossed a river and then followed a smaller creek. But when he tried to cross this, an alligator bit off one leg. He crawled on, on one leg, to a place called Yagaljida, near the present site of Yarrabah. And died there.

It was a long and powerful story, that took most of the day to transcribe. As usual, a group had gathered around us as we worked, listening while the tape was replayed and nodding as Moses explained each point and corrected my pronunciation. "That's a terrific story," I commented. And Moses said "Yes."

I was totally organised in working on Yidiny (unlike the situation with Dyirbal, where in the early days I seemed to change systems each month). Each notebook bore an identifying letter — A was texts, B questions to ask, C the answers obtained, D vocabulary arranged by semantic fields, E a draft grammar, F more texts, G more responses, and so on. Each numbered page bore the date, and the initials of the informant I was working with. Everything was cross-referenced so, for example, when I came to work on relative clauses, cumulative notes indicated that there were interesting examples on pages B25, C42, C55 and F41, and it was a matter of moments to turn these up.

Perhaps most important of all, I had from the start put vocabulary items onto six-by-four-inch cards. Before leaving Canberra, I'd made out cards for all the words obtained from Dick Moses the previous year, from Alec Morgan in '67, and from Jack and Nellie Stewart in '63. Ken Hale had also passed on to me the couple of hundred words he'd recorded at Yarrabah in 1961. I had sorted these into semantic sets to go through systematically with Moses.

We'd do reptiles one day. I'd warn Moses the night before, and he'd have a score or more species to name, some of which I would already have cards for, but others of which would be new. Then if I had any names he hadn't mentioned, I'd ask him about those. We'd take it slowly and he'd gradually recall a few more. And the next day he might add another one or two. Over a period of several weeks, we covered the entire class of nouns — body parts, kin terms, marsupials, birds, fishes, insects, terms for celestial objects, weather, parts of the environment, artefacts, trees and grasses, noises, and various abstract nouns. After each set of cards had been dealt with, I entered them on a left-hand page in Book D, with a column ruled out for the Jalnguy equivalents. The right-hand page was left blank for any further words of this semantic type that might come to light later on. Book D eventually contained all the words I had collected, arranged semantically. I couldn't resist labelling it a "semanticon" (out of lexicon, by way of phonicon).

For each noun, we'd get a couple of sentences describing some important characteristic. Often Moses would volunteer these, after he got the hang of what I wanted (and that took no time at all), or else I would set him off by asking, "What does a grey frog, *yalburr*, eat?" or something similar. Moses seemed to know almost everything there was to know about every species of living thing (he very rarely had to say "I don't know.") *Yalburr* like to eat cockroaches *jiyarrjiyarr (yalbuudu jiyarrjiyarr bugang)*. The big black goanna, *gugar* (same name as in

Dyirbal) will eat *minya bulu,* stinking meat. And curlews like snails.

After each semantic field had been exhausted, the cards were filed away alphabetically, in wooden boxes. Information on a card could be simply cross-referenced by putting the head word within square brackets. There were interesting relative clauses on the [*manil*] , [*guny-jin*] and [*yangar*] cards for instance, and it was an easy matter to locate these.

So I was building up a reasonable dictionary entry for each word from the beginning. New words would continually come up – in texts, in the sentences given on lexical cards, and in answers to my grammatical questions (although, as before, I kept the latter to an absolute minimum in the first stages). I'd check through all the data I had gathered – on the same day, if possible – and make out a card for any new word. These would be saved up for a couple of weeks and then sorted into sets and put to Moses. It was more sensible to go through six new animals, four trees, seven adjectives and twelve verbs, in that order, than to have them all muddled up. A verb might have occurred in a text with a rather particular sense, but then when I put the Yidiny form to Moses the following week he'd give a more general statement of its meaning, with four or five illustrative sentences.

This field procedure would not necessarily suit every circumstance. Dick Moses was, I believe, unique. He had the mentality of a true scholar, thinking through every point absolutely carefully, with infinite patience. Sometimes a question I asked would start him off on a dialogue – if someone said this, you'd reply so-and-so, then the first man would answer back like this . . . After having dictated perhaps a full foolscap page, he'd have me read it back, partly to check my transcription and pronunciation, but mostly to check that he had himself got everything correct, with the right sort of felicitous phrases. He'd ask me to read out a bit in the middle again, think a bit, then provide an alternative formulation.

"That what you got there," Moses would say, pointing with the stem of his pipe at the page, "that all right – but this way be bit more better." And he must have spent every evening going over what we'd done during the day, for more often than not he'd start the morning with an addition, or perhaps a correction, to something covered the previous day.

From knowing the dates of the early missionaries, and which of them Moses remembered, I calculated he had been born in about 1898.

(He himself said, in 1975, that he thought he must be about eighty-five; but the circumstantial evidence is against this.) He volunteered more texts. A few more traditional stories, although he had to ransack his memory quite hard for these, unlike Chloe and George, since the culture of the Dyirbal-speaking tribes had disintegrated much more slowly and less dramatically than that of the Yidinyji. And he told autobiographical stories — about the first plane the Yidinyji saw, and what they thought about it; and about how Moses was brought to the mission as a young boy, and what his feelings were.

Some of the other old men at Yarrabah told me Moses had been "a hard case". He'd refused to go to school, running away to talk to the old Yidinyji and Gungganyji elders, absorbing all he could from them. Moses had acquired none of our learning — couldn't read or write — but he alone of the men of his generation had retained a classic knowledge of the Yidiny language and the social milieu in which it functioned.

When I knew him, Dick Moses would always wear long trousers, no shoes, and a white shirt — the buttons not fastened, sleeves rolled up almost to the elbow. In winter he'd also have an undervest. He invariably had an incipient cold and would be continually sniffing deeply and blowing his nose on a sodden handkerchief that he kept clenched in his hand. Every few minutes he'd spit out phlegm into the grass a few feet away, a quite natural — almost graceful — habit. Moses preferred a pipe to cigarettes and would either smoke or fiddle with it all day. A couple of times during the four years we worked together, his pipe degenerated into a stub, with no more than a half-inch of stem. I bought him a new one at the store, which Moses accepted with gratitude. But he still used the old stub for a couple of weeks more until it really did fall apart — he was attached to it, he explained apologetically.

It's lucky I had someone like Dick Moses, because Yidiny is a *really* hard language. It is quite different from Dyirbal. About a quarter of the vocabulary is the same (mostly from loan words in both directions, probably in fairly recent times), but the grammars are totally dissimilar. Each affix seemed to have two forms — a longer and a shorter one. The genitive suffix (marking a possessor, just like English *'s*) was *-ni* with a noun ending in a consonant, or a three-syllabled noun ending in a vowel. "Mother" is *mujam* and "mother's" is *mujam-ni*; "man" is *waguja* and "man's" is *waguja-ni*. But for a word with two syllables ending in a vowel, the genitive lengthened the final vowel and added just -*n*: "father" *bimbi* and "father's" *bimbi-in,* "woman" *bunya* and "woman's" *bunya-an.*

It was the same with verbs. Past tense was -*nyu* with verbs that have three syllables — *majinda-nyu* "walked up". But if the verb had only two syllables, it lengthened the final vowel of the root and added just -*ny* — *gali-iny* "went", *gada-any* "came". (Here *ny* represents a simple sound, like Spanish *ñ,* — more-or-less like saying *n* and *y* simultaneously.)

The phonetics was harder than Dyirbal, because one had to distinguish between long and short vowels, and work out where the stress came in a word. The structure of the words was much more involved — apart from anything else, there were lots of irregularities. And the way in which words were combined to form sentences was also less straightforward than in Dyirbal. I was glad that I'd cut my field work teeth, as it were, on Dyirbal. I could just about handle Yidiny now, but if I'd started off on a language with this degree of complexity, I shudder to think what might have become of me.

Good as Dick Moses was, it was still important that I find other speakers who could give texts and answer critical questions. Moses mentioned his sister, Ida Burnett, who lived in White Rock, just behind the Cairns meatworks. In fact I had called on her in 1964 and taken down a page or two of Yidiny. I couldn't think why I hadn't followed it up, and got more material, while we were living in Cairns during that first field trip.

I soon remembered why, after spending another hour with her. Ida Burnett was a prototypical cranky old Aboriginal lady (the sort who'd take two cigarettes when you offered her one). She wasn't exactly unhelpful, but it was difficult to get very much out of her. There was no chance of texts, that was clear. And after a couple of questions, she'd go off on a tangent, a non-linguistic tangent, in such a way that I'd appear to be rude if I tried to continue. Also her Yidiny was inextricably mixed with Jabugay, the language from north of Cairns. Moses took tremendous pains to keep his Yidiny pure, excluding Jabugay (although he knew a bit) and even eliminating some established English loans! But not his sister. It was hard to tell whether Ida Burnett was a bit stupid or whether she was playing games with me; I suspect the latter. But I did appreciate how she fitted her Yidiny name, *Ngujun* — this is simply based on the particle *nguju* "not, no".

Moses had also recommended Pompey Langdon, in Edmonton. Pompey lived, appropriately enough, next to Blackfellow's Creek, just on the north side of town. This had presumably been a favourite camping place in the old days – now only Pompey and a couple of younger Aborigines lived there. It wasn't at all easy to find – the Edmonton policeman confessed he often had trouble himself. One had to count the number of telegraph poles north of the creek, on the main road, and then, just across the railway line, follow a barely discernible track through the long grass. It led to what must at one time have been a pleasant whitefellow house, but odd bits had been removed, or had fallen off, and Pompey camped out in the remaining shell.

Pompey and Dick Moses, both full-blood Yidinyji, were the last people to have been initiated. Pompey opened his shirt to show rows of deep scars across the lower chest. Even they hadn't been put through the ceremony by Yidinyji elders – the culture had disintegrated too far by 1910 for that to be possible. Moses had been initiated together with a group of young Jabugay men, over at Redlynch, while Pompey, who came from the tableland group of the Yidinyji, had been done with some Ngajanji boys at Malanda.

Pompey seemed older than Moses and he certainly wasn't mentally as spry. But he was helpful and thoughtful, so that it was worthwhile going back to see him for an hour or so now and then. When I asked if he would tell stories, he said he'd have to think about it. And then when I did put on the recorder, Pompey launched into a mourning dirge – not unlike the one John Haviland and I had heard in the Cooktown settlement – incanting like a preacher as he recited the deeds and character of a departed tribesman. It was a powerful performance, which affected Moses and his friends at Yarrabah when I played it to them.

Alec Morgan, who had given me a bit of Yidiny Jalnguy in 1967, was still alive but now totally senile. He'd been living by himself for too long, his daughter said, drinking incredible rotgut, so she'd had to bring him into Gordonvale to look after him. He was fast asleep in a hammock, with a long white beard, looking twenty years older than when I last saw him. The daughter offered to wake him up, but warned that he wouldn't say anything coherent; I said not to bother. She did, however, recommend that I try Katie Mays and her sister Tilly Fuller, who lived in an old cane barracks the other side of Aloomba.

It didn't take me long to realise that I'd found another fine informant. Katie Mays was a fat, jolly lady who'd left her Ngajanji husband, Billy Mays, for Charlie Ibuai, a benvolent Torres Strait Islander. Katie had spoken Yidiny in her youth and she could tell me words and a few stories. The find, though, was her elder half-sister, Tilly. Mrs Fuller had had an English father (from York), but she had been brought up with the tribe and I'm sure that she still thought almost entirely in Yidiny. She was certainly more at home in that language than she was in English.

Tilly was also plump – although not so fat as Katie – with white hair and a double chin. She must have been born about the same time as Moses. Under their heavy lids, her eyes were keen and active, looking me up and down, working out just what I was after. I played a short text by Moses while Tilly and Katie listened and approved. Then Tilly said she could tell one. It began at a place called Dulubirr, a fighting ground, and concerned a man called Gulibunyjay. I switched on the machine and she began slowly, pronouncing a couple of words, and then pausing, thinking, before giving another phrase. Then there was a long gap – what seemed an eternity as I was sitting there (although it

Fig. 13. Tilly Fuller, left, and Katie Mays (Yidiny), outside their barracks at Aloomba. (1972)

was in fact only ten seconds!) — and I wondered whether Tilly had dried up, whether I should switch off. But she continued, and now became more fluent, telling of how Gulibunyjay threw his son, called Wangal "boomerang", towards the coast, and then followed its track down, naming places according to the trees Wangal had grazed.

Tilly didn't feel she could tell me the same story in English, in the way Moses had. But her stepson Ranji Fuller (who was all of sixty) knew a fair bit of Yidiny and he volunteered to do that part. Then Katie told a short story about an old man trying to catch a cassowary. The spear missed the bird and hit a waterhole. As a result, Katie recounted, even today "if you dive in it you never come back." But she spoke in a hybrid blend of Yidiny and English — *bama burrgiiny minyaagu young fellow wanggaajinyu*. When it was replayed, Katie was surprised.

"I thought I talk in Yidiny. I never knew I put all that English in. Fancy, I didn't know I was doing that." Katie's voice was melodic, with impish rises in pitch. "You better stick to Tilly, she give you that Yidiny language straight. She older than me. She had more chance to learn it right through from old people."

I went back to see Tilly pretty regularly, when I wasn't at Yarrabah. We'd have a good session of two or three hours before she'd tire — checking one text or recording another, going through bits of grammar, or getting some Jalnguy.

I'd found in 1967 that the Yidinyji, like the Dyirbal, had a "mother-in-law" speech style, and that they also called it Jalnguy. But it had ceased to be spoken a long time ago. Dick Moses said he'd heard it used a bit, though he had never picked it up himself. Only Pompey Langdon and Tilly Fuller remembered something of it. They didn't remember anything like as much as Chloe or George but — very, very gradually, over four years — I built up a corpus of about two hundred forms.

Just like Dyirbal, the Yidinyji Jalnguy had the same phonetics and grammar as the everyday speech style, but all of the lexical words — nouns, verbs and adjectives — were different. And there would be a single general term in Jalnguy corresponding to a number of specific words in the everyday style. Jalnguy noun *wuruny* translated both *jungi* "freshwater shrimp" and *binduba* "crayfish", for example. Each word that Tilly gave I took care to check with Pompey, and vice versa (and in this way discovered that some of the forms Alec Morgan had rattled off in 1967 were in fact from the Mamu everyday style, and not Jalnguy at all.)

With the friendship and cooperation of Dick Moses and Tilly Fuller, and some assistance from Pompey Langdon and Katie Mays, I had the makings of a reasonable description of Yidiny. And could relax, take a day off, and enjoy Christmas 1971.

11

"Happiness and fun"

Yarrabah has a superb physical location, right on the coast with a view over Trinity Bay and Green Island in the distance. It has soft, silver sands, and shady trees, with jungle-covered hills as a backdrop. But I have never been anywhere that was more socially depressed and depressing. At Palm Island, there had been an autocratic administration and covert ripples of defiance among the wards of the State; at Yarrabah in 1971 there was almost nothing, on either side, save sheer, dull apathy.

In the early days of the mission, a dozen little villages were spread over the considerable area of the Yarrabah reserve. The people had grown paspalum grass, cotton, peanuts, bananas, potatoes and turnips, and there had been some dairying and poultry farming. They must also have resorted to their traditional vegetables and fruits from time to time, despite the missionaries' negative attitude towards these.

In 1971, almost every one of the thousand inmates lived in the central settlement, as they were required to do by the Queensland government. Recent attempts to establish "outstations" — both here and at other settlements in the State — had met first with equivocation and finally with blank refusal. There was nothing for most of the people to do at the settlement. A few worked in the sawmill or looked after the steadily dwindling dairy herd. (One manager calculated that it would be cheaper to put them on the dole than to continue with the dairy business — no account at all being taken of the psychological value of working.) Some were employed going around the town picking up bits of paper. Not that they were expected to do it very vigorously

— these men spent most of the day listening to Dick Moses and me, and we were glad of their company.

Some new houses were being built at the old folks' home by a firm from Cairns. They may have employed one or two Aborigines to help dig the foundations, but all the actual building was done by white workmen. They were even painted by white men from Cairns. When I asked why greater use couldn't have been made of the idle manpower at Yarrabah, the answer was that the contract had been advertised in accordance with standard government practice and the successful tenderer had been this firm from Cairns. No one from Yarrabah had tendered. But how could they, when the government — their guardian and protector — had not taught anyone how to put in a tender? Traditional Aboriginal life, and all its skills and values, had been blasted away, in the name of Christianity and Civilisation. But absolutely nothing had been put in its place. Were the Aborigines supposed to work out the intricacies of our way of life on their own? They aren't stupid, but no one is *that* clever.

Even the people who worked didn't get paid much. The minimum basic wage in Australia, which is laid down by the federal government, applies to every worker, in any sort of job; except on Aboriginal settlements in Queensland. After a few weeks, I thought I should mention to Joe Rogers that I was paying Dick Moses $40 for a full week's work (of twenty-five to thirty hours, quite apart from all the hours in the evening he spent thinking things through.) "Don't tell anyone," warned Joe, "we'll have a riot on our hands." I later found that the top wage paid by the Queensland government to an Aborigine at Yarrabah in 1971 was $34 for a full forty-hour working week. Well, at least it was better than the average wage of $2.50 per week at Palm Island in 1964, although of course these were not directly comparable since at Yarrabah there was no free issue of rations (just a midday meal provided for the schoolchildren).

I never discussed money with Dick Moses, just as I never did with anyone else. On the one day we'd had together in 1970, I'd passed over a note in thanks, and now at the end of the week I'd just give him two twenties, rolled up and passed from palm to palm so that no one knew exactly how much he was getting. (The spectators always nodded, approvingly.) This was the way Moses wanted it. He showed me his bankbook, into which a lot of the money went, and said he didn't want any of the layabouts at Yarrabah knowing how much he had or they'd be forever scrounging off him.

In his attitude to money, Moses was quite untypical of Aborigines. Pompey Langdon was much more normal. One day when I was at his place, there was a younger woman who asked me for a couple of dollars for bread for her daughter (what she really meant was for cigarettes for herself). I declined, gently, but said that I would of course be paying Pompey, which satisfied her completely. When I gave him a five-dollar note, Pompey ran after me asking if I could exchange it for five ones, so that he could share it with all of his friends there.

Moses was essentially a solitary, almost a secretive, person. We had an ideal working relationship, meeting every day from 8.30 or 9 until about 11.30, and then from 2 until 4.30 or so. He never expected to work on Sundays, perhaps from long years of living in the mission. But if I excused myself any weekday afternoon — as I sometimes had to, to catch up with assessing and filing the information he'd given — Moses would be quite disappointed. That was *all* we had, though — a working relationship. I'd drunk and eaten and camped out with George; Chloe and I knew as much about each other's lives and families and beliefs and ideas as any two people could; but I never got really to know Dick Moses as a person.

Dick belonged to the Gurrabana moiety, which was associated with the wet season and went back to Damarri, the cussed brother in that important legend. Each moiety has a number of animals and celestial and material objects associated with it — its "totems" — and personal names would often be related to an appropriate totemic entity or activity. Dick's Yidiny name was Jarriyi, based on the verb *jarri-* "disappear, sink down, become lost", here referring to the rainbow (an important Gurrabana totem) sinking down out of the sky. And that was about all I knew about him. His wife came by now and then and said hello. Her language was Jirrbal, Dick said, although she scarcely remembered any of it. They conversed in English.

There was a story behind that. Moses explained that, way back in his youth, the old men had become concerned that the local tribes were so depleted in numbers, through introduced diseases and murder. No one tribe had sufficient people to continue as a viable political entity. So the old men decided they should pool their resources, as it were, and develop a single macro-tribe, encompassing Jabuganyji, Yidinyji, Ngajanji and the tablelands group of Jirrbalngan. Marriages were purposely arranged across tribal boundaries, which was how Moses had acquired a Jirrbal wife. What the old people of that day hadn't bargained for was the language barrier. Neither Moses nor his wife knew each other's native tongue (Jirrbal and Yidiny are, in fact, as different as English and Welsh), but they both had some English and it was this that blossomed. (A different pattern was evolving at Murray Upper where a macro-tribe had spontaneously evolved from the southern Jirrbalngan and the Girramaygan. However, these two tribes, which had in precontact days been politically as distinct as Jirrbal and Yidiny, spoke mutually intelligible dialects, and in this instance intermarriage did reinforce traditional culture, life-style and language.)

It worried me at first that Dick and I spoke only of linguistic matters. I ventured to ask whether he had any children at Yarrabah; he said he hadn't. I suspect that he had no children at all, although that is just a guess. After a while, I accepted that he wanted only a working relationship with me. Every morning when Dick and I sat down under the big fig tree together, he'd expect to go straight into the serious business of linguistics. This was what he was interested in – thinking back, and working out all of the involved intricacies of Yidiny. He knew he was the last real speaker, the final repository of thousands of years of linguistic evolution, and he was concerned that it should be properly and exactly recorded for posterity. That was his aim; and it was much more important than gossip.

Yidiny has particles, similar to those in Dyirbal, which modify the meaning of a complete clause and don't take any case or tense endings, as do words in other parts of speech. There is *nguju* "not" (which also functions as the negative interjection "no"), *giyi* "don't", *biri* "done again", *yurrga* "still", and one particle in common with Dyirbal, *mugu* "couldn't help it", referring to something that is quite unsatisfactory but which it is impossible to avoid doing.

Dyirbal has a particle *ngurri* "in turn", used to indicate retribution or revenge, or just a reciprocal gift. "He hit me and so *ngurri* I hit him." Sometimes *ngurri* could go with both clauses: *"Ngurri* I'll give you my boomerang, *ngurri* you give me your fishing line." Yidiny has a particle with a similar meaning – in fact two of them, *jaybar* and *jaymbi*. Both seemed to mean "in turn". The puzzle was to try to discover the difference between them.

It might be the sort of action involved – one particle for reciprocal hitting and the other for reciprocal giving, perhaps? No, both of them checked out with both types of verbs. I had a few examples of each particle in texts, and some more in sentences on vocabulary cards or information Moses dictated in response to other questions. But I just couldn't see *any* pattern.

I've always found it's best not to worry about problems one can't solve during field work. Just put them to one side and work on something else that you can make some progress with. A solution to the tricky problem will probably turn up by the time you've done everything else.

So each morning I devised two or three new "retributive" sentences and got Moses to translate them, just doing five more minutes on it and gathering a bit more data until I could perceive what conditioned the use of one particle rather than the other (it was plain from Dick's responses that there *was* some conditioning). Eventually it came. The key was whether it was the speaker or someone else who delivered the retribution. If I did something back to someone else it was *jaybar*, whereas if someone else did something back to me, then *jaymbi* was the particle to use. "I hit him and he *jaymbi* hit me," but "He hit me and I *jaybar* hit him." I looked back over all the examples that had accumulated — this hypothesis explained them perfectly. Remembering things that Moses had said earlier on about these particles I saw that time and again he'd been trying to explain to me the difference — but somehow I was too dense to take it in. I suddenly let out a controlled whoop, and explained back to Dick what he'd told me so often. He relaxed and smiled, with the satisfaction of a patient teacher who has at last got a point over to an eager but slightly dull student.

Tilly Fuller was always glad to see me, but it was best to come in the week, she said, when all the men were at work and it was quiet enough for us to concentrate. She, Katie, and Katie's extended family lived in a four-roomed shack that had originally been intended for itinerant cane-cutters (in the days before cutting was mechanised). It was built of corrugated iron, of course, supported by some incredibly thick, gnarled, ant-eaten wooden posts. Tilly had a cool room at the end which she shared with Ranji when he came down at weekends from his job on the tablelands. There were always people around, on any day — Katie's pretty, fresh-complexioned teenage granddaughter Curly, with her white boy friend, or smaller children calling in for a biscuit or something.

Tilly had no less than eleven names, in the Yidinyji way. Her main name was Buruuny, but there were also Dalganday "eaglehawk nest",

Buri "fire", and a scatter of other names. She chatted happily, and with complete frankness, about her life. Her husband had been, like her father, from England, from Cambridge. I said I knew the place — it was flat and marshy, quite unlike Yidinyji territory, but with beautiful old college buildings. "I was having his baby," Tilly confided, "so he did the right thing and married me."

Like Moses, Tilly Fuller felt a responsibility to describe the old ways, so that I could get them down on tape before it was too late. The next text she recorded told of tribal life in her youth, and the different foods that they ate. When the tail feathers of the willy wagtail bird, *jigirrjigirr,* turn white, it is time to gather rickety nuts, *badil,* on the hills in coastal country. Then when the black scrub locust first cries out, around Christmas, it is a sign to go up to the tablelands to feast on black pine nuts, *gubuum.*

As we went through the text, transcribing it, Tilly expanded on some of the points. When camp was pitched, the children would eat, and then bathe in the river.

"Always swim after eat," she explained, "happiness and fun." But they must only bathe downstream from the camp. "If we bogey upriver they might throw spears at us, and stone us," Tilly said. "Might make water by the camp dirty." Then she mused on: "That was the law when I was girl. We wouldn't dare bathe up from camp. But these white people nowadays — they just bathe anywhere. No rules at all. I don't know what our old people would say if they could see it."

The first stories I'd recorded from Moses had one peculiar characteristic: the narrator would set the scene for a few sentences, using third person pronouns, and would then take on the identity of the main character, telling the rest of the legend in the first person. Dick had told the tale of the first Yidinyji man to come into the territory, named Banggilan or Yidi. Moses first assumed the identity of Gulmbira, an old Yidinyji man who travelled around the country naming places. After Gulmbira died, he took over the role of Gindaja, the cassowary, who had been a minor character in the story until then.

The story of Damarri and Guyala, the brothers who gave people their vegetable foods and started the moieties, had two main characters. It was told in the third person until near the end, when Guyala went north and the story continued with just Damarri. At this point, Moses had quietly slipped into first person, himself taking on the identity of Damarri.

Dyirbal stories had nothing like this. Chloe and George and Paddy Biran had all used third person right through. I thought at first that Moses's method was a personal style, but then I found that exactly the same thing happened in the traditional stories Tilly Fuller told – she also took on the role of the central character as often as not. "First person orientation" was plainly a general convention in Yidinyji story-telling. It was yet another important difference from Dyirbal, and surely just as significant as all the phonetic, grammatical and lexical differences between the two languages.

We had taken the flat in Cairns for three weeks and after getting to know Joe Rogers I asked if we could then all come to stay at Yarrabah. Sure, no difficulty at all. He thought a bit – we could stay in the male schoolteachers' residence, none of them would be back for another three or four weeks.

Yarrabah is eight miles across the bay from Cairns, and in 1964 you could only get there by boat. Since then, electricity had been brought in and the electricity access track gradually upgraded into a road over the mountains. It was much further than by sea – round the inlet, up the mountains and then zigzagging between the peaks was forty miles from Cairns, about an hour's drive.

We headed south from Cairns on the main highway, past the racecourse and the meatworks, and then through Edmonton with its Hambledon Mill, sweaty, noisy, tall-chimneyed, right up by the dark mountains (a far cry from cricket in Hampshire). Ahead, on the right of the road, are the first hills of the Bellenden Ker Range – Walsh's Pyramid, called Jarrugan in Yidiny because it looks like a giant incubating mound built by *jarruga* "scrub-hen". There were no signposts for Yarrabah; you just had to know to turn left where it said "Kamma Pine Creek Road". The road crossed the railway line and then, narrow but still bitumen, snaked round cane fields just beginning to sprout, past Green Hill (Murubay in Yidiny) which even in precontact times was covered only in grass, and over a narrow bridge that cars share with cane trains, the tram lines just running through the middle of the bitumen. We rattled over an old covered bridge and jolted off the end into potholes and dirt and dust. Past Bessie Point where a group of Aborigines from Yarrabah had been "resettled", as the government put it. What really happened was that after a bit of an uprising at the mission – sometime in the fifties, I believe – the ringleaders were made to go out to Bessie Point to live. It was typical of Queensland's authoritarian "divide and conquer" policy.

Our laden station wagon made the steep ascent up the Murray Prior Range, two thousand feet high, still a dirt road but just now dry and navigable. The track is a ledge cut out of the mountain side, with sharp U-turns. We glimpsed Mission Bay and then began the steep, spiral low-gear descent to Yarrabah. A bumpy ride to the wooden cattle grid across the road at the sawmill and then very, very slowly into town, careful of the children playing in and out of front gardens.

The male schoolteachers' house had five little bedrooms with glass-slatted windows – half of the slats missing – and a kitchen and bathroom. The toilet was across the garden. Venture onto the back step – mind that snake, I'm sure he's still living there under the house – jump down to the path and thread through a battalion of toads. The house itself was filthy; Alison washed the walls (you could almost peel them), whereas I wouldn't have bothered.

Although there may have been three hundred or more people at Yarrabah who called themselves Gungganyji, and about the same number of Yidinyji, just two people were able to speak the language – Moses and Richard Hyde. The others might know a couple of score words – which would be symbols of group identification within their attenuated version of English – but they couldn't put together a sentence in Yidiny or Gunggay. Richard Hyde was friendly, though not as good as Moses. Rather like Katie Mays, he introduced English words into each sentence of the textlets I recorded and he had to think a lot longer than Moses about each question, and then only sometimes produced an answer. He also didn't have the powers of concentration of Moses, or the same urge to get the language down before it was too late.

When Moses listened to the tape I'd recorded from Richard Hyde, he slapped his thigh in derision. "He make me laugh, all that English in there. Why can't he keep that language straight?"

Richard Hyde was helpful on some points, and the money I paid helped buy food in his daughter's house. In fact he was always coming around for a loan "until I get my pension on Thursday". Of course he didn't mean a loan, but a gift that would tide them over until the government money came in. He was often sick, so I couldn't do all that much language work with him. Richard Hyde died in 1974.

Back in 1963 I'd begun by taping everything, using the recorder as one would a rough notebook. But then it took a long time to transcribe it afterwards, and it's not always easy to transcribe without the speaker there to assist. So on Yidiny I only kept the recorder for texts and for bits that I wanted to study from a phonetic point of view. I used only seven tapes in the whole five-year study of Yidiny, from December 1970 until December 1975 — whereas for Dyirbal I'd used sixty-six tapes in 1963/64, nine in 1967 and three in 1970.

If one just tapes responses to questions, there's no necessity to understand them absolutely fully at the time and there is little feedback to the speaker. The keenest informant will get tired of talking into a machine after quite a short time. But if the investigator can repeat the words correctly, if he can make up new sentences and engage in dialogue, then everything becomes worthwhile. When the message can be seen to be getting through, enthusiasm will banish tiredness.

Both Dick Moses and Tilly Fuller set out to teach me how to talk Yidiny — properly, felicitously, appropriately. There is a considerable skill to being able to "answer back" in Yidiny. Here again I found a great difference from Dyirbal, where replies will often be as short and elliptical as possible. "Why are you going out?" "For wallabies." "Can I come?" "Yes."

In Yidiny each answer to a question, or comment on a statement, must be a full sentence, with a subject and a verb. If someone asks, "When shall we go walkabout?", you could answer. "We'll go walkabout tomorrow." The reply could not be simply "tomorrow"; well it could, but it wouldn't be good Yidiny. And while the response must be a full sentence, it must not mechanically repeat all the words from the original utterance — there must be some, but not too much, variation in the words used or in the grammatical constructions employed — rather like someone asking, "Do you want to come and hunt wallabies?" and receiving the reply, "Yes, I'll come and spear marsupials". It is probably to this end that the language has a number of pairs of synonyms (many more than Dyirbal). *Burrging* and *yajil* both mean "go walkabout". The only difference Moses would acknowledge between them was "if someone tell you *burrging* then you answer him back *yajil*", or vice versa.

Both Moses and Tilly dictated long strings of statements and responses, and questions and answers. I had to read them back. And then I would be tested. If someone said such-and-such, how would you answer him back? So, slowly and patiently, I was taught how to speak the language. Not just to pronounce it properly, not just to use the

right words and put them together in the right grammatical patterns —
although that was a sine qua non — but how to construct good
discourse in Yidiny, so that I could take my place around a long-past
campfire without fear of embarrassment.

I never had the opportunity of hearing Yidiny just being spoken
around the place (quite unlike the situation with Dyirbal). I was able
simply to pick up how to converse in Dyirbal, but for Yidiny there was
a demanding course of instruction which really took precedence over all
the other things Tilly Fuller and I — or Moses and I — were doing.

We moved across from Cairns to Yarrabah just in the nick of time.
Two days later the rain started. And what rain! It rained for roughly
twenty-three hours of each day for the next five days. Real tropical
wet season torrential rain, so loud that it made conversation difficult.
When it stopped, for an hour now and then, I spent the time bailing the
water out of the car — there was usually a depth of two or three inches,
dribbled in through the ventilator grilles and suchlike.

The road over the mountains was washed away the second day. This
happened every year, I was told by a member of the Aboriginal
Council. "They spend the dry season putting the road back in and
grading it ready to put bitumen on. Then the rains come and wash it
away and they have to start all over again. That's our money they're
using, you know, DAIA pays for that road every time." (It did
eventually get bitumenised, but this comment was true enough at the
time.) They had to get the boat out to try and get across to Cairns for
supplies. We had no bread for several days — and not even the where-
withall to make our own — but there were plenty of packets of crackers
in the store!

Dick and I needed somewhere dry to work and he suggested asking
Father Brown if the church vestry would be available. The concrete
floor in the vestry wasn't very inviting, so we used the table and chairs.
It was a relief to me, after a month of sitting on the ground under our
tree and Dick didn't seem to mind — for a day or two at least.

I was gradually working out what most of the affixes meant.
Ergative case on nouns, marking agent of some action, was *-nggu*
— as in Dyirbal — except that there were complex rules for its being
reduced in certain circumstances: *waguja-nggu* "man did it", but
bunya-ang "woman did it". The ablative case, meaning "from", was
-mu on some nouns and *-m* on others. The past tense was *-nyu,* while
-ng covered both present and future. And so on.

But there were a couple of things I couldn't work out. And they really did haunt me. When Alison asked what I wanted for Christmas, all I could mumble was "to find out what *-Vli-* and *-Vlda-* mean". (How did she put up with it?) Anyway I asked a few more examples every now and then, to add to the considerable number of instances from texts, trying to discover what the significance of these two affixes might be. They lengthened the last vowel of a verbal root (I wrote this as *V*) and tense was added after them. There was *magi-* "climb up" and then, with one of these affixes and past tense: *magi-ili-nyu* and *magi-ilda-nyu*. And it was the same with every other verb except *gali-* "go" and *gada-* "come", which for some reason couldn't take *-Vli-* or *-Vlda-*.

I think Moses must have despaired. He kept on dictating sentences which, when I looked back later, perfectly showed the meanings. And then he explained it in English and I wrote it down, but still I couldn't understand. Finally, one day the penny dropped. *-Vli-* meant "do while going" and *-Vlda-* was "do while coming", *magiilinyu* was "went up, climbing" and *magiildanyu* was "came up, climbing". And that was why they couldn't go with the verbs "go" and "come". My joy at discovering — after three weeks of effort — the import of these common affixes was as nothing to the relief Dick Moses showed. "Thank goodness for that," he plainly thought, as I bubbled over with "my" discovery. "Now I shan't have to try to explain that again, day after day."

Not everyone at Yarrabah was totally sunk in apathy. A number of concerned Aborigines worked as hard as they could to try and make something of the place. Alf Neal, for instance. He was a leading light in the co-operative which, with help from a church group in New South Wales, was trying to establish a bakery at Yarrabah. Alf's son was then doing his apprenticeship as a baker in Sydney — and doing extremely well by all accounts — and they were hoping to build their own oven at the settlement before long.

The Aboriginal Council was keen for people to have the opportunity of regaining something of their heritage — which had been lost during the long years of dormitories and suchlike. Specifically, it wanted the people to learn and revive their own languages. I was given permission to work at Yarrabah with this aim in view. The plan was that I should learn as much as I could from Moses and Richard Hyde, and then write lessons so that everyone — adults and children — could start to learn it.

Alf Neal was Muluriji himself, from beyond Mareeba (he said his mother had known that language; unfortunately she was by that time utterly senile). But Alf now belonged to Yarrabah, and he himself was keen to learn Yidiny. So I worked with this in view. Next time I came, it would be with a stack of lessons and some ideas on how they could be taught (I wouldn't be able to stay for more than a few weeks, during the university vacation).

What dialect actually to teach was a somewhat tricky problem. Originally just one language had been spoken over the country south and south-west of Cairns with, as far as I could discern, four different dialects. There were two varieties of Yidiny itself — the coastal dialect, now represented by Moses and Richard Hyde — and the dialect spoken by the Yidinyji groups who had lived up on the mountains, towards Lake Barrine, which included Tilly Fuller, Katie Mays, Pompey Langdon and Jack and Nellie Stewart.

Then there was Wanyurr, on the coastal plain around Babinda. One old lady speaker had been alive in 1964, but I'd never been able to find her in. Now there was no one who remembered any Wanyurr and I had only two old word-lists, both taken down at Palm Island — one by Norman Tindale in 1938 and the other by Father Worms in the late forties.

Finally there had been Gunggay, spoken on Cape Grafton Peninsula where Yarrabah is now situated. The last speakers had died just a few years back, and again all I had was a few old vocabularies by the Reverend Mr Gribble, Dr Roth and Norman Tindale — no more than three hundred words in all and virtually no grammar. It was quite plain that Yidiny, Wanyurr and Gunggay were all dialects of one language, sharing about 80 per cent vocabulary and, by all accounts, being mutually intelligible.

Tribal jealousy was strong between the Yidinyji and the Gungganyji at Yarrabah. Whenever the possibility of land rights came up (a somewhat theoretical question, given the type of government Queensland has nowadays), the Gungganyji said that the land should be theirs. Moses and the other Yidinyji used to get very indignant about this and quote the last Gungganyji "King" as having declared that anyone born at Yarrabah belonged equally to the country.

I decided to write lessons in the "Yidiny-Gunggay language", and to try to quote the Gunggay forms as well when they were different, insofar as these could be discovered from old word lists. Moses sometimes remembered a bit about the Gunggay language, but mostly he was just contemptuous of the Gungganyji — he said they were small, weak people "like a midget".

I was glad to have this goal, the hope of being able to give some positive feedback to the community. The field trip was certainly turning out to be the most enjoyable I have ever undertaken. I knew what I was doing, which I didn't when I began work on Dyirbal. Yidiny was a fantastic language, much more complex than Dyirbal, and it posed a remarkable intellectual challenge. Formulating the problems and discovering solutions to them gave me as much sheer mental thrill as I might get in ten years of poring over books at an office desk. Also I had Alison and the children with me; doing fieldwork on one's own can be all right, but always a little lonely.

I was getting to know something of the character of Yidiny. There seemed to be a preference that as many words as possible should have an even number of syllables, perhaps to get a regular rhythm to each word — tum-ti-tum-ti . . . Past tense was -nyu with a verb root that had three syllables, producing a word that had four syllables: *majinda-nyu* "walked up". But with a disyllabic root it just lengthened the final vowel and added a palatal nasal *ny* — the past tense of *gali-* "to go" was *galiiny*, a word with just two syllables. The same applied to genitive — *waguja-ni* "man's" but *bunya-an* "woman's", both having an even number of syllables.

I had scores of examples of things like past tense, and understood the most frequent affixes fairly well. But there were some verbal endings that had come up just a few times in texts. I'd take these less common affixes one at a time, and try to get more examples. The technique was to try to make up new Yidiny sentences, putting the affixes on verbs different from those they'd occurred with in texts, and then see if they were acceptable to Moses. Even if I hadn't got a sentence quite right, he would usually see what I was trying to do and give me the correct way of saying it.

I remember one morning I took the affix -*nyun* and looked forward to an interesting hour of getting more examples before trying to discover the conditions under which -*nyun* was used and what it meant. I noticed that, in each of the three instances I had, -*nyun* was added to a trisyllabic root. And then a thought occurred. -*Nyunda* marked the verb in a relative clause and — checking — I found that all examples of this were onto roots of two or four syllables.

I really was disappointed when it took only about five minutes to work out *-nyun*. I tried putting it onto a disyllabic root within a sentence, *gali-nyun*, and Moses corrected this to *gali-nyunda*. Then I put *-nyunda* onto a trisyllabic root *majinda-nyunda* and that was corrected to *majinda-nyun*. It was just another manifestation of the preference for words to have an even number of syllables. If the root had two or four syllables, then *-nyunda* was used, giving a word with four or six syllables. But if the root had three or five syllables, then it must take *-nyun*, again producing a word of four or six syllables. (And it was actually *-nyuun*, not *-nyun*. If the last syllable was lost from a word — which is what seemed to be happening — then the vowel of the preceding syllable was lengthened. The same thing happened with past tense, and with the genitive ending.)

No contrast could have been greater than that between the sheer intellectual pleasure Moses and I obtained from exploring the structure of Yidiny, and the nature of life at Yarrabah.

One of the schoolteachers had plainly been friendly and approachable during term, and a bunch of Aboriginal kids still came by each day to play through the house we were staying in. There were footballs, and a model railway. It was good; all of our children joined in. Then, after we'd been there a week or so, Eelsha's eighth birthday came up. She invited a group of her new friends to a party. A white-style children's party. They had some games, which went off all right. And then tea — big piles of sandwiches and cakes. It was almost instantly demolished — someone said could they take a bit home for a brother or sister and so did someone else. Suddenly, the house was empty. Everyone was gone, mouths bulging, food in paper bags.

The date was the thing. A Tuesday, two days before the fortnightly Thursday when pension and social security checks were payable (the day when the Australian government makes all its salary and benefit payments, all over the continent). The money from the past payday, twelve days before, was quite gone, so that the children of Yarrabah and their families, were — simply — just hungry. But it was something of an experience. One minute there was a party, the next there wasn't.

Linguistic work also had its lighter side. The word *jurrujurru* came up in one text and I asked what it meant.

"Oh," Moses replied, "that's middle-aged man — like you."

Now I'd known that middle age was somewhere around the corner. I must admit, however, that I hadn't expected it to pop up for a while yet. After all, I was only just coming up to 33. But there comes a time . . . Anyway, I carried on with field work. A little sadder, a bit wiser — and appreciably older. Until a couple of weeks later the same word, *jurrujurru*, came up once more and, forgetting, I again enquired its meaning. This time Moses said "young buck". I must make it clear that he didn't add "like you", but it did cheer me up. (Later on I found that *jurrujurru* refers to any man in his prime, between eighteen and sixty — when he can hunt actively, before old age starts to set in.)

We'd been marooned at Yarrabah while the rains fell, and for a week or so afterwards. But that was fine, it was where we wanted to be at that time. Finally the road over the mountains was repaired and we gingerly eased along it. We popped in to see Pompey Langdon and Tilly Fuller for another session or two, and said hello to George and Chloe on the way down, and to the Cowans. And then the long drive, two thousand miles back to Canberra.

12

"It's not"

Working at the Australian National University was getting to be as exciting as I'd hoped it might when we'd taken the considerable decision to leave London. During 1972, I taught a full-year course on "Australian linguistics" – three hours a week for twenty-six weeks. The first term we spent in detailed study of Dyirbal – going through texts and generally getting to understand the structure of its nouns, pronouns, verbs and sentences – as a vantage point for the main endeavour, a comparative overview of the two hundred different Aboriginal languages of Australia. The aim was to see what sorts of features recurred across the continent and, eventually, to discover whether all the Aboriginal languages of Australia could be proved to be genetically related as one language family, descending from a unique ancestor language that must have been spoken some tens of millennia in the past.

I'd done some reading around what had been written on Australian languages from all parts of the continent – although not much work had been done, and a lot of it was of pretty mixed quality. But until now I hadn't really tried systematic comparison of languages. In that 1972 course we made all sorts of serendipitous discoveries. These were improved and refined as I taught the Australian course again, in 1974, 1975 and 1977, until they were eventually tied together in a long book called *The Languages of Australia,* published by Cambridge University Press in 1980.

The first topic we took was verbal systems in Australia, chosen because it was the thing I knew least about, and wanted to work on most. We looked at verbs from a number of languages from Western Australia — Warlpiri (from an unpublished paper by Ken Hale), Walmatjari (from material written by Joyce Hudson, a missionary linguist who had just spent a term in Canberra), and so on. These languages had five or six verbal conjugations. That is, there were five or six different classes of verbs, each having different kinds of tense endings — just as in English we have one class with *sing/sung, ring/rung,* etc., another with *bleed/bled, feed/fed* among others, and so on.

Some of the verb conjugations in western languages had just a few members, all just one syllable long. There were roots like *nya-* "to see" and *yu-* "to give". This is quite different from languages like Dyirbal and Yidiny where every verbal root had to have at least two syllables.

Then John Haviland, who had just come back from a second trip to Hopevale, gave one lecture on verbs in Guugu Yimidhirr. This language also had a few monosyllabic forms, and some were very similar to those in languages from the west — *nhaa-* "to see" and *wu-* "to give", for instance. Other examples can be found of *ny* corresponding to *nh, a* to *aa* and *y* to *w*. Also, the inflections these monosyllabic verbs took were similar in the two areas. This was quite unexpected, and it was really exciting. Then I remembered that Dyirbal has *nyagi-* "to see" and *wuga-* "to give". Perhaps the original Australian ancestor language had monosyllabic verbs, some of which were retained in languages from the west, and only in Guugu Yimidhirr from the east coast. Dyirbal and many other languages in the east seemed to have added a syllable, so that now every root had at least two syllables — *nyagi-* from *nya-* and *wuga-* from original *wu-*. Maybe the extra syllable was added to satisfy a rhythmic pattern of pronunciation.

I also settled down to work on Yidiny, going through the ten good texts given by Moses and Tilly Fuller and typing them up. I wrote draft chapters on the sound system (phonology) and on the structure of words (morphology). Then, as soon as lectures were finished in late October, I took off for a few weeks' field work, while the students did last minute revision and wrote the end-of-year examinations.

Now that Yidiny was pretty well under control (or so I thought) I wanted to try to do some more on Warrgamay, the language immediately to the south of Dyirbal. Alf Palmer had provided a bit of data, back on Palm Island, but he had had difficulty separating out Warrgamay from Warungu and Dyirbal.

George Watson had mentioned a couple of Warrgamay speakers in Ingham, Arthur Wild and Alec Dennis. A young linguist called Peter Sutton, from Macquarie University, had done some field work on the Gugu-Badhun dialect of Warungu and reported that a speaker of Warrgamay named John Tooth could be ·found at Minnamoolka Station, on the tableland south of Mount Garnet. I wrote to Vernon Atkinson at Minnamoolka, who replied that John Tooth was now at Glen Ruth, run by his cousin Robert Atkinson. My letter there brought a telegram saying: Yes, I was quite welcome to call in and do linguistic work.

I flew up to Townsville one Friday, picked up a vehicle and drove north to Ingham. Alec Dennis was said to be visiting in Innisfail, but I did track down Arthur Wild, living half-way between Ingham and Halifax. He was helpful and gave a few score words, but senescence limited his usefulness − no texts, and he really couldn't dictate more than the odd sentence.

At mid-morning on Saturday, I set off for Glen Ruth. Just north of Cardwell the forestry track went inland, through bananas and grazing land, then climbed, winding up the wooded range. It was unmade, narrow and very steep, so progress was slow. Then a junction, with no signposts. Three miles brought me to a homestead, and back again to the junction, this time with some directions. Over Blencoe Creek. A good place for lunch − peaceful, clear water moving unhurriedly over the rocks, birds alighting for a drink, drinking from their reflections.

Then the track seemed to disappear into an outcrop of rocks. The only way was to drive over them, very gingerly, the Land Cruiser swaying up and down like a boat, as first one side and then the other negotiated an embedded boulder.

After that it was back to the old holey, tree-rooted track which now seemed − in contrast to the rocks − quite pleasant. Sixty miles from the coast road took two and a half hours, not counting the stop to eat. But at last there was Glen Ruth. From the wide track down from the turn-off I had a view of the homestead, its name painted in large white letters on the roof (for aerial identification). Fat cattle, and beautiful thoroughbred stallions were grazing in the paddocks. Over a couple of wide metal cattle grids and then through a wooden gate, into the home paddock. There was only one person at home − a middle-aged Aborigine. John Tooth − oh, he'd driven into Garnet for the day, to spend some of his pay. Easy to find him there, just ask anyone at Lucey's pub.

Mount Garnet was another sixty miles on, but this was easier, only an hour and a half on a straight, flat track, just a few gates to open, and watch out not to skid in the sand.

John Tooth was in the pub. Yes, he'd tell me some language, but not today. He was a bit drunk, not too much, but he needed a clear head for thinking about Warrgamay — long time since he'd had anyone to talk to in it. What about tomorrow — could I come out to Glen Ruth then? Quieter out there, no drink, and we'd be able to do a bit on the language. I only had a couple of weeks away from Canberra and couldn't bear to waste time, but there seemed no alternative (and that day hadn't been completely wasted — I'd got a bit from Arthur Wild). There was nothing for it but to relax in Garnet for the remainder of the day — although goodness knows I hadn't done anything to earn a rest, at this stage in the trip.

John Tooth and I hit it off at once. We had a drink, and a talk about friends in common, and then drove down to the cafe for something to eat. It was just a big square room with a concrete floor, and there was a building at the back labelled "motel", although it didn't look exactly motel-like. The owner was an interesting man — a Norfolk Islander who'd emigrated to Queensland. His Tahitian ancestry was apparent and I could hear just a trace of Norfolkese vowels. We had fish, huge pieces, really too much for one man, and then a game of bar billiards. John had to teach me how to play it. I potted a high number and was then going for "three" before he explained that I should now take all the highs and he'd have to deal with numbers one to seven. I could discern a doubt, as John wondered what sort of person could be ignorant of the rules of bar billiards!

Back at the pub, John's wife Lala had just arrived from Innot Hot Springs, which is half-way to Ravenshoe. John had lent his car to some friends to go to some place beyond Hot Springs, and he couldn't return to Glen Ruth until they brought it back. So we sat and drank a bit more.

Aborigines could go into the bar at Lucey's — John and I had, for a while — but generally they didn't. They sat instead in a sort of wide corridor, leading up to the lavatories, with a couple of small tables and some old chairs. That was the way the publican preferred it, and perhaps the way they did too, at that time. We were chatting and drinking and someone was strumming on a guitar when suddenly the policeman appeared in the doorway that led to the garden. A young, "tough", raw lout of a man, he stood with his hands on hips, surveying the group. Everyone stopped – drinking, talking, playing.

"Right," said the policeman, "you, you, you, you – and you as well. You're coming with me. Come on, look lively about it. I'll teach you to come up and frighten my wife while I'm away."

And the five people he'd pointed to got up without any argument, and went with him.

The whole business mystified me.

"What's happening? Where's he taking them?"

"He's going to lock them in a cell for the night, up at the police station," someone offered.

"Why?" my voice rose in incredulity and anger. "What have they done?"

"Nothing. They went up to ask him something but he was out and his wife she don't like dark people so she tells them to go away. They didn't know he was out. Could be they gave her a bit of lip but I don't think so. Anyhow she could have started it."

I protested that he had no right to lock them in jail for that.

"Oh no, he'll let them out in the morning," John said. "Don't go after them. You'll only make things worse. If you try to argue with him then as soon as you're gone he'll come and take it out on us even more. Let it be. That's the sort of man he is. Nothing anyone can do about it."

So we had another jug of beer and the guitar started again. John's Jirrbalngan wife, Lala, looked to be in her fifties, twenty years younger than him.

"I been *nyinanyu balay* long time. Very lonely, *nyuwala*," Lala was saying. Then to me: "You understand Jirrbal?"

"Little bit."

"You know what I'm saying there?"

"Yes."

"Oh no you don't, what's *nyuwala* mean?"

"That means 'all by yourself'," I replied.

"Yes," Lala showed surprise. "*Nga, nginda bala guwal ngamban* all right, *ngaja nginuna nyunjali.*"

I was taken aback by this, and responded instinctively, without thought, "*yimba!*"

Lala was, as well she might be, quite offended at my reaction. No lady likes to have her offer of a kiss spurned quite so abruptly. But I tried to make up for it, and before long she had her hand on my knee, and my work was cut out attempting to stay friendly but at a distance. John's car still hadn't returned and he was grumbling. "Say they want it for an hour and it's three hours already".

The policeman had returned and was still hovering around, in and out of the bar, watching us through the open doors. I felt I might be the next target — there must be something suspicious about a white man who prefers to drink with the Aborigines rather than in the bar with his own kind. But plainly he didn't quite know how to approach it.

Then I went into the toilet. Ah, here was the opportunity. The policeman followed me in and stood at the next urinal, peeing and interrogating. I told him what my job was, recording Aboriginal languages, and felt it must have confirmed his worst suspicions.

"Where are you sleeping tonight? In the back of your truck?"

Ah, so he'd worked out it was my Land Cruiser. The open back was thick with dust, from the roads I'd been along that day. So I told him "No".

Then we both started speaking at once. He said: "There's a pretty nice motel just down the road", while I was saying: "The motel looks pretty crummy."

I went back into the corridor. John and Lala and their friends and I talked and drank a bit more. About half an hour later I suddenly discovered, to my horror, that in the heat of the interrogation I had omitted to zip up my fly fully. What a place to make that oversight! If the policeman had seen it he'd have put me in jail for a week, like as not!!

I was feeling really tired by half-past nine. John's car still hadn't returned, but it couldn't be very long now, he said, and then he and Lala would go straight back to Glen Ruth. They'd expect me there about nine in the morning. So I said goodnight and went down to the motel for a sleep. It was sort of reasonable: three single beds in each room, for groups of stockmen or prospectors or geologists (not the sort of place where couples would choose to travel). Clean, and they aimed to keep it that way. There was a notice on the wall: "Please do not put boots, shoes or feet on the beds." Difficult.

I had breakfast as early as it was served and was on the road by half-past seven the next morning. I followed four miles of bitumen along the road to the west, and then turned off onto a wide dirt track towards the big stations. Just by Gunnawarra there was a pretty girl walking towards Garnet. She looked more like a Torres Strait Islander than an Aborigine. It was a funny place to walk, for she'd have all of thirty miles before she reached town.

The road from Mount Garnet to Glen Ruth goes through different kinds of country and it reflects them all. A few miles of red clayey surface then a rich, black soil. Pebbles, crunching underwheel, and then soft white sand. I got to Glen Ruth just on nine. There was the same man I'd spoken to the previous day. He was quite taken aback. No, he'd already told me yesterday, John Tooth wasn't at home, he was in Garnet.

What a fool I was! I tried to explain that I knew he'd told me that before — but I'd seen John there and he'd said he was returning. It all sounded so lame. Why on earth hadn't I checked in Garnet that he *had* left before driving all the way out here again!

There was nothing to do but drive the sixty miles back, over the sand and pebbles and black soil and clay, past kangaroos looking for a place to sleep out of the sun, into a swarm of locusts that were stunned by the impact of the radiator and trapped between its mesh. When I had to stop to open a gate, they suddenly came alive again and inundated me with their flapping wings and their noise.

Six miles past the Gunnawarra turn-off, the girl was still walking along towards Garnet, wearing a flowered dress and a pair of rubber thongs and carrying just a small bundle. She didn't try to thumb a lift, but I stopped to offer one. She was headed for Cairns. Cairns? That was the best part of a hundred and fifty miles away. I could take her some of the way — to Innisfail, and she'd be able to hitch a lift up the main highway from there.

The engine was noisy and she was naturally soft-spoken, so it was hard to converse except by shouting. She was an Islander, her mother now lived in Cairns, and she'd been working at Gunnawarra as a house-maid. Early that Sunday morning she'd just decided to move on out. I couldn't catch everything she said, but it seemed she'd left her pay lying on the bed — whether accidentally or on purpose was unclear. But she was never going back. What had happened? Had anyone tried any-thing on with her? No — she just didn't like it there, decided to leave.

John Tooth was at the pub in Garnet, playing darts. The car had been returned so late that they'd decided to camp the night in town. He was sorry, but he was already pretty full, too full to do any Warrgamay today. Drunker than he'd been the previous night, in fact. I'd have to come back another day. He wanted to help, but he had to be sober. O.K., I'd be back in a fortnight. Fine, he'd be out at Glen Ruth, waiting for me. I wrote down the planned date, Saturday 4 November, and my name, and made sure the piece of paper was safely stowed in his pocket.

My passenger may have wondered at this, but I didn't attempt any explanation. It would have been far too complicated anyway. We drove on, a straight road through the open forested country to Ravenshoe, and then winding around sloping dairy pastures on the tableland to Millaa Millaa. I was getting hungry and suggested lunch. She said all right, and wanted to wait in the car, but I at least persuaded her to come into the cafe with me. I couldn't persuade her to eat, though. She just sucked at a coke while I tucked in to grilled barramundi. We talked a bit, but there didn't seem much to say.

Another winding hour down the Palmerston Highway, and then I made straight for South Johnstone, where George Watson had moved the previous Christmas, to share a barracks with an old white friend of his, Mick Lonnergan. Mick was away visiting his son in Townsville, but I found George at home, sitting on a bed in the dirty, squalid cabin, watching a tennis game on Mick's large television set. George promised to help me find Alec Dennis and came out to climb in the car. He was very surprised at what he found there.

After I'd introduced them, George started talking to me in Mamu, and I replied in kind. *"Wanya ginyan yibi – nginu?"* I told him she wasn't my woman, that I was just giving her a lift towards Cairns. The girl sat there between us – impassive, as she had been the whole trip. But she was obviously finding things stranger and stranger – the fact of my talking to an old Aborigine in a language she couldn't understand seemed to be the last straw. George talked with her, mentioning some of the Torres Islander families in town, with whom she might be able to stay overnight. Just then we were overtaken by a station wagon full of people, and the girl asked me to attract their attention, and let her out. They were Islanders, and it soon transpired that they had friends in common. Rather dubiously, they took her on board. She seemed awfully relieved when she left us.

George then made me recount the whole story, everything she'd said.

"Don't believe a word of it," he declared.

"Don't you?" I asked (I always was rather gullible).

"No," he continued, "she never come from Gunnawarra. Some truck driver would have picked her up somewhere, had it off with her, and then just put her down in the middle of the bush. Stopped his lorry and told her to get out and walk. That's what they do when they've got what they want."

"She didn't seem that sort of girl," I wondered.

"Maybe not," said George, "but I think it would be the way I said."

Then, after a pause, he added: "You could have had her. She'd have gone with you all right."

"Well, maybe," I agreed, half-heartedly.

"Look, if you get anyone like that again and you don't want her, pass her on to me. I'm not too old."

"All right, I will," I said, to try to end the conversation.

Finding Alec Dennis was easy. We just went to King George V Park, in the middle of Innisfail, to see if anyone could give us a lead — and there were Alec Dennis and his family sitting under the shade of a tree. He didn't know much language, he said, and couldn't be of any help. But George wouldn't accept that, and bullied fifty words out of him. It turned out that Alec Dennis's language was Nyawaygi, not Warrgamay, and he knew so little that it really wasn't worthwhile persevering. But field work is full of dead ends like that. Every lead must be followed up, because it's hard to tell in advance which one may reveal a really good informant. And at least I'd achieved something that day!

I had a few questions to ask George arising out of the Dyirbal part of the course I'd been teaching in Canberra, and then we had a meal and a drink and a chat. I stayed around Innisfail that night in order to call in on Chloe the next day, before starting my main work at Yarrabah. I wasn't doing any serious study of Dyirbal just then — the grammar was being printed and I'd postponed work on getting texts and dictionary ready for publication until after I'd completed a grammar of Yidiny. But I had to call in on Chloe — she'd never forgive me if I didn't. Chloe was still living at Silkwood, but she'd moved over to Edgar and Mamie's place when Eunice went off to work elsewhere. Mamie greeted me with warmth, as she always does, and said Chloe had gone to Innisfail. She was going to the doctor first, and I might just catch her there — the surgery on the left just before the Jubilee bridge. Well, I called at the doctor's, but Chloe wasn't there and she hadn't been near the place. I knew Chloe from old. She never had trusted doctors. If she was feeling unwell, she'd like as not have gone to a Chinese herbalist, only she wouldn't tell anyone. And I didn't know where to start looking. I was so impatient at having done virtually nothing so far — it was now Monday lunchtime and I'd left Canberra early Friday morning — that I had to call it a day. It was time to drive up to Aloomba and Tilly Fuller, to enter again the beautiful, mystic world of Yidiny.

Following my normal practice, I'd sent Tilly Fuller a card the previous month, telling her roughly when I expected to call and asking if she would think back and try to remember as much as she could of the mother-in-law speech style, Jalnguy.

Tilly seemed really pleased to see me. As soon as I could get out my notebook, she was reeling off words and sentences in Jalnguy, saying them faster than I could write them down. The Jalnguy was gushing out of her so fluently that I quickly switched on the tape recorder and just let her talk, entirely in Jalnguy, until gradually she wound down and then stopped. It was as if she had a sudden recall of a huge segment of Jalnguy, a stream of discourse — a noun prodding an appropriate verb and then that the next noun, and so forth. But there was nothing really mysterious in the way it came. Mrs Fuller had been working very hard, thinking to herself in Jalnguy each evening since she'd received my card.

We then went back over the tape, transcribed it, translated each sentence into the everyday style, and then went over a few of the trickier grammatical queries I'd accumulated (as with Dyirbal, I did try to check out most things with two different speakers). Then Tilly was tired and we arranged that I'd come back at the weekend.

I made the familiar drive over the mountains to Yarrabah. Joe Rogers was still there and he put me in the VIP flat, the place where the Queensland minister of Aboriginal affairs might sleep if he stopped over a night at Yarrabah (although I'd be extremely surprised if he ever did). I think it was called the VIP flat because it had a fan in one bedroom. Otherwise you really had to know what you were doing. The shower only had hot water, and the bath only cold — soaping oneself in the former and then jumping into the latter to rinse became quite an art. And the pointer was broken on the temperature knob of the tiny electric hot plate (all cooking in a pan and a half). The trick here was to leave it on high permanently (having located this by trial and error) and to switch off at the wall. But there was an old fridge, and a table to work at and the flat was roomy. All in all pretty good living and working conditions for an Aboriginal settlement in Queensland.

I set out the next morning towards Dick Moses's house and met him half-way.

"They tell me you come in late last night," he said. "They seen your car and they come and tell me."

It was good to be back. We settled under the familiar fig tree, just by the church. I asked Moses how things had been with him and he said he'd had a bit of a bad chest in the wintertime but it was all right now. He got out his pipe and tobacco pouch, and then called up a small boy who was lazing nearby and sent him up to the store to buy a box of matches. Dick blew his nose, crossed his legs and waited for me to begin.

The thing that had been concerning me most, as I'd tried to work over the Yidiny materials in Canberra, was the nature of the vowel that was added to some nouns and adjectives before a case ending. The word for "top-knot pigeon" is *gambiin* with the second vowel long. Ergative case (marking when it "does" something) was *gambin-u-nggu*, and genitive (marking a possessor) was *gambin-i-ni*. These seem to involve a root *gambin*, with both vowels short, and the regular ergative *-nggu* and genitive *-ni*. All this was all right. What worried me was the vowel between them, *-u-* in one instance and *-i-* in the other.

Different words seemed to take different vowels. "Two" is *jambuul* and its ergative was *jambul-a-nggu* and genitive *jambul-a-ni*, the intervening vowel being *-a-* in each case. And sometimes the vowel had a very short, central quality. *Gubuum* is "black pine" (an important food staple in traditional times), but I couldn't decide whether the genitive should be written *gubum-u-ni* or *gubum-i-ni*. The vowel was short and indeterminate, a bit like that in English words like *the*. (And central vowels like this never occurred anywhere else in Yidiny!)

Well, I'd been through all the data gathered on the field trip the previous Christmas, and I *thought* I understood the principles that determined what vowel should come between a certain root and a particular case ending. I had a list of questions to ask which would check this hypothesis, and then there would be oodles of work (about an hour each day, maybe) working out the details for each noun and adjective of this type.

Within half an hour it became quite clear that my hypothesis about the vowels was plain wrong. There was nothing for it but to go back to the drawing board — as it were — and begin all over again. Really, I'd been trying to generalise on too little data. Of the eight or nine hundred nouns and adjectives that had been gathered so far, about sixty or seventy took this intrusive vowel. I should try and get as many case forms as possible (there are seven cases all told) with every one of these words, check them for consistency with earlier data, using both Moses and Tilly Fuller, and only then try to induce a general hypothesis that would explain the data.

I worked hard at this, and by the end of the fortnight had made good progress, although it took another two field trips to be certain that I had the correct description. But it put me under tremendous pressure. The first Yidiny field trip had been little short of euphoric, as I revelled in the beauty of the language, unravelling the more obvious niceties of structure. Now I was trying to get below the surface, attempting to understand *exactly* what was happening and why, and it was hard. My second visit to Yarrabah developed into something of an intellectual nightmare.

We carried on working on all aspects of the language. On the card I'd sent to Moses I'd asked him to think up more stories, and he told a long legend about Gulnyjarubay, a hero from "storytime" (what people in other parts of Australia call "dreamtime"), who went around Yidinyji and Gungganyji territory naming places by what he saw there, or things that befell him at a particular location.

At one place, Gulnyjarubay found water bubbling up out of a pool of mud, bubbles forming and bursting in the mud. He called this place Ngabul, after the noun *ngabul* which describes this "bursting noise". A bit further east a little frog, *wiji*, was crying out, and that place was called Widiy. Gulnyjarubay went north, and as the day darkened he made himself a torch from a tea-tree, *gidi*. Just past a small hill he threw the spent torch away, and named that place Gidila.

Days with Dick Moses had a fixed pattern. I'd originally reckoned to work from about nine till twelve and two till five, finishing when the bell rang for a mealtime in the old people's dining hall. But lunch and tea got to be served earlier and earlier each year. In 1970, it was twelve noon, but by 1972 the bell would go at twenty to or quarter to, and by 1975 it could be twenty past eleven. And the same with tea. So we'd start at about half-past eight, and then again around half-past one. That gave me time for a couple of hours' work on my own early in the morning, another hour at lunchtime, and then two or three hours in the evening — going over what we'd done that day, extracting new vocabulary, checking text transcriptions, assessing the answers to grammatical questions and devising new ones to be gone through the next day. And it gave Moses a bit of a rest after his lunch.

I always tried to vary what we did, never staying with one thing for more than an hour or so at a time. First thing in the morning was a good time for the hardest job of all — checking difficult grammatical points. I might have tried to formulate a syntactic rule and would then work out some types of complex sentences which should be all right if the rule was correct. Moses would give me an opinion on them. Then I'd get more examples of tricky affixes with a representative selection of verbs, and so on.

We might do grammar for the best part of an hour. Moses never had tea-breaks or gossip-breaks, but I'd give us a rest from hard thinking by perhaps playing a bit of tape — a text of Tilly Fuller's that I wanted to check up a couple of points from, or some Gunggay songs from an LP recorded at Yarrabah a few years back by Alice Moyle (the singer had since died). Or Dick might ask me to play something by George Watson, just to hear another language spoken straight and true.

The second half of the morning might be spent going through vocabulary cards, checking a dozen new verbs that had come up the previous week, weighing each one, getting sentences illustrating its various senses, and contrasting it with near-synonyms. Then after lunch there might be another half-hour's grammar, or perhaps playing back another text, something Dick had recorded on the previous trip. Although I might have it pretty well transcribed, there could be still a couple of points where what I heard on the tape seemed different from what I had on paper, and a couple of words used in a metaphoric sense that required further clarification. Finally, I might ask Moses if he was ready to record a new story, one he'd been thinking about for the past few days. He would tell it in Yidiny, then, after playing that back, would go over the same story in English.

Transcribing a new text took a fair time — about half an hour for each minute of story. So a twelve-minute text would take a full day to go through the first time. But to spend a whole day on one thing could be a bit stultifying. To avoid that I might start the transcription after lunch, do half that day, and then finish it off the next morning.

All this took place under the same old fig tree, between the church and the old people's cabins. Dick and I always arrived within a few minutes of each other. Other people would sit down with us for half an hour, or even a whole morning, listening and approving, very occasionally making a suggestion. Sometimes children would sit there and giggle when Moses and I exchanged sentences in Yidiny; now and then Dick might have to tell them to "listen more quiet" — then they might learn something.

If it rained, we moved over to the verandah of Dick's house. I'd once suggested going over to where I was staying, and we did have half a day there, but Dick was obviously uncomfortable. He preferred his own territory. Each old folks' cabin was for two people — a married couple, or a pair of widows or widowers. There were two small rooms joined by a verandah on which were a couple of chairs and a small metal table. They were modern and functional — each room with a single bed, built-in wardrobe and drawers, and a big mirror on the wall. *On* the wall, not inside a cupboard door. Moses had hung a blanket over his (as I would have) — presumably he didn't care to see himself every time he turned around.

One afternoon the ground was wet from a lunchtime shower, so Dick swept the verandah before we settled down at the table. I wanted to ask more examples of the suffix -*Vji*-. It could mark a verb as reflexive, but it had all sorts of other functions too. The first thing was to get the suffix with a variety of verbs, of all semantic types, and see what effect it had with each. And after an hour of that I reckoned we deserved a treat, so we finished off the day with classifiers.

Yidiny doesn't have genders, as Dyirbal has, but instead it has about twenty generic terms, or classifiers, things like "person", "edible animal", "ant", "tree", "vine", "stone", "drinkable liquid". To speak felicitous Yidiny, one should use the appropriate generic before a specific noun. Rather than "the girl dug up yams", a Yidinyji would say "the *person* girl dug up the *vegetable* yams", and so on. I was trying to work out the scope of each classifier. *Minya* "edible animal" would be used with *yalburr* "grey frog species", since that can be eaten, but never with *wiji*, a smaller inedible frog. *Bulmba* is the classifier "habitable place" and can be used with *burray* "cave"; but *burray* can also co-occur with another classifier, *walba* "stone", since it is made of stone.

Classifiers are highly revealing of the semantic organisation of Yidiny vocabulary, and of how its speakers view the world. They were easy to work on, not requiring terribly much analytic thought, something that was fun to do when both Moses and I were feeling tired, and a bit jaded.

I'd come armed with the first five lessons of "Learning the Yidiny-Gunggay language", fifty copies of each. Alf Neal and two other members of the council called around one evening to discuss how we could organise the lessons. As luck would have it, one of the Yarrabah schoolteachers, Sue Chinnery, had done a bit of linguistics in her teaching course and was really excited by the idea of teaching the language. We had a couple of good chats, and the first class was arranged for next Wednesday evening, in the school. I'd conduct that — and then Sue would take over the lessons. Both of us would of course have the considerable assistance of Dick Moses.

There seemed to be more general interest in language than I'd noticed the previous year. Robert Patterson, or Nyalmbi, was one of the most articulate and determined of the Gungganyji. He greatly regretted not having learnt more than a few odd words of Gunggay from his parents. I'd got copies of Gribble's Gunggay vocabularies (published in *Science of Man,* 1900) and read these out — trying to make as much sense as I could of Gribble's transcription — to Moses and Nyalmbi. Dick recognised some words, and Robert thought a few others rang a bell, from way back in his childhood.

When Nyalmbi had gone off, Dick used to laugh at him, and at all Gungganyji — a relic of age-old tribal jealousines.

"He doesn't know nothing. He think he know. He think he remember them but he just imagine. Too late now. Should have listened to old people when he was boy. Plenty people speak Gunggay then. He could have learn. But no good now, all gone."

When Nyalmbi was actually there, though, Dick was pleasant and helpful. Robert told me about a cave over on the other side of the peninsula, at the end of King Beach, with an old map painted on the rock which showed the journeying of a storytime woman named Bindam. We arranged to drive out to see it on Sunday. Moses said he might come along as well. He'd see how he felt.

When I went across to Aloomba on Saturday, as arranged, Tilly and Katie were out. Shopping in Gordonvale, someone said. I found them all right, bustling in and out of grocers and they said that since I was here with my "truck" they'd get a few big things it was difficult to take home in a car. Brooms and things. We had a pleasant morning, sitting on the bench waiting for one another and chattering away. Tilly told someone that I was like a son to her — I was looking after her and she was helping me — which was nice. We hadn't much time for language when I got them home, but we did a bit — some of those intrusive vowels in between noun roots and case affixes. Every bit helps.

Tilly was going up to the tableland to see a doctor there. He might tell her to stay up top — the mountains were better for her chest than the humidity of the coast country, especially with summer just round the corner. She'd be staying in a house just opposite McGillicudy's shop in Kairi (pronounced Kee-rye). I could call there on Friday, after finishing at Yarrabah, and she'd tell the story of Bibiyuwuy, a story-time man who started death. Ask Moses if he knew about Bibiyuwuy, too. That old man might have heard it. He did know a lot.

Then up to Blackfellow Creek and Pompey Langdon. Pompey was home, but he was a bit drunk. My heart sank — he was never very articulate or clear when sober (although the more I learnt, the better he was — Pompey understood my Yidiny better than my English). Still, I was able to get confirmation of most of the new Jalnguy words Tilly had remembered, and Pompey managed to drag up a few new ones himself.

I also asked a few other questions, things which had been worrying me for ages and which I hadn't been able to work out with Moses, such as the two words *wanyi* and *wanyirra,* both of which translated as "what". Was there any difference in meaning or function? Or were they real synonyms, freely interchangeable? I'd tried and tried to get at the difference, if any, but without success. Then suddenly, from Pompey's half-inebriated explanation, it became clear. *Wanyi* was the more general word, used when one had no idea at all what something was. *Wanyirra* was more specific, to be employed if one knew what classifier an object fell under, but not what species it was. *Yingu wanyi?* I asked. Pompey translated it as "what's this?". And *yingu wanyirra?* That was rendered as "what *kind of* sugar or meat or anything?"

Hearing a noise one might say *wanyi gadang* "what's that coming?". The reply could be *minya gadang* "an animal is coming" using the classifier *minya* "(edible) animal" And the next question might be *minya wanyirra gadang* "what sort of animal is coming?", to which a reply could be *minya gurrili gadang,* "a kangaroo is coming". Back at

Yarrabah I looked through my list of examples of *wanyirra* — almost every one of them was next to a classifier, like *minya wanyirra*. I checked it out a bit further with Moses on Monday, and he seemed relieved that that was another thing we didn't have to keep coming back to, over and over again.

On Sunday afternoon, we went on the trip to the painted rock — Robert Patterson and Alf Neal and I and a couple of others. Moses decided to come too, although he said he might not be able to walk very far. We made a couple of stops on the way to look at interesting trees and Moses explained how the fruits were prepared, where bark was taken from for water-bags and canoes, which tree to use for spears. He showed me how to roll up a leaf into an efficient drinking vessel. Robert and Alf lamented that the children at Yarrabah didn't know the names of most of these trees — neither the English nor the Yidiny/ Gunggay names, nor what the trees were good for.

We drove out along the rutted track to the other side of Cape Grafton Peninsula, and along King Beach until the sand looked too soft ahead. Then we walked for maybe two miles, but after less than half that distance, Dick Moses had to stop, even though we'd been going very slowly.

"I got no more breath," he told us. "You fellow go on to cave. Bring back picture. I wait here for you."

It was more of an overhanging ledge than a real cave, but on the underside — four feet above the ground — was a faded design. Photographs wouldn't be likely to show much, so I tried to reproduce the drawing onto a six-by-four-inch vocabulary card. Alf and Robert helped, pointing out what was a mossy patch (to be ignored) and how the lines of dots went, across the solid splashes of colour. We were all excited that it had been found so easily, a relic from the real tribal Gungganyji who would last have touched up the colours more than half a century before. Robert had a good idea of the significance of the different types of mark, but he wanted to discuss them with Dick.

Moses had made his way slowly back to the vehicle. He and Robert sat on the sand, poring over the card, each remembering another bit of the Bindam legend, reinforcing and correcting each other. I don't think I've ever seen two people more genuinely enthusiastic about something, elated with the spirit of discovery, a sort of religious discovery (an escape from the drab certainty of life at Yarrabah).

Fig. 14. Robert Patterson (Gunggay) standing by the rock that bears a map of Bindam's travels, at King Beach, Yarrabah Reserve. (1972)

The following day Moses told me, in Yidiny, the full legend of Bindam, as it had been remembered and reconstructed on the beach that Sunday afternoon. Bindam had run away from her husband, Gamburrguman, and the dots represented her path around the beach; the solid lines in the diagram were geographical features she encountered. Like many — indeed, most — other legends Dick told, this was essentially a travelogue, a list of the places Bindam visited and the names she assigned. The mouth of a creek bounded by high rocks was called Jalja, after the adjective *jalja* "full", because the water rose high within this narrow opening. And then to Bubunji, so called because there were many silky-oak trees, *bubun,* growing there. Finally Bindam went across to Murubay, Green Hill, and then settled down at Jarrugan, known to white people as Walsh's Pyramid.

Moses wanted to keep the card on which I had copied down the design. I wanted to make a photocopy of it in Canberra, and then pass the original back to Dick — he plainly set a high value on it and told me he'd spent some hours examining the routes, and so on. But Sue Chinnery also wanted to have a look, and somehow I never did get a copy for myself.

That business about which vowel would go between some roots and a case ending was still occupying my mind. Too much. Maybe it was also living alone in the VIP flat — although I did talk to people, and was even invited to a party on King Beach one night by the schoolteachers. But I seemed unable to relax. Looking back over the notebooks from that trip, I seem to have asked questions in an odd order, jumping about nervously from one page to another, whereas I would normally go through things in a more settled and logical manner.

Some previous VIPs had left a stack of paperbacks in the flat and I started *The Quick Red Fox* by John D. McDonald. Instant escapism. It seemed to work, a bit. I rationed myself to quarter of an hour after lunch and half an hour at night (and then another half-hour or so when I couldn't sleep, and then another when sleep still eluded me, and so on . . !) I'd never read a detective story before — preferring science fiction and mainstream novels and travel books — but that turned me on, and ever since I've always had a Dick Francis or Raymond Chandler around, to turn to in times of out-of-the-ordinary stress and pressure.

Then we had the first Yidiny lesson, on Wednesday evening. I'm always a bit scared about talking to a new type of audience, but this time I was plain petrified. Would I be able to get things across to a group of Yarrabah Aborigines? How did they regard me, a white man, working on their own language — their own tribal heritage, with a history that undoubtedly went back far beyond the shallow history of the English language? This didn't make sleep any easier.

Sue and I and Moses went along to the school early. The desks had been put in a circle. One family sidled in, trying to be inconspicuous, to sit down right at the far end. Then another three people, sitting down

half-way between them and us. And gradually the number built up to
about twenty-five or thirty. Everyone had a copy of Lesson One. An
introductory paragraph emphasised that the only real way to learn a
language was to use it, and encouraged them to speak in Yidiny to Dick
Moses or Richard Hyde, who would then reply to them in the language.

The first thing was the sounds. Some of these are the same as English
– *b, d, g, m, n, l* – but others are different. English has *ng* (two letters
represent a single sound) at the end of words – the sound after *i*
in *sing* – but in Yidiny this sound starts many words, important words
like *nguju* "no", *ngayu* "I".

And then there are the two *r* sounds.

"What's the word for 'nose'?" I asked Dick.

"Jingay."

I'd forgotten that he'd given me two words, and this one didn't have
any *r*. "No, the other one.'

Dick looked blank. My mind raced. "You told me *digirr* was also
'nose'."

"Oh, *digirr*," Moses repeated after me. And then I'll swear that he
said "It's not."

When I heard this, everything seemed to close in around me. I've
tried to brazen things out often enough in my life – when I found I
hadn't explained something absolutely correctly in a class in London or
Canberra. But no way out seemed possible here. Perhaps playing for
time I asked him to repeat it.

"Sorry?"

And then Moses said the same thing. By denying this he seemed to
be casting doubt on the whole lesson, the project, my very presence
there.

Suddenly, out of my despair a light shone – exploded into a
thousand coloured flares. What Moses had actually said was not "It's
not." He'd said "snot", indicating that *digirr* could be used to refer to
"nose" and also, more specifically, to "nasal mucus".

We had quite a good lesson, from then on. Moses was really a terrific
support. Everyone around the room practised the sounds, and in the
process learnt several dozen of the more important words. The contrast
between long and short vowels was crucial enough to emphasise early
on: *malan* "flat rock" as against *malaan* "right-hand".

After an hour and a quarter, I felt that was enough for the first
night. We'd covered half the first lesson. Someone asked. "What about

simple sentences?", which were in the remaining part. Oh, it would take two weeks to cover each lesson, I said, although in fact I hadn't really known in advance how much we'd be able to do at a time. Moses seemed very satisfied with the evening, and Sue Chinnery was enthusiastic about carrying on from there. Certainly it could have been a lot worse. But I still didn't get to sleep until close to dawn.

I outlined to Sue what lessons six to twelve would cover, and promised to write these up and send copies along as soon as needed. By all accounts, she did very well on this project. The adult classes in the evening carried on for a few months, but numbers gradually dropped off. There was no real impetus to learn the language — nothing they could do with it. And it was always hard to work up enthusiasm for anything in the atmosphere that prevailed at Yarrabah.

But Sue also taught Yidiny to some of the children in school, and that seems to have been a decided success. Their normal curriculum had virtually no Aboriginal content — it was the same as that used for white children in Brisbane. In fact, the schoolbooks may very well have included veiled derogatory comments about the autochthonous peoples of Australia. But the lessons Sue conducted enabled them to see something of their own heritage, and that they did have a language of their own, with a beautiful and intricate structure. It must have helped the children's self-image, and kindled a little pride. Living there, they'd need that.

Then Sue Chinnery was moved away, or she left (I'm not sure which) and no other teacher continued the work. But Robert Patterson, our middle-aged Gungganyji consulant, started going up to the school. I supplied photocopies of everything written on the Yarrabah language and culture and artefacts, from Gribble's books and Roth's *Bulletins*. And I sent up duplicated copies of a sizeable Yidiny-Gunggay vocabulary. By 1977, Robert was being paid to go round all the schools in the Cairns area, giving a talk, once a fortnight, on Aboriginal traditional life and language. It was a small contribution to the Queensland educational system, but a most valuable one.

I'd mentioned to Moses that Tilly Fuller had promised to tell me the story of Bibiyuwuy, and he said he'd heard that story, from an old Yidinyji woman at Yarrabah. He recorded it for me, and on Thursday, my last day at Yarrabah, we were able to transcribe the legend. We also went through some last bits of grammar, and a final instalment of vowels between noun roots and case endings. My head was like a sieve from lack of sleep, things chasing each other around as if it were a race — a randomised race — and I had to concentrate really hard to pronounce the Yidiny words and sentences even half-way correctly, so that Moses could comprehend them. At lunchtime, I just lay down and rested, and finished *The Quick Red Fox*, to gather strength for the afternoon.

Around five o'clock, Moses and I said goodbye, until next year. I did a couple of hours' work, cooked some supper, and then went to bed early, exhausted. And, of course, couldn't sleep. I began reading another VIP book, *Lost Horizon* by James Hilton. Good book, but it didn't help. By four in the morning, I was quite desperate. I couldn't continue. A plan formed in my restless mind: if I left at seven, I could drive straight down to Townsville, drop the vehicle off at the Department of Works, and catch the midday plane to Canberra. Appointments with Tilly Fuller on Friday and John Tooth on Saturday would simply have to go by the board. I just couldn't continue in this state.

Then I did sleep, from five until seven. Just enough, and deep enough, to make me feel relaxed and able to carry on. After all, I had never before run out on a situation like this. So, going very slowly and steadily, I drove over the Murray Prior Range to the sugar fields of the Mulgrave River. I spent a couple of hours with Katie Mays, and then went up the Gillies Highway to Kairi. A cassowary peeked out from the forest just past Little Mulgrave, then ran in front of me — as I slowed down — and away into the bush the other side. That was cheering — you don't see cassowaries on the road very often.

The shop had been owned by McGillicudy twenty or thirty years before; Tilly Fuller just hadn't kept up with the change of owners. Eventually I found it, and Tilly, who had rented a room in a house just across from it. "Twenty dollars a week they ask for this room and food," she complained, and I agreed that it was a lot. She was going to stay up on the tableland now — much better for her health and nearer Ranji's work anyway. And they'd live in the back of McGillicudy's shop — for eight dollars a week, a much more reasonable rent.

She was interested to hear Dick's Bibiyuwuy, which began with a child being found inside a giant white apple, *gurubal*. It was good Yidiny, Tilly decided, but he'd got the story wrong. That hadn't been the way she'd been told it, anyway. And then Tilly told me her version. She sat on one chair and I was on the other in the chintzy front room, looking through the open doorway onto the street. There was no table and I held the microphone quite close as Tilly told the story, in a soft low voice, consonants lightly aspirated because of her chest condition. It was the last story Tilly ever told me, and it was a good one.

Two male children had been born. When they grew up, one had two wives but the other none. The married brother went out one day. He cut an ash tree, took out a grub and tasted it. It tasted of semen, telling him that his wives were being made love to by his brother, back at the camp. He returned and accused his brother, who denied the charge. The married man hit him in the back of the neck, killing him. He dug a hole to bury the body — but their mother first cut off the dead man's head, and kept it in a bark container.

The spirit of the murdered man went and bathed in the salt water. Then he returned, bringing a black bream on a small stick, for all the people to eat.

"You murdered me," he said to his brother, "but I've returned."

Then he enquired: "What's this stink around the camp?"

Everyone sat silent.

When the spirit had gone away, they spoke among themselves. "What can we do? The head must be buried. It should have been done long ago."

When the spirit returned with the same question, his mother told him the truth. "I cut off your head after you died, wanting to gaze on the skull of my dead child."

The spirit groaned: "Now that I've seen my own skull, I'm returning to my spirit-home in the water. Leaving you all. Going away."

And as he went through the trees, jumping over logs, he called out "Wuy, wuy, wuy", and was known as Bibiyuwuy from then on.

"You can eat the black bream I brought," he called back, "but in three days you'll follow me. I'm the first one to go the spirit-home, crying as I travel."

And that was the beginning of death, Tilly said. There was a bit more to the story — the married brother repented of what he had done, now blaming his wives for having seduced the brother, and everyone mourned the dead man, recounting his virtues. Their mother got headaches and felt dizzy; then they all moved camp and she recovered. But this seemed a somewhat gratuitous coda. What struck me quite forcibly was the similarity to the Mamu legend of Gijiya, which George Watson had recorded on Palm Island eight years before. The two stories were by no means identical but there were many points of similarity.

We then went through the text, transcribing it. How do you think Tilly would describe, in English, the unmarried brother's misbehaviour with the wives? She wouldn't use anything as chi-chi as "make love", nor as erudite and soulless as "copulate with", nor as crude as the normal four-letter word (although she would have known this). One gets a certain insight into the white social world with which Tilly had contact from the expression she used: "he interfered with her".

It would have been anticlimactic to have attempted anything else that day. I wished Tilly good health and she said to come back soon — between us we'd get that language straightened out before it was too late.

I stayed at the Mount Garnet motel for another night (but this time I didn't go anywhere near the hotel). After an hour finishing *Lost Horizon* — as brilliant and relaxing a story, in its different way, as the one Tilly had told — I actually slept for eight hours, putting the puzzles of Yidiny vowels far away.

At Glen Ruth, John and Lala Tooth were waiting for me. John had been thinking over his Warrgamay. And Lala, now that she was sober, was a charming hostess. They lived in a corrugated iron shack opposite the stables, but Lala had contrived to make it cheerful and pleasant. It was fairly clean, for one thing. And she had her best crockery, out of the tin trunk, to offer me tea and a piece of cake.

John Tooth was born, probably a few years before 1900, of a Girramay mother by way of a Malay father. But he'd been brought up by his Warrgamay grandfather, at Lannercost and Stone River. Although he regards Warrgamay as his native language, John is also proficient in Girramay. For the last few decades there had been plenty of people to talk to in Girramay or Jirrbal (Lala, for instance), but no one else who knew any Warrgamay, so his Warrgamay was far from fluent. John had to think quite hard to answer almost every question. But this was compensated for by his intelligence and application. He also had a fine linguistic sense. If I presented him with a putative sentence which wasn't perfectly acceptable, John would query it with the words: "It don't seem to rhyme". He might then alter the grammar slightly so that an acceptable piece of Warrgamay was produced, something that "did rhyme".

One of the most useful techniques of field work I had learned on my

Fig. 15. John Tooth (Warrgamay) and Lala Tooth (Jirrbal) outside their quarters at Glen Ruth Station. (1972)

second or third day, back in October 1963: if anyone says he can't give texts, play him a text by another speaker, extol its virtues, and imply that he couldn't do as well if he tried. This had first stung Chloe into action, when she heard the inane ramblings of Birdy Curtis's three old ladies and immediately produced five beautiful stories. And it had worked a few times since (although of course it didn't *always* work). I played to John and Lala one of George Watson's texts (which they could of course understand). And then John recorded a text, quite short and rather hesitant, but it was a text in Warrgamay, the first I'd obtained. It was about a time when John and some friends had been drinking, and they thought they saw a ghost; a funny little autobiographical snippet.

We had a good Saturday, working through names for birds and animals and fishes and parts of the environment, and checking and filling out the pronoun paradigm I'd got from Alf Palmer. The Tooths invited me to come back the next day, since it was clear there were many more things I wanted to ask.

There seemed nowhere to stay at Glen Ruth, so I drove back to Mount Garnet for the night and another long deep sleep. Then on Sunday, John gave another brief text, a traditional story about two black wallabies (dreamtime men) who had two parrots as wives, and about the two eaglehawks who stole them away. And after that we went through adjectives and verbs and lots of tenses and cases.

Since John also knew Girramay — but was sufficiently intelligent and organised to keep the two languages apart — I was able to ask questions in Girramay, sometimes checking in both Girramay and English to make sure I'd understood some tricky point properly, such as words referring to locations. *Yala* is "here" in Warrgamay and *yalangga* "there". Then *nyagu* is "to here; hither" and *nyagungga* is "to there, thither". This seemed to be unusual. Dyirbal had *yalay* "here", *yalu* "to here", and *balay* "there", *balu* "to there". But, John affirmed, *balu* would be translated by *nyagungga, balay* by *yalangga, yalu* by *nyagu* and *yalay* by *yala*. That was the way it was.

I finally left them at four o'clock on Sunday, intent on getting down the rough track to Cardwell before dark. We'd had a most enjoyable and relaxing couple of days, and had made tremendous progress with the main facts of Warrgamay. John said that there was one other speaker he knew of — Lambert Cocky, who lived somewhere around Ingham. So I drove straight there and called at the police station to see if they knew where Lambert lived. Yes, sure, he was at Sheahan's farm, fifteen or twenty miles out along the road to Abergowrie. It was now pretty late, but I rang Mr Sheahan from Ingham. Certainly, I could come out early in the morning and talk to Lambert if I wanted to.

I was there before eight to meet Lambert, who was quite tall, and with shoulders and bodily frame that were wide for an Aborigine of those parts. He had a dark skin, darker than anyone at Murray Upper, and was about the same age as John Tooth. Lambert was moving around the farmyard with a deliberative shuffle, doing the jobs that had been entrusted to him. I said who I was and who had sent me.

"Johnnie – he still up at Glen Ruth? Yes, I know Johnnie, Johnnie Tooth." Lambert drew out his vowels and seemed to spit the stressed words, like "Tooth". He didn't have any objection to helping me, but I'd have to wait until he'd finished his jobs. That seemed fair enough.

So I sat in the shade and went over some of the points John hadn't been totally sure of, and for which he had suggested Lambert as a second authority. Lambert took a bucket to get feed for the hens, went across to the coop and gave it to them, a handful at a time, talking, muttering all the time. Then another sack and something else for the hens. And water for them. Then something else. After half an hour I walked across to where Lambert was feeding the cockatoos. I called their Warrgamay name, *"gayambula"*. Lambert seemed pleased.

"They *gayambula* all right. Johnnie tell you that, did he?"

A few more minutes. I asked Lambert again when he'd be ready.

"Got to finish these job," he muttered.

But I mentioned that I had to drive sixty-odd miles to Townsville, drop off the vehicle, and catch the one o'clock plane. So I would have to leave at about half-past ten. One of the white men – a Sheahan – working in the yard heard this.

"Come on Lambert," he half-urged, half-ordered, "talk to this fellow now. You've got all day to feed the animals after he's gone."

Lambert didn't seem to mind much, although he continued muttering to himself as he put the pails away, wiped his hands, pulled up two upturned kerosene tins and sat down by the fence, just outside the tiny hut (almost a hutch) in which he lived.

I began by playing John Tooth's two texts. Then I asked a few lexical questions, things John had been a bit dubious about, and one or two points of grammar. Then Lambert recorded a short text. His father and grandfather had told him of massacres by the Native Police, just before he was born, when the Warrgamay tribesmen were chased into the bush and shot at. Simply murdered.

Since the recorder was on, Lambert offered a song, one which he said had been made up by John Tooth's father (stepfather?), about "chucking spears and dancing." Then a song about a ghost, looking at itself in a glass – "good dance – oh we dance there in Hawkins Creek." A song about a Chinese girl brushing her hair. Then a Girramay song about "telegraph, when you ringing up, want to listen who that fellow talking somewhere else, that's what he mean. We dance — dance in Tully."

By this time, two white men had come up, leaning over the fence enjoying the concert, pretending not to, covering up with ribald comments. Lambert didn't want to stop singing, but there were a few more points I hoped to clear up. Some bird names. The white men stayed on to listen. Then Lambert couldn't remember the English name of *garamgaram.* "That *garamgaram,* he tell us when cyclone come, in old days, before white people here."

This slayed our audience. "Go on Lambert," they kidded him, "you got a bird that tells you about cyclone. Pretty smart bird that, eh? Tallest story I ever heard."

Lambert continued, seemingly unperturbed. And I explained to them, quite simply, that when seagulls are seen this far inland it did indeed presage the coming of a cyclone. These birds will vacate the coast at the first hint of a high wind.

Mocking comments were suddenly replaced by half-respect. I had to go, since it was already eleven o'clock. As I backed out of the driveway, I saw Lambert shuffling around, arranging the kerosene tins back tidily against the wall of his hut. And I could see he was still muttering to himself.

13

"Those are good for you"

While I'd been in America, Ken Hale had imbued me with the importance of training native speakers in the principles of linguistics, so that they could describe their own languages. It is much more satisfactory to have a native speaker analyse a language, than for people like me to do it. And of course this could fulfil an important social role, involving people in their own bilingual educational policies, and providing jobs for them.

In 1971, very soon after arriving in Canberra, I'd tried to interest the Australian National University in a scheme to bring a couple of bright, well-motivated native speakers of Australian languages to the university, to teach them linguistics. A special programme would have to be devised, since scarcely any Aborigines had had the opportunities for secondary schooling. It was a proposal that demanded educational courage, and special funding. Unfortunately, the top brass at the ANU couldn't be persuaded. Our university coat of arms includes a boomerang across the middle of the shield. But the only interpretation I could advance was that (at that time, at least) proposals concerning Aboriginal education just came flying straight back.

Then, in late 1972, a Labor government was elected, for the first time in twenty-three years. It didn't do everything right, by a long way, and it only lasted three years. But it changed the face of Australia, for the Aboriginal people most of all. When the Liberals got back in, they retained a number of the best Labor initiatives.

Australian politics had for decades been extraordinarily boring, but those first two weeks after the 1972 elections were in the real humdinger class. It would take time before all the Labor parliamentarians could meet to elect a cabinet, so Whitlam persuaded the governor-general (Sir Paul Hasluck) to swear in a two-man government for a fortnight — Whitlam and his deputy, Lance Barnard. They divided the twenty-seven ministries between them, and Whitlam devoted one day to each of his. On 14 December, he made a number of important policy announcements concerning Aborigines. They were to be given rights to some of their traditional tribal lands, for one thing. And bilingual education was to introduced, for another. Children would no longer have literacy lessons in English forced on them from the time they began school, if English was not their native language. Schooling would begin in the local language, and the children would learn to read and write in it before transferring these skills to English. (The policy could, of course, only be implemented in the Northern Territory, where the federal government had full authority.)

During the early Whitlam years, money flowed — as never before or since — for any good social cause. Rather than resurrect the idea of getting native speakers of Australian languages to Canberra to learn some linguistics, it seemed an appropriate moment to press for something much more ambitious: a School of Australian Linguistics, based in Darwin, the town nearest the largest number of viable language communities. The aim of the school would be to teach linguistics to native speakers of Australian languages, so that they could write grammars of their own languages, devise orthographies, and plan and implement bilingual education schemes. And eventually they would take their places on the staff of SAL, and perhaps of universities down south.

The establishment of this school was approved in late 1973, as a part of the new Darwin Community College. Unfortunately, the first director wasn't very experienced; it was a case of making some appointment or perhaps seeing the job disappear. Luckily, as it turned out, the whole thing was blown away by the great Darwin cyclone of Christmas Day 1974 — and the director left. It was restarted at Batchelor, sixty miles to the south, and eventually a new director was appointed — Dr Kevin Ford, who had lots of sound experience from both West and East Africa. SAL is now doing a steady and useful job. It's just a pity it hadn't been established fifty years earlier.

The other thing that suddenly became distinctly possible was land rights. I wrote a letter to the new minister for Aboriginal affairs about the people I knew. Yarrabah was gazetted as an Aboriginal reserve, but the Queensland government had complete control over it. The people wanted to own their own land, and run the settlement — they should surely be helped achieve this goal.

And then there were speakers of Jirrbal and Girramay, who'd never had even a government-owned reserve. All their traditional territory had simply been seized, and they had had to find a kindly farmer who would allow them to squat on a corner of land that had been theirs for millennia. My letter set out the case, and offered to supply any more information that might be needed. Minister succeeded minister with alarming rapidity in the Whitlam government, and I wrote to them all, making the same points.

Meanwhile *The Dyirbal Language of North Queensland* had been published — a couple of weeks after Labor won — by Cambridge University Press. I posted off hardback copies to Chloe and George, and put aside a paperback to take to the Cowans. I carried on working with Yidiny, typing up the new texts and completely rewriting the draft chapter on phonetics and phonology. It was now three times as long, and much nearer accounting for all the facts I'd observed. I was also drafting a grammar of Warrgamay, with a list of points that still required attention.

Now that both Yidiny and Warrgamay were under control — although they both needed quite a lot more steady work — it seemed the right time to go back to Nyawaygi, originally spoken to the south of Warrgamay. I'd got a bit of data from Long Heron and Willie Seaton in 1963/64, and then in 1967. Seaton was still alive. Bev Haydon, Mrs Cowan's daughter, who now lived in Ingham, told me she'd seen him walking around town, a tall, erect, blind man with a high-crowned pork-pie hat. So I went over my old notes, trying to work out the inflections on nouns and verbs and to decide which things needed clarification.

In 1973, I snatched a field trip during the three-week August break between second and third terms. Willie Seaton, the first Aborigine I'd ever spoken to, back in October 1963, greeted me warmly. "Oh, Mr Dixon, I remember you. Haven't seen you for two or three years." In fact it was more than six years. The last time we'd talked was during a thunderstorm in Long Heron's leaky iron hut, Seaton explaining Heron's slurred sentences. Now Heron was gone.

But Willie Seaton was as bright and helpful as ever. He'd used

Fig. 16. Willie Seaton (Nyawaygi) at Toobana, near Ingham. (1973)

Nyawaygi in his childhood and remembered some hundreds of words. He could translate simple sentences from English, but there were no texts. I started going quite systematically through the vocabulary slips, checking the pronunciation of each. And Seaton did something that no one had ever done for me before: he mentioned other words that were phonetically very similar to a particular form, and which an English speaker might be likely to confuse.

Like most Australian languages, Nyawaygi has two *r* sounds. When I asked "worm", Willie Seaton not only gave the form *rrubi,* with a rolled initial (as in Scots), but cautioned against confusion with the imperative of the verb "to swallow", *rubi,* with a continuant *r* (similar to the *r*-sound in Australian English). Then *gurrijala* "eaglehawk", not to be muddled with *wurrijala* "barramundi". *Gawiga* was another word for "barramundi". Willie didn't know the term "synonym", but he explained the concept expertly, through an example from English. *"Wurrijala* and *gawiga* that's just the same thing, just like you say *man* or *bloke."*

"When did you leave Canberra?" Seaton asked.

"This morning, seven o'clock. Plane got me to Townsville about one o'clock. Picked up this vehicle and I was here by 3.30. Not bad?"

"Oh," said Willie, *"mali gaambijam, bulbayma."* Which means: don't do that, you might fall down (i.e., crash) — about the longest sentence he ever gave spontaneously.

I went back to Seaton the next morning and we had another most productive session. Then I spent an hour on Warrgamay with Arthur Wild.

Lambert Cocky was still at Sheahan's and we had another animated session. I called quite late in the day, after his fowl-feeding chores were over, but he still seemed preoccupied by having to cook tea soon, and it was only his curiosity concerning what I'd learnt about other languages that made Lambert break off from his self-imposed schedule of jobs to talk to me.

I made an early start on the difficult drive up the range towards Kirrama, with its steep, winding forest track and then the road that got lost among piles of boulders. John Tooth had received my card and gave me a good welcome. But Lala had died in the autumn. John was just going through her things. He didn't feel he had any use for the best crockery, so it was packed up carefully and wrapped in newspapers in a tin trunk, which I promised to take to John's son in Cairns.

Long vowels were one of the main topics on my agenda. In Yidiny, they could occur in any syllable except the first, but in Warrgamay long vowels are found only in the first syllable. *Julu* is a noun meaning "buttocks", but *juulu* is the adjective "black". The verb *badi-* means "to hook a fish", but *baadi-* is a quite different verb, "to cry". A few words from last time which I wasn't sure about. "Wallaby" had been taken down as *jijin* on one page and *jiijin* on another. "It's *jiiijin*," John said, emphasising and drawing special attention to the long first vowel.

Warrgamay needed great care, to separate out extraneous Dyirbal elements. La Mont West had passed on a lot of material he'd recorded from Jimmy Johnson, and I'd got over five hundred words from Alf Palmer; but these contained a fair admixture of forms from the Girramay dialect of Dyirbal. John Tooth also knew Girramay, although Lambert didn't. For every word I tried to get at least two people — one of them John or Lambert — confirming that it definitely was Warrgamay. I'm fairly confident that, by really careful checking, almost all the non-Warrgamay words were eliminated. My final vocabulary is, I'm prepared to bet, 99 per cent correct Warrgamay.

The housekeeper at Glen Ruth invited me to join them for meals, which was welcome. There were two eating places. I could go in the dining hut nearest the serving hatch with the white stockmen – as befitted my colour. Or in the next hut, where John and the other "darkies" ate. I chose to eat with John, and the white people didn't seem too offended.

Then John invited me to stay the night, which was doubly welcome. He had a bed in a spare room at his shed and some blankets. He even produced a sheet – unexpected luxury. We put the notebooks away at tea-time, and then sat by the fire, listened to the seven o'clock ABC news, and yarned. The previous year, I'd told John about Carl Lumholtz's book *Among Cannibals,* based on the year he spent living with the Warrgamaygan people at Herbert Vale in 1882/83. It contained accounts of daily life and customs, and a bit about the language. John had mentioned this to Robert Atkinson, owner of Glen Ruth, who scoffed and – it seemed – doubted that a book about John's tribe had ever been published. Could I get him a copy of it? I said I'd try. (Unfortunately the second-hand price was over a hundred dollars, and I wasn't able to fill that request until a reprint came on the market in 1981.)

I'd stupidly left the tape-recorder switched on after using it in Ingham, so the storage battery was flat. We plugged it in to the Glen Ruth supply, to recharge, but the generator never seemed to be on for long enough at one time. They'd put it on as often as the freezer required it, and then off for an hour, John said. We got a trickle of juice, enough to play back the texts made on my last visit and to check some points, but not enough to play things like George Watson's texts, which John had requested. John excused himself from telling any more stories this time; he didn't feel up to it since Lala had died.

The next day, Sunday, John suggested driving a few miles to the Herbert River, where some Jirrbalngan people from Mount Garnet were having a weekend camp. On the way he remarked – looking at the wide-bodied gums behind which in the old days a warrior might have been waiting, spear in hand – that things were different now. If you moved around too much in earlier times, you stood the risk of being killed by strange men, but not any more. I was a bit slow on the uptake: "You mean killed by a white man?"

"Oh no," John said grimly, "they still would. I mean by Aborigines, from another tribe."

I was quite taken aback by the matter-of-fact way John commented on white proclivities. But he meant it. I think everyone in Queensland accepts that if a black person is murdered, the police investigation is unlikely to be so intensive or thorough as if the victim were white. But I hadn't heard things put quite so bluntly before.

Four or five Jirrbal families were camping on the sandy shore just where a log bridge crossed the river, the children diving into the water and some of the men wandering a mile upstream to a deepish water-hole, to fish. John and I sat by the river and finished off the questions I had left — pronouns, ablative case ending, continuative forms of verbs, and a few more.

The previous year, John had refused to accept any money from me. He'd been quite adamant. When I said the university gave me money to pay people who helped with information on languages, John and Lala instructed me to give it to a charity. But now he was paying off the cost of Lala's funeral and was glad to accept both this year's money and last year's (although of course I didn't say it was that). Then it was time to go. I'd said I was hoping to make another trip in the summer.

"Nginda banaga garrimara!" shouted one of the Jirrbal men, who'd been bemoaning the fact that although they spoke their own language, the children just wouldn't use it, preferring English instead.

"Nga, garrimara," I called back, "in the summer."

I drove straight to Atherton that night, and in the morning called at the room in the back of McGillicudy's shop, in Kairi. No one was home, although there were signs that it was lived in; the shop itself appeared to have closed down. Then a neighbour told me that "the old lady" was in hospital at Atherton, because of her chest.

She was sitting up in bed, just next to a verandah. Tilly's eyesight was failing, but she could recognise a voice.

"Hello, do you remember me?"

"Yes, I know you. You're school teacher from Canberra. Man who writes down all my language."

Whenever people ask me what I do, and why I can't come up north more often, I explain about having to teach students at the ANU. Tilly's was a reasonable designation, one that I rather liked.

We went out onto the wide wooden verandah and talked for three-quarters-of-an-hour. Bits of Jalnguy, and a little grammar. And then Tilly was tired. I promised to call in next week, and carried off messages to her sister Katie, and to Pompey. Katie was now in a barracks at Edmonton, surrounded by fields of six-foot-high cane. I hadn't felt able to play the recorder in hospital, so Katie went through Tilly's Bibiyuwuy story, explaining some of the trickier bits as best she could.

Pompey was also in hospital, at Cairns, with a bump as big as a scrub-turkey egg on his forehead. He'd fallen off the bridge over Blackfellow Creek when drunk, onto the rocks of the dry river bed below. I called in to see him, with some fruit and cigarettes, but it was mostly a social call. With a head like that he wouldn't feel too much like linguistic work.

I'd written to Joe Rogers to expect me the following day. But it was school holiday time, when people from the south flock to Cairns in search of sun. Every single hotel and motel seemed to be full. At about half-past five, after being turned away from the twelfth place I'd tried, I rang Joe. He said to come on over – come straight up to the manager's house, in fact, for tea.

Bitumen had finally made it to the track over the mountains at Yarrabah, although there was still some dirt along the flat. The Rogers family had called on us in Canberra, during a camping tour of the south, so both sides had plenty of questions.

"Come in, Professor," began Joe. And then when I'd sat down. "And how is Mrs Professor. And all the . . . " His voice tailed off, but it was too good to miss.

"And all the little Professors?" I supplied.

Joe had put me up in the VIP flat again, he said, but this time I'd be sharing it with three other people. At last the baker's oven was being constructed, and my fellow-guests were Karl and Jock, two bricklayers from Sydney, together with Clem, the secretary of the New South Wales Bakers' Union. They were at Yarrabah for three weeks. The first couple of days had been spent examining some of the old ovens in Cairns, and work had actually begun the previous day. They'd be leaving when I did.

Clem introduced his team and explained the project. No traditional brick oven – with arching roof, packed around with sand – had been built in Australia for about fifty years. The trend had been towards replacing local bakeries with large, electric, bread factories. A few years ago, Clem had built a rough-and-ready oven at St Paul's, Moa Island, in the Torres Strait. And now he was fulfilling a lifetime's ambition by building a proper, traditional oven, at Yarrabah. Alf Neal's son, who was just finishing his apprenticeship in Sydney, would come home as community baker.

Clem's enthusiasm was infectious. He showed me the plans, worked out last year in consultation with a retired builder in Newcastle who'd helped build one of the last ovens of this type in Australia. When Clem had returned the previous month to discuss a few last details, he had found the man had died. They'd advertised in builders' trade papers and found Karl, who had built bakers' ovens in Germany before he'd emigrated. Jock, from near Inverness, was Karl's regular mate.

Karl and Jock were supposed to share one bedroom, but Karl preferred a couch in the living room. I was in with Clem, who seemed well enough disposed. (Karl and Jock regarded me with a suspicion that they probably had for anyone who didn't work with his hands — and especially when they couldn't rightly understand what the person actually did.) They were to get up at about 5.30 and be at work by 6. That was a bit early for me. I generally got up around 6.15 and started work soon after 6.30. Clem promised they'd have a quiet breakfast, so as not to disturb me.

The first morning it worked — there wasn't a sound. I strolled down just before half-past eight, and found Dick Moses sitting under the familiar fig tree, waiting for me. A couple of minutes' small-talk, and then we were into the agenda. Yidiny kept on throwing up irregularities. Ergative inflection was *-nggu* on words of three syllables ending in a vowel. Thus *mularri* "initiated man" became *mularri-nggu*, with ergative case, when describing someone who does something to someone else. But *gurrili* "black-nose wallaby" unexpectedly had ergative form *gurrili-nyju*. It seemed that "black-nose wallaby" was really *gurriliy* and that it was the final *y* that triggered ergative *-nyju*. But *y* wasn't pronounced after *i* at the end of a word, so the name of the animal was said simply as *gurrili*. All nouns that had three syllables and ended in *i* had to be checked, to see if they were regular like *mularri*, or irregular like *gurrili(y)*.

It wasn't too hard to locate all words of a certain type, since my Yidiny materials were still very efficiently organised. The vocabulary card index was too big to bring back into the field each time, but before the second trip I'd copied out an alphabetical list into notebook H. It wasn't in conventional alphabetical order, since I still chose to put close together things that were phonetically similar — *bambi* was next to *banbi* and a fair distance from *bama*. Only the top half of each page was used in this "phonicon"; as new words came up they would be added in the lower part. Cards would be made out for any new words that came up in the field, and then they would be incorporated into the general file back in Canberra. Interesting new uses of old words were cross-referenced onto a six-by-four-inch paper slip, which was then filed behind the master card for that word when I returned home.

So it was easy to pick out the two dozen trisyllabic nouns ending in *i* and check their ergative and other case forms. Just one other word was like *gurrili(y);* this was *jumbari(y)* "grandchild". There was also one place name, Wungaji(y). And a personal name. An Aborigine called John Barlow had been appointed "King" by Gribble around 1900, to help him maintain discipline at the mission. John's Yidiny name was Minmini(y), with irregular inflection. Moses later recorded a story about how he and another boy had once stolen potatoes from the mission garden, and of the thrashing they had received from Minminiy.

Half-way through the morning, while we were having a bit of a break, Moses asked what day I'd left Canberra and what I'd been doing on the way. Warrgamay sounded interesting, he'd never heard of that language before. What was it like? Well, a few words were like Yidiny (whereas Dyirbal, which intervenes, has something quite different). "Red bream" is *wayiil* in Yidiny and *wayili* in Warrgamay. For "possum", Yidiny says *gajaarr*, whereas Warrgamay has *gajarra*.

And then I told Dick about the Warrgamay verb "to go", which has root *gaga-*. Imperative adds *-ga* to intransitive verbs, and so a command "go!" is *gagaga*. This really broke him up. It sounded more like the cry of a kookaburra bird than telling someone to go away. He kept on coming back to this unbelievable word in Warrgamay, getting me to repeat it whenever anyone came to sit in.

It was a good morning, but somehow I hadn't fully enjoyed things. It was hard to tell why. Field work was always the high spot of my year. I looked forward for months to escaping from the antiseptic life in Canberra — to just sitting under a tree with Moses. Even when I hadn't been able to sleep, the previous year, the work itself had never palled. Now, on the first morning, here I was feeling restless, wondering how long it would all take, having to force myself to move on to the next topic.

At lunchtime, a telegram arrived from Canberra. We'd just made a new faculty appointment in my department, and I'd asked the administrator in charge to let me know when it had officially been approved, and the formal letter sent out. It was all rather tricky. Effectively a replacement for a quite unsatisfactory member of staff — someone I'd inherited — who just wouldn't go. The only person I've ever known who had been replaced *twice* and still he wouldn't resign! I was very relieved to get confirmation that the new appointment had been approved.

That telegram must have done the trick, because from then on I was back in my normal rut of enjoyment. I did not experience the sheer exhilaration of the first Yidiny field trip, or the tense frustrations of the second one, when hypotheses weren't working out, but from now on it was as it had been with Dyirbal, just a steady, hedonistic delight in the linguistic round — texts, vocabulary and grammatical description.

New insights were always coming up, about the most unexpected words. Like *bunggu,* for instance. On the very first day, in 1970, I'd got this with the meaning "knee". Then it turned up as the name for the hump in a snake's body, as it moves along the ground, and for the bend in the tail of a crocodile. An accurate definition of *bunggu* seemed to be "that part of a body whose movement is the major factor in propelling the entire body along the ground". This fitted in well with a further sense. *Bunggu* is used to describe a particular part of a motor car or tractor — "wheel". It is plainly the wheels that propel a vehicle.

One afternoon, Moses and I had been talking in Yidiny for a couple of hours when he suddenly lapsed into English, to describe something from European culture: "Look at that car! It's got a flat knee." This brought howls of mirth from those of his friends who were sitting around listening, and even Moses had to smile at himself.

Clem and I got on well together. He was that typical Australian contradiction, a very strong member of the Labor party but also a rip-roaring capitalist. Clem was thinking of buying a block of land in Cairns, in addition to his substantial property holdings down south.

We got to talking about what you could do with bread. Clem recounted how in the army they'd been told to add a certain substance that temporarily restrained the male sexual drive. But the bakers themselves knew what to eat — as a result they had a free run with all the girls in the unit.

That seemed perhaps justified (time of war and all that), but what I couldn't accept was Clem's story of Moa Island, after the bakery had been built there. Most of the young men had left the island to find work and opportunities on Thursday Island or the mainland, with the result that the middle-aged and old men who were left had a fine time with all the young girls. Then higher authority sent instructions that the old army additive should be used, to put a stop to such behaviour. The result, Clem said, was that most of the girls then left the island too.

There'd been some changes at Yarrabah. Newspapers were now being brought over each day from Cairns and sold in a kiosk attached to the hall. It was good for the people to know what was happening in the world and to use some of the literacy that had been acquired (often rather painfully).

And there was now a beer canteen, open from 6.30 until 8.30, six nights a week. Beer in glasses, for consumption on the premises only. The canteen was in many ways a good thing. People had always smuggled in booze, and then been liable for a few days in jail if the police raided at the right time. It was only right that the Aborigines in Yarrabah should have the same privileges as anyone else in Australia.

I asked Moses if he went down to the pub — maybe I could buy him a beer some time.

"No," he said. "When pub open I go down there every night. No good. Spend all my money. Get drunk a few time. So I stop going." Just like that. He now had no interest at all in frequenting the canteen.

But the brickies did. The VIP fridge was full of stubbies. They had two or three each at lunchtime, and more than that before tea. Clem had organised one of the local girls to cook lunch and tea, and she agreed to put an extra potato in the pot for me. After tea, all three of them would go straight down to the pub, the moment it opened. I'd have peace — for a couple of hours' solid work on the day's materials — and then I'd join them at the pub just before closing time. The beer I put away in that fifteen minutes — maybe three glasses — would affect me about as much as the two or three jugs that Karl, Jock and Clem had each consumed. I've never known people drink so steadily through the day with so little visible effect.

One night there was a dance in the hall, as soon as the pub shut. Clem and I yarned a bit around the perimeter, while Karl and Jock looked over the local talent. One girl persistently tried to drag Clem onto the dance floor, and it was only after a few minutes that I realised she was deaf-and-dumb. Suddenly, he was able to get rid of her. Amongst his other skills, Clem knew a bit of deaf-and-dumb language.

"It's easy enough," he said. "I just told her I had my balls shot off in the war and she scarpered."

I went to bed about ten, but kept being wakened by girls chasing or being chased through the house, or round the side. Next morning there was a fair amount of noise and laughter at breakfast, swopping experiences. I got up as soon as they left and went for a shower-and-bath (alternating hot and cold). It was only after getting dressed that I found I'd several times walked past a girl fast asleep, on Karl's couch.

And so it went on — drink and girls, and drink and drink and more girls. Clem just tried to keep the oven being built. "I've been married for thirty-five years and faithful for more than half that time," was his peculiar boast. Jock, no more than about twenty-one, took a week to really attach himself to a girl and then kept to her. (Clem thought she might have been his first.) But he was working hard to catch up. Clem told me that after he'd knocked on the wall to wake Jock in the morning, there was a significant time-lapse — and tell-tale scuffles — before Jock appeared for breakfast.

Karl was the one, though. He made it quite clear that he'd agreed to do this job mostly because of the chances of crumpet, and there was someone to share his bed just about every night. Five different girls in all, I think. Clem asked him how they measured up.

"That dark-haired one with the big nose," Karl told him, "she could buy and sell the rest six times over."

"That's what I figured," agreed Clem. "She's not too pretty, but I guessed she'd know what it was all about."

And beer. I was going into Cairns one afternoon to pay another visit to Pompey, and Clem asked me to pick up a few stubbies at Fiorellis.

"A carton — two dozen?" I enquired.

"Oh no, we've got to be realistic with these boys. They can't work unless they get their cold stubbies. Better make it three cartons." So I did.

A few days later, Clem went into Cairns and got another four cartons. I calculated how much beer was consumed during the fortnight I was there: something like 450 thirteen-fluid-ounce stubbies and about an equal quantity of draught beer from the pub. I wouldn't have had more than about fifteen stubbies in all, and Clem drank a lot less than the other two.

Their work did suffer. Starting time in the morning got to be nearer seven than six, and lunch breaks tended to be extended. Another cold stubby would make it easier to work in the afternoon, went the story. On Sunday — with just a week to go — Clem was writing to a friend in Sydney. "I told him I'd send them both back if I could — on the next plane." After that things did pick up a bit and, although they didn't actually finish the oven, all the really tricky arch-work was done, and Clem said he'd return with a couple of workmen from Cairns to finish it off.

I went up to Atherton again to see Tilly Fuller. She was almost better, but the doctor had said she should stay in for a few more days just to be safe. There was so much I wanted to ask her — grammatical points that needed a second source. She and Moses were the only really fluent, intelligent speakers who could see what I was after and explain it clearly and precisely.

Tilly discussed the various verbs for "heat", "cook", "burn" and "radiate". And then she explained how a man would always sleep between his wife and the fire she had made for them; the baby would sleep on the other side of its mother. This was in fact fairly chivalrous, since there was always a distinct possibility of rolling into the fire in one's sleep.

That visit went on a little too long. Three-quarters of an hour was quite enough in the constraints of the ward.

"Don't be too greedy!" Tilly warned me. I could come back next day and, yes, there was something I could bring her — a piece of grilled fish from a shop she named in the main street. Didn't have to be hot, just a piece of fish, but mind it was grilled not fried.

That night I went across to Mareeba, to catch Slim Dusty's show with his travelling country band. It was quite a contrast from recent evenings at Yarrabah. Then, the next day, I couldn't find any fish shop in Atherton with the name Tilly had mentioned. But there was Fergie's Fish Bar on the main street. Yes, that was what she meant. I should have remembered Tilly's tendency to identify shops by the names they had many years before. The grilled fish was exactly right. She had a couple of nibbles and then put it aside to enjoy properly after I had gone.

A few vowels still needed thorough checking. And Tilly, getting the idea of what was needed, began reeling off paradigms, the first person who'd ever indulged me in that way. Causal inflection "as a result of, from" added different bits to different words. *"Ngayu duburrji* (I'm full up)", Tilly recited, *"jabanmu, yagunyumu, gajaramu, mabiim, wurgulumu* (from eating eel, porcupine, possum, tree kangaroo, pelican)."

Down at Yarrabah, Robert Patterson was getting more and more interested in what Dick and I were doing. He'd spend as much time as he could sitting under the tree with us, listening as I checked points from last year's texts, and as Dick recorded new ones. One recurrent theme was that the sea level used to be lower, the coast being where the Barrier Reef now is. This accords exactly with historical facts at the end of the last Ice Age, some ten millennia ago. Green Island used to be about four times as big as it is now — Dick maintained — only the north-west corner remains above water; this is quite consistent with the water depths around.

Even the word for "island", *jarruway,* has an interesting second sense: "small hill". What were originally the tops of small hills became islands as the sea level encroached. The name of Fitzroy Island is Gabar "lower arm", because most of this geographical feature was submerged and only one limb remains above water today. And, perhaps most significant of all, Moses told us of a place, Mudaga, named after the pencil cedar trees that at one time grew there. It was half-way between Fitzroy Island and King Beach, and is now completely submerged.

Anthropologists currently find it fashionable to doubt that such stories have any historical basis. But, as with the legend of the origin of the crater lakes, these tales simply cannot be ignored. Many of the texts Moses recorded described the sea level rising, and people throwing hot stones into the water to try to stem the inundation.

Moses was gaining more respect for Robert Patterson. His name, Nyalmbi, was — Moses said — based on the verb *nyarrmbi-* "to approach but not quite reach the ground", describing the passage of a totemic whirlwind. This brought us to the subject of cyclones. Lambert Cocky had described how his people had received advance warning through the movement of seagulls unnaturally far inland. But what of coastal dwellers? Certainly there was an indicator, Moses assured me. Watch out for *jalnggan,* a black bird rather like a duck, with a red head. Whenever that bird flew unusually close to the ground (described by the verb *nyarrmbi-*), to avoid the first breath of a high wind, the Yidinyji knew that a cyclone was imminent, and gathered in large, low huts for maximum protection from the wind.

Moses and I talked in Yidiny almost all the time now, as he dictated dialogue, with the right sort of responses, for me to write down and read back. Or as I asked about the acceptability of complex sentences my rules generated. Moses used to hold me up as an example to the young boys who often sat around us.

"Listen to him. He can talk your language properly. Why don't you learn it? You ought to be ashamed of yourselves, you Yidinyji boys."

I was never a very brilliant phonetician, and it's hard to judge one's own performance. Back in 1964, Lindsay Cowan had speculated: "I suppose you must talk their language with a bit of an accent, just like these Italians pronounce English," and I'd agreed that that was probably the case.

George Watson was always the best teacher, brooking no nonsense. He'd occasionally haul me up for not rolling the *rr*'s enough. "You can do that all right. I've heard you. Usually you pronounce it properly but today you been talking like a white man." I'd apologise, and try to keep more in line.

Yidiny was harder, and I'd been trying to pronounce things exactly as Dick specified. So it was encouraging when Robert Patterson told me I spoke just like the old people had, when he was a boy, before there was so much English influence.

One day Robert asked a question of a different sort. The winds of political change were beginning to brush against Yarrabah and he wondered about land rights. What chance was there? What could be done? We discussed it for a fair while and I mentioned the letters I'd written to the government ministers. The next day, Moses told me that Robert had come around to talk to him about it again in the evening. "He pleased with what you tell him. Nyalmbi say that's good. You did right thing. Nyalmbi very pleased about what you say."

The brickies were having a picnic over on King Beach. I got the idea I was being invited mainly because I had a suitable vehicle, and offered Clem the keys to it. But he insisted I come, I needed a break just as much as they did (!) The girl who cooked for us had organised it, and invited along three girls. "The best three girls in the whole of Yarrabah," Clem assured us. She also brought along her boy-friend, who played the guitar and sang — incredibly badly.

We set off at dusk. Two cartons of cold stubbies, some steak to barbecue, and the girls. They were about as far away as it is possible to imagine from being the three prettiest in Yarrabah. Well, I suppose they weren't quite the three ugliest, but they can't have been too far off. One was about Jock's age. They spent the evening looking at each other and holding hands and then he was fixed up for the rest of his stay. The most presentable of the three was Rosie. She was tallish, quite slim, skin only a little bit saggy on her face, but she had a brassy look, a kind of mocking air that mixed defiance and sullenness. Finally, there was Sheila, a typical casualty of Yarrabah, someone who'd been greatly used by life without being able to use it back. Sheila probably was in her thirties, but she looked well over forty — baggy, plumpish, self-effacing and not a little crude (there was no contradiction in this combination of qualities; it would have described others at Yarrabah).

For the first hour we drank, and cooked and ate the meat, and drank some more. Rosie plainly thought I might be a new sort of experience for her (no one at Yarrabah could make out exactly who I was or what I was doing) and alternated between non-verbal suggestion and what she may have thought of as jealousy-inducing provocation. Sheila just drank and waited. And Karl and Jock drank too, as if it were a serious employment.

We had a visitor, one of the young male schoolteachers, with a blanket over one arm and a girl on the other. Someone who probably *was* one of the three prettiest girls at Yarrabah. They'd been for a walk along the beach, enjoying the clear moonlit night.

It now turned out that Sheila had a son, who was being brought up by her brother because she'd never married and had no home of her own. The son was in this teacher's class. Out there on the sand we had a fragment of a parent-teacher evening (or perhaps a parody of one).

"I wish you'd come to the open day, we do like to meet parents, and it can be useful to discuss how things are going. It helps us quite a bit."

Sheila was pleased to be spoken to as an adult, a parent, an equal member of society, but she said she would never go to the school — what would they think of her?

"No," the teacher insisted, before he walked further on along the beach, "you must come. It's not a thing to be shy about. It's important and it'll help your son."

Rosie eventually got fed up and went off along the sand with Karl. (He later gave me his considered verdict: she wasn't much good anyway, but after that much drink it was just nothing. I refrained from asking why on earth he'd bothered.) Meanwhile Clem and I went for a swim, leaving Jock holding hands with his true-love, Sheila with her beer, and our cook pretending she enjoyed the cacophonous sound being made by her boy-friend's guitar.

Bathing isn't easy in North Queensland. During all the summer months, there's too great a risk of being stung by a sea-wasp (or stinger) — it's like a jelly fish, but with tentacles twenty or thirty feet long. One or two people die this way each year. Rivers are mostly out because of crocodiles. And then, of course, the salt-water has its fair share of sharks. But this was outside the bad sea-wasp season, a beautiful cool winter evening, the water just a pleasant temperature. We splashed about a bit in shallow water, where sharks wouldn't be likely to venture.

Then some more beer, against the out-of-tune guitar. By about ten o'clock, I was feeling tired of the party and wanted to go home. So, since it was my truck, everyone packed up. Before driving off, I went round the back to make sure the tailgate was fastened and asked, just to be companionable: "Right. Is everyone back here okay then?"

There was one voice raised in response. "No," said Sheila, "I haven't had a fuck."

On the last morning of this visit, I asked Moses if we could sit somewhere different, under another tree.

"Why?" he asked in surprise and with some consternation. That wide fig tree was an institution, as much a part of our daily ritual as the three blue Mars Lumograph 2H pencils in my top pocket, or Dick's stub of a pipe. My reply must have seemed lame.

"Because I'm fed up with these green ants falling out of the tree on me all the time. They bite."

"Oh, no!" Robert Patterson exclaimed. "Those are good for you."

And Moses agreed most emphatically. He told me of the medicinal properties of *jilibura* "green ants". In the old days, people would squeeze some ants between their hands and mingle the resulting "milk" with clean ashes obtained by burning a blue gum tree, *gawuul*, or a quandong, *murrgan*, or a type of tea-tree, *bagirram*. This would then be drunk as a cure for headache and other ills. Alternatively, a hardy man would effect a cure by putting the green ants directly onto his chest, under his shirt, and allowing them to bite him. One interesting linguistic correlate is that Yidiny has a classifier *munyimunyi* "ant" which includes within its scope all ant species — such as *gajuu* "black tree ant", *burrbal* "red ant" — with one exception: *jilibura*. The green ants had such an important medico-social role that they were looked on as something apart from other kinds of ant.

So we continued under the same tree. I tried to enjoy being bitten, and certainly continued in good health. We gathered more examples of the enigmatic verbal suffix -*Vji*-. Sometimes it formed a reflexive ("he cut himself, on purpose"), sometimes it marked an inanimate agent ("the branch hit me"), and sometimes a human agent who achieved some result accidentally ("I found a stream of fresh water, quite by chance"). And there were more types of use of -*Vji*-, that I was just getting an understanding of.

There was a short Gunggay legend in Gribble's book, *The Problem of the Australian Aboriginal* — published in 1932, but the story must have been recorded at Yarrabah a generation before that. It concerned "Goonyah". Robert Patterson got quite excited about this and said he remembered a story his mother told about Ganya. I said this could well be the correct pronunciation, since Gribble wasn't wonderful at phonetics and I couldn't be certain how one was supposed to interpret his spelling. But Moses wasn't having any. I'd pronounced it as "Goonya" and that was it, he insisted; Gribble took it down from the old people directly, and what he'd put in that book must be correct. Anyway, Moses and Nyalmbi had the story read to them twice, and then they met again and talked about it in the evening.

Finally, on my last morning, Dick said that he really ought to tell the Goonya story in Yidiny (Gribble of course had it only in English). He'd embellished the outline and also changed it a bit. Gribble said that the Great Spirit "Balore" caused the sea to rise against Goonyah, whereas Moses had Goonya stand Balur — the sacred curved woomera — in the prow of the boat, to calm the waves, as the sea came relentlessly on, moving the coastline inland from somewhere near the Barrier Reef to its present location. It was a fascinating story to add to my now quite considerable store of Yidiny texts. And it contained more examples of -*Vji*- and more relative clauses, to feed the emerging grammatical description.

The following April, a team of filmmakers from Sydney went to Palm Island to make a documentary on the strike there in the fifties. They also shot a poignant film at Murray Upper — featuring a lot of Tommy Warren and Joe Kinjun — called "We Stop Here". And they spent a bit of time at Yarrabah that included recording some material from Moses (of which I was given copies). One of the stories he told

them concerned Goonya. Dick does say, on the tape, "You see, old
Gribble, he got that in a paper . . . he been put that down . . . that's
the way I been to get them out of that book, you see", but the significance of this aside might well be lost on some future anthropo-historian
who was not aware of the full chain of events: that a brief outline of
the story had been taken down by Gribble about 1900, published by
him in 1932, then completely forgotten by the Gungganyji and only
revived — probably in significantly different form — after I'd read the
Gribble version to Moses and Robert Patterson in 1973. A folk
tradition had died, but was now on the way to being partly re-
established.

By leaving Yarrabah at lunchtime, I hoped to be able to see George and
Chloe on my way to spend the night at Warrami. George was there, fit
and active as ever, still sharing the barracks with his white buddy Mick
Lonnergan. I had a few questions to ask, mostly things arising from the
work on Yidiny and I wasn't too sure how Dyirbal would handle them.
We went into Innisfail, and George picked out a shady tree in King
George V park. He started telling me a story about how the moon was
once in difficulty and, of all the things in the world, only the grass
would help him. So now, in gratitude, the moon sprinkles cool
refreshing dew onto the grass each morning. Suddenly, it seemed that
something was being sprinkled down on me. And they were biting.
George scoffed at my discomfort. "Those green ants, we call them
ngulbuny in Mamu. They're good for you, good medicine." There
seemed no escape from prophylactic insects that year.

Chloe was now stopping with Ernie, a few miles out of Tully, but
I'd just missed her. She wouldn't be back until very late. This was a
shame, since I'd also missed her the previous year. But I had to get back
to Canberra for the new term and did want to see Lambert Cocky and
Willie Seaton in Ingham. There was nothing to do but leave a message,
saying I hoped to be back quite soon and to look after herself.

Warrami still seemed sad — and somehow incomplete — without
Lindsay Cowan. But Mrs Cowan was as active as ever, running the shop
for nine or ten hours each day, six days a week. Her brother, Arthur
Henry, had sold his own place and was now at Warrami, looking after
the milkers and so on. All of the Cowans' four boys and four girls were
now married, and a new grandchild seemed to come along every few
months. There were always people at Warrami — dropping in, staying

for tea, stopping over the night. It was good to see them all again. And Tommy Warren was now eager for me to sit down and write down everything he had to say (I really believe he might have considered paying *me* twelve pounds!)

Then to Ingham, to Sheahan's cane farm and Lambert Cocky. Old Dan Sheahan, who'd retired a few years back, had a house on the opposite side of the farmyard from his son, and his wife invited me in for a cup of tea while Lambert was finishing off his chores. Dan was a pretty good poet — I'd seen one of his pieces in the *North Queensland Register* the previous week and the newsagents in Ingham had copies of *Songs from the Canefields,* a collection of eighty of Dan's poems from over the years; ditties like "The '27 flood", "Hauling cane trucks to the mill", "The road to Abergowrie" and "Vote Peter White for chairman". Dan's major claim to fame was that he had written "A pub without beer", which was the basis for Slim Dusty's hit record.

I couldn't really refuse when Mrs Sheahan suggested I talk to Lambert at her kitchen table, but he didn't seem to mind (although I think the results might have been better if we'd been on our own outside). Lambert had a really good knowledge of Warrgamay, but he liked to go his own way. It was hard for me to get a direct answer to any question, although mentioning a topic often meant that Lambert talked around it, and might well supply the information I was after, almost inadvertently. I was writing things down as fast as I could, but after a while it seemed best to just switch the recorder on and let Lambert talk.

I couldn't get him to give another text. A story about his childhood ran to three sentences (punctuated by two yawns). For the rest, he preferred to say a sentence of Warrgamay, then an explanation in Lambert's variety of English, then a bit more Warrgamay, and so on. This did provide a rich vein of data which really added to the Warrgamay corpus, and complemented what I had from John Tooth.

When Lambert paused, Dan Sheahan, still sitting at the end of the table, began telling an interesting and involved story. But then Lambert would start up again. Dan was rather deaf (although Lambert had a resounding tenor voice) and Lambert quite oblivious. So they talked on, each over the other, and the tape-recorder picked it all up (although of course the microphone was pointed towards Lambert).

Two hours seemed enough. Although Lambert would have continued, I didn't want to push it that day. I'd come back next morning, I said, but Lambert suddenly became doubtful and said he had many jobs to do.

Willie Seaton, in the afternoon, was as helpful as ever. His language had ceased to be actively spoken many years before, and Willie didn't even know the Nyawaygi name for his birthplace, Waterview Creek. But his keen mind remembered fascinating aspects of the language. For instance, Nyawaygi did not have one word for "moon", nor one for "sun": it had two names for each. *Balanu* is "new moon" and *ngilgan* "full moon". *Bujira* refers to "sun low in the sky, in morning and evening" while *jula* is "hot sun, when directly overhead".

The next morning, Lambert was plainly in a bad mood. He made it quite clear that he'd said everything he had to say the previous day, that he had jobs that would keep him busy for hours, and then there was his meat to cook before it went off. I should go away at once, and not come back. I was used to waiting around for Lambert, but his attitude was different from what I'd seen before, and it didn't bode well. I did sit down, but every time Lambert shuffled past with a new bucket of something or a broom or a rag, he continued to berate me, half under his breath, but loud enough for me to hear.

There were certain things that I really wanted to check before starting on a revised draft grammar of Warrgamay. The more obdurate Lambert got, the more determined I became — the greater the importance of those questions loomed in my mind. I started offering him more money than usual — ten dollars instead of five. This was silly, because I've never known money to buy any Aborgine; field work has to be based on trust, information willingly imparted. Lambert began openly swearing at me. He said there was a sort of head Aborigine in Ingham and he'd tell him of me, tell him to "get" me; he was getting almost vicious.

Later, when I told this story to someone from the Institute of Aboriginal Studies, he suggested one approach would have been to say I came from the government and could use my influence to get his pension stopped if he didn't cooperate. I don't think that would have worked, such was his mood. And it was a reprehensible suggestion.

So after perhaps three-quarters of an hour I went off, insults flying after me. It was an unpleasant and sobering experience. In just on ten years of working in North Queensland, I'd never had an encounter remotely like this. The odd polite refusal from a stranger, but people I knew had always been friendly and pleasant.

Willie Seaton was surprised to see me some hours earlier than I'd said but we had another good session on Nyawaygi. We spent about an hour and a half on words and short sentences, the most Seaton could take at a time, and dealt with words for artefacts, and adjectives, and lots of verbs. It was a productive session, and included another "minimal pair" of closely similar words – *wuruwuru* "frog" must not be confused with *wurruwurru* "ibis".

Although I was due to return to Canberra the following day, there was a bit of time for detective work. Back in 1964, Chloe had told me about a very old lady called (Chloe thought) Maria, living just south of Rollingstone on the road to Townsville. Now both John Tooth and Lambert Cocky (on the day he was being friendly) had strongly recommended Nora Boyd, from Black River, which is between Rollingstone and Townsville. I was sure it was the same person as Chloe's Maria. She was the last surviving speaker of Biyay, the Warrgamay

Fig. 17. Nora Boyd (Biyay dialect of Warrgamay) at Ayr. (1973)

dialect from Halifax, at the mouth of the Herbert. This was supposed to be a bit different from the dialect up towards the Herbert Gorge, that spoken by John and Lambert.

As luck would have it, Nora Boyd had left the small settlement at Black River just a day or two before, to go and stay with a greatniece in Ayr, sixty miles south of Townsville. So I drove down to Ayr, getting there at about three o'clock, and eventually found my way round the fields of tall cane to the wooden house on stilts where "Gran" was staying. She was with a "South Sea Islander" family, descendants of indentured Kanaka labourers brought over to work the sugar eighty years before.

Nora Boyd was a fabulous old lady. Really old — she said she was ninety-three and I had no reason to disbelieve her. She had a son in an old folks' home, at Charters Towers, and used to go up from time to time to visit him. She could get around all right, with a stick, and her mind was still good. Biyay language? She hadn't spoken that for ages, the other speakers had all died a long time ago. We worked for an hour — a few words, some pronouns and verbs and short sentences. Most things were the same as John's and Lambert's Warrgamay, but some words and affixes differed.

It was only half-past four when I said goodbye and took a picture of her at the bottom of the steps. There was plenty of time to get back to Townsville where I wanted to spend the next morning talking to Professor Ron Sussex of the James Cook University. He and I were on a national committee to review the role of languages and linguistics in Australian universities, and I thought it might be useful to swap a few ideas in advance.

Twenty miles out of Townsville, I stopped for a swig of water and to tighten up the rather primitive seat belt, which kept working loose. I'm not quite sure why I did it there, so near my destination. Then, driving into Townsville along Racecourse Road, I was wondering whether to stay in a motel or go up to the university and try for a room in a hall of residence, which would be cheaper. I was in between two cars, going along at about thirty miles an hour. Suddenly the car behind overtook me, and I had to brake to let him pull in in front, because there was a car coming towards us.

*   *   *   *   *

The next thing I remember was a policeman, quite a pleasant policeman, asking for my name, address and driving licence. And for my
recollections of the accident. (Ah, so that was what had happened.)
And then a doctor saying they'd have to shave off the hair at the side of
my head to put in some stitches and was that all right? And X-rays, and
a plaster cast on my broken left arm. Then I complained about the right
arm, an X-ray, and a cast went on that, too. A skull X-ray — but
nothing seriously wrong there. Stitches in my nose and the side of my
face. Both feet cut, and plasters on them.

Lying in a bed in the Townsville General Hospital next morning, I
could hear the local news on a radio three beds away, giving full details
of the accident. Soon Clem called — never was I more pleased to see
anyone. He was in town for the day, and had seen a picture of the crash
across the front page of the *Townsville Daily Bulletin* — I didn't want
to see it. Clem was really shaken, more so than me. Could he do
anything? Well, it would be a help if he could just tell the airline that I
wouldn't be flying to Canberra that day.

After a few hours, I went across to the phone and called Alison,
reversing the charges. Had she had any message about me? Nothing —
neither the police nor the hospital had thought to inform her! I'd
braked to let the overtaking car pull in and must have skidded across
the road, colliding with the car coming from the opposite direction. I
couldn't remember anything about it. My Land Cruiser was a write-off;
the engine had been found twenty yards away from the body. Luckily,
the woman driving the other car also had only fairly minor injuries, and
she'd be out of hospital in a few days' time.

Lying in bed, the thought went through my head that at least I'd
worked out the syntax of the -*Vji*- affix in Yidiny. But what had
happened to all of my notebooks and vocabulary slips?

I rang Ron Sussex and he came round with some fruit and a few
things to cheer me up. Luckily his son Roland, also a linguist, was
holidaying there, and he was tremendous. First of all, Roly took me
around town picking up the bits. My briefcase had accompanied me
into hospital. Another bag of notebooks and the tape-recorder were at a
police station. And the remains of my suitcase had been towed with the
vehicle to the Department of Works depot. They asked if I wanted to
have a look at what was left of the Land Cruiser, but I didn't think so;
Roly went instead. Then we bought a new suitcase from Woolworths
and found that I'd only lost one sock in the whole escapade. The next

day I was able to fly back to Canberra, bestubbled, bandaged and well plastered — but still alert. It was only on reaching home that I really collapsed, and the full import registered.

14

Loss

The plaster stayed on my left arm for almost three months, and it took that long before I was able to work at normal pace. Then I made a thorough assessment of Warrgamay. It had always seemed a bit too similar to Dyirbal to be truly interesting (in the way Yidiny was), and there was the perpetual struggle to separate out bits of Girramay. But suddenly, one day in November, things fell into place. Warrgamay doesn't have anything at all that could be called "tenses" — nothing referring simply to past, present or future time. Instead, it has a number of verbal endings marking "aspect". A final -*ma* refers to something that might happen, purposive -*lagu* to something that should be done, -*gi* to something that is irretrievably finished. And then there is an unmarked aspect -*y* which must be used in circumstances other than those covered by -*ma, -lagu* or -*gi* (for instance, reference to present time); and -*y can* be used in place of any of the other inflections, if the speaker does not want to be too specific.

The materials on Warrgamay were rather slim, with just three short texts, and I could only produce a short sketch of the main grammatical features — perhaps a hundred pages, whereas my Dyirbal grammar had run to over four hundred. I had even less on Nyawaygi, but it was still important to work as intensively as possible on this, since it was so different — in vital ways — from any of the other languages.

Yidiny continued to be the major project, of course. Although I'd never heard it actually used around me, there were now on tape almost twenty texts, of the highest quality, from Moses and Tilly Fuller. And they had explained things so clearly and in such detail that I felt I could write a full account of the language, just about as complete as if it were still spoken every day by hundreds of people. Yidiny is harder than Dyirbal, with more irregularities in its structure, so the description I wrote would be at least as long as the Dyirbal grammar. During 1974 I worked away, revising yet again the chapters on phonetics and phonology and on word structure, and then settled down to the chapter on syntax, the ways in which words can be combined to form sentences.

I didn't get back up north for fifteen months. And then we decided we'd all drive up again for two months over the summer vacation — the children could easily miss the last couple of weeks of school term. It was three years since our last trip together, and now only two could sleep in the back of our station wagon, so we took a bigger tent that could sleep three or four. And this time we made it up north without having to get a new engine fitted half-way there.

Nyawaygi was what I was really excited about just then. In the early data from 1963/64 and 1967, there'd been verb forms *buma* "hit!", *bunjima* "will hit", *buwanya* "did hit" and *bunya* "hitting". I assumed that these must be different verb roots, *buma-, bunji-, buwa-* and *bunya-*, with slightly different meanings. After all, Dyirbal has *balga-* "hit with long rigid object, held on to", *minba-* "hit with long rigid object, let go of", *biji-* "hit with rounded object", and *bunju-* "hit with long flexible object". And I was used to the idea — from Dyirbal, Yidiny and Warrgamay — that every verb root must have at least two syllables.

But working with Seaton in 1973, it became clear that these were all forms of a single verb *bu-* "to hit". Quite unlike all its neighbours, Nyawaygi has archaic monosyllabic verbs — as do languages in Western Australia and the Northern Territory, and Guugu-Yimidhirr, the language John Haviland had studied at Hopevale.

Dyirbal has two classes of verbs, and so does Warrgamay. But Nyawaygi has no less than seven distinct verb classes, one more than Guugu Yimidhirr. And four classes each consisted just of a few mono-syllabic verbs, an archaic feature going back to the original Australian ancestor language, probably spoken some tens of millennia in the past. Most languages in the eastern part of the continent have replaced mono-syllabic roots by new disyllabic forms. Just Guugu-Yimidhirr and Nyawaygi kept some monosyllables. Nyawaygi has *nyaa-* "to see", Guugu-Yimidhirr has *nhaa-* and languages in the west show *nya-*. *Bu-*

"to hit" also occurs in Walmatjari, from the Western Australian desert and *wu-* "to give", in both Nyawaygi and Guugu Yimidhirr, relates to *yu-* in western tongues.

So our first major stop in December 1974 was Ingham. We stayed in quite a pleasant caravan park where we could put the tent up in a corner, surrounded by cane. There was a snake up a tree, but when we mentioned this to John Tooth the next week he said that if they went up trees then they weren't dangerous.

Almost every morning I was able to have an hour and a half with Willie Seaton, and then spend the afternoon going over the material, collating it and working out what was still needed. I got a real thrill seeing the monosyllabic verb paradigms gradually take shape, a bit more each day. *Ya-* "to go" and *yaa-* "to throw", *nyii-* "to sit down" and *yuu-* "to lie down". That week camping in Ingham provided the sort of intellectual discovery that is for me the high-spot of linguistic work.

A good general rule is that every aspect of a language should be checked with at least two people, but this is hard to achieve when there is just one speaker left alive. So I did the next best thing − checked what Seaton said one year with what he gave the next. (And I had got a fair amount from Long Heron, before he died.) So every word had to have been given twice, pretty spontaneously, to be entered in the vocabulary file. And of course every inflection of each of the ten monosyllabic verbs had to be obtained, and then checked on a different occasion (*not* the next day). We took it gradually − each day a few new words, and a few sentences that should throw up a few more verb forms. I recorded almost all of our sessions − the material was so elusive and so important, and my knowledge of the language was so much less good than for Dyirbal and Yidiny (and the phonetics was a little bit trickier), that it was useful to have everything on tape so I could go back over it at will.

Information on Nyawaygi could be critically important to a comparative study of Australian languages, and to an attempt to reconstruct the original ancestor language and trace how the different types of modern language evolved. So there was a transcendent reason for doing as much as possible with Willie Seaton (who was by then about eighty). Warrgamay I worked on because it was there, to get a complete coverage of languages of that region. Nyawaygi is totally different from Dyirbal, with the intervening language, Warrgamay, acting as a sort of buffer. Warrgamay has interesting similarities in each direction, but neither of them is strong enough to say it is a close genetic brother of either its northern or its southern neighbour.

Nora Boyd, who was still in Ayr, gave some more interesting data on Biyay — fishes and birds and verbs and interrogatives. She'd be moving up to Ingham before Christmas, and I promised to call on her there on our way back down south. Lambert Cocky had shifted from Sheahan's to the Eventide Home at Charters Towers, eighty-five miles inland from Townsville. I was a bit dubious about calling on him after our nasty altercation last time, but it was worth a try. He was in fact as nice as pie, just as helpful as could be. Maybe it was because there weren't so many jobs to occupy him at the old folks' home. I also popped in to see Nora Boyd's son, who was confined to bed there. He'd dropped his cigarette stub onto the sheets the previous week and got a few burns. I passed on his mother's best regards, but he just looked at me and grunted, as if the message had barely gone in.

From Charters Towers, we took the back road, mile upon mile of uninterrupted scrub until suddenly we drove into a bright, new, modern town for workers in the Greenvale nickel plant. The road continued for another hundred and forty miles without a house or petrol station and then, just before Mount Garnet, came the turn-off to Glen Ruth.

I'd thought it might be nice to camp for a few days by the bridge over the Herbert River, where the Jirrbal families from Mount Garnet had been for that weekend the previous year. There was no one there now. Stupidly, I drove the car too far down towards the river and it sank to the hub in soft sand. Fortunately, a car came by just at that moment and the driver helped us dig it out. We could probably have done it by ourselves, although it would have taken a lot longer. We'd have to have done — the next car didn't come along that track for two more days.

John Tooth came down from Glen Ruth to spend the days with us. We sat in the shade doing Warrgamay — checking that my idea about no tenses and lots of aspects was correct. Then we'd have lunch and a chat, followed by more Warrgamay. Ten-year-old Eelsha came to listen as I was recording tricky pairs of words — some that differed only in the kind of *r*-sound, like *gambarra* "cyclone" and *gambara* "body" — and differences in vowel length, like *jurra* "cloud" and *juurra* "wipe it!". I think she decided it was all a bit *too* tricky for comfort.

John Tooth had never been near a school, but he could read a bit, almost the only one of the elderly people I worked with in North

Queensland who could. He'd taught himself – there was no other way. He'd once read a book, a western, but it had taken him a while, he said. John had interesting ideas, and he and Alison and I chatted round the camp-fire. A kookaburra called out "ga-ga-ga-ga-ga" as the sun was setting, and John asked if I knew the Jirrbal story of Gijiya, the man who first trod the path of death.

Then a car went by, the first for two days. It was Ruth and Doug Farquar whom I'd met at Kirrama in 1963. They'd now moved to Glen Ann, right next door to Glen Ruth (which had been named for Ruth by her first husband, father of the present owner). They saw John and stopped to tell him that old Alec – the Warungu man whom Chloe and Jimmy Murray had taken me up to Kirrama to see – was ill in Atherton Hospital, and that they were on the way to visit him. (Alec died a few days later.)

We chatted some more. The old Cashmere Telegraph Station used to be on top of that hill, John said. It was moved in 1879, and then Cashmere station was there until old Mr Atkinson moved to the present site of Glen Ruth, as a more fitting home for his young bride.

It came time to drive John back to Glen Ruth. Wallabies and kangaroos jumped about in the early moonlight – I think Fergus and Rowena counted thirty in the ten-mile journey. And two planes. Robert Atkinson's own light plane had been joined by that of a visitor. There was plenty of money in that horse stud at Glen Ruth.

Our next stop was Tolga, the nearest camping site to Kairi, where Tilly Fuller should be. I delayed going to see her, and spent a morning sitting in the shade pondering over the Warrgamay material, trying to harness ideas that had been going through my head the last three days. From what I knew of the other languages nearby, and those in other parts of Australia, it was possible to perceive something of how Warrgamay had changed, in recent times.

Yes, there was no doubt about it, Warrgamay showed a very interesting tendency. As with every other language, it had some irregularities, complications that speakers must just learn but which don't carry any meaning load, don't assist the communicative function of the language – things like the past tense of *come* in English being *came* instead of *comed,* and the plural of *child* being *children* rather than *childs.* I had three clear examples where Warrgamay had eliminated an irregularity. It had either dropped it completely or else had attached some meaning to it – a difference that was there had been made to pay its way. More work would be needed, but at last Warrgamay had become an interesting language for me!

I had a premonition when I went round to the back room of what had long ago been McGillicudy's shop. No one was there. A burly white farmer was fixing a tractor nearby and he knew her. "The old lady died. Couple of months ago. It was her chest."

Obviously, working with very old people one must be prepared for them to die. But preparation never really eases the blow. Tilly Fuller said I was like a son to her, and the loss felt like that of a close relative. There were scores of questions about the tablelands dialect of Yidiny that I'd never be able to clarify now. But that was a minor consideration. I could think only of Tilly's cheerfulness, her warmth, and the personal rapport we had had.

The rest of that field trip followed a fairly routine course. We took a holiday flat in Cairns for a couple of weeks while I commuted across to Yarrabah for a few days each week, and then the whole family moved there for a couple of weeks, staying again in the male schoolteachers' residence. Joe Rogers had left — been transferred away against his wishes. Father Brown had eventually retired — again — and gone down to Melbourne. The bakery was finally in operation, producing beautiful fresh, warm loaves, a change from the sliced and wrapped things that used to be sold in the store. (The supplier in Cairns had been rumoured to send out to Yarrabah a selection of the stale bread that hadn't been sold in town the previous day.) There'd been bureaucratic delays in opening the bakery, I was told. The Department of Aboriginal and Island Affairs had taken out the bread contract with the Cairns firm on a yearly basis, and so the Yarrabah bakery was made to stand unused for six months, until the contract ran out.

Moses was glad to see me back, after more than a year. His wife had died in the winter and he'd had a bad attack of flu, but had thrown it off when the warmer weather came. We still worked five or six hours each day, and he was still a bit disappointed when I took an afternoon off to catch up on analysis and filing. But Dick was more subdued than previously, happy to respond to my questions, but less inclined to take over — to dictate a two-page long conversation and then quiz me on what should be said next.

Everything was finally falling into place in my understanding of Yidiny. Long vowels always bore stress and successive syllables couldn't be stressed. So two long vowels couldn't occur in successive syllables. But the "going affix -*Vli*-, the "coming" affix -*Vlda*-, and the ubiquitous reflexive affix -*Vji*-, all lengthened the preceding vowel (this lengthening is symbolised by *V*). What happened if two of these affixes occurred together? One of the long vowels would have to be shortened. Which one would it be? What was the pecking order?

This question had been intriguing me for years, and I had been accumulating data to try to solve it (and a number of related problems). Finally it became clear that there was no pecking order. Because of the way in which affixes were combined, long vowels could never occur in successive syllables. Certainly, a verb could involve both -*Vji*- and -*Vli*-, but another affix, -*nga*-, must intervene, separating the two long vowels, as in *bunja-aji-nga-ali-nyu*, from the sentence *ngayu jugi bamaanda bunjaajingaalinyu* ' I used a stick to go and hit a person". So the ways in which words were put together were orientated to the requirement on stress being satisfied in a straightforward way. A neat language!

Dick had another story ready, a tale about something that had happened in his childhood. A woman had been bathing in a waterhole on the Barron River, near Redlynch. A crocodile came up and carried her off, holding the victim against its chest with a claw. An old man followed the trail of disturbed, muddy water and finally jumped on top of the crocodile, pinched its eyes, and then pushed a sharp stick into the reptile's mouth, wedging it open. It dropped the woman and fled to its lair, a cave under the water. The woman was suspended with her feet over a branch while her belly was massaged to expel the water she had swallowed. And the crocodile was dug up and despatched.

While Dick was telling this story, an Aboriginal woman walked by, her defiant shouts being clearly picked up on the tape. "I'm drunk, I go, I'm drunk" — the plaintive cry of the new culture, superimposed over Dick Moses' carefully enunciated narrative, the last vestige of the old.

There were always new words to check — some from texts and others from sentences Moses dictated in answer to my questions. My vocabulary now had almost 2,000 entries — less than for Dyirbal but still quite a respectable total. (The number of words checked out as definitely Warragamay was 920, my Nyawaygi notebooks showed 660, and for Mbabaram there were only 250.)

One difference from Dyirbal concerned double entendres. George — and Chloe, after she saw I was getting them from other people anyway

— had mentioned risque senses of many common words. But I had almost nothing of this for Yidiny. It may have been partly a real difference between the languages, although I think a large factor could have been the mission atmosphere. Dick had run away from school and concentrated on learning from the old people, but enough of the Christian ethic had filtered through for him to expect not to work on Sunday, and perhaps to suppress the more dubious metaphors.

Relative clauses were high on my agenda this trip. It's always easiest to ask things that have a strong pragmatic force. George Watson had enjoyed telling me how to say "I speared the man who misbehaved with my wife"; a disadvantage was that when I came to write the grammar, a fair proportion of the sentences were scarcely publishable as they stood. Now, checking up on the rule which I hoped would explain relative clauses in Yidiny, I put a sentence of this type to Moses. He accepted it, and chuckled.

Robert Patterson interjected: "We was just talking about that last night. You never use that word *jumba*."

"No," I defended myself, "but I did write it down from Dick three years ago, got it in the book all the time."

"That's what I tell him," said Dick, "but I never heard you say it, and we think you forgotten it maybe."

The most momentous thing that happened to me at Yarrabah didn't concern Moses or Yidiny at all. One day we were sitting after lunch chatting to a schoolteacher we'd met three years before who had stopped by on a visit, when a telephone message was brought across from the office. It was quite short: "Chloe Grant died yesterday. Funeral in Tully three o'clock today. Message from Ernie." I just read it, and passed the paper over to Alison. The schoolteacher prattled on. We had nothing to say to him. And there was no way I could get to the funeral — it was three hours' drive away, and everything would be over by the time I reached Tully.

We had been going to call on Chloe the next week. This year, not pressed for time, I wasn't going to pass by without seeing her. I certainly owed more to Chloe than to anyone else. She started me off, when I had little idea where or how I was going, and provided the bulk of the Jirrbal material. But, much more than that, Chloe was always available with help and advice and simple kindness. She was a friend, of a very special sort.

15

"I think I like that language best"

Pompey was still around, living in increasing squalor in the hut by Blackfellow Creek. He'd been telling me for years to look up George Davis in Tolga, a younger man who knew Yidiny well. George took a bit of finding – he now lived in Atherton – but it was worth it. And by this stage I'd been working in North Queensland for so long that in any group of Aborigines there'd be likely to be someone who knew me, someone I'd given a lift to a few years back, or someone who knew George Watson, or some other link. I'd almost always be greeted as a friend, and given all necessary help.

George Davis had been born in 1919 and brought up by his grand-father at a farm out along the Goldsborough Road. The old man worked for a white farmer, but he was imbued with traditional ways and spoke mostly in Yidiny to young George, taking him off to the bush at weekends and passing on much of his knowledge about trees and animals and legends. George had learnt about Gambuun, small spirits just a few inches high who can warn their master by whistling when a stranger approaches. George's grandfather told him he had two Gambuun, called Banggurr and Baybaguwarr, but could only see them when he was alone. And the two of them – grandfather and grandson – had drunk opium together.

His grandfather died when he was fifteen or sixteen. George was suddenly hurled into the white world. He went to the school at Butcher's Creek and dismissed Yidiny and Yidinyji culture from his mind. But then gradually, over the years, he went over it all again and came to value the old ideas as much as the new.

George Davis now works as a contract timber-cutter, out by himself in the bush all week long with plenty of time to think. He has a pleasant house in Atherton, and is indistinguishable from his white neighbours in standard of living, general knowledge and articulateness. No, that is doing him an injustice. George is much more intelligent and knowledgeable, and better with explanations, than most people I've met, of any race.

When I said what I was doing, played one of Tilly Fuller's texts and demonstrated that I knew a bit of Yidiny, George became interested in the project. He didn't have much time. When he was in Atherton, he had many obligations, giving advice to local Aborigines or helping with community and political groups. But he was able to make a little time to talk with me, if I'd let him know in advance when I'd be calling. George recorded a text about the origin of fire, not very different from the Dyirbal story that I had in several versions. The small black bird who snatched the fire from the rainbow serpent was called *bajinjila* in Jirrbal, *bajinjilajila* in Mamu, *bajinji* in the coastal variety of Yidiny, but just *bajin* in George's mountainside dialect.

Although I was getting pretty familiar with this story, the full significance had never come through to me before. George explained that when *bajin* took away the glowing coals, the rainbow was told by the birds that he would never again have fire, but must now take to the water – the opposite of fire, and incompatible with it. The rainbow is said today to live in deep water-holes in the river, and children are discouraged from bathing in such pools for fear of the spirit – an admirable safely regulation. Deep water is always found at the foot of a waterfall, and a small rainbow may often be observed in its spray. When the rainbow is seen in the sky, George said, he is travelling from one water-hole to another, or just coming out of the cold water to warm himself in the sunshine, the nearest he can get to the fire he once owned.

George and I had two long sessions together. And were they productive! We covered about as much ground in three hours as I might hope for in three days with an average informant. George was planning one day soon to retrace the steps of Gulnyjarubay, the dreamtime hero who was the first man to go through tribal country, naming all the places. It sounded an exciting prospect.

George Watson was still around, living now in a decrepit barracks at Boogan, still with Mick Lonnergan. His TV had broken down, so we took it into Innisfail to be repaired. While this was being done, George indulged in a bit of refreshment and the technician had to help me carry the set out to the car, George being rather unsteady by this time. He was getting older, and his hair was finally turning white (at the age of seventy-five!), but he was still very alert.

Then we had a couple of days at Warrami, renewing acquaintance with the Cowans. And Ingham again — Nyawaygi with Willie Seaton in the mornings, and the Biyay dialect of Warrgamay from Nora Boyd after lunch. Changing languages part-way through the day wasn't easy — like switching one's mind into a different time-span — but I got a lot done. When I went round to Seaton's place in Toobanna the third morning, he said he couldn't talk that day. An item on the early morning news had reported that his wife's daughter had had a fight with her man, down in Townsville, and stabbed him to death. His wife had already gone to Townsville to look after the daughter's child, and Willie was too upset to think about Nyawaygi just now. I could understand how he would be. It seemed best to call it a day, so far as Nyawaygi was concerned, for that trip.

Finally, a trip back up to Charters Towers and Lambert Cocky. The Towers is an unusual town. It was a rich gold mining centre at the end of the last century, but began a gradual decline from about 1905. Many of the old buildings still stand — sturdy, with fancy, coloured brickwork and intricate wrought-iron railings and balconies. The main industry there now is not gold but schools, boarding schools, mostly run by churches, to which northern pastoralists send their offspring. The Cowan children had all gone there, before a high school was established in Tully.

There are gaps where many old buildings have been pulled down, or fallen down, as the population gradually thinned. Driving in to Charters Towers, one might get the impression of a pleasant, well-planned country town. But a truer picture might be of a nineteenth-century settlement left high and dry when that era ended, and into which modern civilisation has only intruded spasmodically and half-heartedly. The daily papers arrive at six o'clock at night; except Saturdays, when they don't come at all.

The average age of Charters Towers residents must be about twice that of the population as a whole. Two out of every three people in the street seem to be pensioners, and the giggling shop "girls" are forty-five if they're a day. At the Eventide Home, people who are old by Charters

Fig. 18. Lambert Cocky (Warrgamay) going about his chores at the Eventide Home, Charters Towers. (1975)

Towers standards are looked after by people who would themselves be regarded as old in any other town.

Lambert was becoming obsessed with the routine of the Eventide Home, but we still covered a lot of ground. Adjectives and ambitransitive verbs, and checking up on some of the vocabulary from Carl Lumholtz's book *Among Cannibals.* Lumholtz had ámmery "hungry" – that would be *ngamiri.* Boongary "tree-climbing kangaroo" is in fact *bulnggarri,* and what the Norwegian zoologist wrote as g'rauan "scrubhen" is in fact simply *girrawan.*

Lambert got more bound-up in time-keeping as the years went on, and by the time I next called there, driving up from Townsville just for the day in 1977, his preoccupations were almost as bad as they had been out at Sheahan's place.

That day in 1977, I arrived at about a quarter to eleven, hoping Lambert would be friendly today. One of the supervisors threaded his way through the line of little huts to Lambert's. He had the room on the left-hand side, and we could see him through the open door, lying on his bed fully dressed. I was introduced and haltingly wondered if I could ask a few more things about Warrgamay. No reply from the bed. I'd just seen John Tooth, I said, and he sent his regards. He'd given me a lot of help, but there were some things only Lambert would know. Still no response. I just stood by the door.

Then Lambert sat up. "We sit on that seat out there. You wait out there. I got to change my trousers. Put these boots on." The same sliding tenor voice, rising at the end of a sentence although there was no question, almost but not quite a mocking intonation.

I organised my notebooks and tape-recorder and then when Lambert came out, alarm-clock in hand, he wanted to move the wooden bench. So I lifted everything off. He only wanted it moved a couple of feet and I didn't enquire why. Then he sat down, took his boots off, and put the clock on the ground. We went through verbs, checking the sorts of nouns each could occur with. I'd recorded some of what he was saying, and thought he might like to hear a bit played back. Lambert first looked at the alarm-clock. He listened appreciatively to the recording, *marri minya gujugay . . .* , and then commented as if it were by some quite different person: "He right there, that Warrgamay all right."

An old white man on the verandah of the next hut suddenly started to pour out abuse. "Not a bloody radio. Always playing bloody radios. Shouldn't be allowed. Go on, bugger off with your radios, fucking radios all around . . ." and so on. He hadn't objected to Lambert talking Warrgamay to me, the recording wasn't any louder than the original speech, and I'd played it for at most a minute.

Lambert, though, seemed scared silly. "You better be careful," he confided to me, as much sotto voce as was in his nature, "he mad. Never know what he do to make trouble. Switch if off." I already had, and didn't play back anything else.

We made good progress, but Lambert was picking up the clock and looking at it more and more frequently. He talked about the quality of the dinners at the Eventide Home. More and more about meals so that it was difficult to slip a bit of Warrgamay in between courses. One hadn't got to be late, I inferred — well, what time were they served? Twelve fifteen, Lambert said. Then surely if we stopped at twelve — it was only about two minutes' walk away? Lambert didn't disagree with the reasonableness of this line of argument, but it appeared that he did have to stop at twenty to twelve, in order to get there on time. My proposal to return in the afternoon brought no hostility, so I said I'd come at about two o'clock.

Finding somewhere to eat in Charters Towers isn't easy. There's a long main street that would have had a selection of cafes, in any other town. But all I could find was one faded chintzy place that was mostly for morning coffees and afternoon teas. Well, any sort of snack would do. The menu had hamburger, cheesburger, eggburger. I ordered a cheeseburger. When it came, it was a bun with a bit of half-toasted cheese in the middle — no meat at all. I didn't like to say that anywhere else in the world one would get cheese on top of the meat, not instead of it.

There is a beautiful park in the middle of Charters Towers, with well-kept grass and colourful flower-beds, dozens of garbage bins, and a man going round emptying them (every half-hour?). It was a relaxing place to assess the morning's work and decide what to ask Lambert next. Then I walked over to the long Regency-style pavilion in the middle of the neat lawns. It was a memorial to the young men from Charters Towers who lost their lives in the war. I hesitated to look further and see which war. The Boer War. Of course.

I couldn't think why I'd said I'd be back as late as two o'clock, so I returned at half-past one and Lambert, despite his time obsession, didn't complain. I waited again on the bench while he got ready and went through the same ritual, boots off, alarm-clock down. We did two minutes of work and then Lambert made a suggestion. Why didn't we go and sit on another bench, over towards the road? Far away from that bugger — he nodded at the radio-hater who still sat on his minute verandah, viewing us with suspicion. Well, I didn't really think it was necessary, but if Lambert preferred somewhere else . . . Yes, he did. Just wait while he goes inside to change his boots and get a hat. So five minutes more, then we walked across the lawn to an identical bench, boots off, clock on the ground, hat on lap.

Finally, more than an hour of almost solid Warrgamay — reciprocal verbs and verbalised adjectives and checking on the spellings of some nouns, which type of r was used, whether there really was a long vowel. But after every second or third question from me, Lambert would ask something, in his turn. He wanted to know what parts of

Australia I'd been to, learning the languages. And he wanted to know things about other languages. What was the word for "water", for instance. "Water" is *bana* in Dyirbal (which Lambert knew already), and also *bana* in Yidiny. It is *yagu* in Nyawaygi (which he also knew). *Gug* in Mbabaram – that was news to Lambert.

I had students working on languages from South Australia, New South Wales and the Northern Territory – Diyari, Murinjpata, Rembarrnga, Bandjalang, Gumbaynggirr, Ngiyambaa. I didn't know what "water" was in any of those languages, though. Lambert didn't think very much of this. We were able to discuss Warrgamay uninterrupted for ten minutes, and then he asked what I did in Canberra. Learn about different sorts of languages from other parts of the world. What parts of the world? We'd just had a course on American Indian linguistics from Professor Mary Haas, so I mentioned this. All right, how did they say "water" in North American languages?

I didn't know what to say. Lambert wasn't interested in the things we *did* talk of in Canberra – noun incorporation or ergative inflection or obviative marking. He was interested in the word for "water" – what could be more straightforward? So, eventually I made one up. It seemed the only thing to do. I picked sounds typical of the languages of British Columbia, so that at least it was like an honest-to-goodness Amerindian word. "They call it *ƛip'iɣ,*" I said, popping in a lateral fricative, a glottalised bilabial stop and a final velar fricative. Lambert was impressed. "Oh, *ƛip'iɣ,*" he said, repeating the word I had made up, exactly, correct in every detail, although English has no sounds like *ƛ* or *p'* or *ɣ* and Australian languages don't have fricatives at all, no *f* or *s* or *th,* let alone *ƛ* or *ɣ.*

The alarm-clock was consulted from time to time. At a quarter to three, he began to get nervous, and then at ten to three distinctly edgy. Tea, the evening meal, was getting close. This was ridiculous. Most Australians have tea at about six, and even at the Old Folks' Home at Yarrabah it had only moved forward to about four-thirty. The official time for Lambert's tea was, I'm sure, no earlier than four. "Would it be all right if we stopped at three?" I asked. Lambert seemed to accept this, but then at five to three he couldn't wait any longer, and began to put his boots on in readiness for a hasty retreat. I don't really think he was bored or fed up with the questions. It was just a case of being ready for the next meal – as he stressed, if you were late you didn't get any. So I hastily asked two quick, final questions and recorded the answers; no time to write them down. Lambert shook me by the hand, accepted a ten-dollar bill, picked up hat and clock and stomped off across the grass without a backwards glance, leaving a pile of note-books, and tape-recorder, and me, on the bench.

During 1975, I spent every spare minute — when not teaching or attending meetings at the whim of our bureaucrats — writing the final version of a grammar of Yidiny. I had two short field trips, just a week in August and a week in December, to check up on the few outstanding points. The finishing touches were added during the first couple of months of a year's sabbatical, back in London, and the final typescript went off to Cambridge University Press towards the end of March 1976.

There was good news on the land rights front. Whitlam's policy, announced in December 1972, was gradually being put into effect. Not at Yarrabah, which is a Queensland government settlement, outside the jurisdiction of federal power — and the Queensland premier was adamant about his state's competence to look after its own Aborigines. What was in the air was the purchase of a block of traditional land at Murray Upper for the Jirrbalngan and Girramaygan people to live on and work on — and own. The federal Department of Aboriginal Affairs had sent up a representative to decide what was needed, and to make a case to the Aboriginal Land Fund Commission chaired by Professor C. D. Rowley.

Finally, a sizeable block on the Murray River was purchased. Not everything about the deal seemed perfect — the price paid was just over $200,000 whereas some people did say that about $130,000 would have been a fairer evaluation. And they still tell tall stories about the DAA representative, the ventures he got into, debts that mounted up. He certainly did seem to have looked after himself, utilising to the full the generous expenses then allowed by the Federal Government, and even keeping a yacht moored in Rockingham Bay. But, leaving all that aside, at least the Aborigines did benefit. For the first time since the white invasion, they had some land that was recognised to be theirs, where they could live without interference.

At first, Aborigines in Cardwell and Murray Upper, formed a co-operative with the acronym CAMU, the word for "water" in Girramay. Then Murray Upper decided to go it alone, and changed the name to Jambun "witchetty grub". The Department of Aboriginal Affairs built half a dozen houses, of very good quality, and most of the people moved there — old Rosie Runaway, Tommy Warren, Jimmy Murray's old widow Mary Ann, and four or five families of younger people. They cultivated bananas and cucumbers and seemed to be doing pretty well. Some days in 1978 and 1979, they were so busy working that I had to make an appointment to discuss matters linguistic — in the evening or on Saturday morning. It was a change from the old days, and a most pleasant one.

There was just one snag. The Queensland government had to approve the transfer, and when they discovered the land had been bought by the federal government, with federal money, for a bunch of Queensland Aborigines, they had apoplexy. And simply refused to approve the transfer. So the land is still held by the Aboriginal Land Fund Commission, as Trustee, although they have assured the Murray Upper Aborigines that it is to all intents and purposes theirs.

Things at Yarrabah were pretty unchanged when I returned there in late 1975. Father Brown had found he couldn't stand Melbourne, and he and Mrs Brown had been allowed to come back and live in a small house in the old folks' area, taking their meals with Moses and the rest. Pompey Langdon was now at Yarrabah, at George Davis's instigation,

Fig. 19. Dick Moses (Yidiny), Robert Patterson (Gunggay), and Pompey Langdon (Yidiny) on the verandah of Dick's house at the Yarrabah old people's home. (1975)

and he lived in the other half of Moses's hut. It seemed very appropriate — the last two really good speakers of the language, and they could talk to each other as much as they wanted.

Moses had been pretty ill during the winter, Robert Patterson told me, and they hadn't thought he'd pull through. But he had. He was sniffing a bit more than before, if that were possible, but there was still the same intellect, the same curiosity, the same drive to teach me. In fact he seemed better than the previous year, more like his old self. One day Moses took a grammatical question as cue for dictating a long conversation, which led into another and another, taking up the whole afternoon. The next morning he apologised for not having let me get on with what I had to do. No, I assured Dick, I'd much rather have you just talk. Plenty of time for my questions afterwards.

We checked every last point in the completed grammar chapters, and then Moses told another story, a legend about two Burrawungal, who Dick described as being like "water fairies" or "mermaids". A man was once going along a creek near Yarrabah looking for eels when he spied the Burrawungal bathing in the water. He washed his body-sweat off and then approached from the north — since the wind was from the south, the mermaids would not smell his approach. He lined his hands with sand so that when he grabbed the younger Burrawungal, she could not slip away. Her body was covered with slime like an eel, Moses explained. The water fairy was taken home, and eventually settled down to be a good wife. Just one precaution was needed — she must never be sent for water, or she would disappear, back to her old life under the water. But one day, years later, when the Burrawungal's husband was out hunting, someone did send her down to the creek. And that was the last they saw of her.

Americans remember what they were doing when the news came through that Jack Kennedy had been murdered. I remember that too. But for an Australian — even a naturalised one — the day to remember is 11 November 1975, when a governor-general (whose name eludes me) sacked a prime minister who had a majority in the House of Representatives. And also 13 December 1975, when Whitlam was voted out of office by the people of Australia.

I left Yarrabah early in the morning on 13 December, having checked the last sentences in my grammar with Moses the previous night. By nine o'clock I was in Atherton, hoping to have a couple of hours with George Davis. He was out campaigning – for the Labor candidate of course – but Mrs Davis suggested I return at about eleven. Just a few doors up the road lived Helena Cassells, an ex-student from Canberra who'd married a forester. She had asked me to write to the forestry department in Brisbane requesting that he be posted somewhere where Helena could work on a local language. And she had been recording and analysing Jabugay, from Redlynch. We talked about how it was going and cleared up a few points; her husband David was also out campaigning for Labor.

Then I spent a short but useful hour with George Davis, going over the travels of the dreamtime hero Gulnyjarubay and how he had originally come up from the sea as an alligator. At the junction of the Russell and Mulgrave Rivers, Gulnyjarubay couldn't decide which fork to take. He jumped out of the water, took on the form of a man, and continued overland, mapping and naming Yidinyji tribal country.

Now that the Yidinyji grammar was finished, I planned to return to Dyirbal, to work on a comparative dictionary of the ten or more distinct dialects with full information on the meaning and use of every word, and of course its equivalent in the mother-in-law style, Jalnguy. To do the job properly, I would need the help of both a zoologist and a botanist for identification of fauna and flora species. As a preliminary to this I stopped off, that afternoon of the Whitlam defeat, to see Geoff Stocker, head of the Tropical Research Station of the CSIRO Division of Forest Research. Geoff had a farm just south of Malanda, and I only saw the significance of a large notice "Vote Donkey" at the sight of one. In the living room were jars upon jars of orchid plants; Geoff's hobby was hybridizing them. He was enthusiastic about the idea of field trips into the bush, and we agreed to be in touch again in a year, when I returned from sabbatical. In fact the project didn't start until 1979, but then it did give good results. On the first day, in a forest near the South Johnstone River, George Watson gave the Mamu name, Mollie Raymond the Ngajan name, and Geoff Stocker the botanical name for eighty-seven different plants, and I wrote them all down. Both Geoff and I were fascinated to see the similarities and differences between the Dyirbal genus-species taxonomy and that used by botanists. (By November 1982 we had over three hundred and fifty species fully identified, and there are probably another hundred or more to go.)

From Geoff's place, that Saturday in December 1975, I drove down to Innisfail for a quick word with George Watson — plans for the Dyirbal dictionary work, which George thought was long overdue. Then I carried on south. Just as the polls closed, a tremendous storm set in — perhaps the spirits were venting their anger. Then I made a stop in Tully for petrol and the attendant relayed the first voting figures from the south, an hour ahead because of daylight saving. It seemed inconceivable. For me, the manner of Whitlam's dismissal meant that he *must* be reinstated by the people, quite apart from all other issues.

I just drove on. And then stopped at a motel in Cardwell, but had a shower, did some work, delayed switching on the television. Then, by the time I did, the result was quite clear. I switched it off again at once.

Within half an hour I realised that it had been inevitable, and that any thinking person should have seen this. Whitlam was a tremendous social reformer, but he didn't really know how to do his sums. You can't spend vast quantities of money on new projects without cutting back on old ones, somewhere. He had the ability to govern properly, but without the know-how. Nepotism, scandals and sackings, over-rapid expansion that had led to blatant waste of public money counted more to the people of Australia than Aboriginal land rights, or bilingual education, or good relations with Asia. I'd voted Labor on a principle (the principle that prime ministers shouldn't be sacked), but on reflection the Labor party had really shown themselves unfit to govern, at this time. Nothing, though, could take away Whitlam's achievements — he had made more positive contributions to the quality of Australian society in three years than the Liberals had in the previous twenty-three.

At Warrami next morning no one shared my shock and sadness, to put it mildly. So we forgot about all that and just caught up on our families and gossip and such. And then my annual visit for a chat with Tommy Warren — fatter than ever, still unable to stand up, but happy enough in his little hut, with two transistor radios for company. Tommy moved up to the new Aboriginal property at Jambun the following year, and then in 1977 he rolled into the fire and burnt himself. They didn't know what to do with him in the Tully hospital — he couldn't go in a bed. He died there and, like Tommy Springcart the year before, was buried in the old cemetery at Warrami.

I'd had no time to work on Warrgamay and Nyawaygi in Canberra during 1975. Those were two major projects for the coming sabbatical year. But I called in to see Nora Boyd and Willie Seaton anyway.

Nora Boyd seemed a bit less sprightly than before, but we had a useful hour. For some reason my recorder wouldn't function, so a greatniece (or it may have been a greatgreatniece) lent her cassette recorder and insisted on giving me an old cassette. Nora's Biyay interspersed with funky pop, as I checked the spellings of some words that differed between dialects. Nora Boyd died the following year. She was about ninety-five by then.

Willie Seaton, though, is indestructible. I saw him that day after Whitlam's defeat and then again each year from 1977 to 1982 at Murray Upper, where he'd moved (conveniently for me). I finally got all the archaic monosyllabic verbs in Nyawaygi pretty much straightened out.

It was October 1977 before I got into the field again. *A Grammar of Yidiny* had just been published, all 586 pages of it, and I had a copy for Dick Moses. He wasn't able to read, but he would value it as a document of the language, the project into which he'd put so much effort; and it did include two photographs of him.

This trip was mostly for detailed work on the Dyirbal dictionary, with George Watson on Mamu and Mollie Raymond on Ngajan — getting them together helped, with lots of mutual promptings. There were plenty of people around Murray Upper to extend and check all the material Chloe had given — Jack Muriata and Bessie Jerry on Girramay, Mick Murray, Ida Henry and Andy Denham on Jirrbal, and others too. Also some final Warrgamay and Nyawaygi checking with John Tooth, Lambert Cocky and Willie Seaton.

Helena Cassells, the forester's wife in Atherton, had done good work on Jabugay, but there was still much more to tackle — and fast, with only one or two speakers left. Helena wasn't able to undertake this, because of her growing family, so Elizabeth Patz, an ANU student, agreed to continue with the project for her honours year sub-thesis. I arranged to meet Elizabeth in Cairns to start her off. (She was ideally organised, having brought along her husband, Günther, to keep her company, and also her father, to play chess with Günther while she worked on Jabugay.)

The most important event for us at the ANU during 1977 had been the visit of Professor Mary Haas, one of the leading figures in world linguistics. Mary had written a grammar and dictionary of Thai and had worked on many American Indian languages, as well as training a generation of linguists. She'd spent the second semester with us, teaching a course on Amerindian languages, and entering into all our academic pursuits. While the students were completing their final essays, she had come north for a week's holiday, viewing the Barrier Reef and other wonders. And I'd promised to take her on a day's field work, with an Australian language.

The plan was to take Elizabeth and Mary to Yarrabah — a short drive from Cairns — to meet Dick Moses. Alf Neal had been in Canberra recently and said Dick was fit and well and sent his best wishes. Moses might record another text for me, and I knew he could help Elizabeth with some preliminary information on Jabugay. Rather than suddenly descend on Dick with two strange ladies, after a two-year absence, I decided to call in on my own first, just to say hello.

There was another new stretch of bitumen on the road to Yarrabah, but otherwise things looked the same as ever — physically beautiful but, from a social point of view, stagnant. I hadn't been able to get through by phone to ask permission to come, so the first thing was to go to the manager's office. Although I knew perfectly well how to find Moses, the procedure was that someone would take me to the chairman of the community council, and she would then show me the way.

I said who I wanted to see, although she knew me anyway. Her reply was barely audible, and it used the old Yidiny term which had meant "mother's mother" but now, in Yarrabah English, could refer to any old person, a term of deference.

"*Gumbu* passed away last month," she said (the name of a dead person should never be pronounced), "just after Father." (Father Brown, that is.)

He'd died just about the day the book was published, the book into which he'd put so much of his knowledge and spirit, the heritage of his people. Without Moses's help it wouldn't have been a quarter as detailed or complete. I walked over and looked at his grave; it bore a single posy of flowers.

Pompey was still there, sitting on a bench overlooking the sea, puffing on his pipe. We talked for a bit. He was getting old and slow, but still enjoyed life. We didn't mention Moses. But as Pompey spoke Yidiny, melodious sentences, long vowels strategically placed to engender a euphonious rhythm, it became hard to respond. This was Moses's language, and Tilly Fuller's, a mystical magic tongue. And I would never again hear it spoken, hear Yidiny stories, as they had pronounced them.

I took Elizabeth Patz and Mary Haas down to George Watson instead. It was a bit further, and since George hadn't been expecting me just then, he'd been drinking. Not too much, though. The previous week George had suggested a trip to a traditional site, a stone that was said to be a transmuted dog. George had undertaken to tell its story when we got there. Well, he felt it would be a good idea to make the trip that day, so off we went, about another sixty miles along forestry tracks through the bush until a fallen tree blocked our path. Then we walked. Mary, sixty-seven and still suffering from the after-effects of a broken hip a year or two back, trotted along gamely, George pointing out the plants and the tracks of a wallaby — must be camping up there on the bank (but none of the rest of us could discern anything).

After about two miles, Mary stopped, and Elizabeth stayed to keep her company, while George and I struggled on. We found where the dog-turned-into stone should have been, and battled through the jungle,

Fig. 20. Elizabeth Patz (linguistics student from the Australian National University), Mary Haas (professor of linguistics at the University of California, Berkeley) and George Watson (authority on the Mamu dialect of Dyirbal) at Millaa Millaa Falls. (1977)

wait-a-while vines tearing shirts and skin, leeches almost jumping up our legs, mosquitoes stinging, and all sorts of other scratches and bites. And then we couldn't find it. So we all went back, had a huge meal at the Millaa Millaa cafe, and then went on to admire the Millaa Millaa falls. George told the story there, with all three of us — Elizabeth, Mary and I — busily writing it down. When we dropped George off at his barracks, I mentioned that Mary had bought a copy of *The Dyirbal Language of North Queensland,* to which George had contributed so much (and with his photo in it), at the bookstore in Berkeley, California. He was surprised and pleased.

The next day, Elizabeth and I went up to Redlynch and Helena Cassells introduced her to Gilpin Banning, the last man with a good knowledge of Jabugay. Half a dozen people sat down at the bench with us, to help out. One of the men was Yidiny, so I asked him; *"Nyundu yidiny nyanggaajing?"*

"That's very well pronounced," said Gilpin. And then he leant over to confide: "You know my language is Jabugay but I know a little bit of Yidiny, and I think I like that language best." I knew exactly how he felt.

Afterword

The first draft of these memoirs was written in Cambridge, England (30 April — 4 July 1980) entirely from memory. I had kept no journal or diary or other notes.

It was revised in Canberra (11 March — 24 August 1981) and I did then try to check up on as many points as possible, referring to linguistic texts and notebooks, looking at photographs and listening to tapes. During field trips in November 1980 and June-July 1981, I was able to revisit some of the places mentioned, and discuss incidents with others who had been involved. Thanks are due to Muriel Cowan, Dorelle Fox, Ernie Grant, Doreen McGrath, Jack Muriata, Mick Murray and George Watson for patiently answering my questions about things that happened in the past, and about names and spellings. Jack Doolan, Ernie Grant and Doreen McGrath were good enough to read sections of the manuscript, and suggest some necessary corrections.

The material included here has been checked in the manner considered normal for scientific projects. Everything reported in this volume actually happened; just occasionally two related episodes have been merged, to create a more cohesive narrative. Parts of the initial draft for which I could not obtain corroboration were simply deleted (they were very few in number).

The only pseudonyms used are Lachlan, Frank Lawson, Charlie Jericho, Hughie Lawson, Clem, Karl, Jock and Sheila. Everyone else is referred to by his or her real name.

Pronunciation of Aboriginal words

ng is a single sound; it occurs only at the end of a syllable in English — the single sound after the vowel in *sing*, for instance. One way of learning how to say a word like *nga* "yes" (in Dyirbal) is to begin with *sing*, add *a*, and on repetition gradually drop off the *si-*, thus *singa*, *singa*, *singa*, *nga*. (Unlike in the English word *finger*, there is no hard *g* sound in *nga*.)

ny is a single sound, like *n* and *y* pronounced simultaneously; it is like the sound in the middle of English *onion* (and is identical to Spanish *ñ*).

j is like *d* and *y* being pronounced simultaneously, a sharper sound than that in English words like *judge*.

rr is a trilled or rolled *r*, as in Scottish pronunciation.

r is very close to the Australian or English pronunciation of *r*, as in *arrow*.

b, d, g, m, n, l, y and *w* can be pronounced almost exactly as in English.

i is pronounced like the vowel in English *bit*.

u is pronounced like the vowel in English *took*.

a is pronounced like the vowel in English *ban*.

Doubling of a vowel letter indicates an lengthened vowel: *ii* is like the vowel in *beat* only longer; *uu* is like that in *soup*, only longer; and *aa* is like the vowel in southern English pronunciations of *grass*, only longer.

Each vowel should be pronounced carefully and distinctly; they should never be reduced to the vowel sound of English *the*, for instance.

Tribal and language names

The Girramaygan people speak Girramay, the Jirrbalngan (sometimes called Jirrbalji) speak Jirrbal, the Malanbarra speak Gulngay and the Ngajanji speak Ngajan. These four, and also Dulgubarra Mamu (usually called Mamu), Waribarra Mamu (often called just Wari) and Jirru are dialects of a single language, which I refer to as Dyirbal.

The Yidinyji people speak Yidiny and the Gungganyji speak Gunggay. These two, and also Wanyurr, are dialects of a single language.

The Jabuganyji people speak Jabugay and the Yirrganyji people Yirrgay, two dialects of one language.

The Warrgamaygan people speak Warrgamay; Biyay is another dialect of the same language.

Gugu-Yalanji, Muluriji, Jangun and Wagaman are all dialects of a single language.

Mbabaram, Warungu, Nyawaygi, Olgolo, Gugu-Mini, Gugu-Warra, Gugu-Daiban, Guugu Yimidhirr, Lama-Lama and the Flinders Island language are all different languages, distinct from each other and from those listed above.